Advance Praise

This volume is a pioneering and grieving parents who lost childre dren succumbed to drug overdoses. The authors have done a masterful job of blending their quantitative research findings and the anguished voices of parents attending survivor support groups to create a rich and very engaging book. Their scope is huge as they discuss the unique characteristics of traumatic loss, how stigma affects grief and healing, the impact of multiple losses, early and later years after losing a child, the essentials of bereavement support groups (including Internet groups), posttraumatic growth and resilience, gender differences in grieving parents, and how losing a child affects marital function and continuance. Clinicians who read *Devastating Losses* will come away with enhanced empathy, essential new insights, and a skill set that will give sustenance and hope to these shell-shocked yet courageous parents on a bumpy journey of recovery and repair, a journey they never asked for.

> —**Michael F. Myers, MD,** professor of clinical
> psychiatry, SUNY Downstate Medical Center,
> Brooklyn, New York, and author (with Carla Fine) of
> *Touched by Suicide: Hope and Healing After Loss*

Taking a journey out of their own heart of darkness, the Feigelmans, along with researchers Jack Jordan and John McIntosh, have blazed a trail of enlightenment for survivors of sudden, traumatic loss and suicide and for those who work with them. This book breaks new ground while establishing pathways yet needing to be mapped in the landscape of surviving. This is much more than an important book; it is an essential book.

> —**Lanny Berman, PhD.** executive director, American
> Association of Suici

D1319195

Devastating Losses: How Parents Cope With the Death of a Child to Suicide or Drugs is an incredibly important book for many reasons. As a carefully conducted study, it helps bridge the gap between research and practice—truly this is research that matters. This research offers powerful information and clinical tools to assist counselors in helping parents deal with the devastating and disenfranchising losses when a child dies due to his or her own self-destructive behaviors. Clinicians, educators, and researchers will need this book.

—**Kenneth J. Doka, PhD**, professor, The College of New Rochelle, and senior consultant, The Hospice Foundation of America

Devastating Losses is what survivors of suicide have long been waiting for: a compassionate yet scientifically based study on the grief we experience following the loss of a loved one to suicide. The stories, research, and insights in the book helped me personally and will certainly provide comfort and understanding to others as well. By breaking through the stereotypes and stigma surrounding suicide and other sudden and unexpected deaths, the authors open the door for us to begin our healing with both dignity and courage.

—**Carla Fine**, author of *No Time to Say Goodbye: Surviving the Suicide of a Loved One*

Grounded equally on solid clinical practice and uniquely relevant research, and tragically leavened by the personal bereavement of two of the book's authors, *Devastating Losses* sheds new and compassionate light on the experience of a child's death due to traumatic causes. Readers will find in these pages the stories of many who have suffered the unspeakable loss of a son or daughter to suicide, drug overdose, or fatal accident and who have struggled with and often surmounted the subsequent symptoms and stigmatization with the help of family, peer support, online communities, and, sometimes, professional help. This book is for all parents who experience the tragedy of sudden bereavement and all those who try to help them, as they reach through suffering to survivorship and from grief to growth in the journey.

—**Robert A. Neimeyer, PhD**, editor of *Death Studies*

Devastating Losses

William Feigelman, PhD, is professor emeritus and adjunct professor of Sociology at Nassau Community College (Garden City, New York) where he has taught for more than 44 years and still teaches part time. Author and coauthor of six books and more than 40 journal articles, he has written on a wide variety of social science subjects, including child adoptions, youth alcohol and drug abuse, problem gambling, tobacco use and cessation, and intergroup relations. Since 2002, after his son Jesse's suicide, Dr. Feigelman has focused his professional writings on youth suicide and suicide bereavement. His work has appeared in *Suicide and Life-Threatening Behavior, Death Studies, Omega: Journal of Death and Dying,* and *Illness, Crisis and Loss.* He is a member of the American Association of Suicidology and the Association for Death Education and Counseling; a frequent presenter at bereavement conferences in the United States, Canada, and Japan; and a co-facilitator of a survivors' support group.

John R. Jordan, PhD, is a clinical psychologist and grief counselor who has specialized in working with survivors of suicide loss for many years in the Boston metropolitan area. He also regularly provides training for mental health professionals, clergy, and others throughout the United States, Canada, and Australia on working with individuals and families after suicide. He is a consultant for the Survivor Council of the American Foundation for Suicide Prevention and the Grief Support Services of the Samaritans of Boston. Dr. Jordan has authored numerous important publications in the bereavement field and was the recipient of the Association for Death Education and Counseling Research Recognition Award in 2006. He is also coauthor of two books in the suicide bereavement field, *After Suicide Loss: Coping with Your Grief* and *Grief After Suicide: Understanding the Consequences and Caring for the Survivors.* With the sponsorship of the American Foundation for Suicide Prevention, he also authored the foundation's Support Group Facilitator Training Program and manual for survivors and professionals who would like to facilitate self-help support groups.

John L. McIntosh, PhD, is Associate Vice Chancellor for Academic Affairs and Professor of Psychology at Indiana University, South Bend. He has previously authored, co-authored or co-edited seven books on suicide including: *Elder Suicide: Research, Theory and Treatment* (1994); *Suicide and its Aftermath* (1987) and *Grief after Suicide* (2011). Author of many book chapters, journal articles, presentations and keynote addresses at professional conferences, Dr. McIntosh is a past president of the American Association of Suicidology where he was also given several awards for his distinguished service to the field. McIntosh serves on the editorial boards of several of the leading journals in the suicidology field, his work has frequently been quoted in some of the country's leading national newspapers and newsmagazines including: the *Wall Street Journal,* the *New York Times, USA Today, Chicago Tribune,* and *Newsweek.* Dr. McIntosh has also received awards for his distinguished teaching and research accomplishments from Indiana University.

Beverly Feigelman, LCSW, is adjunct professor of social work at Adelphi University (Garden City, New York). She also maintains a private psychotherapy practice, providing family and individual counseling. She is an educational consultant for the Bellmore-Merrick (Long Island, New York) School District, training graduate social work students for work in secondary school settings. Ms. Feigelman is a member of various suicide prevention organizations, including the American Foundation for Suicide Prevention, SPAN-USA, and the American Association of Suicidology and a co-facilitator of a survivors' support group. She is also author or coauthor of several articles on suicide bereavement, addiction treatment, and social work education. Ms. Feigelman often presents on these topics at professional conferences. She is also chairperson of the Long Island Chapter of the Association for the Advancement of Social Work with Groups.

Devastating Losses
How Parents Cope With the Death of a
Child to Suicide or Drugs

William Feigelman, PhD, John R. Jordan, PhD,
John L. McIntosh, PhD, and Beverly Feigelman, LCSW

SPRINGER PUBLISHING COMPANY
NEW YORK

Springer Publishing Company, LLC
11 West 42nd Street
New York, NY 10036
www.springerpub.com

Acquisitions Editor: Sheri W. Sussman
Production Editor: Michael O'Connor
Composition: Absolute Service, Inc.

ISBN: 978-0-8261-0746-6
E-book ISBN: 978-0-8261-0747-3

12 13 14 15/ 5 4 3 2 1

The author and the publisher of this Work have made every effort to use sources believed to be reliable to provide information that is accurate and compatible with the standards generally accepted at the time of publication. The author and publisher shall not be liable for any special, consequential, or exemplary damages resulting, in whole or in part, from the readers' use of, or reliance on, the information contained in this book. The publisher has no responsibility for the persistence or accuracy of URLs for external or third-party Internet websites referred to in this publication and does not guarantee that any content on such websites is, or will remain, accurate or appropriate.

Library of Congress Cataloging-in-Publication Data

Devastating losses : how parents cope with the death of a child to suicide or drugs / William Feigelman ... [et al.].
    p. ; cm.
  Includes bibliographical references and index.
  ISBN 978-0-8261-0746-6 — ISBN 978-0-8261-0747-3 (e-book)
  1. Children—Death—Psychological aspects. 2. Parents—Psychology. 3. Bereavement—Psychological aspects. 4. Drugs—Overdose. 5. Suicide victims—Family relationships. I. Feigelman, William.
  [DNLM: 1. Bereavement. 2. Parents—psychology. 3. Overdose. 4. Self-Help Groups—utilization. 5. Suicide. BF 575.G7]
  BF575.G7D477 2012
  155.9'37085--dc23
                              2012015358

Special discounts on bulk quantities of our books are available to corporations, professional associations, pharmaceutical companies, health care organizations, and other qualifying groups.

If you are interested in a custom book, including chapters from more than one of our titles, we can provide that service as well.

For details, please contact:
Special Sales Department, Springer Publishing Company, LLC
11 West 42nd Street, 15th Floor, New York, NY 10036-8002
Phone: 877-687-7476 or 212-431-4370; Fax: 212-941-7842
E-mail: sales@springerpub.com

Printed in the United States of America by Bang Printing.

*This book is for Jesse and all other children
lost to untimely deaths and their parents who were brought down
to the depths of despair. May their parents be able
to rekindle hope for a better future and sufficient energy to work with
others in society, to diminish the numbers
of these deaths, and spare others the agony and grief
that they know only too well.*

Contents

Foreword

For those who have lost a child to suicide, this book will provide a life ring for their unique journey down this dangerous river of suicide. For the clinician who seeks to be a resource or a guide to those who have begun this journey, it will be a map that can help provide clinical support and understanding necessary for a safer trip. For anyone in a community who wants to be there for those experiencing the bereavement problems associated with a child's suicide, it may help them keep the survivor inside the boat.

Doctors Feigelman, Jordan, and McIntosh, and Beverly Feigelman have taken us into the most treacherous area of bereavement, the loss of a child to suicide. This reality, which impacts so many parents each year, is the tsunami of grief. It is held up as the worst scenario one might ever experience and the most difficult to bear. The generous work compiled in this text will enable anyone in the community seeking to support someone who has lost a child to suicide to accomplish their goal more readily. It will also allow those who have gotten a call or found their child having taken their life to not feel the void of hope and know that they can survive this loss that so many survivors have experienced. Anyone who reads this book can find ways to contribute support to those who receive the sad news of a suicide loss. Parents who lose a child this way become members of a new community of suicide-survivors and they may need a diverse variety of supports to outlast their grief.

The authors bring not only a wealth of knowledge about research and suicide but for William Feigelman and his wife Beverly, this is also their personal story. Their son Jesse's suicide has immersed them in this devastating loss and by their sheer will to understand his death by suicide, they have fought to find a safe passage through their own unique streams of grief and have helped others in the process.

This book will ensure that the reader has the information necessary to not only survive but to manage their lives effectively after their loss–with a renewed sense of self. The loss of a child, especially when it follows a suicide death, inevitably requires the mourning parents to re-invent themselves afterwards. This is not an easy journey nor is the outcome guaranteed; however, like most journeys, preparation and knowledge increase the survival rates of those who are cast into the water.

By using the chapters presented as a guide to deepen their knowledge, parent survivors may be able to avoid some of the pitfalls and barriers that most parents who experience the death of a child to suicide often encounter.

There is also important information for those who want to be supportive to the newly bereaved. Because bereavement following suicide is filled with paradoxes (opposites being true) and those who want to provide much needed support may need guidance themselves—the information in this book can improve the bereavement trajectory of the people they wish to support. In many cultures we do not readily accept oppositional viewpoints. We expect behavior to make sense and be logical. This is not what the research has found. Some seemingly logical assumptions about suicide (for example about finding the body) might not impact on the bereaved in the same way or with the same consequences as assumed by those in supportive roles. Therefore, providing support without more insight can be less than helpful and in some cases may create harm. It is clear to those of us who have had the privilege of working with parents who have suffered this grief that many of those who wish to be supportive do not have the tools they need to provide adequate support. A classic example of one of the paradoxes of this bereavement are attempts to encourage the bereaved to talk openly about the death by asking various questions about "why it may have occurred." Yet, it may be more supportive to a newly bereaved to simply listen to them, similarly offering to do what is helpful ("Just let me know if there is anything I can do") may not be as valued as doing what is needed ("I have brought groceries and will fix dinner for tonight") and especially to listen nonjudgmentally to a story that may need to be told over and over again.

The information offered in this book on the initial days after the loss will perhaps help caregivers more than the newly bereaved, as many survivors are so deeply absorbed in their grief and unable to concentrate enough to read or comprehend each section. However, it will be a valuable resource throughout the grief process, which can predictably last and be revisited for a very long time. Recognizing that what is important in the first year may be less important in the second and later post-loss years will be essential to reducing expectations about grief. It is for this and many other reasons that this book will be a valued resource for the parents and caregivers to return to re-reading sections throughout their lifelong grief journeys.

More than 40 years ago Dr. Edwin Shneidman suggested that the deceased "hang their psychological skeleton in the survivors emotional closet" (p. x, 1972). For the first time in all the intervening years, these authors have provided the reader a well-researched and informed view of the psychological and emotional closets of suicide-bereaved parents. Their work will provide a much-needed compass for those who are cast into this complex bereavement and help steer them safely from the edge of a very dangerous journey.

If *Devastating Losses* ended here the rewards for its readership would be sufficiently bountiful. But, fortunately for those who explore this volume, the wide-ranging perspectives offered here—across different important, neglected subjects in the bereavement field–provide readers with many new insights about grief and bereavement and about the impact of traumatic losses more comprehensively. In many ways this is a ground-breaking work. Among the subjects investigated is drug overdose death bereavement, whose mourners may actually outnumber those bereaved-by-suicide, who again, paradoxically, have attracted little attention among bereavement researchers, despite their many unmet needs for bereavement support and services. For the first time we hear from nearly 50 drug-death bereaved parents who report on their post-loss travails. Initially, we might have expected these mourners to have experienced more supportive responses from their intimate associates than those bereaved-by-suicide, as their children died "accidental deaths," much like automobile accident casualties or victims of drownings. Yet, again, paradoxically, the taint of illegal drug use and its associations with mental illness puts a strong negative spin on these deaths, leading some close friends and family members to recoil and avoid the bereaved parents afterwards or to say thoughtless and even blameworthy things about the deceased child and the parental care prior to the death. Thus, bereaved-by-drug-death parents find themselves placed in a similar boat as the bereaved-by-suicide, isolated, stigmatized, and deeply ashamed of their children's death causes. Like suicide-bereaved parents, many feel reluctant to speak openly about their children's deaths because of the censure it may evoke and assume a posture antithetical to the development of a sense of psychological wellness.

This book also brings into sharper focus a number of other important neglected topics in the bereavement field. These subjects are occasionally mentioned as important ones for study but little empirical data have been collected on them. The authors explore how bereaved parents that sustain multiple losses (either from the loss of two children or from the loss of a spouse and a child) manage their grief afterwards, compared to the parents who lost a single child; how parents who lost their only child adapt afterwards, compared to parents who still have surviving children. Only-child-bereaved-parents must carve out new types of family forms that make sense to them, without any living children. Another topic taken up here is how traumatic child deaths affect marital integrity and cohesion afterwards. These divergent bereavement subjects intersect and overlap with each other. The authors broad-ranging perspectives are valuable for providing all subgroups of traumatically bereaved parents with the best and most appropriate kinds of help needed. In this way *Devastating Losses* helps both the bereaved and their caregivers, by offering a more complete and detailed understanding of the bereavement process, so essential to promoting a smoother healing after the loss of a child.

Another important shortcoming, and another paradox, in the professional bereavement literature that does not correspond well with bereavement realities is fortunately addressed in this volume. Bereavement scholars stand in almost universal agreement on the point that bereavement will be a lifelong process for the mourner. Yet, few studies have extended beyond the reach of 5 years after the loss. Here, for the first-time, we find solid empirical data from almost 250 suicide-bereaved parents who averaged 10 years post-loss, who provide much informative detail about the longer-range impact of child loss.

This analysis leads us two ways. First, it takes us to the unfortunate conclusion that there will remain a small minority of bereaved parents, who suffer from their suicide-losses of children to such an extent that they will remain permanently hurt psychologically from their losses. Higher rates of reported depression and poor mental health were reported among these 10-years-or-longer post-loss survivors than other nonbereaved parents in the general population. For these bereaved parents ready access to professional mental health services will be needed to help them over their lifelong grief adaptation course.

Most longer-term suicide-bereaved, however, will not need such help for their grief-related issues. The majority group of survivors will adapt well after their children's suicide deaths, finding new life goals, a renewal of their sense of purpose and some new friends in their post-loss lives that will be decidedly different from who and how they lived prior to the death. They will experience occasional waves of sadness and yearning for their lost children, especially at holidays and commemorative date times. Yet, with the help from the communities of other survivors and with access to other healing help like professionals, psychics, and clergy, most will manage well. Some will express their new sense of purpose within the bereavement communities, helping the newly bereaved, but many will find other important spiritual or social issues with which to invest themselves beyond the bereavement arena.

Most traumatic-loss bereaved parents start their healing from a perceptual field of feeling utterly vanquished from their losses. Thus, they begin healing facing a challenge that this adaptation may represent the single most imposing trial they have ever assumed in their lives. Yet, as we have heard from so many bereaved parents in this book, and with the profound help they offer each other with their grief and coping struggles, most succeed in finding hope again and are able to move forward, setting new life goals and renewing their sense of purpose. From the many accounts provided by these survivors, we see there are ultimately better days ahead as time after losses passes and a myriad number of small curative social forces bring survivors along on their healing journeys.

Until this book was written many parents had to travel their healing journeys without much assurance that they could survive this trip, believing they were engaged in a mostly singular effort to heal on their own. Now, parents who read this text will know that what they thought was uncommon and rare, may not have been so unusual when contrasted against the responses given by other survivors. They will also see, in sharp relief from other survivors' responses, the uniqueness of their own losses. Thus, each healing journey will differ and not everything experienced will be the same for some, as it may be for others on this same journey.

It is sometimes said that each death has a life of its own, i.e. its distinctive characteristics. Traumatically bereaved parents are especially vulnerable after the death of a child. They often question their judgement and decision-making abilities. Well intentioned, but perhaps less well-informed, friends and family members may advise them, "Isn't it time you gave away your son's clothing now?" and the bereaved parent will wonder whether they should be doing this. Yet, within the bereavement community, and in close association with many other similar mourners, survivors learn there is no timetable for "letting go" of things. Bereaved parents learn they must follow the needs for their own self-care first. Thus, they learn that the uniqueness of their losses will be as complex as the relationships they had with the children they lost. Seeing their distinctiveness, against the contrasting responses of bereaved others, helps survivors from falling prey to feelings of isolation in grief. This, in turn, helps promote more self-confidence, better decision-making abilities, and psychological health; it may also aid survivors from ultimately becoming additional casualties to depression, high-risk and self-destructive behavior patterns and even their own suicides. Thus, what these authors have gathered in this important research effort are the voices of those who have been on this journey and have survived. Other survivors who have found their voices are often the best resource to those who are now starting their own journeys to survive the traumatic death of a child.

Frank R. Campbell, PhD, LCSW, CT
Senior Consultant
Campbell & Associates Consulting, LLC

REFERENCE

Shneidman, E. S. (1972). Foreword. In A. C. Cain (Ed.), *Survivors of suicide* (pp. ix–xi). Springfield, IL: Charles C. Thomas.

Acknowledgments

Many hands and hearts went into this book. We are so grateful to the many bereaved parents, nearly a thousand in total, who generously gave their time to answer our very demanding 27-page survey or who participated in interviews. We are so thankful for the enthusiastic support we received from so many, who wrote in additional comments or added important qualifiers to further clarify their survey answers. Some even went to the trouble of including additional typed pages and stapled these to their surveys to fully explain why they answered particular questions in given ways. We were also greatly helped by the post-loss memoirs that eight respondents generously offered to help us more fully understand the nature of their healing journeys. These demonstrations of enthusiastic interest and support from our respondents helped to sustain us during this long and sometimes arduous intellectual and analytical journey.

In addition, we are keenly appreciative of our many sponsors, people who helped us along the way—some repeatedly, as we sought respondents to complete our surveys. These people showed exceptional support to publicize our study and placed their own credibility on the line to encourage bereaved parents to complete surveys. They helped us find particular types of respondents, such as drug overdose bereaved parents, parents who lost an only child, those who had never used therapies or support groups, and so on. Most of these sponsors came from the ranks of support group facilitators, clinicians, and suicide prevention organization personnel: Karen Anderson, Donna Barnes, Anita Becker, Iris Bolton, Karyl Chastain- Beal, Fred Fox, Gail Fox, Carol Greenberg, Ron Hall, Walter Katz, Marilyn Koenig, Phyllis Kosminsky, Sandy LaCagnina, Ann Marie Mairorana, Karen Marshall, Sherry McGinnis, Melinda Moore, Karen Opp, Jane Quercia, Gloria Schramm, Arthur Silverman, Elaine Stillwell, and Pat Wittberger. Without the repeated help of some of these most generous and committed sponsors, our sample never would have been as large and diverse as it eventually became.

Ana Ruth Colon completed the mammoth enterprise of coding all 575 surveys, reducing each from its original 27 pages into a 3-page form of more than 400 places of bubble-coded markings for scanning. She also diligently transcribed the many comments offered by respondents into machine-readable Excel files for later data analyses. On many occasions, we needed to revisit the original surveys and the accompanying electronic records, and we were always struck by the remarkable correspondence between both, indicating rare coding errors. Bob Reily, of Nassau Community College MIS, also offered us invaluable help with scanning the code sheets into ASCII data files. Bob's perseverance and technological know-how enabled us to get accurate records from antiquated scanning equipment that would have been abandoned by any profit-making company but which, unfortunately, was the best available at NCC at that time.

As an early member of our research team, Bernard S. Gorman, professor of psychology at Nassau Community College, offered us valuable help with our project. Helping to design our research instruments, programming the statistical software to compute our numerous scales and measures, he was an invaluable statistical consultant during the formative stages of this project. Gorman also helped to create tables and graphics displaying our findings, assisted greatly in preliminary analyses of early papers, and offered valuable methodological counsel and support during the formative and developmental stages of this work.

We would not have been able to complete the analysis of Internet support groups in Chapter 11 without the very generous help and support of Karyl Chastain-Beal. She encouraged us to complete a survey of the parents of suicide (POS) group membership and helped to facilitate it by continually posting reminders to members about our survey so that within 3 months, 200 members had completed our survey. We are also grateful to Tom Taylor of the Nassau Community College Academic Computing Services for creating our easy-to-take survey on the NCC file server. Both Taylor and Anthony DeLouise helped us to administer this survey with a maximum of ease and efficiency, fully protecting respondents' confidentiality.

We, our four-author team, assume full responsibility for all errors. For each of us, this project has represented an attempt to advance the knowledge base about how bereaved parents repair their lives after the traumatic loss of a child. Our past experiences have shown us that the information presently available for clinicians and the bereaved themselves is woefully inadequate to the immense challenge presented by a traumatic loss of a child to any bereaved parent. Survivors and clinicians alike deserve a broader perspective and more comprehensive information than what is currently available. None of us were paid to do this work; yet, each of us felt a sense of urgency to provide richer, more detailed, and evidence-based information for all concerned parties—the bereaved, their friends and families, and clinicians/caregivers and researchers—who are concerned with a suicide or a drug overdose death. It is in this spirit of fostering the development of a more solid base of social science knowledge about this important but neglected group of bereaved persons that we offer the present work.

Devastating Losses

Introduction

This book is about ordinary people. People, most of whom, before their lives were upended, clinicians would have regarded as normal and psychologically well adjusted. They come from all levels of society and walks of life. They are physicians, teachers, lawyers, social workers, managers, salespeople, entertainers, and truck drivers. What sets these people apart from everyone else is their sudden, unexpected, and personally devastating experience of losing a child to suicide or some other traumatic event.

(For the case illustrations that follow, we have changed all names and personally identifying information to protect the privacy and confidentiality of our informants.) Susan and Henry Goldfarb, for example, were the proud parents of Ronald. When the boy graduated with honors from his suburban Detroit high school, Ronald's parents thought he deserved a special treat and sent him off on a 2-week, chaperoned trip to England. Tragically, as the group made its way across the country, one of the double-decker sightseeing buses toppled over. The driver had had three pints of beer during lunch and overcompensated on a turn. Ronald and two other children were killed in the accident.

Dick Phillips and Marion Forsythe live in a high-rise condominium apartment in San Francisco. Loretta, Marion's 22-year-old daughter from a previous marriage, lived with the couple. Loretta was a shy and awkward young woman, with few friends and a long history of weight control problems. At age 18, she was diagnosed with type 2 diabetes. After struggling to finish college, she eventually found a job as a trainer in a program for emotionally disturbed children. Three months later, she was let go; the supervisor told her she did not mix well with the troubled youngsters. Loretta was deeply hurt by the firing. A few days after the job loss, in an attempt to cheer her up, Marion and Dick suggested going out to a restaurant for a family dinner. Loretta said, "No. You guys go out. I'm not hungry right now. I've got things to do in my room. Bring me back a sandwich." When Marion and Dick returned, they saw police cars, an ambulance, and many people gathered outside their building. They learned that during their absence, Loretta had jumped to her death from their balcony, 14 stories above street level.

Judy and Marty Abramowitz had remarked to each other, many times, that having a drug-abusing child was much like living with a person with a serious physical handicap—a lifelong project and if your child gets the right treatments, he or she will survive. This is the way they had begun to think about Nicole, their 24-year-old daughter, who had been living on the streets in their suburban community near Seattle. In and out of outpatient and in-patient programs ever since she was 15, at different times Nicole stole their money, jewelry, and had totally destroyed one of their cars. She had tried most every common street drug: heroin, pot, cocaine, crack, and lysergic acid di-ethylamide (LSD). She prostituted, shoplifted, was in and out of county jail at least three times. During her most recent hospitalization, it seemed to the Abramowitz's that she had possibly turned a corner. Drug-free for more than 6 months continuously, she finished her General Educational Development (GED) and was appointed as a trustee at the treatment facility. Judy and Marty were cautiously optimistic about Nicole's recovery when she returned home for her first visit for Christmas holidays. Yet, the next morning after her late evening arrival, they found her limp body in her childhood bed where she had apparently died of a heroin overdose. Although an Emergency Medical Services (EMS) team arrived within minutes after being summoned, Nicole was pronounced dead at the local county hospital 2 hours later.

Janice and Patrick Driscoll, a couple in their mid-50s, live in an upscale Boston suburb. Patrick, an orthopedic surgeon, and Janice, a speech therapist, were parents of Emily and a younger son, Michael. Michael was a good student, athletic, and popular with the girls. After finishing near the top of his high school class, Michael persuaded his parents to send him to the University of Colorado. Although they were at first reluctant because it was so far from home, they eventually agreed. After all, they thought, they could readily afford the costs of Michael's occasional trips home; and how could they deny him when he had done so well in school? They knew Michael was a ski bum and much attracted to the recreational opportunities that Colorado presented. In the early months after Michael left home, he communicated regularly with his parents. But by spring, his calls and letters had become less frequent. The only problem his parents were aware of was that Michael was having difficulties with a college math course. Because he intended to pursue a career in the sciences, poor math grades would have presented a serious obstacle to him. Then, after several days without hearing from Michael, they got a call from the sheriff of a small town about 50 miles from Denver. Michael had apparently shot himself with a handgun that he had purchased a few days before he died. His body was found in a deserted location in a rented car.

How do parents survive the loss of a child and particularly the loss of a child to suicide, drugs, or other traumatic death? Some experts, such as Atle Dyregrov, have claimed that the loss of a child is the most devastating and disruptive of all kinship losses. It puts the survivors (the term used for people who sustain the loss of loved ones) at risk for their own untimely death. If survivors do not succumb to their own premature demises, how do they sustain themselves? Do they conduct their lives in a state of near-perpetual gloom, or are they eventually able to experience joy and laughter, once again? Do they ever completely "heal" after losing a child? And do they want to heal in such ways that they purge their remembrances of loss from memory altogether? Do they sometimes feel marginalized in their grief, encountering a wall of disinterest and avoidance by others that leads them to feel less socially acceptable? What is the psychological impact, if any, of this marginalization? Do suicide survivors encounter more stigmatization and complicated grief than parent survivors of other traumatic deaths or natural deaths? Do some or many suicide survivors experience posttraumatic growth following their tragic losses, and if they do, in what ways is their growth manifested? These are but a few of the important questions about traumatic losses of children that need to be answered.

The field of bereavement studies has generated considerable research on how people adapt after losses of loved ones. Despite the intellectual outpouring, however, relatively little attention has been devoted to the subject of suicide bereavement. Investigations of this subject have been so sparse that in 2003, the National Institute of Mental Health (NIMH) sponsored a conference of experts in the field to stimulate more research in this area and to identify some of the critical knowledge gaps (NIMH, 2003). Although survivors widely use peer support groups in their healing efforts, almost no work has been done to evaluate whether survivors find these groups as helpful as other resources, such as professional counselors or religious advisors (Cerel, Padgett, Conwell, & Reed, 2009). Little work has been done to identify survivors' needs for social services years after the initial loss (called the *postvention period*). Few survivor studies have extended beyond 5 years after the loss. There has been little or no research on the experience of sustaining multiple losses of kinfolk to suicide versus the loss of a single child. No one has studied whether survivors find meaningful help in Internet support groups, how suicide affects families, or whether married couples experience greater discord or cohesiveness following a child's suicide. These are but a few of the many important questions we examine in this book.

Losing Jesse and Making Sense of It, a Reflection by Bill Feigelman

In the bereavement literature, it is often mentioned that survivors, especially in traumatic loss cases, must make sense of their loss if they ever hope to advance their healing (Currier, Holland, Coleman, & Niemeyer, 2008). And in his analysis of the unique bereavement issues associated with suicide loss, Jordan contends there is an essential need for survivors to create a narrative explaining how their loved one was lost (Jordan, 2001).

This book has its genesis in the urgent need Beverly and I felt to make sense of the suicide of our beloved son, Jesse. In order to heal, we needed not only to understand what happened but also to help others struggling with the devastating impact of the traumatic loss of a child. An essential part of this sense-making is the narrative of loss.

I remember the day of Jesse's death—July 12, 2002—as vividly as if it were yesterday. The phone rang at about 6:30 a.m., waking me up. Susan, Jesse's fiancée, was calling from California, where she had gone on a business trip. Sobbing, she said, "Bill, I don't know how to tell you this, Jesse's gone; he's gone." I didn't know what she meant until she finally said, "Jesse's dead. . . . He hung himself. I can't believe it! Evan [Jesse's good friend and neighbor] found him and called the police. Evan felt Jesse's limp body against the closed bathroom door in his apartment. He immediately called 911 and the police found him."

Heartsick, I told Bev what happened. We sat in bed in shocked disbelief. Every parent's worse nightmare had come true for us. As I got dressed, the same thoughts kept swirling in my mind: Why did you do it, my boy? How will we manage without you? How will we live as a family now that our lives have turned upside down? How can we possibly survive this?

Over the course of that first dreadful day, several images and impressions became fixed in my mind. The contrast of our sadness with the beautiful early July day—brilliantly sunny, clear, and dry—was startling. "How could anyone take his life on such a perfect day?" I thought. I felt sorry for Evan, who had had the shock of discovering Jesse. Only a few years earlier, he had discovered the body of his younger brother, who died at age 19 from a first experimental use of heroin. Evan had also lost his father, who died in his mid-50s after a long and painful illness.

I will never forget the yellow crime scene tape draped around the doorway to Jesse's apartment, nor the sight of the bag containing his body being transported through the hallways of the building. Several neighbors stood by while the body was carried out, commenting, "That was the nice young man that lived in 4D. What a horrible tragedy!"

Several family members accompanied us to the morgue at Kings County Hospital, Brooklyn, that afternoon. At the hospital, we were told we had to identify the body and sign the death certificate. We were also told that there would be an autopsy because Jesse had died alone.

We were on automatic pilot, in a daze, preoccupied with the tasks of dealing with Jesse's death, making an appointment to visit a funeral parlor later that evening to arrange for his memorial service and calling the cemetery to get permission to have a grave site allocated to us.

The last things we did that day were to return to Jesse's apartment and go through some of his belongings. We searched his "briefcase," which was in reality a deep red Naugahyde bowling ball bag. Jesse, an aspiring filmmaker, was always ready to defy conventional fashion and taste. He wanted people to know he was an independent thinker, who did not blindly follow traditional practice. The unique briefcase was trademark Jesse.

In the briefcase, we found many telling indicators of the disorder, conflict, and confusion in Jesse's life. There were rumpled scraps of paper listing appointments he had made and a notepad with important phone numbers, sketches, and doodlings. In addition, we found cigarettes, nicotine gum, and several asthma atomizers. (In recent years, he had made several urgent visits to hospital emergency rooms for asthma attacks; and ER doctors had often told him to quit smoking.) We also found Zoloft and Ativan, the most recently prescribed psychotropic medications, as well as Advil and Viagra.

Every survivor resists the reduction of the lost loved one's life to the cause of his or her death. Survivors always want to remember and cherish the memory of their lost loved one's life, personality, accomplishments, and uniqueness, not only their demise. This is heard over and over again at survivor support group meetings and at healing conferences. "Please remember my child by who he was, but not by how he died; this was only one small part of his being." But the urge to seek an explanation for the dreadful event is powerful.

In the days that followed, we tried to make sense of Jesse's death. There were several things that did not quite add up, suggesting little pre-thought on Jesse's part before he took his life. He had told Beverly that he was looking forward to spending the next weekend at the family's country house and asked to be picked up at the late afternoon train on Friday. On the day he died, he had sent off a check covering the next 3 months' rent for his Manhattan writing studio. These facts suggested his death was impulse-driven, perhaps a quick decision, made in an isolated moment, to relieve his extreme pain and sadness.

As we thought about his death, we recalled that Jesse was haunted by the deaths of two close friends in a boating accident 8 years earlier. When he was making his senior year college film, he took a small crew of friends and fellow students to our summer home in the middle of winter. In the early morning hours, after a late night of filming, while everyone else slept, two of Jesse's close friends thought it would be fun to go out in the family rowboat. They rowed out on a seemingly calm sea; but when the wind came up, the boat capsized, and they drowned. Jesse felt tormented by their memory and never forgave himself for not dissuading them from taking the boat out.

Jesse was also caught in a vise of rising expectations. Although he felt pride that, at age 28, he alone had raised half a million dollars to make his first narrative feature film—which was generally well received in the industry—he struggled to get a next film to make or to launch the film scripts he was writing. Even with a Hollywood agent representing him, he felt he was a failure. In the year before his death, to carry him through the slack period of film work, he took a job as a salesman in a fashionable men's clothing store, catering to many in the entertainment industry. Because Jesse aspired to have some of the store's clientele as his personal friends, he felt greatly humiliated to be working there.

Jesse's personality was not ideally suited for a career in film. He was much too sensitive and easily hurt for this kind of work. Film makers and script writers must have thick skins to endure frequent rejections and all those "wonderful meeting you" declarations that rarely result in returned phone calls. Jesse could vividly recall slights many years afterward. He was his severest critic. Sometimes family members, seeing evidence of his low self-confidence, suggested that he pursue a less competitive and stress-inducing career. Jesse invariably resisted this advice. He claimed that filmmaking was his one and only occupational choice, his exclusive career goal; he had little respect for friends who had abandoned film for more modest and readily attainable employments. Although we never thought of it that way at the time, his low self-esteem was a major suicide risk factor.

And then there were the drugs. Jesse had a long history of self-medication. He could never stop smoking, despite his asthma. At certain points during Jesse's life, he could have been described as a recreational drug user. On numerous occasions during his adolescent and young adult years, he tried many different drugs: alcohol, marijuana, LSD, heroin, and cocaine. On other occasions, especially toward the end of his life, he exhibited signs of deep drug dependence. He took risks to his physical health when he knew at any time he could sustain a fatal asthma attack. He persisted in using cocaine even as he observed adverse effects that it created in some of his social relationships. In times of stress and with his somewhat low-frustration tolerance and high impulsivity, he frequently sought the quick relief and oblivion of drugs. And even though he had entered outpatient rehab programs at different times, Jesse never really thought he had a drug problem. He died as he was coming down from a cocaine binge, one that was especially ill-advised, as he combined the cocaine with the new psychotropic medications he was given about 6 weeks before.

Less than 2 months before taking his life, Jesse became engaged to Susan—the love of his life. Susan was the first woman to succeed in capturing his restless spirit. They had lived together for more than 2 years before their engagement was announced. He was enormously proud of Susan. He greatly admired her physical beauty, intelligence, social skills, and enterprise. Susan was a successful freelance graphic artist who had fully transcended the difficulties of growing up in a dysfunctional family. She supervised the rehabilitation of his apartment, transforming it from an undistinguished tenement apartment he had occupied by himself to an aesthetically pleasing living quarters.

One might think that Susan's commitment to him would have diminished his suicide risks considerably. However, in actuality, it may have had precisely the opposite effect. Susan's high energy and achievement orientation for both of them may actually have been stressful for Jesse, who didn't believe that he could keep up. If Susan was not charting their next career milestone, she was planning vacation trips and elaborate, memorable parties for them to enjoy. Susan had little tolerance for Jesse's drug taking, his repeated bouts of cocaine use, and the interference that his treatment had on their social life. Her expectations that he successfully become drug-free may have been another challenge he felt he could not meet. Sometime after his death, we learned from one of his co-workers that Jesse secretly dreaded getting married to Susan. On the one hand, he could not imagine himself living without her. On the other hand, her high performance expectations and his fear of disappointing her frightened him.

Jesse had been on and off various prescribed psychotropic medications. As he saw different psychotherapists from time to time, he believed Valium or Prozac or some other drug could give him the relief he sought. Yet, he found that these drugs decreased his interest in and ability to have sex. Sexual performance anxiety was still another issue he coped with during his last year.

Nearly a month before Susan and Jesse's engagement party, we learned that Jesse had made a suicide attempt in the couple's apartment. While coming down from a cocaine high, he wedged his belt between bathroom door and door frame (in much the same way he did when he later completed suicide). The door opened, and he fell to the floor where Susan discovered him, gasping for breath. The next day, the couple went to a local psychiatric facility where Jesse was evaluated. At this evaluation, he did not show any signs of severe psychiatric impairment. He was asked if he wanted to enter to inpatient care, but as he glanced around the building, eyeing shuffling, disheveled patients in soiled-looking pajamas, he convinced the psychiatric evaluators that his problems could be effectively handled by outpatient care and a different regimen of psychotropic medications. After this crisis passed, Jesse was able to assure Susan and the family that his suicide attempt was an anomaly, a wild, impulsive gesture that would never again be repeated. He vowed to never—ever—try to take his life again.

Two months later, with Susan away in California, Jesse had another cocaine binge. This time, he was on a new and not fully established regimen of psychotropic medications. And this time, with his body full of unfamiliar chemicals, when the cocaine high faded, he felt impelled to take his life.

Jesse Remembered

One of Jesse's best friends recounted their first meeting as they found themselves sharing a college dormitory apartment. Jesse extended a cigarette to his new roommate and said, "Care for a fag, matey?" feigning a distinctly British accent. His new roommate, taken aback, asked, "Are you English?" Jesse smiled mischievously and said, "No, I'm from Queens, as in Queens, New York. I was in England for 2 weeks before I came to school." He loved to surprise and disarm people with gestures like this. Over the years, he made many fast friendships with his playful manner.

Jesse had a great deal of charm. He was genuinely interested in people. He could make conversation and form friendships easily with people from all walks of life: whether they were taxi drivers or highly ranked professionals. He made many friends from his contacts in the film industry and his performing-arts-oriented college and even kept a few from his junior high school years. Among his friends, he was known as someone you could confide in, who would offer thoughtful and sensible advice. He always tried to help his friends who needed emotional support.

Jesse also had close relationships with his family. He was his father's best friend. We often went to movies or sporting events together, talked about film, watched Knicks and Yankees games. He frequently cooked gourmet meals with his mother at the family's summer house. (Jesse knew a great deal about food preparation from his days working as a sous chef in a Mexican restaurant and as a short-order cook in a Seattle fish restaurant.) Jesse also had warm, close relationships with his sister and brother-in-law, his young nephew and niece, his aunts, and cousins.

Jesse gave the people he was closest to nicknames that he felt were terms of endearment. He called me "River," for "Old Man River." Bev was known as "Irmadillo," although she had little use for her middle name, Irma. His sister, who had been adopted in infancy, he called "Ana Banana," to acknowledge her Colombian heritage. His brother-in-law was known as "Johnny Bag of Donuts," commemorating his Italian origins. Jesse came to family celebrations whenever he could. He enjoyed the company, support, and interest of close family members and did not want to miss any special holiday meals. At times, Jesse's playfulness resulted in his being an insufferable tease, but that was part of the package.

Jesse loved film. His filmmaking heroes were Steven Spielberg, Francis Coppola, and Jim Jarmusch. One of Jesse's early productions was a short road film, in which he traveled from New York to Cleveland, to Jarmusch's home, in the hope of meeting one of his idols. The film ends with Jesse standing in an outdoor telephone booth having a phone conversation with Jim Jarmusch's mother.

Jesse also loved to travel. He had been to Europe five or six times, usually in conjunction with screenings of his films in Berlin, Lugano, London, and Oldenberg, Germany. He seized every opportunity to join the family on our vacation trips—to Mexico, Puerto Rico, Dominican Republic, and Costa Rica. Jesse loved the outdoors, loved to sunbathe, swim, body-surf, play tennis, and bicycle. He liked to read great works of literature and popular contemporary work. He had little interest in current events, barely opening the newspaper except to follow the latest film openings or sports results.

Jesse was a man of principle, deeply committed to his filmmaking art. Although he had feelings of low self-worth, he almost always presented himself with confidence and self-assurance. He readily talked to strangers, who usually found his humble and nonpretentious manner engaging. Jesse was a man of action to his core, not a brooder. Those who knew him will probably never forget him.

The Winding Path of Healing

The sense-making associated with bereavement leads survivors to the important tasks of creating two narratives for themselves. First, survivors must develop an understanding of the death of their loved one. Second, survivors are drawn to the task of explaining how they are managing after the loss. Every survivor recognizes that the preloss image of himself or herself no longer fits. Survivors must reinvent themselves to adapt to the enduring absence of their child. They must create new goals, replacing the ones that seemed appropriate when their child was alive.

During those early days after Jesse's death, I was haunted by the conviction that this was the low point of my life. No tragedy I had ever experienced came close to this one. During those early grief days, I often did not feel like getting out of bed in the mornings. My legs felt leaden, almost as if they were paralyzed. Life seemed pointless and devoid of meaning. I was glad it was summer, and I did not have to appear on campus everyday. I kept wondering how I would feel in September, when classes resumed, and I would be seeing all those young men around campus, some of whom would remind me of Jesse. Would I be able to handle that experience without bursting into tears or getting angry?

During those early months, I had a very vivid recurring dream. I dreamt Jesse was still alive, holed up in the attic bedroom where he lived as a high school student. In the dream, I would go up there, and we would have long talks or watch movies together. Occasionally, we would go out for walks. No one recognized that he was there with me on our walks. Bev was the only other person who knew that Jesse was still alive. It was our secret. Then, I would awaken to the sad realization that this was a preposterous, wish-fulfillment dream, and the tragedy of his absence pummeled me once more. There were also instances in real life where I thought I had seen Jesse somewhere—boarding a subway train off in the distance, getting into a car on the street somewhere, or riding a bike. These images of people resembling him were strong and frequent during those early days; fortunately, as time passed, they subsided.

I also remember occasionally feeling that life was so abysmally sad and meaningless that I could readily accept my own death. On more than one occasion, as I rode a subway train, I thought I could easily fall into the track bed, where all my miseries would be over. On other occasions, I thought of steering my car into an oncoming 18-wheeler. What stopped me from acting on these self-destructive fantasies was the realization that I might not accomplish my goal and would become a helpless invalid. I was so into myself then that I did not give a single thought to the effect my suicide would have had on my loved ones. If there is anything I have learned in my post-loss years, it is the huge, devastating impact that a suicide has on surviving family and friends.

During those early days after loss, I could not stop blaming myself for missing crucial signs about Jesse's vulnerabilities. If he had not died by suicide, he could have overdosed on some of the drugs he was taking or fallen asleep at the wheel while driving when he sometimes pushed himself beyond his endurance level. I kept playing over in my mind the would-haves and should-haves. After his first suicide attempt, we should have insisted that he enter one of the country's best psychiatric clinics. If only we had. . . .

Bev also experienced many of the same painful symptoms associated with loss that I did. Yet, she had some unique issues. As a practicing psychiatric social worker, she began to doubt seriously her abilities as a psychotherapist, questioning her competence. She was overcome with guilt that, although she had been able to save several patients from suicide during her many years as a practitioner, she had missed the signs in her son. There were many days when she thought she should give up her practice altogether to assume a less demanding line of work. She was also reluctant to disclose the loss of her son to her patients, fearing that some would lose confidence in her and that others would focus on her loss, at the expense of their own treatments. In her intense pain, she found it difficult to listen to some patients' problems, especially their complaints about personally troublesome but seemingly superficial matters.

Our "blame-game" routine extended beyond ourselves and at times included others. At that time, we were united in our anger and extreme disappointment in particularly important people in Jesse's life. Why had not Susan alerted us to his drug use on so many occasions when we thought he was drug-free? Why had she not participated more actively in supporting his treatment-seeking efforts? We were also extremely angry with Jesse's therapist and conferred with a lawyer about pursuing a suit against him. We felt he did not monitor Jesse's medications sufficiently closely, did not mobilize the family adequately in his treatment plan, and did not appear to show the slightest caring interest to our bereaved family afterward.

What kept me going during those early days were the many tasks associated with loss. Writing letters to people who had sent sympathy cards or to those who had attended the funeral, and *Shiva* kept me occupied. Susan created several poster boards for our living room with large recent photos of Jesse. It was comforting to glance around at the photos as I took care of my many correspondences. We also created a memorial scholarship for a gifted film student to be offered yearly at Jesse's alma mater. There were donation solicitation letters to compose and distribute; and there were thank-you letters to write. We also scheduled two screenings of Jesse's feature film: one at his alma mater and another at my college campus. Invitations had to be sent out to family, friends, and colleagues. It was also comforting to keep score of the many responses that we received: contributions to the scholarship fund, condolence letters, and so on.

Most people were kind and supportive, recognizing our grief and generously supporting the memorial scholarship. But there were other responses that were deeply disappointing. Some so-called friends never said a word of sympathy to us, passing over the death as if it never happened. For example, a few months after the death, we received a personalized Christmas greeting card from a formerly close friend who thoughtlessly wished our family "a joyous holiday season." And there were others who attended the funeral but never called us again afterward. Still others made thoughtless remarks about

Jesse's suicide or about suicide in general, like those who said officials may have been mistaken in claiming that Jesse died by suicide.

After Jesse's death, I decided to memorialize him by trying to preserve his artistic legacy. Jesse died around the time the DVD was beginning to eclipse videotape as the most popular film distribution format. I commissioned one of Jesse's friends to make a DVD master from the AVID outtakes of his feature film. Jesse's friend also made a DVD copy of Jesse's 16-mm short films, some of which had won prizes at film festivals. If someone had a further interest in any of Jesse's work, I was prepared to act as its facilitator. I also thought I might be able to work over his three film scripts, to ready them for his California-based agent but was soon forced to acknowledge my own scriptwriting limitations. My plan to memorialize Jesse would have to take place in a different arena. I decided then that I would apply my social science research skills to study suicide and began digging deeply into the vast behavioral science literature on the subject.

At about this same time, Bev and I were active participants in a local support group for survivors of suicide. We found the group greatly helpful. About two years after Jesse's death, an opportunity presented itself for us to take a support group facilitator's training course in Philadelphia. Although at that time we had no desire to lead our own group, we thought it would be valuable to gain more knowledge about how these groups work and how survivors get the best healing benefits from them. The suicide information clearinghouses such as American Association of Suicidology (AAS), American Foundation for Suicide Prevention (AFSP), and Suicide Prevention Action Network (SPAN) recognize peer support groups as one of the primary resources survivors use to help themselves following suicide losses. This course was taught by Dr. Jack Jordan, one of the foremost experts on suicide bereavement. When I had an opportunity to speak to him during a break, I was stunned to learn that almost no research had ever been done to evaluate the effectiveness of support groups in helping suicide survivors.

After learning about this important knowledge gap, I began to focus my reading more directly on suicide bereavement. I talked over the possibility of planning a survey of suicide survivors with my longtime friend and frequent collaborator, Dr. Bernard Gorman. Over the years, Gorman and I have worked together on a great many different behavioral science research projects. He and I usually complement each other's academic strengths. There are few who know research methods and statistics better than Gorman, and he has always found a way to temper my theoretical flourishes with solid methodology. Some months later, when we had developed a rudimentary plan for the survey, I approached Jack Jordan again in the hope he would join us in collaboration. It was a long-shot idea because he hardly knew me. But much to my surprise and exhilaration, he generously agreed to work with us. With Beverly bringing her therapeutic perspective, we had a well-balanced team of collaborators to study this important neglected subject. I now had an important mission to complete, one that would honor my son's memory in a way that seemed approachable and, indeed, extremely exciting.

As the early work progressed, our team produced a series of research articles that appeared in some of the leading bereavement journals: *Death Studies*, *Omega: Journal of Death & Dying*, and *Illness, Crisis and Loss*. We also began to see our preliminary work laying a foundation for a larger, more comprehensive and unifying work that we now present here. Unfortunately, Dr. Gorman's many previous commitments left him unable to devote the necessary time and attention for producing this book. Yet, very fortunately, we were able to gain the support of Dr. John McIntosh. Dr. McIntosh is one of the suicide bereavement field's most experienced and knowledgeable scholars, and his careful research and methodological skill has often been praised. We are honored to have him join us in completing this much-needed work, to help healing professionals and the bereaved better understand how grieving parents recover after losing a child.

The Research

We created and repeatedly revised a survey draft, including well-established instruments used in grief studies, indicators of grief difficulties, complicated grief, PTSD, depression, and suicidality, among other criteria for mental health problems. Wherever possible, we also attempted to include measures that had been employed in representative sample surveys—measures of depression, mental health dysfunctionality, spousal cohesion—so that we could have comparison points for our data and those for nonbereaved peers in the general population. We also developed a social stigmatization scale, something that had not been used before in studies of suicide survivors. We include our survey instrument in the Appendix.

In the chapters that follow, we present our findings on how parent survivors adapt after the upending loss of a child, and especially, after a child's death from traumatic circumstances such as suicide or drug overdose. We take the point of view of parent survivors themselves and trace how they change during their early years of grief to many years later after the loss. We examine how and what healing aids are used over time and whether these parents show any greater mental health service needs than others who did not experience the loss of a child.

We also offer an in-depth exploration of how survivors' socially significant others often fail to understand the nature of their grief. Most survivors will, at some time or other after their loss, hear the remark from nonsurvivors, "Isn't it time you moved on?" If there are any words that signify to survivors the degree to which they are misunderstood and inspire in them an oppositional mood, these are precisely the words. For most, the thought of expunging or diminishing the memory of their lost loved ones is something they never, ever want to do, however painful the burdens of remembrance may sometimes be.

This is one of the important challenges every survivor faces: carrying forward the memory of their lost loved one in a society that finds it more convenient to forget the deceased and especially those that died under less morally unacceptable circumstances like suicide or drug overdoses. Survivors face a lifelong task of carrying the burden of their loss with them in a society that only dimly understands their grief. Our task throughout this volume has been to identify the many challenges that parent survivors who have lost children to traumatic loss inevitably confront.

Portions of earlier versions of this work have appeared in the following publications: Feigelman, W., Gorman, B. S., & Jordan, J. R. (2009). Stigmatization and suicide bereavement. *Death Studies, 33*(7), 591–609, used by permission of Taylor and Francis; Feigelman, W., Gorman, B. S., Beal, K. C., & Jordan, J. R. (2008). Internet support groups for suicide survivors: A new mode for gaining bereavement assistance. *Omega, 57*(3), 217–243; Feigelman, W., Jordan, J. R., & Gorman, B. S. (2008–2009). How they died, time since loss, and bereavement outcomes. *Omega, 58*(4), 251–273; Feigelman, W., Jordan, J. R., & Gorman, B. S. (2009). Personal growth after a suicide loss: Cross-sectional findings suggest growth after loss may be associated with better mental health among survivors. *Omega, 59*(3), 181–202; Feigelman, W., Jordan, J. R., & Gorman, B. S. (2011). Parental grief after a child's drug death compared to other death causes: Investigating a greatly neglected bereavement population. *Omega, 63*(4), 291–316, used by permission of Baywood Publishing Co., Inc.; Feigelman, B., & Feigelman, W. (2008). Surviving after suicide loss: The healing potential of suicide survivor support groups. *Illness, Crisis & Loss, 16*(4), 285–303; Feigelman, B., & Feigelman, W. (2011). Suicide survivor support groups: Comings and goings, part 1. *Illness, Crisis & Loss, 19*(1), 57–71; Feigelman, B., & Feigelman, W. (2011). Suicide survivor support groups: Comings and goings, part 2. *Illness, Crisis & Loss, 19*(2), 165–185, used by permission of Baywood Publishing Co., Inc. We are grateful to the publishers and copyright holders for permission to reprint this material.

REFERENCES

Cerel, J., Padgett, J. H., Conwell, Y., & Reed, G. A. (2009). A call for research: The need to better understand the impact of support groups for suicide survivors. *Suicide and Life-Threatening Behavior, 39,* 269–281.

Currier, J. M., Holland, J. M., Coleman, R. A., & Neimeyer, R. A. (2008). Bereavement following violent death: An assault on life and meaning. In R. Stevenson & G. Cox (Eds.), *Perspectives on violence and violent death* (pp. 177–202). Amityville, NY: Baywood.

Jordan, J. R. (2001). Is suicide bereavement different? A reassessment of the literature. *Suicide and Life-Threatening Behavior, 31,* 91–102.

National Institute of Mental Health. (2003). *Research on survivors of suicide workshop. May, 2003.* Retrieved from rarediseases.info.nih.gov/asp/html/conferences/conferences/suicide

1

Theoretical Issues Guiding This Study and How the Data Were Collected

THE PLAN OF THIS BOOK

This chapter focuses on the theoretical issues guiding this research and explains how the data were collected. In this first chapter we set the stage for our remaining analyses, which focus on how parents cope and repair their lives after the traumatic death of a child.

Part I, which includes Chapters 2 through 5, focuses on the nature of the trauma that parents experienced. In each of these chapters we investigate how a different kind of traumatic death or the distinct circumstances of the death can bring about differences in outcomes for parent survivors, leaving some with greater grief difficulties, complicated grief, posttraumatic stress, and mental health problems compared to other child-loss survivors. Chapter 2 covers suicide stigmatization, widely discussed as an obstacle in any survivor's healing course, as survivors struggle with their loss being discredited in the eyes of some (or many) of their socially significant others. In Chapter 2 we investigate the pervasiveness of stigmatization as it affects suicide survivors, wherein particular significant others are likely to stigmatize the survivor and whether this shunning has a measurable impact on a survivor's healing processes, grieving, and mental health problems. In Chapter 2 we also compare whether suicide survivors experience more stigma than other child-loss survivors. Chapter 3 investigates the bereavement difficulties of parents who experienced the loss of children from drug overdoses and other drug-related deaths. We compare this group of parents to suicide survivors and parents sustaining losses of a child from other causes of death. In Chapter 3 we gauge the pervasiveness of drug overdose deaths compared to other deaths of young adults. We also compare and contrast the stigmatization experienced by these parents and examine whether they confront any greater or different challenges of stigmatization compared to other parents experiencing traumatic and non-traumatic losses of children. Chapter 4 delves into some of the additional death circumstances surrounding a suicide that may have an impact on bereavement—for example, whether the bereaved parents found the body, had a history of prior suicide attempt experiences with their child before suicide completion, or had a close or conflicted relationship with their child before the death—and how these experiences may be associated with different bereavement outcomes. In Chapter 4 we also evaluate how time after the loss is associated with reductions in a suicide survivor's grief difficulties. Chapter 5 explores another poorly understood bereavement phenomenon: parents who sustain the loss of their only child and the question of whether they experience any different or greater bereavement difficulties compared to bereaved parents with surviving children. In addition, we also explore whether parents who sustained multiple death losses in their families (e.g., the death of two children or of a parent and a child, closely following each other) experience any greater or different bereavement problems compared to parents who lost one child.

In Part II we investigate the different kinds of help-seeking resources survivors use along their healing journeys as they cope with their grief and try to advance to a new normal after the death of a child. Recognizing the profoundly disturbing pain of early loss, we devote Chapter 6 to the help-seeking behaviors survivors usually pursue in their first years after a loss. Early grief often brings survivors to a desperate quest to seek help from a wide variety of sources: grief counselors, support groups, pastoral counselors, psychics, and so on, or sometimes several different support groups or counselors are visited at the same time. In Chapter 6 we examine survivors' usage patterns during these early difficult years and the resources perceived as most and least helpful to them. In Chapter 7 we turn our attention to the later years after loss, another poorly researched and understood subject, when most survivors accept their grief as an enduring feature of their lives. Most available studies cover bereavement adaptations taking place within the first 5 years after the death. In Chapter 7 we focus on bereaved parents who averaged 10 post-loss years. In later years after loss, we find survivors usually narrow their help-seeking to fewer resources and diminish their attachment to any single resource. In Chapter 7, we also pose the question whether longer term child-loss survivors experience more enduring mental health problems when compared with their peers in the population at large who have not experienced child losses. Chapter 8 takes us to a close-up look at peer support groups for suicide survivors, one of the most popular arenas where survivors seek grief help after a suicide loss. Chapter 8 takes an overview of the many psychosocial needs of survivors addressed in peer support groups, examining the many benefits survivors experience through participation in such groups. In Chapter 9 we identify the characteristics of those survivors for whom these groups offer little grief help, and we also explore the transition process and the social characteristics of those survivors who are more likely to rely on these groups. In Chapter 9 we also explore support group termination and how, as the time after a loss passes, many survivors outgrow these groups and withdraw from them, whereas a smaller number of survivors assume positions of support group leadership. Chapter 9 also delves into the qualities of support group leadership and other group features that promote beneficial group functioning. Chapter 10 focuses on the posttraumatic growth that many survivors experience years after their loss. Our findings suggest that posttraumatic growth is associated with better mental health for survivors. In Chapter 10 we identify those social characteristics associated with the development of survivors' posttraumatic growth. Chapter 11, the last chapter in this section, examines a relatively new resource for survivors: participation in Internet support groups. In Chapter 11 we contrast the social and loss-related differences between those seeking grief help from other survivors in online groups with others who seek grief help exclusively in face-to-face groups or from other sources. This analysis generally shows that Internet support group affiliates devote much more time to their groups than members of face-to-face groups. In addition, Internet affiliates have usually experienced greater stigmatization, grief, and other mental heath difficulties than face-to-face members. Thus, Internet support groups appear to offer these survivors valuable help that is not readily available to them elsewhere.

In Part III we investigate the impact of a child's traumatic death on married couples. Chapter 12 explores how men and women deal differently with grief after the loss of a child and how this may affect spousal relationships afterward. In Chapter 12 we explore the differences between men and women regarding grief difficulties, complicated grief, posttraumatic stress disorder (PTSD), and mental health problems after losing a child. We also explore gender differences in seeking grief help and support. This analysis of gender differences sets the stage for the next chapter, Chapter 13, where we examine spousal relationships after the traumatic loss of a child. We explore whether the loss brings a married couple closer together or drives a wedge between them. In Chapter 13 we also investigate those shared social characteristics that may have an impact on marital discord (or harmony) after the loss.

In Part IV, our final chapter, entitled "Where Do We Go From Here?" we suggest directions for future research based on our current findings. In Chapter 14 we also sum up the important practical implications of this study as it suggests better ways for survivors to cope with loss and to advance their healing afterward.

THEORETICAL ISSUES GUIDING THIS RESEARCH

If there were an array of questions propelling us forward with this inquiry, it was to investigate whether parents sustaining the traumatic death of a child stand at a higher risk of premature mortality and whether they are more likely to have any greater mental health, grief, and other problems than other child-loss survivors.

With our heavy reliance on our bereaved parent survey and interview data, we knew we would be unable to say very much from these sources about the premature mortality of parents who lost children to traumatic deaths. Yet, this is a question that often arises in the mind of a bereaved parent: Are they at risk for dying prematurely? We, therefore, felt it necessary to review the available literature on this important question.

First, we should clarify our terms of what may constitute "a traumatic death" of a child. Arguably, it might be advanced that any death of a child is a traumatic one because it goes against the natural order of life where parents ordinarily expect to predecease their children. Yet, when a child dies after repeated unsuccessful surgeries to treat a faulty heart valve or a progressive decline in functionality associated with an aggressive cancer, an inoperable brain tumor, an acute asthmatic attack, or diabetic complications, such cases usually offer parents advanced warnings of their child's mortality risks. In many of these cases, parents may have had long and painful histories of witnessing declines in their child's health, as he or she may have been shuttled from home to hospital (or to hospice care) and to eventual death. Probably a substantial portion of child deaths recorded on death certificates as attributable to natural causes could be termed less traumatic deaths, where parents had varying degrees of awareness of their child's fragile health and diminished ability to survive. Of course, some natural deaths leave parents totally surprised and unprepared for the fatality, such as a single lethal attack from a brain aneurysm.

In this research *traumatic deaths* are defined as those listed on death certificates occurring with varying degrees of suddenness and violence. Sudden, unexpected, and violent deaths bring about more traumas. The standardized U.S. death certificate lists five different death cause classifications: natural causes, accidental deaths (such as automobile accident deaths, drownings, poisonings, etc.), homicides, suicides, and deaths under ambiguous circumstances ("undetermined" deaths; Hetzel, 1997). It is our assumption throughout this study that most parents accept the definition of their child's death designated by their local medical examiner or coroner. They may not share this information fully and correctly with everyone they know, but they will usually share it accurately with many, if not most, of their socially significant others.

Let us take a look at the frequency of individuals who experience traumatic and natural deaths among the U.S. population who are likely to have living parents. We computed these numbers from the Web-based Injury Statistics Query and Reporting System (WISQARS) website, maintained by the Centers for Disease Control and Prevention. The WISQARS database enables users to investigate deaths occurring in 2008. If we look at the deaths of people surviving the first year of life and dying by age 50 (and thus likely to have living parents), we see almost as many traumatic deaths cases ($N = 97,457$) as those dying from natural causes ($N = 106,477$; Centers for Disease Control and Prevention, 2011). Thus, there are substantial numbers, probably close to 200,000 parents every year who will be added to the ranks of traumatic death survivors, having lost one or more of their children to a suicide ($N = 21,652$), homicide ($N = 14,988$), or an accidental death ($N = 60,817$), dying within the age range of 1 to 50 years. These numbers quickly mount to the millions as the total of youth and adult child deaths accumulate over the years.

When we began this inquiry into traumatic child death bereavement, with our somewhat less conventional method of gathering a sample primarily from the ranks of various general bereavement support groups and from the rosters of survivor of suicide (SOS) support groups, we expected to draw in at least some bereaved parents who had lost children to homicides. We expected this for several reasons. One of our principal resources for our respondents was The Compassionate Friends, a general bereavement group with many local chapters explicitly offering grief support to parents sustaining losses of a child to homicide (www.compassionatefriends.org). Given the relatively high frequency of U.S. homicides among the young, we anticipated some of these parents would inevitably become respondents in our sample. In addition, drawing upon (SOS) support groups, we anticipated some numbers of parents who had experienced a murder/suicide death of a child to inevitably join our sample. Given the extensive media coverage of murder/suicide cases, we thought (SOS) groups would attract at least some of these bereaved parents to seek grief help.

Yet, oddly, as our sample rose to more than 500 cases, only four parents who had lost a child to a homicide were included, and we did not encounter a single parent from a murder/suicide case. Despite its frequent media coverage, we discovered the reality of murder/suicide is exceedingly rare. As suicides themselves are relatively uncommon events in the United States, with an annual rate of approximately 11 per 100,000 persons, the murder/suicide rate is especially rare, with a rate of 0.2 to 0.3 per 100,000 or about 1,000 to 1,500 cases yearly (Marzuk, Tardiff, & Hirsch, 1992). Had we extended our recruitment efforts of traumatic loss survivors to the dedicated support groups serving the bereavement needs of parents sustaining homicide losses of children, such as the U.S. Parents of Murdered Children (www.pomc.com) or Loved Ones Left After Murder in Great Britain (www.lolam.org), we would have been able to recruit potential respondents from these organizations. However, because of the small number of homicide survivors who became part of our sample, it was not possible to provide any useful information about this important subgroup.

Let us now return to the important questions stimulating this inquiry. What does the previous research tell us about whether parent survivors from all child deaths stand at a higher risk for their own premature mortalities (compared to nonbereaved parents)? Do parents of traumatic death losses have higher mortality than people whose children died from nontraumatic causes? Only three previous studies were found that attempted to answer these questions. One early study of child loss conducted with a British sample of more than 900 cases found excess mortality for bereaved parent survivors compared to their nonbereaved peers (Rees & Lutkins, 1967). However, these results contrast sharply with an Israeli study that found no differences in mortality between bereaved and nonbereaved parents (Levav, Friedlander, Kark, & Peritz, 1988). More recently, a Danish study (Li, Precht, Mortensen, & Olsen, 2003) based on a national registry matched a sample of more than 21,000 bereaved parents against a control group of more than 29,000 nonbereaved peers and found the following: "(T)he death of a child is associated with an increased mortality from both natural and unnatural causes in mothers, and an early increased mortality from unnatural causes in fathers" (p. 363). Thus, these results are mixed and do not help us arrive at any firm conclusion regarding whether any premature death of a child is associated with a diminished life expectancy and whether a traumatic death of a child has any special significance in this respect. Thus, these important questions remain unresolved and deserve further exploration in future research.

STUDYING A MORE APPROACHABLE QUESTION

A more approachable question for us to consider is whether parents experiencing traumatic deaths of children stand at higher risk for grief and other mental health difficulties as compared to others sustaining nontraumatic losses of children. Up to this time, those wishing to review this issue within the context of drug overdose deaths and drug-related deaths have not been able to find much guidance from previous research. The question has never been considered explicitly within this population. Now, if one wishes to approach this question in relation to suicide bereavement, there are at least some opportunities to gain an overview of how suicide survivors compare against other groups of survivors. However, one will need to be especially cautious before making any inferences from this research record because of the many differences between previous suicide bereavement studies. Past studies have yielded many diverging findings and all these are perfectly understandable, considering the many studies being completed at different times and focusing on diverging objectives, having differing samples, sampling methods, control populations, and loss relationships, and using differing measurements, along with the existence of very few longitudinal studies.

In an ambitious synthesis of many of the diverse research findings on suicide bereavement, Sveen and Walby (2008) were able to extrapolate several convergent themes from this confusion. Scouring all similar studies cited in MEDLINE from over a 60-year period and from an even longer period from psycINFO and applying minimalist criteria for inclusion (studies had to include suicide survivors, include another bereaved group as controls, be quantitative, and be published), they found 43 studies to fit their criteria. Their assessment of overall findings showed no significant differences between suicide survivors and people bereaved by other causes of death in terms of general mental health, depression, PTSD symptoms, anxiety, and suicidal behavior.

The comparisons on overall levels of grief were less clear. When measures developed specifically regarding suicide bereavement were included, the suicide survivors reported higher levels of rejection, shame, stigma, and a need for concealing the cause of death than controls.

As helpful as Sveen and Walby's (2008) results may be in summarizing overall patterns, they do not reduce the confusion when we examine a particular type of loss relationship, such as the loss of a child. Of the 43 studies fitting their minimalist criteria, only seven explicitly focused on parents sustaining the suicide death of a child. One of these seven focused on family functioning and did not deal explicitly with grief and mental health issues. Six others of the seven studies of parental suicide bereavement drew comparisons to other traumatic child-loss populations, such as to parents bereaved by homicide and accidental deaths. We would consider both of these bereaved parent populations as traumatic death survivors. Thus, only one previous study (Miles & Demi, 1991–1992) explicitly compared parent suicide survivors ($N = 62$) to natural death survivors ($N = 38$) and found higher guilt among the suicide survivors compared to their natural death–surviving counterparts. Throughout our investigation we will use all available previous bereavement studies to help us better illuminate how our specific findings may mesh with the past research record.

What is striking about the Sveen and Walby (2008) work is the relative paucity of studies collected from their extensive online searches. Only 69 studies were uncovered that had any potential for inclusion in their review, of which 43 were chosen when selection criteria were met. Previous research offers a meager number of studies—seven in all—that have dealt with the matter of parental suicide bereavement, a matter that affects some 40,000 to 60,000 surviving parents each year based on the yearly suicide frequencies among decedents who might be imagined to have living parents. This says a great deal about the virtual neglect of suicide survivors by behavioral scientists in their choice of participants. It is no small wonder that in 2003, the National Institute of Mental Health (NIMH) sponsored a special conference among suicidologists to help stimulate more research on suicide bereavement (National Institute of Mental Health [NIMH], 2003).

Suicide survivors appear to be a greatly neglected population in the field of suicidology. Sometime ago, Edwin Shneidman estimated six survivors for every case of suicide (Shneidman, 1969), which probably was a drastic undercounting of survivors because a more recent random-digit-dial phone survey implied approximately 13 million Americans knowing someone who took his or her their life in the past year, of whom 2.2 million knew an immediate family member or other relative who had taken his or her life (Crosby & Sacks, 2002). Research has also documented that suicide survivors have a higher risk of self-harm and suicide compared to the nonbereaved (Agerbo, 2003; Mościcki, 1995; Runeberg & Asberg, 2003). Yet, despite their demonstrated greater risk of self-harm, relatively little research has been conducted with this population.

If one were to undertake a similar literature review of all studies of people dying by suicide compared to people dying by other causes of death over a 60-year period (much like the review Sveen & Walby, [2008] conducted—but on suicide directly) one would uncover many times more studies on this topic than the paltry number of 69 found on suicide bereavement. Any cursory examination of the journals devoted to suicidology shows that the bulk of the work generated has been devoted to suicide explicitly, with very few articles focused on bereavement after suicide.

Drug overdose bereavement, another substantial problem affecting hundreds of thousands of new mourners each year and rivaling suicide as a frequent cause of death among youth, is another greatly neglected subject. We made exhaustive online searches on MEDLINE and psycINFO and were able to find only two previous studies on drug overdose bereavement. Both studies were preliminary studies, undertaken on small samples, completed outside the United States: one, a Brazilian study based on six cases (da Silva, Noto, & Formigoni, 2007) and the other, a British study based on four cases (Guy, 2004). This very meager previous research record contrasts very sharply with the hundreds of epidemiological studies of overdose drug decedents themselves, examining the diverging combinations of drugs consumed, differing locales where the deaths occurred, treatment exposures, social characteristics and life histories of the decedents, and so on. Somehow, bereaved families sustaining the loss of family members to drug overdose appears to have failed to attract the interest of researchers. Why behavioral scientists have ignored these risk populations is an interesting and important question to which we will return at a later point in this introduction. Readers less interested in the details of how the data were collected, characteristics of survey sample, measurements, and additional data sources may wish to scan over or skip this next section and go to the final part: "Thoughts on the Difficulties of Doing Traumatic-Loss Research."

STUDY METHODS, SAMPLE CHARACTERISTICS, AND MEASUREMENTS

Quantitative Data Sources and Methods

Before seeking to distribute our survey among different groups of bereaved parents, the study protocol was reviewed and approved by the Nassau Community College Institutional Review Board. Each respondent received a mailed survey kit consisting of a cover letter outlining the overall goals of the research, a consent form, a survey form, and a postpaid return mail envelope.

As we began this study, we sought to gain a large and diverse sample of parents who lost children to traumatic and nontraumatic death causes. We also sought to better represent survivors in the community at large who used peer support groups. Suicide survivors were an important targeted population for our research, and we sought to better represent survivors participating in peer support (SOS) groups. Thus far, only one survey research study has been conducted specifically with this population (Callahan, 2000). With the listings of support groups from the American Association of Suicidology (AAS) and the American Foundation of Suicide Prevention (AFSP), we attempted to include support group members from most regions of the country. Several facilitators were initially contacted and were asked either to furnish their membership lists or to publicize information about the study at meetings, in their newsletters, or on their electronic list serves. Typically, support group facilitators posted announcements in their newsletters calling for volunteers to participate in a confidential and anonymous survey of parent survivors. Volunteers were directed to contact the first author who was identified as both a sociologist and a survivor of his son's suicide.

In seeking contrast populations for the parent suicide survivors investigated here, we sought to include parents who lost children to other sudden death causes, such as automobile accidents, drug overdoses, accidental drownings, homicides, and so on. We also sought to include cases of child death from natural causes, such as brain aneurysms, cancers, heart disease, AIDS/HIV, and so on. To represent these additional groups of other traumatic and natural death cases, we also made contacts with chapters of The Compassionate Friends groups from where we acquired not only cases of parents losing children from other-than-suicide-death causes but also additional parent suicide survivors. The Compassionate Friends groups, existing throughout the nation, are general bereavement support groups open to parent survivors of all types of child deaths.

We also sought to include traumatic loss survivors using Internet-based support groups. Two such suicide survivor groups were contacted and these furnished respondents: The Parents of Suicide Support Group (www .parentsofsuicide.com) and the Parents Grieving Children of Suicide Group, which presently no longer functions. We also contacted and gained respondents from two Internet support groups serving survivors of drug overdose deaths: Angels of Addiction, Inc. (www.groww.org/Branches/angelsofaddiction.htm) and Grief Recovery After a Substance Abuse Passing Group (widely known as GRASP; www.grasphelp.org). The present survey is the first ever to investigate survivor support affiliates using the Internet.

The following newsletters and list servers played crucial roles in circulating information about our survey: the SPAN USA list server, the Friends For Survival Inc. Newsletter, and the "Surviving Suicide" newsletter published by AAS. These outlets reached large audiences of survivors and clinicians. In addition, several bereavement counselors and psychologists also asked to distribute copies of the survey among their patients. Also, many survivors who learned of the study by word of mouth spontaneously offered names of additional respondents who they thought would want to complete the survey.

By drawing our sample primarily from the ranks of those with past or present affiliations to support groups, there may have been bias overrepresenting survivors with more mental health difficulties. This possibility has been advanced in two earlier analyses (Levy & Derby, 1992; Stroebe & Stroebe,

1989–1990). We sought to correct this possible bias in the following manner. Almost every respondent was asked, in the course of our data collection, to furnish their e-mail addresses, and close to 400 e-mail addresses were collected from this solicitation. Using a "snowball" technique, toward the end of the data collection period, all respondents were sent an e-mail asking if they knew of another child-loss survivor who, to the best of their knowledge, had neither used support groups nor had seen professional mental health or bereavement counselors. They were asked to contact this person, and upon obtaining that person's permission, they, in turn, would be sent survey kits. Eight more survivors became survey respondents from these additional recruitment efforts. When these respondents were added to the numbers that we obtained from the marital pairs subsample (to be described in the next few pages) and from those who learned about our study because they were newsletter subscribers, the data collection eventually included 37 respondents who reported never participating in a peer support group or having any form of post-loss professional counseling. Bereaved parents who never had peer support group contact or professional help have rarely been studied previously. In Chapter 6 we investigate the distinctive characteristics of this lesser known bereaved parent population.

We also encouraged respondents to have their spouses or partners complete surveys. The cover letter accompanying every survey stated that if any respondent wished to have an additional survey mailed to his or her home for a spouse or partner, we would gladly send one. Of all respondents to the first wave of data collection ($N = 540$), 60% ($n = 327$) reported being married at the time of the survey. Only a small percentage of that number, less than 15% ($n = 45$), elected to receive a second survey for a spouse; and of these, only two spouses who had requested second surveys did not complete them. It is possible that the imposing length of our survey instrument (see Appendix) led some to feel their responses were already covered by their partners' responses. In other cases, a parent's grief problems may have diminished his or her ability to complete the survey. Yet, we were still able to gain completed surveys from 13% of all married respondents, which represented a total of 43 cases of marital pairs whose responses were later analyzed both separately and comparatively. Comparative evaluations were made both between the husbands and wives in our survivor sample and between our sample's marital pairs and nonbereaved husbands and wives from the Wisconsin National Survey of Families and Households (NSFH) Study (Bumpass & Sweet, 2001). Four marital cohesion questions were selected from the NSFH surveys and were administered to our respondents for comparative purposes.

Quantitative surveys were collected at two separate time intervals. The first, extended from March 2006 to September 2007. During this early phase, 754 surveys were sent out and 540 surveys were returned, yielding a response rate of 72%. We thought this was a more than satisfactory return rate, considering the difficulty of conducting surveys on grief issues and considering the length of the research instrument, a 27-page mailed survey form. Typically in mailed questionnaire surveys, responses rates fall below the 60% mark (Hopkins & Gullickson, 1992; Kaplowitz, Hadlock, & Levine, 2004; Smith, 1995). Although we never planned it this way, from the outpouring of cooperation received from survivors, our study ($N = 462$) became the largest sample of suicide survivors ever collected.

Within the first data collection wave, there were also 24 natural death survivors, 11 drug overdose death survivors, and 43 other parents who lost children from all other traumatic death causes, such as vehicular accidents, drownings, homicides, military casualties, and ambiguous deaths. As we also sought to further investigate drug overdose bereavement, it became clear that we had insufficient numbers for any preliminary analysis of this important bereavement subgroup. Starting again in March 2009 and extending until September 2009, we contacted three different chapters of The Compassionate Friends groups in the New York metropolitan area to find additional respondents who had lost children to drug overdose or to drug-related deaths. We also made contact at this time with the two Internet support groups serving the drug overdose death bereaved: Angels of Addiction and GRASP. At that time, 42 potential respondents names were given to us, 35 of whom completed surveys, yielding an 83% response rate for this subgroup.

Characteristics of the Sample

Our final sample included 575 respondents. Females outnumbered males by a huge margin, 85% to 15%. By age, 74% of respondents were between the ages of 46 and 65 years; 18% were 66 years or older; and 8% were 45 years of age or younger. The sample also overrepresented upper-status respondents: 34% had household incomes of $90,000 or higher; 43% had incomes between $40,000 and $90,000; and 23% with incomes below $40,000. In addition, 53% of our respondents reported having managerial or professional occupations; 41% reported completing 4 or more years of college; 42% reported some college; and 17% had high school degrees or less schooling. Religious affiliations included 35% Protestant, 26% Catholic, and 11% Jewish, 18% affiliated to other faiths, and 9% with no religious affiliation. The sample was predominately White and native born with 94% of respondents U.S. born, 95% White, and 5% from all other races. Respondents came from every state in the United States, and seven were from Canada.

Of the 575 cases, survivors of suicide outnumbered all others at 80% (462 cases); there were 46 cases of overdose drug death survivors, 24 natural death survivors, 34 other traumatic death survivors such as drownings and auto accidents, 4 homicide deaths, and 5 cases where it was reported that a child had died under ambiguous circumstances. Based on all the information provided, two of the five ambiguous death cases were subsequently reclassified as drug overdose cases, and the three remaining cases were incorporated into the other traumatic, mostly accidental death, survivors group. For 10%, their loss had been sustained within the past 12 months, 39% between 1 and

4 years ago, 35% between 4 and 10 years ago, and the balance, 16%, more than 10 years ago. A total of 18 respondents reported experiencing multiple untimely death losses of either two children to suicide, the loss of a child and a partner to suicide, or some other combination of accidental and/or natural death losses of nuclear family members occurring close each other. Decedents ranged narrowly in age, with 7% being 15 years or younger, 30% between 16 and 21 years, 36% between 22 and 28 years, 18% between 29 and 35 years, and 9% older than 36 years. Clearly, adolescent and young adult deaths predominated in our sample, with over 80% of respondents ($n = 478$) reporting the loss of a son or daughter between the ages 16 and 35 years.

Measurements

To measure grief difficulties we used an abbreviated version of The Grief Experience Questionnaire (GEQ; Barrett & Scott, 1989). The original GEQ scale consisted of 55 items. Following the lead of Bailley, Dunham, and Kral (2000) who performed a factor analysis of the scale and identified eight distinct factors within it, we selected the two highest factor-loaded items for each of the eight factors to form our 16-item abbreviated scale. Our abbreviated scale yielded an internal consistency (Cronbach's alpha) coefficient of .87. The brief GEQ scale was answered by 522 respondents, yielding a mean of 39.1 ($SD = 11.5$) with scores that ranged from a low of 16 to a high of 80. Although we had no way of verifying how closely this abbreviated scale correlated with the full 55-item scale, we did find it correlated highly with other grief problems indicators that were also administered to our respondents: the Impact of Events Scale (Horowitz, Wilner, & Alvarez, 1979) and the Complicated Grief scale (Prigerson, 2002). The correlations between the abbreviated GEQ scale were .77 with the Complicated Grief scale and .69 with the Impact of Events Scale. The Complicated Grief scale was answered by 541 respondents, yielding a mean of 27.9 ($SD = 8.9$), with scores ranging from 11 to 51. The Impact of Events Scales, a measure of PTSD, was completed by 522 respondents showing a mean score of 33.3 ($SD = 8.9$) and a range of 14 to 56.

We used the same single-item depression screening question that was asked in the 1998 Midlife Development survey (Wethington, Kessler, & Brim, 1998): "During the past year, was there ever a time when you felt sad, blue, or depressed for 2 weeks or more in a row?" with possible answers of "yes," "no," or "not depressed because of taking antidepressant medication." We found that overall depression was widely reported by our respondents, with 67% reporting current depression. In comparison with the same question, only 32% of a nationally representative sample of middle-aged adult women and only 17% of men reported depression. In our sample, the comparable depression rates by gender were 70% for women and 52% for men.

This 1998 Midlife Development survey also included an eight-item measure of depression that we administered to our respondents. It was based on responses to the previous screening question: "During the past year, was there ever a time when you felt sad, blue, or depressed for 2 weeks or more in a row?" Those answering affirmatively were asked seven additional questions.

1. During this period, did you lose interest in most things?
2. Did you feel more tired or low on energy than is usual for you?
3. Did you lose your appetite?
4. Did you have more trouble concentrating than usual?
5. Did you feel down on yourself or worthless?
6. Did you think a lot about death—either your own or someone else's or death in general—during this time?
7. Did you have any sleep disturbances?

An 8-point scale ($no = 0$; $yes = 1$) was created for responses to these eight questions. In our sample, the alpha coefficient for the scale was .92. The depression scale was completed by 506 respondents with a mean of 4.34 ($SD = 3.1$), with scores ranging from 0 to 8.

We also created an index of personal psychological problems by combining several questions that had been asked in the Midlife Development survey. The survey asked respondents to self-rate their mental or emotional health: "How about your mental or emotional health? Is it poor, fair, good, very good, or excellent?" Then, we also counted the previously mentioned depression screening question. Survey respondents were also asked to count the number of days in the past 30-day period when they were unable to go to work or had to cut back normal household activities because of mental health difficulties. In addition, they were also asked a life satisfaction question: "At present, how satisfied are you with your life—a lot, somewhat, a little, or not at all/none at all?" We administered these same questions to our respondents and found responses associated with one another that had correlation coefficients ranging from .20 to .52. Summing together responses of (a) poor or fair mental health reports, (b) self-reported depression, (c) one or more days lost to work or housework during the past 30-day period, and (d) life satisfaction reports of little or none at all, we placed respondents along a continuum from 0 to 4 on our mental health problems scale, which yielded a Chronbach's alpha of .70. The total score of our respondents on the personal psychological problems scale was 1.6 out of a possible 4 ($SD = 1.3$, $N = 556$). For the national sample, midlife survey women older than 46 years (and thus representing over 75% of our survey respondents), the reported mean was only 0.5 ($n = 1,051$).

Respondent suicidality was measured by three items. (These same items have appeared in the National Survey of Drug Use and Health [2010] and various other general mental health surveys.) The first item assessed suicidal thoughts, "How often during the past 12 months did you think about taking your own life?" Respondents could answer from 1 to 5: *almost never or never, rarely, occasionally, frequently,* or *very frequently.* Respondents reported rare-to-occasional suicide thoughts, with a mean of 1.8 ($SD = 1.1$) among the

567 respondents that answered this question. The second item assessed suicide plans. Respondents were asked, "Had you made any specific plan for suicide during the past 12 months?" Of our respondents, 10% ($n = 59$) reported making a suicide plan during the year prior to the survey. The third item assessed suicide attempts and nine respondents (1.6%) answered affirmatively to the query: "Had you made any suicide attempts during the previous 12 months?"

To assess positive growth after the loss, we also included the 7 items that had the highest factor loadings from a 12-item set of personal growth questions that formed part of the Hogan Grief Reaction Checklist (HGRC; Hogan, Greenfield, & Schmidt, 2001). The included items were "I have learned to cope better with life; I feel as though I'm a better person; I have a better outlook on life; I have more compassion for others; I am stronger because of the grief I have experienced; I care more deeply for others; I am a more forgiving person." These 7 items yielded an alpha coefficient of .91 among the 536 respondents that offered useable responses to this abbreviated personal growth scale where responses ranged from a low of 7 to a high of 35, with a mean of 24.0 ($SD = 7.1$).

Another important measure, our stigmatization scale, which appears throughout many of our analyses, is described in detail in the next chapter.

Additional Qualitative Data Sources

Besides the previously described survey administered to the largest number of our respondents ($N = 575$), two supplemental surveys were also collected during the course of this investigation. As we examined survivors' attachments to Internet support groups, we developed an online survey that we administered to 200 Internet support group members who belonged to an online parent (SOS) support group. More details on how this survey was conducted and our findings will be found in Chapter 11. For Chapter 9, devoted to transitioning and use of peer support groups, we collected 24 additional follow-up interviews by telephone with survivors who had withdrawn from peer support groups.

In addition to numerical survey materials, this study is also based on several different qualitative data sources. Our survey included several open-ended questions where respondents could offer more information on the nature of their particular bereavement experiences, in addition to the previously mentioned scales. For example, respondents were asked to enumerate any troublesome stigmatizing situations encountered or any particular socially supportive (or hindering) experiences that advanced or retarded their recoveries. In addition, many respondents offered lengthy comments and qualifications to survey questions. From among our respondents, eight had written memoirs or pamphlets detailing their loss and healing journeys since the death of their children and supplied these materials to us. We examined and analyzed all this information and, wherever relevant, cross-checked it with the survey data findings.

We also collected participant observation data from more than 200 other survivors, from monthly peer support meetings of suicide survivors, and from various survivor healing conferences over an 8-year period. Because the first and fourth authors were survivors of their son's suicide, they were able to regularly attend monthly meetings of a peer-led, (SOS) support group for over 5 years—from 2002 to 2007. Findings based on this field observation experience are described in detail in Chapter 8. Both investigators provided a cross-check on one another, making sure observations were accurately recorded. All names and personally identifying information about these respondents were changed to protect respondent confidentiality. Wherever necessary, nonessential details of observations and persons were changed to safeguard each participant's privacy and confidentiality.

Additional participant observations were also collected over a 3-year period when the first and fourth authors led their own support group situated close to a large metropolitan center. Whereas most participants in the first support group were aware they were being studied (and the majority had offered signed consent forms before completing their surveys), few participants in the second group were aware that observations were being collected on them at the group's meetings. The researchers identified their research objectives and obtained respondents' permissions for study participation among all individuals who gave interviews. Again, in the second group, all names of individual informants have been changed, and nonessential details of the observations and the persons have been changed to safeguard each participant's privacy and confidentiality.

THOUGHTS ON THE DIFFICULTIES OF DOING TRAUMATIC-LOSS RESEARCH

If any answer can be found to the question why so little research has been conducted among traumatic loss survivors and the suicide bereaved in particular, it leads back to the widely held belief that survivors are an especially vulnerable population, easily hurt by any questioning that would take them back to reviewing their loss experiences. In one early discussion of the capacity of bereaved individuals to offer informed consent to participate in research, Macklin (1978), a bioethicist, questioned whether any bereaved individual can offer their informed consent to participate in research given their trying personal circumstances. More recently, Wortman and Silver (1989) framed this question somewhat differently, suggesting that "normal" grieving may present few difficulties for bereavement survey research participation. Yet, the authors claimed some survivors may have difficulties freely making consent decisions when they have lost close relatives, such as a spouse or a child, or in cases of traumatic deaths when the death occurred under violent circumstances.

Beliefs claiming that suicide survivors may be unable to freely offer their consent to participate in research have a wide currency among behavioral science professionals and clinicians. At a 2003 conference sponsored by NIMH dedicated to expanding the knowledge base of suicide bereavement, experts in the field concluded that one of the important methodological and ethical challenges in doing survivor research includes the potential risk of retraumatization (NIMH, 2003). With pervasive fears of harming survivors by doing survivor research, researchers have often encountered difficulties in gaining approvals to do survivor studies by institutional review boards (IRBs) at universities, hospitals, and other research institutions (Ceci, Peters, & Plotkin, 1985). Recently, an incident was reported to us of two very experienced and respected researchers in the suicidology field who were turned down in their initial application to administer pencil-and-paper tests (consisting of established grief problems measures) to groups of suicide survivors by a university human subjects review board. The board rendering this decision was at one of the larger research universities in the country, regularly reviewing hundreds of similar behavioral science proposals yearly (although not often with survivor populations). The board claimed that answering these grief experience questions would be too upsetting for these very fragile respondents.

In another case, taking place at another large research university, a graduate student completing doctoral studies was initially denied IRB approval to do a survey research of suicide survivors. This student/researcher had survived a family member's suicide and intended to impart this information to potential respondents. The IRB committee initially told this student that it was not proper for her to tell research subjects she was a suicide survivor. By doing so, she would lead some respondents into study participation out of pity for her. She was advised that if she did not disclose her survivor status, she could proceed with the research. The student objected to being considered "pitiable" by the IRB committee and was especially troubled by the restriction being placed on her study that would deny her an important rapport-building opportunity (from appropriate self-disclosure), thereby diminishing the trust and support that would have otherwise been available to her. With help from more experienced suicide bereavement researchers from across the country, she was eventually able to persuade the committee to withdraw its prejudicial procedural requirements. These cases are just two of many in which bereavement researchers may be discouraged or thwarted altogether from doing grief studies, usually without any well-founded empirical justification. At professional conferences, bereavement researchers often swap their hard luck stories of trying to persuade human subjects review boards to accept their survey research proposals.

The accepted protocol for most any survey research is to clearly tell potential respondents they do not need to answer all questions and to skip over all items found as personally troublesome. And if they wish to leave parts of their surveys uncompleted, they are also free to do so. They are also routinely told if any parts of the survey questions are personally upsetting, the researcher will refer them to a professional counseling resource for assistance. Yet, despite these very clear and protective stipulations about research participation (which as we noted are common practice in many investigations), many review boards still remain skeptical that survivor research can be completed without harmful incidents.

In sharp contrast to these widespread beliefs about reluctant and easily damaged respondents, we found a very keen willingness on the part of our respondents to complete the lengthy 27-page surveys. Although we made only a single follow-up effort to secure cooperation from delaying respondents, in deference to beliefs about respondent fragility, we still obtained a 72% rate of cooperation from the first wave of survivors we approached. Some respondents returned surveys many months later, offering profuse apologies for their delays, stating they had mislaid their forms. We are confident that had we made a subsequent follow-up effort, response rates would have been higher, even closer to the 80% rate, which is considerably higher than that found for most mailed surveys (Kaplowitz et al., 2004). Such a rate would have rivaled those for household interviews (Siemiatycki, 1979; Smith, 1995).

Many of our respondents voluntarily expressed their willingness to be contacted in the future at the end of their surveys. Many commented how thankful they were that this research was being conducted. Some said they felt honored and privileged to be selected as respondents. Many also wrote in or typed long and detailed qualifications to their survey answers. Some also transmitted copies of books, journals, or memoirs they had written since their loss. A few of our more articulate respondents also commented that they found the survey experience to be cathartic. Of course, there were others who refused to complete the surveys. They often sent back notes stating that answering the questions was too painful for them now. Statements of apologies frequently accompanied these survey refusals.

We should also acknowledge that another important element enhancing cooperation with this study was the fact that the principal investigator was himself a survivor of his son's suicide. Had this fact been withheld, it could be argued that it is doubtful that as many respondents would have been as keenly motivated to complete surveys or available for future assistance. As it was, many respondents expressed condolence wishes to the principal investigator as they returned their surveys. The survivor/researcher also helped to engender trust and a sense of importance about the research enterprise. This sentiment cannot be more vividly documented than by the acts of one especially cooperative respondent who insisted on conveying to the principal investigator her only copies of her son's last letters, a photo memory book, and newspaper clippings about her son that she insisted must be seen and evaluated by the researchers in completing this study.

The responses to our survey were comparable to those obtained from another survey of child-loss survivors, whose deaths were attributable to three causes: SIDS, suicides, and accidents (Dyregrov, 2004). In this Norwegian study, a subsample of 64 parents from the larger sample of 262 was reinterviewed, and 100% reported their research participation was a positive or very positive experience and none regretted participating. Respondents to this Norwegian study linked their positive experiences to being allowed to tell their complete stories and to having a hope that telling their stories might help others. Everyone in this smaller group of respondents to the follow-up survey had participated in open-ended interviews, lasting between 1.5 and 4 hours, where respondents had the opportunity to talk about whatever bereavement subjects they wished to of personal importance. Many, approximately three-fourths, reported feeling varying degrees of pain in talking about their traumatic losses; yet, because most felt they would be thinking about their lost children everyday anyway, there were no added dangers from having the research interviews. Many expressed feelings of satisfaction at being able to vent their feelings for the first time, having a sympathetic and supportive listener, and gaining a therapeutic experience from their research participation.

These findings converge closely with several other studies of survivor populations cited by Alicia Skinner Cook (2001): Cook and Bosley (1995), Dyregrov, Dregrov, and Raundalen (2000), Lehman, Ellard, and Wortman (1986), Pennebaker, Barger, and Tiebout (1989), and Pennebaker and O'Heeron (1984). In each of these cases, bereavement research respondents welcomed the opportunity to openly discuss their feelings of loss; it offered grievers an outlet for thoughts and feelings not previously shared with available support systems, and they also felt sharing their sorrows would educate others and promote a better understanding of the impact of death on survivors. Some of this research also suggested that when survivors talk more about the death, this is associated with better long-term health outcomes (Pennebaker et al., 1989).

Dyregrov (2004), reviewing several similar studies, concluded

> a growing body of research has started to point out that research participation may even serve the interests of the participants and not only those of the researchers. Instead of causing distress, research may be educational, enriching, therapeutic, or empowering for vulnerable populations. (p. 392)

Talking about their bereavement experiences is believed to help people heal and find meaning to their loss and recovery (Neimeyer, 2000; Neimeyer, 2001; Steeves, Kahn, Ropka, & Wise, 2001). This is especially true in cases of traumatic deaths where respondents find fewer opportunities to openly discuss their losses among most significant others. In the next chapter, we will be examining how stigmatization associated with suicide and other traumatic deaths complicates survivors' grief experiences.

Based on the previously mentioned findings, although most survivors will probably find bereavement research to be personally beneficial, some may not. It is possible that a small number of cases of highly troubled psychiatrically impaired survivors may find that the opportunities to participate in research only exacerbate their psychic difficulties. Yet, the reader is asked to consider the alternatives: ignoring this group of psychologically needy persons altogether or inviting this group to participate in a research task. It seems plausible that by answering survey questions, people will probably gain more help through the attempts to engage them, rather than by being bypassed altogether. Invitations to participate in research may also help troubled individuals identify their needs for gaining psychological services, if they are not already engaged in receiving this kind of aid.

In this opening chapter we outlined the theoretical directions for this research on bereaved parents suffering from diverging types of child losses. Our consideration embraces child deaths from suicides, drug overdoses, other accidents, and natural causes. We described our large and diverse study group, some of whom had lost children just weeks before we encountered them, whereas others experienced losses more than a decade ago. In our attempt to better illuminate the directions bereaved parents take in attempting to cope with their losses, we employed various quantitative and qualitative methods. Some of our methods included precise written measurements with professionally recognized scales of bereavement and mental health difficulties scales, and others involved the direct observation and interviewing of bereaved parents at their support group meetings, healing conferences, and other gatherings and by examining some of their writings about loss. Hopefully, all this will help to form a clearer picture how bereaved parents restart their lives after loss and how this process changes as bereaved parents move from early grief until later years after loss. In this chapter we also approached the question why previous researchers appear to have paid scant attention to these mourners. It is hoped that in the chapters that follow we will present some new and insightful thinking to help guide future research on this neglected and important subject.

REFERENCES

Agerbo, E. (2003). Risk of suicide and spouse's psychiatric illness or suicide: Nested case-control study. *British Medical Journal, 327*(7422), 1025–1026.

Bailley, S. E., Dunham, K., & Kral, M. J. (2000). Factor structure of the Grief Experience Questionnaire (GEQ). *Death Studies, 24*(8), 721–738.

Barrett, T. W., & Scott, T. B. (1989). Development of the grief experience questionnaire. *Suicide & Life-Threatening Behavior, 19*(2), 201–215.

Bumpass, L. L., & Sweet, J. A. (2001). *National survey of families and households, waves I, II & III.* Madison, WI: University of Wisconsin-Madison, Center for Demography and Ecology.

Callahan, J. (2000). Predictors and correlates of bereavement in suicide support group participants. *Suicide & Life-Threatening Behavior, 30*(2), 104–124.

Ceci, S. J., Peters, D., & Plotkin, J. (1985). Human subjects review, personal values, and the regulation of social science research. *American Psychologist, 40*(9), 994–1002.

Centers for Disease Control and Prevention, National Center for Injury Prevention and Control. (2011). *Web-based Injury Statistics Query and Reporting System* (WISQARS). Retrieved from www.cdc.gov/ncipc/wisquars

Cook, A. S. (2001). The dynamics of ethical decision making in bereavement research. In M. S. Stroebe, R. O. Hansson, W. Stroebe, & H. Schut, (Eds.), *New handbook of bereavement research: Consequences, coping, and care* (pp.119–142). Washington, DC: American Psychological Association.

Cook, A. S., & Bosley, G. (1995). The experience of participating in bereavement research: Stressful or therapeutic? *Death Studies, 19*(2), 157–170.

Crosby, A. E., & Sacks, J. J. (2002). Exposure to suicide: Incidence and association with suicidal ideation and behavior: United States, 1994. *Suicide & Life-Threatening Behavior, 32*(3), 321–328.

da Silva, E. A., Noto, A. R., & Formigoni, M. L. (2007). Death by drug overdose: Impact on families. *Journal of Psychoactive Drugs, 39*(3), 301–306.

Dyregrov, K. (2004). Bereaved parents' experience of research participation. *Social Science and Medicine, 58*(2), 391–400.

Dyregrov, K., Dyregrov, A., & Raundalen, M. (2000). Refugee families' experience of research participation. *Journal of Traumatic Stress, 13*(3), 413–426.

Guy, P. (2004). Bereavement through drug use: Messages from research. *Practice, 16* (1), 43–53.

Hetzel, A. M. (1997). *U.S. vital statistics system. Major activities and developments: 1950–95* (DHHS Publication No. [PHS] 97-1003). Hyattsville, MD: National Center for Health Statistics. Retrieved from http://www.cdc.gov/nchs/data/misc/usvss.pdf

Hogan, N. S., Greenfield, D. B., & Schmidt, L. A. (2001). Development and validation of the Hogan Grief Reaction Checklist. *Death Studies, 25*(1), 1–32.

Hopkins, K. D., & Gullickson, A. R. (1992). Response rates in survey research: A meta-analysis of the effects of monetary gratuities. *Journal of Experimental Education, 61*(1), 52–62.

Horowitz, M., Wilner, N., & Alvarez, W. (1979). Impact of Event Scale: A measure of subjective stress. *Psychosomatic Medicine, 41*(3), 209–218.

Kaplowitz, M. D., Hadlock, T. D., & Levine R. (2004). A comparison of Web and mail survey response rates. *Public Opinion Quarterly, 68*(1), 94–101.

Lehman, D. R., Ellard, J. H., & Wortman, C. B. (1986). Social support for the bereaved: Recipients' and providers' perspectives on what is helpful. *Journal of Consulting and Clinical Psychology, 54*(4), 438–446.

Levav, I., Friedlander, Y., Kark, J. D., & Peritz, E. (1988). An epidemiologic study of mortality among bereaved parents. *New England Journal of Medicine, 319*(8), 457–461.

Levy, L. H., & Derby, J. F. (1992). Bereavement support groups: Who joins; who does not; and why. *American Journal of Community Psychology, 20*(5), 649–662.

Li, J., Precht, D. H., Mortensen, P. B., & Olsen, J. (2003). Mortality in parents after death of a child in Denmark: A nationwide follow-up study. *Lancet, 361*(9355), 363–367.

Macklin, R. (1978). Studying grief without consent: Commentary. *The Hastings Center Report, 8*(4), 21–22.

Marzuk, P. M., Tardiff, K., & Hirsch, C. S. (1992). The epidemiology of murder-suicide. *The Journal of the American Medical Association, 267*(23), 3179–3183.

Miles, M. S., & Demi, A. S. (1991–1992). A comparison of guilt in bereaved parents whose children died by suicide, accident, or chronic disease. *Omega: Journal of Death and Dying, 24*(3), 203–215.

Mościcki, E. K. (1995). Epidemiology of suicidal behavior. *Suicide & Life-Threatening Behavior, 25*(1), 22–35.

National Institute of Mental Health. (2003). *Research on survivors of suicide workshop.* Retrieved from rarediseases.info.nih.gov/asp/html/conferences/conferences/ suicide

Neimeyer, R. A. (2000). Searching for the meaning of meaning: Grief therapy and the process of reconstruction. *Death Studies, 24*(6), 541–558.

Neimeyer, R. A. (Ed.). (2001). *Meaning reconstruction and the experience of loss*. Washington, DC: American Psychological Association.

Pennebaker, J. W., & O'Heeron, R. C. (1984). Confiding in others and illness rate among spouses of suicide and accidental-death victims. *Journal of Abnormal Psychology, 93*(4), 473–476.

Pennebaker, J. W., Barger, S. D., & Tiebout, J. (1989). Disclosures of traumas and health among Holocaust survivors. *Psychomatic Medicine, 51*(5), 577–589.

Prigerson, H. G. (2002). *Measuring complicated grief*. Retrieved from http://info.med .yale.edu/psych/cgrief/measure_CG.htm

Rees, W. D., & Lutkins, S. G. (1967). Mortality of bereavement. *British Medical Journal, 4*, 13–16.

Runeberg, B., & Asberg, M. (2003). Family history of suicide among suicide victims. *American Journal of Psychiatry, 160*(8), 1525–1526.

Shneidman, E. S. (1969). "Prologue: Fifty-eight years." In E. S. Shneidman, (Ed.), *On the nature of suicide* (pp. 1–30). San Francisco, CA: Jossey-Bass.

Siemiatycki, J. (1979). A comparison of mail, telephone, and home interview strategies for household health surveys. *American Journal of Public Health, 69*(3), 238–245.

Smith, T. W. (1995). Trends in non-response rates. *International Journal of Public Opinion Research, 7*(2), 157–171.

Steeves, R., Kahn, D., Ropka, M. E., & Wise, C. (2001). Ethical considerations in research with bereaved families. *Family & Community Health, 23*(4), 75–83.

Stroebe, M. S., & Stroebe, W. (1989–1990). Who participates in bereavement research? A review and empirical study. *Omega: Journal of Death & Dying, 20*(1), 1–29.

Sveen, C. A., & Walby, F. A. (2008). Suicide survivors' mental health and grief reactions: A systematic review of controlled studies. *Suicide & Life-Threatening Behavior, 38*(1), 13–29.

United States Department of Health and Human Services, Substance Abuse and Mental Health Services Administration, & Office of Applied Studies. (2010). *National Survey on Drug Use and Health, 2009*. Ann Arbor, MI: Inter-university Consortium for Political and Social Research. doi:10.3886/ICPSR29621

Wethington, E., Kessler, R. C., & Brim, O. G. (1998). *Midlife development in the United States (MIDUS): Psychological experiences follow-up study*. Ann Arbor, MI: Inter-university Consortium for Political and Social Research. Retrieved from http://www.icpsr.umich/icpsrweb/ICPSR/series/203

Wortman, C. B., & Silver, R. C. (1989). The myths of coping with loss *Journal of Counseling and Clinical Psychology, 57*(3), 349–357.

Section I

Factors Associated With the Loss Experience

2

Suicide Stigma and Compounding a Survivor's Grief Difficulties

INTRODUCTION

In this chapter, we investigate the intense stigma that surrounds suicide and the complications this presents for families losing a loved one to suicide. We suggest that the stigmatizing responses of significant others often serves to impede the bereaved parent's ability to grieve and thereby adds to the survivor's grief difficulties and mental health problems. In our discussion of stigma and stigmatization, we apply a sociological definition of the term, referring to stigma as "a deeply discrediting attribute, reducing a person from a whole and usual person to a tainted and discounted one" (Goffman, 1963, p. 3). Many bereaved parents feel greatly rejected by some of their significant others who seem to distance themselves after the suicide.

Our respondents often reported in the open-ended survey questions their experiences of stigma and stigmatization in many different ways after the loss of their child. For most, being stigmatized was expressed in subtle and nonobtrusive ways. For example, Tim E. offered this response to our query about hurtful (and/or helpful) responses from significant others.

> People never said anything really bad to me [after Bobby hung himself]. It was not what they said; it was what they didn't say. Some people who I thought would offer solace remained quiet. And most people just said nothing [after my son's death] and seemed to try to avoid any discussion. It was as if my son never existed.

In another case, Larry P. offered this comment about a neighbor's response to him shortly after his daughter's suicide death.

> I was taking a walk in the neighborhood, and there in the distance, not more than 100 ft ahead of me was my next-door neighbor, Charlie. He was coming down the street in my direction on my side of the street. I saw him look up, spot me, and quickly shift his direction to the other side of the street. Then, as we passed each other, he burrowed his head deeply into his newspaper and didn't respond to my waves to him. It was so obvious and transparent that he was avoiding me. Does he think I am a moron or something, not to notice such things? I remembered that he and his wife didn't come to our daughter's funeral either, though everyone on the block knew about it. And we supposedly were friends, occasionally playing golf together and shoveling each others' sidewalks after a snowfall.

In other instances, actions taken were more overt and obvious. The next case presents a clergy member who denied a bereaved mother a privilege that would have been available to most everyone else.

> Betty Lou J., a 59-year-old physical therapist, remarked that when her son took his life, she hoped to have his funeral service in the local Catholic parish that she regularly attended. Her priest, however, said the service could not take place in his church and that she would have to go elsewhere. Later on, Betty still attended this parish but felt that the priest acted unfriendly to her and showed some reluctance to engage in any further communication.

Surprisingly perhaps, some respondents encountered rejecting responses as they sought grief help from clinicians and other bereaved persons. Subsequently, one survivor reported her experience of rejection in a newly formed therapy group for recently bereaved mothers suffering child loss. At the initial meeting of the group, after the introductions, one of the mothers remarked to the therapist and to the others:

> I can't be in this group with her [the parent sustaining the suicide loss]; this is not possible. My 5-year-old died of a brain tumor. He wanted to live. What good can I ever get from being in the same group with someone whose child wanted to die?

Typically in many cases, survivors reported that they received little acknowledgment of their losses. Such is the case of Tim H., a 63-year-old community college chemistry professor, who told this story about how one of his supposedly close friends reacted after the death.

> We had known each other for more than 25 years, did carpooling together, went together to professional meetings, and always invited our families to each others' parties. Yet, when I saw him at the office a week

after the funeral, he apologized for missing the service and claimed he was "away." Then, he said that we must sit down together and talk, sometime very soon. I suggested now would be fine. He looked visibly upset and said, "Now is definitely not a good time; I have to go home and check my mail." I didn't hear from him again; he never sought me out as he said he would. A couple of months later, he sent our family the traditional holiday card wishing us a joyous Christmas. We were flabbergasted that a so-called friend could act so insensitively and send such a meaningless card without any personal comments of support or condolence to a family that had experienced such a profound recent tragedy.

Respondents reported that the attempts of some people to offer comforting words often showed little empathic sensitivity. Roberta M., a 54-year-old real estate saleswoman, heard the following remark from a close friend 6 months after the death of her 20-year-old son.

It's been 6 months. Get over it. You're not the only parent who lost a child. He's in a better place. He will have his birthdays with the Lord and what could be better than that? And he's not suffering now; that's got to be some consolation. And at least you still have your daughter.

In still other cases, survivors detected insincerity in people's bland comforting statements. Although rarely, they even detected sheer hypocrisy, as Clara S. did. Clara, a divorced 52-year-old single mother, who held a managerial position in a large international bank, reported some awkwardness when she shared with some of her immediate coworkers the information that her only son recently died by his own hand. She said,

These two young women just seemed to act a little inappropriately at that time. I tried not to pay much attention to it. Yet, a couple of days later, when I was in one of the stalls in the women's restroom, I heard them come into the restroom. They were talking about me and laughing. One of them said [I] probably must have [driven] him to take his life. I wanted to jump out at them and tell them off but I thought better of it. Now, it pains me to put on a poker face whenever I see them. I'd love to let them have it, but making a scene would be difficult since I stand in authority over them.

In still another case Leslie I., a single mother who recently lost her 28-year-old son, Derek, to a gunshot suicide, reported a hurtful response she experienced from her older brother after her son's death. Derek took his life at the family's summer home. Although Leslie found it difficult going back to the family's summer home alone afterward, she was looking forward to the prospect of returning there with her brother's family to celebrate July 4th, an annual family tradition. She hoped this visit would help the family reminisce about Derek and enable her to integrate his death with being at the house again.

Leslie's brother, Bob, however, had difficulty with this plan and told her he was "creeped out" by the thought of being at the summer house. Leslie was stunned when she learned of her brother's unavailability to be supportive to her. She felt her brother was abandoning her at a crucial time. Luckily for Leslie, her brother's wife and children committed themselves to sharing the weekend together. But Leslie felt deeply disappointed and hurt by her brother's withdrawal.

In our discussion, it should be understood that stigmatization brings forth a wide variety of different behaviors, which, from the perspective of the bereaved parents, are perceived as ranging from unhelpful to harmful, as well as deficient in providing them with the comfort and caring they so desperately seek. Although stigmatization is not simply a monolith of mean-spirited condemnation of the bereaved parents and their loss, in some cases it may indeed reflect bald-faced prejudice against the mentally ill and addicted populations, blaming the victim, so to speak. In others situations, the hurtful responses may reflect a clashing of different grieving styles between family members or close friends, such as the example of Leslie suggests. In addition, the withdrawal of significant others may reflect profound fear that such a tragedy could possibly occur in their own families. It could also represent significant others' uncertainty about how to behave in such normatively unfamiliar and unusual circumstances, after the traumatic death of a friend or family member's child. For some significant others, assuming a posture of "benign neglect" may seem appropriate, to offer the bereaved "space," rather than to acknowledge the death with more supportive actions. In some cases, too, bereaved parents' reports of stigmatization may be products of their own imagination, projections of their sense of shame, and how they expect others to respond after such tragic events. All these and perhaps other motivational sources may inspire the rejection-appearing responses that we will call here stigmatization.

The literature on suicide bereavement has long recognized suicide survivors as a highly stigmatized group (Cvinar, 2005; Dunne, McIntosh, & Dunne-Maxim, 1987; Harwood, Hawton, Hope, & Jacoby, 2002; Jordan, 2001; McIntosh, 1993). When families lose a loved one to suicide, they usually report that they feel that the foundation of their lives has suddenly disintegrated and vanished. A tempest swirls within the mind of the survivor. They report confusion, numbness, disbelief, feelings of self-blame, anger toward the deceased for abandoning them, and profound wonder why the loved one who they thought they had known so well could act so uncharacteristically (Jordan, 2001). In Chapter 6, we will discuss the experiences of early traumatic grief and identify many of the common feelings accompanying the sudden and unexpected loss of a child or other close relative. Suffice it to say for now that most survivors see this event as the worst tragedy they ever experienced.

Survivors expect that their socially significant others will understand the immense tragedy that has descended on them and therefore will offer the survivor responses that are comforting and supportive. As survivors find that some of these close relatives and friends say thoughtless and inconsiderate things about the loss or say and do nothing compassionate or comforting, the survivor may feel deeply hurt, a victim of "disenfranchised grief" (Doka, 2001). Neimeyer and Jordan (2002) discuss disenfranchised grief as essentially an empathic failure between the mourner and their larger social network in which they fail to have their experience understood by those around them and instead often feel offended, wounded, or abandoned by a lack of an empathic response to loss.

For our quantitative analyses, we developed a stigmatization scale in which we asked our respondents to tell us whether they received or experienced harmful responses from socially significant others. We also asked them if they perceived strains in their relationships with these individuals following the loss of their children. We also asked respondents to tell us about both the helpful and hurtful things other people had said and done to them following their losses.

Stigma associated with suicide has a long and torturous history for families suffering suicide losses (e.g., Colt, 1987). Historical records show that during the Middle Ages, suicide stigmatization was fully institutionalized. Suicide corpses were regularly mutilated to prevent the unleashing of evil spirits. The bodies of people who died by suicide were denied burials in church cemeteries, and the property of their families was confiscated and put into the control of local agents, with the excommunication of these families from the community (Cvinar, 2005). Dunne-Maxim (2007) notes that after a suicide loss, families often lost their land holdings because they were unable to pay the heavy tithes exacted by the church, which caused their pauperization and emigration.

Although such repressive practices no longer apply today in the United States, there is still a vestige of their existence found in the insurance industry where policies generally will not be paid (except for premiums and interest) if an insured dies by suicide within the first 2 years after issuance. Insurance companies have occasionally denied the claims of suicide survivor families on the grounds that the policy was invalidated because the insured consumed illegal and/or controlled substances (Bleed, 2007). Of course, drug consumption occurs in many instances of suicide. Today, however, it seems likely that the biggest obstacles suicide families confront are acts of informal social avoidance and disapproval. The suicide survivor family may be suspected of being partly blameworthy in a suicide death and consequently may be subjected to informal isolation and shunning.

Today, some analysts suggest that the stigmatization experienced by survivors may greatly complicate their bereavement experiences (Cvinar, 2005; Dunne et al., 1987; Jordan, 2001; McIntosh, 1993). One early empirical study conducted by Reed (1993) was based on medical examiner records and a mailback survey of survivors. It found evidence consistent with these assertions showing that more grief-struck survivors reported greater detachment from their families than those who were less grief-struck.

Until now, few researchers have explicitly quantified stigmatization and systematically examined its association with grief difficulties. Barrett and Scott (1989) developed a 55-item scale measuring grief difficulties, including 10 items pertaining to stigmatization:

> *feel like a social outcast; feel like no one cared to listen to you; feel that neigh-bors and in-laws did not offer enough concern; feel avoided by friends; think that people were gossiping about you and the person; think that others didn't want to talk about the death; feel somehow stigmatized by the death; feel that people were probably wondering what kind of personal problems you and the person had experienced; think that people were uncomfortable offering their condolences to you; and feel like the death somehow reflected negatively on you and your family.* (pgs. 211–213)

These items have face validity, but they are repetitive and do little to clarify the most important elements in stigmatization.

Because of these shortcomings, in the present investigation we sought to develop our own measurement of stigmatization. First, we asked all survi-vors an open-ended question where they could enumerate both the helpful and hurtful things that were said and done to them since the loss of their child. Second, societal stigmatization was defined by a composite stigmati-zation scale consisting of two subscales: a family and social strain subscale and a family and social harm/help subscale, both 11 items. The family and social strain subscale questions asked respondents, after the loss of their child, whether relationships changed with any one of seven different family mem-bers (spouse, ex-spouse, parents, in-laws, children, siblings, and other rela-tives) or four social groups (coworkers, closest friends, less close friends, and neighbors). Respondents could choose between *not applicable, remained the same, became closer/stronger,* or *became weaker/strained relations.* Strain subscale scores were calculated as the sum of the number of relationships that were reported as weaker/strained, ranging therefore from 0 to 11. Responses of no change or closer/stronger relationships were not part of the subscale.

The family and social harm/help subscale was in general logically similar to the strain subscale. It queried respondents' experiences with these same 11 different family and social relationship groups in terms of how harmfully or helpfully the groups had acted during the past 12-month period. Respondents answered on a 5-point scale, from *very harmful* to *very helpful.* We scored any responses of 1 and 2 as *harmful ones.* Again, harm subscale scores were the sum of the number of relationship groups that demonstrated harm and could range from 0 to 11. Responses of 3, 4, or 5 were not part of the subscale.

These two subscales were moderately correlated ($r = .55$, $p < .001$). The strain subscale ($\alpha = .72$), harm subscale ($\alpha = .73$), and overall stigma scale ($\alpha = .76$) were internally consistent. About half of present respondents (55%, $n = 301$) reported one or more strained family relationships after their loss; 47% ($n = 268$) reported one or more strained social (i.e., nonfamily) relationships.

Harmful responses from one or more family member groups were reported by 53% ($n = 291$), and 32% ($n = 199$) reported harmful responses from at least one non-kin group during the past 12 months. Among all respondents, the mean scale score was 3.4, ($SD = 3.2$) with a range of scores that extended from 0 to 17 (from a possible range of 0–22).

It is a debatable point whether reports of greater stigmatization (perceived from their significant others) is associated with greater grief difficulties compared to reports of fewer acts of condemnation and shunning. We tested this hypothesis in the present investigation along with the question of whether greater stigmatization is associated with heightened depression and suicidal thinking among survivors.

We also explored whether suicide survivors stood at a higher risk for stigmatization than survivors of other traumatic and nontraumatic deaths. Most discussions of suicide stigmatization imply that the suicide survivor is likely to be subjected to greater social isolation and stigma than other survivors, such as accidental or natural death survivors. Yet, two early studies yielded results somewhat inconsistent with this expectation (Cleiren, Diekstra, Kerkhof, & van der Wal, 1994; McNiel, Hatcher, & Reubin, 1988). In addition, we attempted to identify which significant others among a survivor's associates were most likely to offer hurtful responses and which particular groups were most likely to respond helpfully. We explored all of these questions with our survey data, among all respondents.

FINDINGS ON STIGMATIZATION

Approximately 85% of all respondents ($n = 460$) offered additional comments in the open-ended questions on our survey forms. They gave us personal accounts of the helpful and hurtful kinds of things said and done to them following their loss of their children. In all, there were 2,421 comments offered on our forms. More than twice as many comments mentioned hurtful things said or done to them as those that mentioned helpful things.

Table 2.1 presents a display of associations between reported stigma and various grief difficulties and mental health problems. Correlation coefficients are measures of association between hypothetically related things and show the strength of their association, that is, how they "go together." Typically, a correlation coefficient of 0–.30 would represent a weak relationship, a correlation of .31–.49 would indicate a moderate relationship, and a correlation of .50 or above suggests a strong relationship. Usually, when a correlation coefficient falls below .10, it is interpreted to mean that the association between the measures is essentially by chance. An examination of Table 2.1 shows correlation coefficients ranging from a low of .23 (with attempted suicide) to a high of .47 (with complex grief) showing that grief difficulties, psychological problems, and suicidality are all significantly associated with each other and with the exposure to stigma. This offers some preliminary confirmation

Table 2.1
Correlation Matrix of Stigma Scale, Grief Difficulties, Psychological Problems, and Suicidality

	STIGMA SCORE	GEQ SCORE	COMPLEX GRIEF	IMPACT EVENT	PSYCH PROBLEMS	DEPRESSION SCALE	SUICIDE THOUGHTS	ATTEMPTED SUICIDE
GEQ score	0.45***							
Complex grief	0.47***	0.77***						
Impact of event	0.30***	0.69***	0.69***					
Psych problems	0.43***	0.60***	0.69***	0.52***				
Depression scale	0.37***	0.57***	0.62***	0.50***	0.78***			
Suicide thoughts	0.35***	0.52***	0.54***	0.35***	0.54***	0.49***		
Attempted suicide	0.23***	0.31***	0.30***	0.19***	0.31***	0.29***	0.60***	

Note. GEQ = Grief Experience Questionnaire.
***$p < .001$.

of our claim of an association between stigma, grief difficulties, and mental health problems. We can see that some of the associations between variables in the matrix are very high, such as between grief difficulties and complicated grief, at .77, indicating a strong relationship between these two variables or between depression and psychological problems, at .78. Almost all of the grief difficulties and psychological problems criteria correlate highly with suicide thoughts and were statistically significant at the .001 probability level. Table 2.1 presents all significance tests for all the variables in the matrix. All were statistically significant and unlikely to have occurred by chance. One must realize, however, that correlation does not necessarily establish a cause-and-effect relationship. At this point, all we can say is that the measures are associated (i.e., certain levels on one measure tend to be observed with specific levels of the other).

It may also mean that some of our correlations are mediated and moderated by other variables, such as the time that had passed since the loss or whether the death was a natural or a traumatic one. Thus, a more meaningful test of these associations takes into account these potentially confounding variables of time since the death and the type of death that could be confusing factors in determining the nature of the relationships under examination. We put stigma and grief difficulties into a multiple regression analysis along with time since the loss and whether the death was a traumatic one or not to predict Grief Experience Questionnaire (GEQ) scores (the dependent/predicted variable). This is displayed in Table 2.2. This regression equation explains 27% of the differences in grief difficulties and showed that stigma made the largest single contribution of all three predictors. We attempted to gauge the relative importance of stigma in predicting GEQ scores by rerunning this same equation

Table 2.2
**Multiple Regression Analysis of Grief Difficulties (GEQ Scores)
by Stigma Scale Scores, Time Since Death, and Type of Death**

GRIEF DIFFICULTIES	CORREL. COEF.	BETA WEIGHT	SIG. PROB.
Stigma score	.45	.44	0.000***
Years since death	−.32	−.21	0.000***
Type of death	.16	.12	0.003**

Note. $**p < .01.$ $***p < .001.$
Number of obs = 481
$F(3, 477) = 58.45$
$p > F = 0.0001***$
$r^2 = 0.27$

without stigma present. The result (not presented here) showed a sharp drop in explained variance from 27% to 12%. Clearly, stigma goes a long way toward explaining differences in grief difficulties. We performed an analogous multiple regression (again, not presented here) with the Complicated Grief scale as the dependent variable and the same set of independent variables, and a similar drop in explained variance occurred from 28% with the inclusion of stigma, but down to 11% without stigma in the equation.

Readers unfamiliar with the meaning of the term "explained variance" should know that if 0 was the explained variance, it would mean that the offered predictive model does not help in any way at all to explain the differences between those at the high or the low end of some measurement scale. If the explained variance was at 80%, for example, it would mean that you could correctly predict the scale's scores with 80% accuracy from knowing the other predictors' values. That would be a wonderful result that does not happen all that frequently in most behavioral science research. Actually, a 30% to 40% explained variance rate suggests that your prediction accuracy is that much better than not knowing anything in trying to make an accurate prediction.

Tables 2.3 and 2.4 offer evidence of stigma, making a significant contribution to explain differences in depression and suicide thoughts (dependent variables) among our respondents. Table 2.3 presents the multiple regression of depression with stigma, grief difficulties, time since the death, and type of death as independent variables. The model explains 37% of the differences in depression scores. In this equation, stigma makes a similar statistically significant contribution with time since the loss. Type of death proves to be redundant (i.e., does not significantly contribute to the prediction) in this multicausal model. Table 2.4 shows that the predictors of suicide thoughts yielded a model that explains 33% of the differences in suicide thoughts, with 5 independent variables: stigma, grief difficulties, depression, time since the loss, and type of death. Again, even in the company of powerful predictors like depression and grief difficulties, stigma continues to make a statistically significant contribution to explain differences in suicide thoughts. These tables support

Table 2.3
**Multiple Regression Analysis of Depression Scores
by Stigma Scale Scores, Grief Difficulties, Time Since Death, and Type of Death**

DEPRESSION SCORES	CORREL. COEF.	BETA WEIGHT	SIG. PROB.
Stigma score	.37	.16	0.000***
Grief difficulties	.57	.44	0.000***
Years since death	−.35	−.19	0.000***
Type of death	.08	−.04	0.27

Note. ***$p < .001$.
Number of obs = 437
$F(4, 432) = 62.49$
$p > F = 0.0001$***
$r^2 = 0.37$

our hypotheses of an association between stigma, grief difficulties, depression, and suicidality.

Which family members are most and least supportive after a suicide death of a child? This is a question on which our stigma scale sheds light as suicide survivor respondents ($N = 462$) registered their hurtful and helpful responses of significant others. Table 2.5 displays each of the 11 different family and social relationships and the levels of strain and improvement reported for those groups. Table 2.6 displays the relationship groups ordered by those who offered the least (to the most) hurtful responses following the suicide death of a child. Data for the relationships and helpful responses are also tabulated there. There is a general similarity between Tables 2.5 and 2.6 showing an essential similarity between the results, such that groups with whom strained relationships were observed were also those for whom hurtful responses were reported (and those for whom improved relations were reported were basically the same as those who were helpful).

Table 2.4
**Multiple Regression Analysis of Suicide Thoughts by Stigma Scale Scores,
Grief Difficulties, Depression Scores, Time Since Death, and Type of Death**

DEPRESSION SCORES	CORREL. COEF.	BETA WEIGHT	SIG. PROB.
Stigma score	.35	.10	0.030*
Grief difficulties	.57	.31	0.000***
Depression score	.52	.25	0.000***
Years since death	−.26	−.08	0.054
Type of death	.07	−.009	0.81

Note. *$p < .05$. ***$p < .001$.
Number of obs = 436
$F(5, 430) = 42.55$
$p > F = 0.0001$***
$r^2 = 0.33$

Table 2.5
Percentage of Parents Experiencing Strained and Improved Relationships With These Significant Others Following the Loss of a Child to Suicide (N = 462)[a]

RELATIONSHIP	PERCENT REPORTING STRAINED RELATIONS	NUMBER[1,2]	PERCENT REPORTING IMPROVED RELATIONS
Children	16.5	407	63.9
Neighbors	18.6	388	22.9
Other relatives	19.3	383	24.8
Coworkers	22.1	339	28.6
Closest friends	22.1	440	48.4
Siblings	22.7	392	41.1
Spouse	23.6	339	58.1
In-laws	23.8	235	21.3
Parents	26.6	267	27.7
Less close friends	33.1	411	15.6
Ex-spouse	38.4	177	23.7

Note. From Survivors Child Loss Survey, 2006–2009.
[a]Each relationship group is listed in order of its occurrence of strained relations and unhelpful responses by percentage from lowest to highest.
[1]Each percentage was calculated from the number reporting a weaker or strained and/or harmed relationship divided by the total number reporting having that type of a relationship.
[2]Each percentage was calculated from the number reporting an improved relationship and/or helped response divided by the total number reporting having that type of a relationship.

Respondents indicated that over two-fifths of ex-spouses and nearly one-third of in-laws expressed harmful responses to the parent survivor following the suicide death of a child. Given the remoteness of family ties between these individuals, this finding may not be all that surprising. More unexpected, perhaps, was the finding that more than a quarter of parents acted hurtfully. One of our respondents, Jane T., shared an example of this type of a compassion-lacking response from a parent: "My mother told me this past Mother's Day we could go out together for dinner if I didn't cry or mention Eddie's name. She said it was a day for the living."

This response may illustrate some competitiveness and invidious comparisons made between mothers and their daughters in evaluating parents' merits in raising their children and in their abilities to show and deal with grief (85% [$n = 490$] of our respondents were mothers).

Close to half of suicide survivors reported closer relationships with children, spouses, and close friends, with about two-thirds of these groups offering helpful responses. Children appeared to be the most accepting and helpful category, even more than spouses, with only 10% acting in ways that were unhelpful. Close friends appeared to be the second most helpful category, with only 13% acting unhelpfully. Generally, across all relationship categories between 10% and 20% of respondents reported harmful responses and around 20% reported strain. Thus, the suicide loss of a child

Table 2.6
**Percentage of Parents Experiencing Unhelpful and Helpful Responses
From These Significant Others Following the Loss of a Child to Suicide (N = 462)[a]**

RELATIONSHIP	PERCENT REPORTING HURTFUL RESPONSES	NUMBER[1,2]	PERCENT REPORTING HELPFUL RESPONSES
Children	10.0	398	69.6
Closest friends	13.2	426	63.4
Spouse	16.6	331	67.4
Less close friends	17.0	407	24.3
Coworkers	17.4	310	40.0
Other relatives	17.6	353	27.8
Neighbors	17.7	362	24.3
Siblings	21.6	380	43.4
Parents	28.4	232	36.6
In-laws	31.8	211	30.8
Ex-spouse	44.0	141	21.3

Note. From Survivors Child Loss Survey, 2006–2009.
[a]Each relationship group is listed in order of its occurrence of strained relations and unhelpful responses by percentage from lowest to highest.
[1]Each percentage was calculated from the number reporting a weaker or strained and/or harmed relationship divided by the total number reporting having that type of a relationship.
[2]Each percentage was calculated from the number reporting an improved relationship and/or helped response divided by the total number reporting having that type of a relationship.

may strengthen the relationship of a parent with his or her child (or children), spouse, and close friends; whereas it may have the opposite effect on relations between ex-spouses, in-laws, and to a lesser extent, surviving parents' own parents.

It is important to examine the many different manifestations of stigma that our parent survivor sample confronted. Therefore, we carefully read over the many negative responses offered to us by approximately 85% of our respondents. These comments were stated by all bereaved parents and not exclusively by parent suicide survivors. Initially, as we looked over the comments, provisionally we were able to group them into one of seven different types. Our initial scheme was as follows:

- *Avoidance* (expressed most frequently) for example,
  - "People avoided me."
  - "Friends or family didn't call me afterwards."
  - "People who I thought would be at the funeral or send a sympathy card didn't show any acknowledgment of the death."
- *Unhelpful advice* (expressed by a majority) such as
  - "It's time to move on."
  - "Are you still going to that support group, now?"
  - "Haven't you grieved enough already?"

- *Absence of a caring interest* (expressed by a majority) for example,
  - "No one asked me how I was feeling afterward."
  - "If I started talking about my lost child, they quickly changed the subject."
  - "People just passed over my tragedy as if my child never existed."
- *Unempathic spiritual explanations* (expressed by a majority) in such statements as
  - "God called him."
  - "He's in a better place now."
  - "It was meant to be."

  Although at first it might seem these remarks were ambiguous, respondents did not appear to take them that way. One male physician said, "If there was anything I found exasperating, it was people saying 'He's with God now.' How do they know I'm a Christian?" An office manager said, "I was annoyed with people saying he's with God. I wanted him here with me now, alive."
- *Blaming the child* (expressed by a minority), for example,
  - "That was a cowardly thing he did."
  - "He was selfish."
  - "He was so reckless in how he lived."
- *Blaming the parent* (expressed by a minority) in statements like
  - "Didn't you see it coming?"
  - "Why didn't you get him into therapy?"
- *Other negative* (expressed by a minority) with examples such as
  - "Well at least he didn't kill anyone else when he died."
  - "At least you have other children."
  - "I know how you feel; I felt very sad like that when my dog died" and
  - "He could have shot himself—I guess that would have been worse" (said to a parent whose child died by hanging).

This provisional scheme proved helpful to us when we later tabulated respondents' comments systematically by death cause. These tabulations appear in the next chapter.

As we compared and contrasted the responses presented to survivors of different modes of death of their children, we noted that responses that included *blaming the parent* or *blaming the child* were never heard by natural death survivors. However, all the remaining five types of comments were offered to suicide, accidental death, and natural death survivors.

Another contrast we made was between the various groups of bereaved parents: We explored whether suicide survivors were any more likely to be stigmatized than any of the other groups of survivors. All respondents were asked to categorize the cause of their child's death, using the widely understood scheme, applied by the National Center of Health Statistics from the U.S. Standard Death Certificate form: (a) accidental death, (b) death from natural causes, (c) homicide, (d) suicide, and (e) death under ambiguous circumstances or pending investigation (Hetzel, 1997).

Table 2.7
Overall Stigmatization Means by Type of Death (*N* = 575)

SUICIDE/ACCIDENTAL/ HOMICIDE AND AMBIGUOUS DEATHS	NATURAL CAUSES	TOTAL	F VALUE/(*df*)	p
(*n* = 551)	(*n* = 24)	*N* = 575		
	Mean/*N* (*Std. Dev.*)			
Stigma Scale Score				
(Actual range 0–17)				
3.47/514	1.78/18	3.41/532	4.85 (1,530)	.028*
(3.2)	(1.7)	(3.2)		

Note. From Survivors Child Loss Survey, 2006–2009.
*p < .05.

With only four cases of reported homicide deaths in our sample and five reported cases of deaths under ambiguous circumstances, we regrouped these cases, along with other reported cases of accidental deaths into a single category of traumatic (nonsuicide) deaths. Then, we compared the 24 cases of natural deaths with 89 cases of traumatic deaths and 462 suicide deaths. In the next chapter, we will regroup these data again into a different subsetting, placing the drug-related deaths into a separate category.

Table 2.7 presents the one-way analysis of variance (ANOVA) test of the differences in means of stigmatization by type of death. We investigated possible group differences in two ways. In the first calculation, we divided the sample into three groups: the suicide-bereaved parents ($M = 3.5, SD = 3.2$), all other traumatic death bereaved parents ($M = 3.3, SD = 3.3$), and those who lost children to natural death causes ($M = 1.78, SD = 1.8$). The calculation showed a trend in the direction we expected, but it showed no significant difference between the three different subgroups, with a nonsignificant *p* (probability) value at .07. (This finding is not presented in the table.) Then, we reran the ANOVA, regrouping the suicide survivors and the other traumatic death survivors together into a single category ($N = 514$) and compared this mean of 3.5 ($SD = 3.2$) against the mean for natural death survivors, $M = 1.78$. The second test, presented in Table 2.7, shows a statistically significant difference between the two means: $F(1, 530) = 4.85, p < .03$. This ANOVA compares and contrasts differences in group means to evaluate whether any differences between them can be said to have occurred by chance or whether the differences are not likely to have occurred by chance. The .03 probability level suggests that the differences in means for the two groups are unlikely to have occurred by chance.

Thus, after losing a child, traumatic-loss survivors (suicide combined with nonsuicide traumatic deaths) reported moderately higher levels of rejection and shunning by significant others than was reported by parents after a child's natural death. However, the results also suggested little difference in this respect between suicide survivors and other traumatic (nonsuicide) death survivors.

IMPLICATIONS

Our assessment of stigmatization offers empirical support for the important, but previously unexplored assumption that stigmatization is associated with problems in the mourning process after suicide, as well as with other traumatic losses. Suicide survivors may not be surprised by this conclusion, knowing full well the damaging influence of societal stigmatization on their healing.

Actually, more than four-fifths of present respondents had stigma scale scores of 6 or less (scores ranged from 0 to 17), and it is important to note that the majority of our respondents reported improved relationships and helpful interactions with many of the important people in their social networks after the death of their child. Thus, it does not appear that stigmatization across all their social relationships is a common experience for most survivors. What does seem likely, however, is that survivors *expected* their significant others to act supportively and helpfully following what many felt was the most devastating tragedy of their lives—the loss of their child. Even one significant others' negative response may have been experienced as very troublesome to a survivor. As survivors found themselves in great psychological pain after the loss of a child or other loved one, and then experiencing strain or unhelpfulness where they expected solace and support, it was not surprising that empathic failures with friends and family may have exacerbated the grief of survivors (Neimeyer & Jordan, 2002). This analysis also suggests that the heightening of survivor grief difficulties may additionally place survivors at greater risk for depression and suicidal thinking.

Our qualitative data shed additional light on how survivors are stigmatized following the loss of a child. From a review of more than 2,000 comments, three recurrent themes stood out: (a) "a wall of silence," where significant others studiously avoided all further discussions about the deceased child; (b) "the absence of a caring interest," where significant others rarely asked about survivors' well-being; and if they did, it was superficial, despite the fact that survivors had experienced what they thought was the most devastating tragedy of their lives; and (c) "unhelpful advice," where suggestions completely disregarded the long-term and transformative nature of the grieving process after suicide, through statements such as "Isn't it time you moved on?" or "Why are you still going to that support group?" The qualitative comments these survivors expressed suggests that some encountered extreme scorn from significant others.

These findings point to important clinical implications. First, as a matter of course, therapists need to query their bereavement patients about the kinds of social support they are receiving from their significant others following any traumatic death losses. It is precisely in those cases where supportive responses are missing, that a survivor's grief difficulties may be greatest. Second, mental health practitioners may also need to encourage their patients to take stock of their intimate associates and help them evaluate which relationships may be worth preserving and which ones may need to be temporarily avoided or even discontinued, given the toxicity of maintaining further association. Third, mental health practitioners also need to offer guidance on how survivors can "teach" their important intimates, who may be unable to get past their own fears and lack of familiarity with loss, regarding how to better support them. Clinicians and support group facilitators may also need to encourage survivors to show socially significant others how to act more supportively and allow these close associates sufficient opportunities to act more helpfully. In short, survivors may have to educate people in their social networks and show them how they can help while also accepting the possibility that some close associates will have a limited capacity to offer comforting responses. Fourth, interventions that directly involve members of the social network, such as couple, family, and network interventions, may also have the potential to ameliorate some of the distress documented in this study (Jordan, 2001). It may seem paradoxical for grief-stricken survivors to have to take a lead role in guiding their personal support network. However, it seems likely that, if they can marshal more caring responses from their significant others, instead of avoidance and scorn, their healing can be facilitated.

Our findings also suggest that after a loss, adult survivors can generally expect to find their most important grief support from children, spouses, and close friends. When, as our study suggests, these groups fail to offer the kinds of support needed, survivors will feel obliged to look for help elsewhere, probably from bereavement professionals and support group memberships. In Chapter 11, we compare and contrast suicide survivors who were members of Internet support groups with those who belonged exclusively to face-to-face groups. The Internet support group affiliates usually spent much more time in their support groups than the face-to-face group survivors did. The Internet group affiliates also reported greater grief difficulties and stigma from their close associates. These findings suggest that as survivors encounter more stigma and grief difficulties, their needs for support group participation will rise as well.

Our findings that one-fourth of the parents of survivors said something harmful and induced strained relationships may appear surprising and perhaps mistaken. Yet, this finding emerged twice in our results, once when respondents reported on their strained relationships, and again when they reflected on the groups presenting the most harmful responses. This suggests that the results were not a statistical anomaly. These responses may have occurred because older parents (the parents of those who lost a child to suicide) may hold traditional stigmatized views of suicide and may be more inclined to hold their adult children responsible for the deaths of their grandchildren than would younger persons. Alternatively, there may be generational differences in coping styles, with older people employing more stoic and avoidant coping styles in dealing with traumatic events, as has often been noted about the parents belonging to the depression era and World War II generation. These are speculative explanations, suggesting another important topic for future research, namely, to systematically investigate the general population to see how views of suicide and suicide stigmatization may be shifting across generational cohorts.

An additional important finding from the present investigation was the convergence with other studies that have shown more similarities than differences in the grief trajectory of survivors of different types of traumatic deaths (Jordan, 2001; Sveen & Walby, 2008). Our findings about the general similarities in the reported social stigmatization of suicide survivors and other types of traumatic death survivors support the observation that there may be many similarities between the experiences of various types of traumatic-loss survivors. They also confirm some of the recent work of Murphy, Johnson, Wu, Fan, and Lohan (2003), who noted more convergences than differences in the grief experiences of these two populations. Accordingly, we would suggest that the acts of suicide and those of homicide, drug overdose, vehicular accident deaths, and other traumatic accidental deaths generally evoke similar responses among the significant others of survivors. Such traumatic losses may elicit fear, dread, and a sense of impending danger that "It could have happened to us, too," and for that reason, result in similar avoidance responses on the part of people in the social networks surrounding the survivors.

An equally plausible explanation for some of the responses from others is that suicide and other traumatic deaths create what might be called a great deal of "social ambiguity." People are most comfortable relating to others in situations where there are more or less agreed upon norms about how to behave. Such norms do not exist for how to interact with a parent who has experienced the sudden, unexpected, and often violent death of a child. This ambiguity and lack of clear-cut rules creates psychological discomfort for many people who then avoid situations that make them feel that way. It is also possible, therefore, that some of the social withdrawal reported by our respondents comes less out of condemnation and more out of social awkwardness. This leads to our final point.

Previous research has suggested that some traumatic-loss survivors may engage in "self-stigmatization" (Dunn & Morrish-Vidners, 1987–1988), where they may assume that others are condemning them and thus either perceive the actions of others as reflecting negative judgments, or even act in ways that elicit avoidance and rejection from other people. Our participant observation data collected at support group meetings did occasionally show some survivors whose feelings of intense shame at the loss of a child from suicide, drug overdose, or another traumatic cause led them to misrepresent the cause of their child's death. Such acts of secret keeping and the associated discomfort from hiding the true death circumstances could also contribute to a misperception of others' responses to the death.

Therefore, an important caveat must be noted to all the analyses that we have provided in this chapter. Because our survey data are "cross-sectional," we cannot say definitively that stigmatizing interactions with others directly cause more mental health and grief problems. That is, the "direction" of the causality may go the other way, meaning that it is also possible that survivors who have greater mental health and grief problems may be more likely to misperceive social situations, perceiving more social rejection and abandonment from others, or even to act in ways that might elicit those responses from friends and family. Although our experience with survivors in clinical and support group settings generally does not support this idea, it cannot be ruled out solely by our data.

The present correlational data do not permit the investigation of the complex and quite possibly circular causality in the social stigmatization processes that may occur after traumatic losses such as a suicide. Instead, these findings, as well as the others presented here, deserve further investigation and confirmation in future research.

REFERENCES

Barrett, T. W., & Scott, T. B. (1989). Development of the Grief Experience Questionnaire. *Suicide & Life-Threatening Behavior, 19*(2), 201–215.

Bleed, J. (2007, February 19). Howell's life insurance payout not a sure bet. *Arkansas Democrat-Gazette.*

Cleiren, M., Diekstra, R. F., Kerkhof, A. J., & van der Wal, J. (1994). Mode of death and kinship in bereavement: Focusing on "who" rather than "how." *Crisis, 15*(1), 22–36.

Colt, G. H. (1987). The history of the suicide survivor: The mark of Cain. In E. J. Dunne, J. L. McIntosh, & K. Dunne-Maxim (Eds.), *Suicide and its aftermath: Understanding and counseling the survivors* (pp. 3–18). New York, NY: Norton.

Cvinar, J. G. (2005). Do suicide survivors suffer social stigma: A review of the literature. *Perspectives in Psychiatric Care, 41*(1), 14–21.

Doka, K. J. (Ed.). (2001). *Disenfranchised grief: New directions, challenges, and strategies for practice* (2nd ed.). Champaign, IL: Research Press.

Dunn, R. G., & Morrish-Vidners, D. (1987–1988). The psychological and social experience of suicide survivors. *Omega: Journal of Death and Dying, 18*(3), 175–215.

Dunne, E. J., McIntosh, J. L., & Dunne-Maxim, K. (Eds.). (1987). *Suicide and its aftermath: Understanding and counseling the survivors.* New York, NY: Norton.

Dunne-Maxim, K. (2007, April). *Survivor history panel: Past, present and what's ahead.* Paper presented at 19th Annual Healing After Suicide Conference, New Orleans, LA.

Goffman, E. (1963). *Stigma: Notes on the management of spoiled identity.* Englewood Cliffs, NJ: Prentice Hall.

Harwood, D., Hawton K., Hope T., & Jacoby, R. (2002). The grief experiences and needs of bereaved relatives and friends of older people dying through suicide: A descriptive and case-control study. *Journal of Affective Disorders, 72*(2), 185–194.

Hetzel, A. M. (1997). *U.S. vital statistics system: Major activities and developments, 1950-95* (DHHS Publication No. [PHS] 97-1003). Hyattsville, MD: National Center for Health Statistics. Retrieved from http://www.cdc.gov/nchs/data/misc/usvss.pdf

Jordan, J. R. (2001). Is suicide bereavement different? A reassessment of the literature. *Suicide & Life-Threatening Behavior, 31*(1), 91–102.

McIntosh, J. L. (1993). Control group studies of suicide survivors: A review and critique. *Suicide & Life-Threatening Behavior, 23*(2), 146–161.

McNiel, D. E., Hatcher, C., & Reubin, R. (1988). Family survivors of suicide and accidental death: Consequences for widows. *Suicide & Life-Threatening Behavior, 18*(2), 137–148.

Murphy, S. A., Johnson, L. C., Wu, L., Fan, J. J., & Lohan, J. (2003). Bereaved parents' outcomes 4 to 60 months after their children's deaths by accident, suicide, or homicide: A comparative study demonstrating differences. *Death Studies, 27*(1), 39–61.

Neimeyer, R. A., & Jordan, J. R. (2002). Disenfranchisement as empathic failure: Grief therapy and the co-construction of meaning. In K. Doka (Ed.), *Disenfranchised grief: New directions, challenges, and strategies for practice* (pp. 95–118). Champaign, IL: Research Press.

Reed, M. D. (1993). Sudden death and bereavement outcomes: The impact of resources on grief symptomatology and detachment. *Suicide & Life-Threatening Behavior, 23*(3), 204–220.

Sveen, C. A., & Walby, F. A. (2008). Suicide survivors' mental health and grief reactions: A systematic review of controlled studies. *Suicide & Life-Threatening Behavior, 38*(1), 13–29.

3

Drug-Overdose Deaths and Survivors' Grief:
A Greatly Neglected Subject

INTRODUCTION

Amy Weiner, a pseudonym for one of our survey respondents, encouraged us on her form to telephone her if we wanted to learn more about her son's death. Her son Adam died at age 28 from a drug overdose. When we spoke, Amy said,

> Adam had a love affair with drugs for much of his short life. When he was in high school, he was into marijuana and alcohol. We couldn't control him, and he was eventually expelled from high school for selling drugs. He experimented with a lot of different drugs at that time and afterward. He was on and off heroin for several years. He went into several different residential rehab programs, then jail, then back again to treatment programs: That was the cycle. Eventually, Adam obtained a GED, went on to complete a program at a culinary institute, but he never worked in the food industry for long because of his drug taking. It was like a roller-coaster ride to hell. He died from a lethal mixing of OxyContin and cocaine. Adam took his last fatal dose at a friend's house.

Amy continued,

> I feel somewhat blameworthy for his death. During the last few years before he died, I gave him a great deal of money. I actually went into debt helping him. Sometimes, I can't believe how stupid I was at the time. But, my son was a very convincing liar. During the last 5 years

of his life, he gave me an elaborate cock-and-bull story about being pursued by the police. He claimed he was being victimized by different groups, couldn't defend himself, and couldn't go to the courts to seek relief. He really was paranoid, and I didn't see it. I kept giving him additional funds and support. I have mixed feelings about it now. But some of my friends say his life was extended from the help I gave. Now, I truly wonder.

I was his only resource. No one else in our family accepted him. His drug problems made him a pariah. His father, who I divorced 13 years ago, wrote him off 8 years ago and rarely if ever communicated with him. Our differing ways of dealing with Adam was one of the many things that drove his father and I apart. My family also has been very disappointing, not offering me any support since Adam's death. They usually have nothing to say about Adam and certainly never a kind word about him. Thank God for my friends and the support group. If it weren't for them, I'd probably be a basket case.

I work in the drug and alcohol field. And drug deaths are so sad and blame riddled. These deaths drag us down so low. But I can't blame myself for Adam's death. I saw the handwriting on the wall, but only he could have stopped taking the drugs, and he couldn't bring himself to do that. They say surgeons shouldn't operate on members of their own families, and I accept that line of thinking. But we don't see it coming. We think these things will just be another bump in the road that our children eventually will get past. But in my case, he didn't. My son was very well liked. He could be very charming. Several of the correction officers who he worked with during his last years came to his funeral: He was that well liked.

Amy Weiner's long and torturous story of dealing with her son's drug problems—full of false starts and eventual disappointments—was common among our respondents. This chapter focuses on the less well-understood population of parents losing children to drug overdoses and to drug-related deaths. In this first-ever comparative analysis, we pose the question whether these grieving parents face bereavement challenges that are similar to parents who have lost children to suicide. In this chapter, we also investigate whether the parents losing children to drugs, suicide, other accidental causes, and natural causes differ from one another in any other important ways. As we emphasized in the last chapter, suicide stigma adds complications to the bereavement process for families sustaining the suicide loss of a child. We were curious as to whether parents who lose children to overdoses and to other drug-related deaths would encounter similar stigmatization problems to those of the suicide-bereaved parents. And if the stigma against drug users matched the shame associated with a family member's suicide, then we wondered whether both these groups would be more troubled by grief and other mental health problems compared with bereaved parents who lost children to accidents and natural causes. These were the primary questions we wished to explore in this chapter.

Although the subject of overdose deaths appears to attract substantial attention among the public at large, in the media, and from epidemiologists, surprisingly, it has sparked scant interest among bereavement researchers. Little has appeared in print on this neglected subject in the research journals. An exhaustive search for entries on grief or bereavement and overdose (or drug) deaths from MEDLINE, PsycInfo, and the Social Science Index yielded only two research notes on the topic. Both studies were done outside the United States: one, a Brazilian study (da Silva, Noto, & Formigoni, 2007) and the other, a British study (Guy, 2004).

The Brazilian study was based on six cases, three of whom were aware of their family members' drug use prior to the death and three who of whom were not. The Brazilian researchers concluded that overdose death is a highly stigmatized behavior because of the loved one's "immoral" and/or criminal behavior, leaving their survivors to feel guilt and shame. When survivors were aware of the loved one's drug use prior to the death, there was a veiled preparation for the death, bringing about ambivalence associated with relief and guilt. Otherwise, there was more substantial shock and surprise at the death. In both cases, survivors needed substantial psychological support following the loss.

The British study, based on four cases, found that when people used illegal drugs, rather than alcohol or tobacco, the deaths were met with social censure. The user was perceived as having had a soiled identity because of the illicit nature of the drugs, which left their survivors blameworthy in other people's eyes. Drug deaths were usually seen as "bad" deaths. Parents were often seen as being at fault in these deaths. A child's heroin use left one parent feeling more blameworthy in the death, than the parents in another case, where the child died from ecstasy use. Parents were often confused about how to act with their drug-abusing child—firmly or in a conciliatory way. Media coverage, which can sensationalize the death, increased the perception by others of the parents as deficient. Parents felt guilty for not succeeding in stopping their child's drug use and were often left with long-standing regrets. The author concluded that the cause of death carried with it a stigma for the deceased, invalidating their lives, and suggesting it may not be legitimate to grieve for them. These two studies offer an abundance of insight into the stigmatizing experiences linked with drug abuse deaths, suggesting that they are a phenomenon rife with victim blame by others and potentially self-blame by the survivors.

Given the paucity of work devoted to the subject of bereavement in drug-overdose deaths, one might conclude that it represents a statistical rarity. Yet, this is hardly the case. The popular press and mental health professionals often emphasize the pervasiveness of youth suicide, frequently mentioning this as the second leading death cause for the college aged. However, the media rarely displays commensurate attention to the yearly totals of drug-related youth deaths, which probably exceed those from suicide. A visit to Centers for Disease Control and Prevention's (CDC's) Web-based Injury Statistics Query and Reporting System (WISQARS) website showed 17,304 suicide deaths for the 13- to 45-year-old population in 2008 (CDC, 2011). (The WISQARS website enables users to identify the number of deaths for various International Classification of Diseases [ICD] death code categories for selected U.S. regions, age, gender, and race groups from 1999 to 2008.) The same website also showed 17,707 poisoning deaths, where most drug overdoses are enumerated. Of course, not all poisoning deaths are drug overdoses. Some may be from the inadvertent consumption of toxic chemicals or pesticides. Yet, if we were to add together all drug-related poisoning deaths, with the car accident death totals involving alcohol or other drugs, either in the deceased driver, passengers, or pedestrians, the combined totals would put more than 12,000 additional cases into the equation each year. Thus, we can readily see drug-related deaths easily eclipsing suicide as a more imposing cause of youth mortality.

Yet, it must be acknowledged that there is a considerable overlap between suicide and drug abuse mortalities. One study conducted in New Mexico, among a predominately Native American population, found that heavy alcohol consumption had occurred among two-thirds of the suicide decedents studied (May et al., 2002). A recent Australian toxicological study of over 1,400 suicides (that excluded cases of deliberate overdoses on psychoactive substances) found substances detected in two-thirds of all cases, with illicit drugs in 20% and alcohol in 40% of the suicide decedents (Darke, Duflou, & Torok, 2009). Another British study found that 45% of their sampled suicide cases tested positive for alcohol, with about 20% who had consumed twice the legal blood alcohol limit when they had died (Crombie, Pounder, & Dick, 1998). Another study of New York City suicide decedents, who had died within a given year, showed that 20% had cocaine within their bodies, and this percentage rose to 45% among young Hispanic males (Marzuk et al., 1992).

Clearly then, there is a considerable overlap between drug consumption and suicide. Therefore, it is often a daunting challenge for medical examiners to ascertain whether a given individual's death was an intentional suicide or an accidental drug overdose. Medical examiners often struggle greatly with the cases that straddle the ambiguous line between these two poles. Envisioning considerable stigma being applied to suicides, medical examiners usually apply what has been deemed "the 51 percent rule," insisting that a preponderance of evidence show a death as a suicide before that classification is offered as the official death cause (Timmermans, 2006). Once an official death cause is given, surviving family members usually try to accept that definition of their loved one's demise. Official death definitions help to clarify and reinforce the meaning of their loved one's death in the survivor's mind. With a firmer grasp of how their loved one died, survivors are then able to begin their sensemaking efforts as they proceed to accept their loss and move forward with their healing journeys (Currier, Holland, Coleman, & Neimeyer, 2006).

As medical examiners struggle with the complexity of understanding the ambiguous nature of a partly self-inflicted, drug-induced death, so too did our respondents. One of our survey respondents, Annette Sanfino (a pseudonym), articulately commented on this ambiguity. "The medical term of my son's cause of death was 'acute asphyxiation' from a result of an overdose of Xanax and heroin. Although his death was not classified as a 'suicide,' it is my personal belief that his actions (although not intentional) caused his death. It is also my personal belief that there is a fine line between suicide and accidental death that involves intoxication."

In this research, we accepted parental self-definitions of their children's deaths (see later discussion). We did not have access to official death certificate records. Especially because most of our respondents were drawn from the ranks of support groups (which the respondents had freely chosen to join with other survivors), we assumed that they accepted the official death certificate designations issued to account for their children's deaths. Such determinations distinguished whether the deaths resulted from natural causes, suicides, homicides, accidents, or ambiguous causes. As our findings will later show, there is a relationship between differences in parental conceptions of their children's deaths and their grief and mental health problems.

THE TRAJECTORY OF GRIEF AFTER DRUG-OVERDOSE DEATHS

There is no one typical drug-overdose death. These deaths take many different forms, and yet they unify bereaved family members in sharing a common consciousness of kind that their loved one died from drugs. One of the parents who participated in our bereavement survey reported that her son died from ingesting a toxic combination of steroids, purchased on the Internet, as he pursued his own bodybuilding program. Another parent reported that her son's fatal overdose resulted from taking too many of his prescribed psychotropic medications. Another reported on their child's death from a bad lysergic acid diethylamide (LSD) trip that triggered a fatal jumping episode. The most commonly reported cases were heroin-overdose deaths and multidrug-abuse deaths from toxic combinations of recreational drugs and prescription medications.

The drug-overdose death reports of their children provided by our parent respondents matched epidemiological findings. Evidence converged with epidemiological findings from statewide studies of drug-overdose deaths in West Virgina (Hall et al., 2008), Georgia, (Graham & Hanzlick, 2008), and New Mexico (Shah, Lathrop, Reichard, & Landen, 2007). Overdose deaths differed from one state to another; West Virginia led the others in having the highest percentage of drug deaths because of the divergence and nonmedical uses of prescribed drugs. In Georgia, cocaine and other drug combinations represented the single largest category of overdose deaths, whereas in New Mexico, opiates and other combinations of drugs predominated. Overall, the intermixing of heroin, cocaine, alcohol, and/or prescription drugs represented the predominant form of all drug deaths across these four states and nationally. CDC evidence also suggested rising drug deaths because of the intermixing of prescriptions with recreational drugs, which underwent a 55% increase in the period from 1999 to 2003 (Wysowski, 2007). The statewide data appear to converge with this national trend.

This chapter focuses on the bereavement consequences of drug-overdose deaths. If we accept the implicit assumption about the damaging effect of a label of a suicide death behind the medical examiners "51 percent rule," one might expect that the most intense stigmatization would be experienced by suicide survivors. Indeed, it is well established that suicide survivors experience more stigmatization from their social networks than do many other bereaved populations (Cvinar, 2005; Sveen & Walby, 2008). By contrast, in general, an accidental death does not directly challenge societal values with the same blunt force that a suicide does. However, consideration of the general attitudes toward "drug addicts" in American society, along with the already mentioned available literature on overdose death bereavement, we had reason to expect considerable stigmatization to be experienced after drug-related deaths, such that there is likely to be a linking of them with immorality and criminality on the part of the deceased. We suspected that when the perceptions of criminality and immorality were weighed against the disparagement of a mental illness or the simple perception of "selfishness" associated with suicidality, few differences would be noted in stigmatization responses. Accordingly, we investigated this with our stigmatization scale, discussed in Chapter 2, and examined whether the differences in death designations between drug deaths and suicide are linked to differences in stigma.

We investigated whether differences between four major subgroups of bereaved parents based on the mode of death—drug overdose, suicide, other traumatic deaths, and natural deaths—are associated with differences in grief and mental health problems among parent survivors. In Chapter 2, we included drug-related death cases in the same category with accidental deaths for purposes of analysis, and we found that both this mixed group of bereaved parents and the suicide-bereaved parents were generally at greater risk for stigmatization, mental health, and grief problems than the parents losing children to natural causes. For this analysis, we disaggregated the drug-death cases from the other accidental death cases and carefully compared and contrasted all four categories of research interest: drug-related, suicide, accidental-death, and natural-death bereavements.

Previous theory has suggested that *disenfranchised grief* plays a vitally important part in stigmatization (Doka, 2001). In our last chapter, we suggested that as socially significant others avoided mention of the survivor's loss, as they refrained from expressing caring interests in the survivor and as they expressed derogatory remarks toward the decedent and placed blame on the survivor for acting as a contributing agent in the death, people in the survivor's network essentially disavowed the survivor's right to receive solace and support. We also maintained that some acts of stigmatization are more stress inducing to the bereaved than others. We expected that overt expressions of direct blame toward parents are especially troubling to the survivor because they reinforce the parent's own self-accusations of ineffectiveness in saving their child's life. Blaming children for their own demise is another direct assault on the survivor, suggesting that the deceased is unworthy and does not rightfully deserve to be honored and remembered. Such expressions of disapproval are likely to be more distressing to a bereaved parent than any acts of avoidance or offers of unhelpful grief advice. If we are correct in our suppositions that both suicide and drug-overdose deaths are more stigmatized than accidental deaths, then we expected to observe greater numbers of child- and parent-blame comments coming from the significant others of the former group of parent survivors than the latter.

Some bereavement analysts may claim that the theory of disenfranchised grief is sufficiently broad based to account for the unique grief difficulties of the suicide and drug-overdose death bereaved, in much the same way that Guy (2004) explains how overdose death bereaved parents are left with a feeling that it may not be legitimate for them to grieve for their deceased children. Yet, we would contend that drug and suicide deaths may bring with them a sense of intense shame and humiliation. Worden (2009) claims, in a chapter devoted to special types of losses, that AIDS-related deaths can be ones that bring with them "socially unspeakable losses," where because of the associated stigma, some survivors fear they will be rejected and judged harshly if the cause of their loved one's death becomes known. So they may lie and attribute the death to cancer or something other than AIDS (Worden, 2009). Behaviors such as these are repeatedly reported by suicide and drug-overdose death survivors at support group meetings and at sharing sessions during bereavement-healing conferences. Many suicide and drug-overdose death bereaved parents routinely misrepresent the cause of a family member's death to other close family members, coworkers, and friends, fearing that the person's reputation will be greatly diminished by the revelation of his or her death cause. In one dramatic example (taken from a support group meeting observation), a father of a 20-year-old son remained reluctant and unwilling to disclose his own father's death (by suicide) to his son, fearing that the boy would no longer respect his deceased grandfather knowing that he had taken his life. The intense shame that these bereaved experience points to a perceived need to preserve the good reputation of their deceased relatives. Not only does the bereaved feel that others won't acknowledge and legitimate their grief but also they fear that the memory of the deceased loved one will be permanently tarnished, and they fear that they, too, will be ridiculed, avoided, and even judged blameworthy by the revelation of the death cause. We believe that this process goes beyond the concept of disenfranchisement, which is simply a lack of social validation of a loss, to active processes of social stigmatization.

To summarize, as we began this analysis, comparing all four subgroups of bereavement research interest—drug-death, suicide, accidental-death, and natural-death survivors—we started with two hypotheses: (a) We expected that we would find similarity in the responses between the suicide and drug-death bereaved in stigmatization, grief difficulties, posttraumatic stress, and psychological difficulties. (b) When we compared a combined group of suicide and drug-death bereaved to accidental and natural-death bereaved, we would find the former groups significantly higher on stigmatization, grief difficulties, posttraumatic stress, and psychological difficulties than the latter two groups. Thus, for the present analysis, we hypothesized that parents whose children die from drug overdoses would show outcomes similar to suicide survivors, and that both the drug and the suicide bereaved would experience greater grief and mental health problems than the parents losing children to other accidents and natural-death causes.

METHODOLOGICAL CONCERNS

Chapter 1 mentions the two-stage process of collecting our sample, first collecting 540 surveys nationally between March 2006 and July 2007, and then collecting 35 additional surveys primarily from the New York metropolitan area between March and September 2009. This was necessitated when we sought to further investigate drug-overdose death bereavement and discovered that with only 13 such cases in our original sample, we did not have nearly enough cases for any preliminary analyses. Thus, we sought to augment our initial sample of drug-death bereaved parents so that we could make more valid generalizations about this population. We concentrated our data collection efforts among The Compassionate Friends chapters in the New York metropolitan area. We asked chapter facilitators to solicit potential respondents from among their membership rosters of those losing children to a drug-related death. In addition, we also made contact with two Internet-based survivor support groups serving parents losing children to drug-related deaths: Angels of Addiction, Inc. and the Grief Recovery After a Substance Abuse Passing group (widely known as GRASP). A total of 42 names and addresses of potential respondents were offered to us from these contacts. Of these, 35 completed surveys, yielding a response rate of 83% for this subset.

As the first sample yielded a population with certain demographic characteristics, described in Chapter 1, we were concerned as to whether the 2009 supplemental parent sample, sustaining child drug-related deaths, would be generally similar to the earlier larger sample. Any great demographic disparity between the drug-related death cases and the others could produce differences in some of the issues under investigation (such as levels of grief or mental health problems) that might be attributable to the demographic differences rather than to the manner of death. We compared overdose death survivors to all other bereaved parents in our sample, and we also compared the four essential bereaved parent subgroups to each other in terms of differences in gender, age, education, religion, and socioeconomic status. We also compared all four subgroups in terms of the time since the loss and the age of the child at loss.

Chi-square tests that compared the overdose-death respondents to all other respondents and to the other three bereaved parent subgroups (suicide, natural death, and other accidental deaths) showed great similarity between the groups, and no statistically significant differences in terms of gender, education, or socioeconomic status. Overdose-death parents were generally like other bereaved parents in terms of age, although parents sustaining natural deaths of a child reported themselves as being significantly younger or older compared to the other loss categories who reported themselves as middle aged. The religion comparison showed significantly more Catholics and Jews among the overdose death parents compared to all other subgroups. We suspected this may have resulted from our sampling procedures because we drew overdose drug-death cases disproportionally from the New York City metropolitan area where more Catholics and Jews were located. In the larger sample, with a more nationally representative constituency, there were more Protestants. Although there were more Jews in the natural-death loss subgroup, in all other respects, time since the loss and age of the child at the time of death, the four bereaved subgroups were virtually indistinguishable from one another, and there were no statistically significant differences between these groups of bereaved parents. These demographic comparative data are not presented in any of our tables.

MEASURES

Type of Loss

The type of loss experienced was assessed by survivor self-definition. All respondents were asked to categorize the cause of death of their child into the widely understood scheme, applied by the National Center for Health Statistics from the U.S. Standard Death Certificate form: (a) accidental death, (b) natural causes, (c) homicide, (d) suicide, and/or (e) death under ambiguous circumstances or pending investigation (Hetzel, 1997). Our survey forms contained two lines after natural causes and accidental deaths where respondents could fill in their child's specific death circumstances.

The aforementioned categories were mutually exclusive. All child deaths were given a single death cause code based on the parent's response. If a parent deemed a child's death as a drug-related suicide, we counted this only as a suicide. If a parent checked off the accidental death cause box and indicated "drugs," "overdose," or mentioned a specific drug such as "heroin," these cases were counted as drug-related deaths. (One parent indicated "death under ambiguous circumstances" but stated drugs were the primary cause; we counted this case as a drug death.)

All 462 suicide death cases checked the suicide death box and filled out seven additional questions about the suicide method, finding the body, and other death circumstances. All 48 drug-death cases filled in the accidental death box (except the one case mentioned previously) and indicated "drugs," "overdose," "drug asphyxiation," "drug interaction," "heroin," or other similar language as the fill-in words. All 37 cases in the other accident category checked off the accident box and most indicated vehicular accidents, such as "car accident," "automobile," "motorcycle," and "hit by drunk driver" as the predominating fill-in words. A smaller number indicated "drowning," "boating accident," "electrocution," "plane crash," or "falling accident." Two additional respondents checked off the accidental death box to report military casualty deaths. We also folded the four cases reporting ambiguous death circumstances into the accidental death category. All 24 natural death cases checked off the natural death cause box and filled in such words as "heart attack," "brain aneurism," "lung cancer," "breast cancer," "diabetic complications," "died from complications during childbirth," and so forth. We excluded from this analysis the four cases where a parent reported the homicide death of a child. We felt the stigma associated with these deaths held a potentially unique importance, and it would have been erroneous and misleading to consider these cases within any of our other categories. The frequency distribution of deaths for our finalized tabulations was as follows: 48 drug-related deaths, 462 suicides, 37 other mostly accidental deaths, and 24 cases of child deaths by natural causes.

Having already discussed our measures for grief and mental health problems (in Chapter 1) and our stigmatization scale (in Chapter 2), we will not repeat these here. The only other procedure, not already described, was the method by which we counted blaming-child and blaming-parent responses.

Our interview survey forms included several open-ended questions in which respondents were asked to provide additional information about their bereavement and stigmatization experiences. Respondents' comments shed additional light on their experienced stigma. They were explicitly asked to list troublesome things said or done to them by significant others since their loss. Approximately 85% of respondents provided information in response to this query. In the previous chapter, we presented a preliminary coding of the negative responses most frequently given: (a) avoidance (e.g., "People never mentioned my child again after the death."), (b) unhelpful advice (e.g., "Don't you think it is time you moved on?"), (c) absence of a caring interest (e.g., "Friends and family never asked how I was feeling afterward."), (d) spiritual responses (e.g., "He's with God," or "He's in a better place."), (e) blaming the child (e.g., "He was so reckless in how he lived."), (f) blaming the parent (e.g., "Didn't you see it coming?"), and (g) other negative responses (e.g., "I know how you feel. I felt that way when my dog died.").

We tabulated all responses, and a total of 2,421 were given. Because we encouraged respondents to report their negative experiences, there was nearly a 2 to 1 ratio of negative comments ($n = 1,541$) to positive ones ($n = 880$).

For the present tabulation, we did not count cases where respondents offered a mixture of both positive and negative responses. We focused primarily on the coding and tabulating of negative response frequencies. We only counted the positive cases when a respondent reported a completely positive response from their significant others, such as when a respondent filled in the blanks, stating something like this: "My family and friends only acted supportively to us." Approximately 7% gave answers such as this. A similar percentage left their forms blank to this part of the survey.

It is important to note that we were counting comments, not respondents. Some respondents left this question blank, and others offered as many as seven or eight comments about how their friends and families had acted. We grouped responses slightly different from our preliminary coding scheme. The finalized coding system was as follows: (a) avoidance, (b) you have other children, (c) unhelpful advice, (d) with God/in a better place, (e) other negative, (f) blame child, (g) blame parent, (h) bereavement problems with work, and (i) left question blank or reported positive responses only. A small number of responses, fewer than 20 overall, could not be readily coded into one of the eight categories of this scheme; they were left uncoded. In the next section, we present frequency tabulations as they were reported by all four death type subgroups.

The 202 survey records that were examined in the qualitative data comparisons were initially coded by the first author. Because blaming comments (whether to express blame to the parent or to the deceased child or to express neither of these sentiments) formed the essence in the examination of the selected surveys, a second evaluator, a trained behavioral analyst, holding a master's degree in social work, independently examined and coded blaming comments made by these respondents. Judgments of the blaming comments were later compared for consistency between both evaluators. Cohen's kappa between the two raters was .93 ($p < .001$).

RESULTS

Stigma, Grief, and Mental Health Problem Behaviors

Table 3.1 presents the means, standard deviations, and *t* tests for the two groups of interest—suicide and drug-overdose death-surviving parents—on the stigmatization scale, Grief Experience Questionnaire, Complicated Grief Scale, Impact of Event Scale, Index of Personal Psychological Problems, and our 8-item Depression Scale. As we compared these two groups on the six problem behavior criteria, we did not observe any statistically significant differences between the means for the suicide bereaved and the drug-death bereaved. Thus, Table 3.1 showed great similarity and convergence between both groups on the six grief and mental health problems criteria.

Table 3.2 performed the same analyses found in the first table. However, this time the drug and suicide-death survivors were combined and contrasted

Table 3.1
Stigmatization, Grief, and Mental Health Problems Among Suicide and
Drug-Death Bereaved Parents

OUTCOME MEASURE	TYPE OF DEATH	N	M	SD	t	df	SIG.
Stigmatization	1 Suicide	433	3.51	3.23	.65	476	.51
	2 Overdose	45	3.18	3.44			
	Total	478	3.48	3.25			
Grief Experiences Questionnaire	1 Suicide	426	40.18	11.12	1.06	469	.29
	2 Overdose	45	38.33	11.03			
	Total	471	40.00	11.11			
Complicated Grief scale	1 Suicide	437	28.02	9.01	.99	480	.32
	2 Overdose	45	29.4	7.82			
	Total	482	28.15	8.91			
Impact of Event Scale	1 Suicide	420	33.53	8.86	.65	460	.52
	2 Overdose	42	34.45	8.02			
	Total	462	33.61	8.78			
Index of Personal Psychological Problems	1 Suicide	450	1.67	1.31	1.05	493	.29
	2 Overdose	45	1.89	1.30			
	Total	495	1.69	1.31			
Eight-Item Depression Scale	1 Suicide	413	4.41	3.13	.75	453	.45
	2 Overdose	42	4.79	2.46			
	Total	455	4.45	3.07			

Note. From Survivors Child Loss Survey, 2006–2009.

with a combined group of natural and other accidental death bereaved. Table 3.2 shows an altogether consistent pattern with significantly higher reports of grief and mental health problems for the suicide and drug-overdose bereaved, as compared to the natural death and other accidental-death bereaved. The only test that was not statistically significant was in relation to reports of being stigmatized. Here, the means differed in the predicted direction, but the differences felt slightly below the .05 significance criteria.

Controlling for Potential Confounding Variables

Having established various bivariate associations in Table 3.2, it is still uncertain whether these associations would remain in the presence of potential confounding variables. One potential confounder, for example, is the well-known association between grief difficulties, psychological problems, and time since the loss. Gender, too, is another well-established correlate of grief difficulties and psychological problems, with women being more likely to report more of these problems than men. Although our study found women reporting more stigma experiences than men, we found no bivariate associations between stigma and time since the loss (not shown). Our preliminary screening

Table 3.2

**Stigmatization, Grief, and Mental Health Problems Among Combined Groups
of Bereaved Parents**

OUTCOME MEASURE	TYPE OF DEATH	N	M	SD	t	df	SIG.
Stigmatization	Natural/ accidental death	50	2.62	2.75	1.80	526	0.07
	Suicide/overdose	478	3.47	3.25			
	Total	528	3.40	3.21			
Grief Experiences Questionnaire	Natural/ accidental death	47	30.42	11.29	5.62	516	0.000***
	Suicide/overdose	471	40.00	11.11			
	Total	518	39.13	11.45			
Complicated Grief scale	Natural/ accidental death	55	25.0	8.37	2.50	535	0.01**
	Suicide/overdose	482	28.15	8.91			
	Total	537	27.83	8.90			
Impact of Event Scale	Natural/ accidental death	57	30.39	9.22	2.60	517	0.009**
	Suicide/overdose	462	33.61	8.78			
	Total	519	33.26	8.88			
Index of Personal Psychological Problems	Natural/ accidental death	57	1.12	1.23	3.13	550	0.001***
	Suicide/overdose	495	1.69	1.31			
	Total	552	1.634	1.31			
Eight-Item Depression Scale	Natural/ accidental death	52	3.31	3.05	2.53	505	0.011*
	Suicide/overdose	455	4.45	3.07			
	Total	507	4.33	3.09			

Note. From Survivors Child Loss Survey, 2006–2009.
*$p < .05$. **$p < .01$. ***$p < .001$.

of demographic associations did not show any distinctive differences between loss type, gender, and time since the loss. Yet, it remained to be seen whether an analysis of covariance (ANCOVA), controlling for gender and time since loss effects, would confirm whether these bivariate associations could be accepted when the control variables were also taken into account. For these tests, we contrasted the 85 males in our sample against the 490 females. Time since the loss was divided into two contrast groups: the under 5-year survivor subgroup ($n = 318$) contrasted against those passing the 5-years post-loss benchmark ($n = 244$).

Table 3.3 presents the ANCOVA showing the mean differences comparisons for all six problems criteria, taking gender and time after the loss into account. The ANCOVA of stigma and loss type showed that the association of stigma and loss type was significant at the .03 level. It remained significant

Table 3.3
Analyses of Covariance of Psychological Variables as a Function of Cause of Death, Years Since Death, and Gender

VARIABLE	SOURCE OF VARIANCE	df	MS	F	p
Stigmatization	Cause of death	1	47.76	4.72	0.03*
	Years since death	1	17.82	1.76	0.18
	Gender	1	97.20	9.60	0.02*
	Error	515	10.12		
	Total	519	10.37		
Grief Experience Questionnaire	Cause of death	1	3436.23	31.22	< 0.001***
	Years since death	1	4873.52	44.28	< 0.001***
	Gender	1	2375.48	21.58	< 0.001***
	Error	505	110.07		
	Total	509	131.01		
Complicated Grief scale	Cause of death	1	406.88	5.93	0.02*
	Years since death	1	3118.07	43.32	< 0.001***
	Gender	1	2970.87	34.61	< 0.001***
	Error	522	68.58		
	Total	526	79.42		
Impact of Event Scale	Cause of death	1	428.18	6.17	.01**
	Years since death	1	2914.72	42.00	< 0.001***
	Gender	1	1683.84	24.26	< 0.001***
	Error	504	69.40		
	Total	508	79.16		
Index of Personal Psychological Problems	Cause of death	1	17.70	11.76	< 0.001***
	Years since death	1	80.82	53.72	< 0.001***
	Gender	1	31.02	20.62	< 0.001***
	Error	536	1.50		
	Total	540	1.74		
8-Item depression Scale	Cause of death	1	57.47	6.81	0.01**
	Years since death	1	373.59	44.24	< 0.001***
	Gender	1	150.22	17.79	< 0.001***
	Error	495	8.44		
	Total	499	9.60		

Note. From Survivors Child Loss Survey, 2006–2009.
*$p < .05$. **$p < .01$. ***$p < .001$.

when gender was considered (at .002), but did not with time since loss in the comparison (at .185). Because there was no bivariate association between time since loss and stigma, this finding is not at all unexpected.

The ANCOVA of grief difficulties (on the GEQ measure) and loss type, controlling for gender and time since loss, showed that the association remained significant when potential confounders of gender and time since the loss were considered. Table 3.3 also showed that these results were also confirmed in the measures of the Complicated Grief scale, the Impact of Event Scale, the Index of Personal Psychological Problems, and the eight-item Depression Scale. When the controls of gender and time since loss were taken into account, the higher problems reports for the drug and suicide bereaved still remained when they were compared with accidental and natural-death bereaved.

Table 3.4 shows the frequency distribution of negative comments tabulated in the four bereavement subgroups. We counted all cases in the categories of natural deaths, accidental deaths, and drug-related deaths. With such a large sample of suicide bereaved, it did not seem necessary to examine and count all 462 cases when a careful investigation of a randomly drawn subsample of suicide bereaved might suffice. First, we sorted all responses on the stigma scale from lowest to highest, including all missing data cases. Then, we took every fifth record of all suicide-bereaved cases on this list, which yielded a random sample of 93 suicide-bereaved respondents from our entire sample.

Table 3.4
Negative Comments by Types of Death

TYPE OF NEGATIVE COMMENT		TYPE OF DEATH				
		1 NATURAL	2 ACCIDENTAL	3 DRUG-DEATH LOSS	4 SUICIDE	TOTAL COUNTS
1 Avoidance	Count	12	24	21	51	108
	%	11%	22%	19%	47%	100%
2 Have other children	Count	6	5	4	4	19
	%	32%	26%	21%	21%	100%
3 Unhelpful advice	Count	4	14	20	55	93
	%	4%	15%	22%	59%	100%
4 With God/in a better place	Count	7	14	14	16	51
	%	14%	28%	28%	31%	100%
5 Other negative	Count	6	3	0	10	19
	%	32%	16%	0%	53%	100%
6 Blame child	Count	0	1	13	31	45
	%	0%	2%	29%	69%	100%
7 Blame parent	Count	0	1	7	22	30
	%	0%	3%	23%	73%	100%
8 Bereavement problems with work	Count	1	2	12	2	17
	%	6%	12%	71%	12%	100%
9 Blank or positive only	Count	4	5	7	15	31
	%	13%	16%	23%	48%	100%
Total counts		40	69	98	206	413
		10%	17%	24%	50%	100%

Note. From Survivors Child Loss Survey, 2006–2009.

As we tabulated the responses for natural-death survivors, a comment was noted that was unique to these cases, and it was only expressed to a minority of the natural-death bereaved. People sometimes were told, "Well you have to be grateful that the suffering is over now." No significant others from any of the other three subgroups expressed any comments like this one, which referred to the ending of the sometimes long and deeply agonizing dying process of many illness-related deaths. And also, there was a comment, uniquely expressed to the suicide bereaved, asking, "Why did your child do it?" This query was almost invariably followed by a comment by bereaved parents themselves, that he or she was deeply puzzled by that very same question.

Parents whose children died from drug-related causes also offered a unique negative response that only a minority of them had heard expressed. Several offered comments, much like Patricia Goldstone (a pseudonym) did. Patricia said,

> It is bothersome for me occasionally to hear friends and coworkers talking about drug abuse and addiction in my presence. They seem to forget I'm there and that my son Jimmy died from an overdose. They demonize all addicts as "born that way," "mentally defective," and as "hopelessly incorrigible." I deeply resent their holier than thou attitudes and indirectly their disrespect for my Jimmy.

It is clear from the data presented in Table 3.4 that both the suicide and drug-death bereaved heard many more child- and parent-blaming comments. None were articulated to natural death survivors; one of each was expressed to accidental-death case respondents, whereas a total of 20 were made to the drug-related death bereaved, and 53 made to the random subsample of suicide bereaved. These differences were statistically significant (chi-square [24] = 88.475, $p < .0001$). When one takes into account the differing numbers of cases within each subgroup category, many of the other comment types seem to match up consistently with one another in each of the subgroups, except those for blaming, which were much different. Compared to almost none among natural death and accidental-death survivors who reported hearing blaming comments, between 40% and 50% of suicide and drug-overdose death survivors heard blaming parent or child statements from their significant others.

DISCUSSION

This first-ever investigation of how bereaved parents cope and are impacted by the drug-overdose death of a child has yielded many meaningful insights. The evidence suggests that parents losing a child to a drug-related or drug-overdose death report much the same stigmatization that suicide survivors confront. The evidence also suggests that these bereaved experience the same grief problems and mental health difficulties as those bereaved by suicide. Although some might have believed that an "accidental drug-death" designation would have spared these bereaved family members from the intense stigma and associated grief and mental health problems associated with a suicide death, this research did not find support for such expectations.

Comparisons on five criteria of grief and mental health problems—grief difficulties, posttraumatic stress, complicated grief, depression, and psychological problems—did not show the drug-death bereaved to be any less troubled on these dimensions than the parents who had lost a child to suicide. Both of these groups showed greater grief and mental health difficulties than parents who had lost children to accidents and natural-death causes. These differences still remained when we took into account important potential confounding variables, such as gender and time since the loss.

As we suggested in the last chapter, stigmatization is associated with greater bereavement difficulties because survivors fail to find the bereavement support they expected among their significant others. Unfortunately, many of our respondents—approximately half—found one or more of their close kin failing to offer them the support they expected. Empathic failures such as these seem likely to exacerbate a survivors' grief (Neimeyer & Jordan, 2002).

When significant others' responses assign blame for the death—blaming the deceased or the parent—we believe this may heighten distress levels for the bereaved parent and bring a person's distress beyond what it would have been, had a significant other simply avoided them or failed to show them a caring interest after the loss. In these cases, the parent who encounters a close associate's statement that his or her child is perhaps better off dead because he or she was already doomed from his or her lifelong mental illness or drug addiction is challenged in a fundamental way to defend the value of their lost child. Such statements carry an inference that the child is/was unworthy to be mourned (Guy, 2004). In the cases where blame is assigned to the parents for not finding the right treatment program for their child or for being an instigating factor in the death, these accusations add to the guilt that suicide or drug-death bereaved parents experience and may compound the obsessional review of their own blameworthiness after a sudden and traumatic death of a child (Jordan, 2001). Close to half of our drug and suicide-bereaved parents encountered blaming responses from one or more of their significant others.

The following are several examples of some of the typical blaming comments that respondents reported. Olivia Thornton (a pseudonym) reported,

> My ex-husband blamed me for (our son) Kevin's death. He has never let up on his accusations of me for not supervising him closely enough. He even claimed I did drugs with Kevin, which was totally untrue and ridiculous; he has been simply outrageous in his accusations. Unfortunately, I still have to deal with him from time to time.

Linda McManus (a pseudonym) reported,

> I couldn't believe my cousins' response. They have a son close in age
> to my Michael. Their son also has a history of mental illness and is in
> recovery. They have been through years of up and downs and hurts
> caused by their son, much like I had with Michael. When Michael
> died, they said to me that it is almost better that he went that way,
> sparing us all a lifelong saga of reverses and disappointments. I was
> shocked and angry they could say that to me, especially since they, of
> all people, should know better.

Betty Lou Boudreau (a pseudonym) commented that she mentioned to
some friends the thought that her deceased son is now with God and in a
safe place.

"The friends said they hoped she was right but expressed doubt to her,
suggesting that her son could be in a different place, away from God, because
of how he lived and his drug taking."

Mary Masterson (a pseudonym) mentioned being totally surprised by her
parish priest's response to her daughter's death.

> The priest said my daughter might not be going to heaven to live
> among the angels because of all the bad things she did during her life
> and because she wasted her life away with drugs. I feel like writing
> a letter of complaint to the archbishop or something else to get this
> damaging man out of there. How smug he was; how does he know
> where my daughter is going?

Such negative experiences may add to a survivor's distress, helping to
sustain a mood of shame, reticence, and extreme caution for these bereaved in
their interactions with nonsurvivors.

This empirical demonstration of blame and its differential association
with different kinds of child losses calls for further investigation of this factor
of stigmatization and an inquiry into whether it has direct associations with
other bereavement-related problems, such as relational strain and perceived
harmfulness. Further investigation is also warranted as to whether blaming
experiences are associated with differences in individual bereavement and
mental health difficulties. Until now, discussions of blaming in stigma have
been offered more or less theoretically. As we have seen here, blaming can be
quantified, and the importance of the assignment of blame as a complicating
factor in individual bereavement adaptations and subsequent mental health of
survivors remains to be demonstrated.

Overall, our findings have shown that, much like the suicide bereaved,
drug-overdose death parent survivors experience substantial levels of "psychache" associated with the traumatic deaths of their loved ones and must cope
with elevated levels of stigmatization accompanying a drug-overdose death.
The very limited literature on drug-overdose death bereavement puts clinicians
treating these individuals at a decided disadvantage. Our findings suggest

that clinicians need to pay particular attention to the social condemnation drug-overdose death survivor parents often confront among their significant others. Advising some to avoid "toxic" relatives and/or encouraging others to openly challenge unhelpful but well-intentioned efforts among intimate associates may help these survivors establish more supportive environments for their healing among their families and friends. It is not simply a matter of dealing with a survivor's grief and depression. Social stigmatization interpenetrates the grief issues that many drug-overdose death survivors must confront.

Reviewing the limitations of this investigation, we need to acknowledge that our mostly correlational data do not permit a full consideration of the complex and sometimes circular causality in social stigmatization and the development of distress symptoms after bereavement. Without longitudinal measurements, we had no ready means to assess levels of psychiatric difficulties among survivors that may have preceded the deaths of their children. Some respondents' avoidance of others may have resulted from their own "self-stigmatizing" withdrawal from contacts with family and friends, who may have been overwhelmed with their own feelings of shame and unworthiness (Dunn & Morish-Vidners, 1987–1988) or the numbing and traumatizing nature of their loss. Some survivors may have created impressions of unavailability or disinterest in maintaining future associations with significant others after their loss.

A number of our respondents remarked that their intense shame about the loss of a child to drugs or suicide prevented them from acknowledging this publicly with significant others until many months had passed. Other survivors never reached a point where they could comfortably talk about their loved one's death truthfully. We can readily imagine that when survivors misrepresent the facts of the death, they then more readily fall into the trap of self-stigmatization. A response of anticipated scorn and ridicule impacts on their various relationships in differing degrees, bringing with it increased bereavement difficulties and suffering for the parent. As a point of contrast, the natural or accidental-death loss of a child seemed to be a situation where the survivor's significant others more often offered what was perceived as appropriate compassionate responses to the bereaved parent. For these survivors, our findings suggested that they rarely, if ever, encountered blaming responses, although they often were exposed to avoidance responses and to statements that their loved one's demise was an act of God.

We also acknowledge other limitations of this exploratory research. With a sample of research volunteers disproportionately drawn from the ranks of support group members and also from clinical patient rosters, newsletter, and listserve subscribers, we cannot claim this sample is representative of the entire U.S. parent survivor population. Only with a sample drawn from official death records where a proactive attempt was made to contact all survivors (and not just those who attend support groups) could we ever hope to adequately provide for representativeness. Yet, for now, there is some consistency between our findings and the previous published record, to suggest that the present results are not anomalous (Dyregrov, Nordanger, & Dyregrov, 2003; Murphy, Johnson, Wu, Fan, & Lohan, 2003).

In addition, some readers may wonder whether there were retrospective recall problems on at least a few of the questions discussed in this report. We do not imagine these problems to have been all that substantial for this survey sample. Slightly more than half of all respondents within each loss type subgroup reported losing their child within the past 4 years, a sufficiently short time span for accurate recall.

CONCLUSION

Although many parents struggle with the challenges of losing a child to a drug overdose, it is surprising and troubling that so little research has been devoted to identifying the unique bereavement needs of this large under-served population. What makes this knowledge gap all the more distressing is the near-constant attention drug-overdose deaths earn among the public at large, as these deaths occur among media celebrities. Within the past 2 years, with the deaths of Heath Ledger, Anna Nicole Smith, and Michael Jackson, an outpouring of media attention has appeared, attesting to widespread societal interest, if not fascination, with this topic. Yet, it is a remarkable disconnect that so many give such great thought and discussion to the subject of drug-overdose death generally, with little more than a perfunctory glance at the impact these deaths have on surviving family members, as they attempt to cope with their losses. It is hoped that this study will help to encourage more scholarly attention and empirical research on this important and disenfranchised group of parental mourners and the impact this tragic mode of death has on the subsequent adjustment and functioning of this too long neglected group of bereaved parents.

REFERENCES

Centers for Disease Control and Prevention, National Center for Injury Prevention and Control. (2011). *Web-based Injury Statistics Query and Reporting System* (WISQARS) [Online]. Retrieved from www.cdc.gov/ncipc/wisqars

Crombie, I. K., Pounder, D. J., & Dick, P. H. (1998). Who takes alcohol prior to suicide? *Journal of Clinical Forensic Medicine, 5*(2), 65–68.

Currier, J.M., Holland, J.M., Coleman, R. A. & Niemeyer, R.A. (2006). Bereavement following violent death: An assault on life and meaning. In R. G. Stevenson & G. R. Cox (Eds.), *Perspectives on violence and violent death* (pp. 177–201). Amityville, NY: Baywood.

Cvinar, J. G. (2005). Do suicide survivors suffer social stigma: A review of the literature. *Perspectives in Psychiatric Care, 41*(1), 14–21.

da Silva, E. A., Noto, A. R., & Formigoni, M. L. (2007). Death by drug overdose: Impact on families. *Journal of Psychoactive Drugs, 39*(3), 301–306.

Darke, S., Duflou, J., & Torok, M. (2009). Toxicology and circumstances of completed suicide by means other than overdose. *Journal of Forensic Sciences, 54*(2), 490–494.

Doka, K. J. (Ed.). (2001). *Disenfranchised grief: New directions, challenges, and strategies for practice* (2nd ed.). Champaign, IL: Research Press.

Dunn, R. G., & Morrish-Vidners, D. (1987–1988). The psychological and social experience of suicide survivors. *Omega: Journal of Death and Dying, 18*(3), 175–215.

Dyregrov, K., Nordanger, D., & Dyregrov, A. (2003). Predictors and psychosocial distress after suicide, SIDS and accidents. *Death Studies, 27*(2), 143–165.

Graham, J. K., & Hanzlick, R. (2008). Accidental drug deaths in Fulton County, Georgia, 2002: Characteristics, case management and certification issues. *The American Journal of Forensic Medical and Pathology, 29*(3), 224–230.

Guy, P. (2004). Bereavement through drug use: Messages from research. *Practice, 16* (1), 43–53.

Hall, A. J., Logan, J. E., Toblin, R. L., Kaplan, J. A., Kraner, J. C., Bixler, D., . . . Paulozzi, L. J. (2008). Patterns of abuse among unintentional pharmaceutical overdose fatalities. *The Journal of the American Medical Association, 300*(22), 2613–2620.

Hetzel, A. M. (1997). *U.S. vital statistics system. Major activities and developments, 1950–95* (DHHS Publication No. [PHS] 97-1003). Hyattsville, MD: National Center for Health Statistics. Retrieved from http://www.cdc.gov/nchs/data/misc/usvss.pdf

Jordan, J. R. (2001). Is suicide bereavement different? A reassessment of the literature. *Suicide & Life-Threatening Behavior, 31*(1), 91–102.

Marzuk, P. M., Tardiff, K., Leon, A. C., Stajic, M., Morgan, E. B., & Mann, J. J. (1992). Prevalence of cocaine use among residents of New York City who committed suicide during a one-year period. *The American Journal of Psychiatry, 149*(3), 371–375.

May, P. A., Van Winkle, N. W., Williams, M. B., McFeeley, P. J., DeBruyn, L. M., & Serna, P. (2002). Alcohol and suicide death among American Indians of New Mexico: 1980–1998. *Suicide & Life-Threatening Behavior, 32*(3), 240–255.

Murphy, S. A., Johnson, L. C., Wu, L., Fan, J. J, & Lohan, J. (2003). Bereaved parents' outcomes 4 to 60 months after their children's deaths by accident, suicide, or homicide: A comparative study demonstrating differences. *Death Studies, 27*(1), 39–61.

Neimeyer, R. A., & Jordan, J. R. (2002). Disenfranchisement as empathic failure: Grief therapy and the co-construction of meaning. In K. Doka (Ed.), *Disenfranchised grief: New directions, challenges, and strategies for practice* (pp. 95–118). Champaign, IL: Research Press.

Shah, N. G., Lathrop, S. L., Reichard, R. R., & Landen, M. G. (2007). Unintentional drug overdoses death trends in New Mexico, USA, 1990–2005: Combinations of heroin, cocaine, prescription opioids and alcohol. *Addiction, 103*(1), 126–136.

Sveen, C. A., & Walby, F. A. (2008). Suicide survivors' mental health and grief reactions: A systematic review of controlled studies. *Suicide & Life-Threatening Behavior, 38*(1), 13–29.

Timmermans, S. (2006). *Postmortem: How medical examiners explain suspicious deaths.* Chicago, IL: University of Chicago Press.

Worden, J. W. (2009). *Grief counselling and grief therapy: A handbook for the mental health practitioner* (4th ed.). New York, NY: Springer.

Wysowski, D. K. (2007). Surveillance of prescription drug-related mortality using death certificate data. *Drug Safety, 30*(6), 533–540.

4

Differences in the Suicide Death Circumstances and How They May Affect a Survivor's Grief

INTRODUCTION

The last chapter led us to a deeper understanding of how a child's death—whether by suicide, accidental drug overdose, other accidents, or natural causes—may be associated with differences in a parent's bereavement and linked to differences in a parent's grief difficulties and also to their overall mental health. We have seen how greater levels of stigma associated with losing a child to suicide or a drug overdose were also related to parents experiencing greater grief complications when compared with parents whose children died from accidents or natural causes. In this chapter, we will focus primarily on some of the circumstances surrounding a suicide death that may impact the intensity of the grief response in suicide-survivor parents—for example, whether a parent had closer contact with the body at the death scene, whether the parent was more or less surprised at the death, whether parents had a positive or conflicted relationship with the deceased child prior to the death—and whether any of these experiences are associated with diverging bereavement outcomes.

Let us begin at an early grief starting point, with bereaved parents sharing their loss stories together at a peer support group meeting. In later chapters, we will have a great deal more to say about how these groups help survivors cope with the traumatic loss of a child. Let us begin by taking a long lens look at a support group meeting with survivors sitting around in a circle. Usually, they start their meeting with a brief "go around," where each member gives his or her first name, mentions the name and relationship of the person who died, the length of time since the death occurred, and the manner of the death. The sharing of these facts serves to create a bond between participants. As Lawrence Shulman describes it, "support groups bring people together to help each other address tabooed topics," what Shulman calls the "all in the same boat" phenomenon (Shulman, 2006, p. 272). At support group meetings, usually much time, attention, and importance is devoted to discussing the manner of a loved one's death.

Bob A., a 54-year-old accountant, who lost his 23-year-old son 2 months earlier, described to his support group the experience of discovering his son's body.

> Betty (his wife) and I came back home from grocery shopping; we pulled the car up to the back of the house and there was David hanging by an electrical extension cord from the branch of a tree in our backyard. I had no idea how long he had been there. All I could think of was cutting him down as fast as I could and trying to do CPR on him; which I did do. (I'm a trained ambulance corps volunteer in our local community.) Betty called 911, and I just kept at doing CPR on him till the ambulance came. When they came, they pulled me off David and told me he was already dead.

As he recounted this experience, Bob's legs shook and there was a quiver in his voice. He said, "I will never forget the shock of discovering David dangling from that branch in our backyard."

At another support group meeting, the facilitator asked the participants whether anyone experienced any "flashbacks." Karen A., a first-time participant, volunteered,

> Whenever I hear a train whistle, it sends shudders down my spine as I recall my husband's death. About 2 months ago, he jumped in front of a commuter express train. His body was shredded into thousands of pieces. After the incident, the railroad people let me go down on the tracks at the death scene. All I could see there were tiny fragments of his clothes and blood-stained mush, although I did find a piece of his St. Christopher's medal. I've tried to return to the scene, but the railroad people threatened to arrest me if they ever see me there again. The coroner's office doesn't want to do DNA testing of his remains. Although his car was parked at the train station, I can't help thinking that he is still alive somewhere and that someday he'll walk in the door and tell me he found a stand-in for him that day.

Stillness fills the room as Karen's sadness is keenly felt by all participants. Reggie M. finally breaks the silence by saying:

> I know how you feel about wanting to go back to the tracks. My wife and I lost our son 8 months ago in a similar situation. Oddly, we found it comforting to go back again, too. We set up a little shrine along the fence near the tracks; we found that very helpful. We also went to a psychic several times. I can give you her name if you want it.

Survivors, whether of a suicide or another traumatic death, attach a great deal of importance to the manner of the death of their loved ones and to how it may be affecting their grieving process. In the popular press, especially since 9/11, much has been written about grief complications arising for survivors from the loss and mutilation of bodies of lost loved ones. In the bereavement literature, much has been written about posttraumatic stresses arising from violent deaths (see Asaro, 2001; Ehntholt & Yule, 2006; Tang, 2006; among many others).

This appears to be well understood in the suicide bereavement literature with one of the primary bereavement assessment tools consisting of a measure of posttraumatic stress, the Impact of Event Scale (Horowitz, Wilner, & Alvarez, 1979). It could be claimed, perhaps, that all suicide deaths comprise violent self-killings. Yet, if we take suicide survivor behavior at face value, it suggests that some suicides are more violent than others, and possibly, by their more violent and troublesome characteristics, likely to generate more grief difficulties.

Thus, the questions we wish to explore here are "Do grief process outcomes vary when the suicide death circumstances differ?" and "How do they differ under diverging circumstances?"

As we reviewed the past research literature, we found limited work devoted to explaining why some suicide survivors have more grief difficulties than others. Jay Callahan (2000), in one of the few studies completed with suicide survivor support group affiliates, found that direct confrontations with the death, either in witnessing the act, finding the body, or seeing the body at the scene of the death increased grief difficulties for survivors. The Callahan study was conducted among a mixed group of survivors consisting of parents, children, spouses, partners, and other close relatives.

Another study, completed among a small Australian sample of suicide-bereaved parents, found that grief difficulties and distress are likely to be greater when survivors were unprepared for the suicide death of their child (Maple, Plummer, Edwards, & Minichello, 2007). These findings lead us to speculate that more surprised parents and those whose children's death represented a first-suicide-attempt suicide would be likely to experience greater grief difficulties than other parent survivors who were less surprised at their child's death and where the decedent had made several prior suicide attempts prior to completing suicide. In addition, and consistent with Kosminsky's (2006) claims, we anticipated greater grief difficulties to occur when survivors reported more conflicted or uncertain relationships with the decedent prior to the suicide.

Accordingly, we expected that the following subgroups would show higher grief difficulties: (a) parents who had closer contact with the body at the death scene, (b) more surprised parents whose child's suicides represented a first suicide attempt, and (c) cases where a conflicted relationship between the decedent and the parent had preceded the death.

MEASURES OF INTEREST

Finding the Body

Suicide-bereaved respondents were asked a series of three yes-no questions to determine whether they had witnessed the suicide act, found and saw the body at the death scene, or saw the body prior to cremation or burial. Witnessing the suicide was an extremely rare event with only seven of our respondents reporting being present at the time of the suicide. A much larger number ($n = 144$), approximately a third of all suicide death cases, reported finding the deceased's body, usually at the family residence. In many of these cases, the decedent took his or her life when other family members were at home asleep or in another part of the residence at the time of the death. We combined the 7 death-witnessing cases with the 144 others who found the body into a total group of 151 cases. We anticipated that respondents who found the body (or who had directly witnessed the event) would experience the highest levels of grief difficulties.

We found the largest number of our respondents fell into a second category, $n = 210$, that is, those who did not find the body but who had seen it prior to burial or cremation. We anticipated intermediate levels of grief difficulties for those in this subgroup, and we anticipated the least grief difficulties for the remaining respondents who reported not seeing the body prior to burial or cremation, $n = 104$.

Surprise at the Death

Respondents were also asked to respond on a 5-point rating scale about their degree of surprise at the suicide death of their child, using the following points: (1) *extremely surprised,* (2) *very surprised,* (3) *somewhat surprised,* (4) *slightly surprised,* or (5), *not at all surprised.* Clearly, great surprise was the most common response with 80% reporting being very or extremely surprised at the death. Consistent with the Maple et al. (2007) hypothesis, we anticipated higher grief difficulties for this very surprised majority of respondents, compared to the less surprised minority. Respondents were also asked to report to the best of their knowledge the number of previous suicide attempts made by their child prior to taking his or her life. Again, consistent with Maple's hypothesis, we anticipated that more surprised parents, whose children were first attempters, would show the highest levels of grief difficulties.

Prior Relationships

Respondents were asked to describe the relationships they were having with their child immediately prior to the death and asked to rate their relationship on the following 5-point scale: (1) *extremely positive,* (2) *somewhat positive,* (3) *unclear or uncertain,* (4) *somewhat negative,* or (5) *extremely negative.* The majority of respondents (82%) reported having a somewhat or very positive relationship with their child prior to the death. Consistent with the Kosminsky (2006) hypothesis, we speculated that those reporting negative or uncertain relationships would show higher grief difficulties than the parents reporting positive relationships.

Suicide Method

Although no prior research has identified any patterns of association between the methods employed in self-killing and grief difficulties, we also investigated whether any differences between these two phenomena might be found.

RESULTS

We examined our hypotheses on three grief problems criteria: the Grief Experience Questionnaire (GEQ), the Inventory of Complicated Grief (ICG) scale, and the posttraumatic stress measure of the Impact of Event Scale (IES). We completed single factor analysis of variance (ANOVA) tests to compare the means of grief difficulties among the subgroups of interest on our hypotheses. Results were generally consistent with each other on these three criteria and, given their similarity, we only present the data for our hypotheses of the means on the GEQ scale differences.

Results contrasting the different methods of suicide are displayed in Table 4.1. They suggest no significant differences in parent's grief difficulties when children died from different suicide methods. Again, when we compared self-inflicted gunshot caused deaths to all other suicide deaths (not displayed in Table 4.1), the grief difficulties means showed great similarity.

Initially, it was our expectation that parents who found the body would report the greatest grief distress compared to all other subgroups: those who did not find the body but saw it prior to burial and those who did not see the body at all prior to burial. This was not supported on any of the three grief difficulties measures, and Table 4.1 shows virtually identical GEQ means for those who found the body and for those who did not find the body but saw it prior to burial. Yet, when we compared those who saw the body prior to burial with those who did not, results suggested any finding or seeing of the body prior to the burial was associated with greater grief difficulties than for those who reported not seeing the body prior to burial or cremation. This result, too, was supported on all three grief difficulties measures. Table 4.1 shows our hypothesis approaching statistical significance with the ANOVA p value at .051 comparing GEQ means of all three subgroups. When we applied the Scheffe paired means comparison test, contrasting those with greater body contact following the death to those with the least contact, results showed no significant differences between these subgroups. Yet, when we combined the saw-the-body subgroup and the found-the-body subgroups, statistically significant results were noted at the .01 level when we compared these 331 respondents

Table 4.1

Differences in Grief Difficulties as Measured by GEQ Scores by Suicide Death Circumstances (*N* = 462)

DEATH CIRCUMSTANCES	*M*	*SD*	*N*	*F*	*df*	SIG.
Suicide method			462	0.70	6, 417	0.66
Gunshot	39.8	11.5	205			
Hanging	40.7	10.0	134			
Overdose	42.4	15.7	20			
Asphyxiation	37.5	11.5	28			
Jumping	41.1	10.3	12			
Drowning	38.2	11.2	9			
Other	42.6	8.9	16			
Finding the body			426	3.01	2, 423	0.051*
Found body	40.8	11.8	140			
Saw body before burial	40.9	10.7	191			
Not found/not seen	37.7	10.8	95			
Prior suicide attempts			423	4.94	2, 420	0.007**
First attempt	39.2	10.8	278			
Second attempt	40.2	9.7	75			
Third or greater	43.8	13.1	70			
Surprised at the suicide death?			423	.55	2, 420	0.57
Extremely	40.2	10.4	225			
Very	39.4	11.9	117			
Somewhat/not at all	41.1	11.8	81			
Previous relations			423	11.4	1, 421	0.001***
Positive	39.3	10.7	348			
Negative/uncertain	44.0	12.1	75			

Note. From Survivors Child Loss Survey, 2006–2009.
* = *p* < .05. ** = *p* < .01. *** = *p* < .001.

with the 95 others who had not seen the body prior to the burial. (This latter result is not displayed in our tables.)

This ambiguity led us to consider gender as a possible confounder to these associations. An analysis of gender showed contradicting trends for parents with differing degrees of contact with the body after the death. Among women who reported finding the body, their grief difficulties scores averaged 43 (*n* = 115) on the GEQ test, 5 points higher on this scale, compared to those without any exposure to the body before the death, who showed a mean of 38 (*n* = 79), a statistically significant difference (*F*[2, 354] = 5, *p* = .007). This significant association was confirmed with the Scheffe means comparison test.

For the men, the least grief troubled subgroup (with a mean of 30.4, *n* = 25) were those who reported finding the body, compared to the other two subgroups of male respondents, which showed higher means of 36 (*n* = 16) for those who neither found nor saw the body prior to burial and 37.5 ($n = 28$) for the men who did not find the body but saw it prior to burial. Fathers also showed significant differences in this respect between one another ($F[2, 66] = 4.3, p = .02$), contrasting the 25 fathers who found the body and the 44 others who did not find the body and had not seen it prior to the burial. This association was also confirmed with the Scheffe means comparison test.

We suspect that fathers may be inclined to respond in a chivalrous spirit, feeling better with themselves if they had found their deceased child's body rather than their wives, children, or other family members first encountering the body. These gender differences in regard to finding the body deserve further exploration in future research.

None of these gender-related associations with finding the body are presented in Table 4.1. In Chapter 12, we will return to the gender and grief issue in greater depth, but we make reference to this now because it appears relevant and associated with the opposing directions of experiencing grief difficulties and finding the body after the death. We examined all the remaining associations presented in Table 4.1 separately by gender and found no other similar gender differences and inconsistencies. This instance, showing gender contrasts regarding the viewing of the body, suggests that gender should be separately considered in all our forthcoming multivariate analyses of grief difficulties.

Table 4.1 also shows the grief difficulties means for parents reporting on whether their child's suicide represented a first, second, or a subsequent attempt. Two-thirds of these respondents perceived their child's suicide as a first attempt; 18% more perceived it as a second attempt; and the balance— 16%—judged their child was making his or her third or more frequent suicide attempt when he or she died. The number of prior attempts was a significant factor. In particular, having a child make a third or greater suicide attempt was associated with significantly greater grief difficulties. Separate Scheffe paired comparison tests showed that parents whose child had made three or more suicide attempts had greater grief difficulties than parents of those children who had never before attempted or those who had made a single previous attempt. Here, too, this association held on both the ICG and IES differences tests.

Table 4.1 also displays the mean differences in grief difficulties between those reporting differences in being more surprised or less so at the death. Those reporting less surprise at the death ("somewhat/not at all") reported slightly higher grief difficulties (with a mean of 41) than those reporting greater surprise ("very" or "extremely") at the death, reporting a mean of 40. Both GEQ and ICG tests showed nonsignificant differences on the surprise element of the death, although significant differences were noted in this respect on the IES test of posttraumatic stress. In this single instance, the mean for surprised parents ("very" or "extremely") was at 33, whereas less surprised parents ("somewhat/not at all") showed a mean of 36, significantly higher with a probability equal to .04.

The test of prior relationship differences did show that parents reporting negative or uncertain relationships with their child prior to the death also reported more grief difficulties, with a mean of 44 on the abbreviated GEQ scale, compared to a mean of 39 for those reporting more positive relationships with their child. The ANOVA test confirmed this relationship, $p < .001$. This result held up on all tests of the three grief difficulties measures.

As we have already seen in earlier chapters, it is important when examining differences in grief difficulties to consider whether time since the loss confounds the relationships being investigated. Therefore, we further investigated the bivariate relationships of interest here with time since the loss in a multiple regression equation to see whether, in the company of this potential confounder, the relationships we observed still held up. In addition, we included gender as another potential confounder to the relationships now under review.

Table 4.2 shows the multiple regression analysis of GEQ scores for parent suicide survivors on the five potentially important bivariate predictors: time since the death, gender, the number of prior suicide attempts, heightened exposure to the death event, and prior relations with the decedent. The regression results showed the time span variable to be the largest contributor to this model, with a beta weight of $-.28$. When the time span variable was removed (results not tabled here), the explained variance dropped considerably from 17% down to 9%, showing its importance in accounting for differences in grief difficulties. We also ran the same regression equation with the time span variable alone, omitting each of the other predictors, and the explained variance diminished minimally, by less than a single percentage point, again suggesting the limited explanatory powers of these other factors alone in the same multivariate model without the time span variable. We also computed these same multivariate models in two equations with the ICG and IES as dependent variables replacing the brief GEQ scale. The findings yielded identical results with 11% declines in the variance explained, mostly from the time since loss variable. (These analyses are not displayed in any of our tables.)

Table 4.2
Multiple Regression of Grief Difficulties, by Time Since Death, Gender, Prior Suicide Attempts, Exposure to the Body and Prior Relations With the Deceased

Number of obs = 419
$F(5, 413)$ = 16.057
r^2 = .17

INDEPENDENT VARIABLES	CORREL. COEFF.	BETA	P
Years since death	$-.32$	$-.28$	.0001
Gender	.22	.21	.001
Number of prior attempts	.13	.05	.27
Exposure to the body	.10	.09	.04
Prior rels. with decedent	.17	.17	.001

Note. p = level of significance. From Survivors Child Loss Survey, 2006–2007.

Table 4.3
Multiple Regression of Grief Difficulties by Time Since Death, Gender, Prior Suicide Attempts, Exposure to the Body, Prior Relations With the Deceased Among 3-Year or Less Post-loss Survivors

			Number of obs = 174
			$F(5, 168)$ = 5.74
			r^2 = .15

INDEPENDENT VARIABLES	CORREL. COEFF.	BETA	P
Years since death	−.11	.04	.54
Gender	.23	.21	.004
Number of prior attempts	.18	.19	.01
Exposure to the body	.07	.10	.18
Prior rels. with decedent	.27	.17	.03

Note. p = level of significance. From Survivors Child Loss Survey, 2006–2007.

We suspected that some of the variables under investigation were potentially important during the early phase of suicide bereavement. It is repeatedly mentioned in the grief literature that the time since the loss assumes an overriding importance in affecting a survivor's grief difficulties. With the passage of time after the death, grief difficulties begin to fade. What if the passage of time were removed (or at least minimized) from this equation and we considered only those bereaved parents who were all less than 3 years past their losses. Perhaps, without the overriding influence of the passage of time after the loss, we might begin to see that the circumstances surrounding a suicide death have a stronger association with a survivor's grief difficulties. To investigate this possibility, we computed the same equation for the 174 suicide cases, where their children's deaths took place within the previous 3 years prior to filling out the surveys. This is displayed in Table 4.3. Within this narrower sample of relatively recently bereaved suicide survivors, the regression equation showed three statistically significant predictors of grief difficulties faring significantly in contributing to the differences in grief difficulties: gender (with a beta of .21; with mothers showing more difficulties), number of prior suicide attempts (with a beta of .19), and poor relations with the decedent (with a beta of .17). All these correlates account for 15% of differences in grief difficulties. Not surprisingly perhaps, during this first 3-year time frame, the time span variable did not yield a significant association with grief difficulties. In a further test, not presented here, we widened the time frame to the first 5 years after the loss and observed the time span variable once again becoming a significant predictor. During the early loss period, the exposure to the body variable appeared to be redundant when it was included in this same model with these other significant predictors of grief difficulties. Both prior suicide attempts and poor previous relations with the decedent appeared to offer modest explanatory value—explaining 8% of the variance of grief difficulties alone—during these first early years after a loss.

We further investigated the relationship of the time span variable in regression analyses with each of the three indicators of grief difficulties included in this survey: the abbreviated GEQ scale, the ICG, and the IES. We do not present these data in the tables, although we summarize these multiple regression findings. In each case, with one of these three variables as the dependent variable, and time span as the independent variable, when we narrowed the sampling frame to include only those survivors where 4 or fewer years had passed since their loss, the time span variable yielded a non-significant association with grief difficulties. This suggests relatively high grief difficulties persisting during the early loss years and little overall variability in grief difficulties during this 4-year-long period. Rather, other variables appear to play a larger role in differentiating the response that parents make to the suicide of their child. Our data appear to show parents bereaved by suicide not experiencing any significant abatement of their grief difficulties during these 4 years. As a group, they appear to fit the criteria for a prolonged grief disorder by having their symptoms persist for longer than 6 months. Yet, as we altered the sample frame to include more survivors, who spent at least 5 years since their loss, we noted significant associations between time since loss and grief difficulties. As we expanded the sample frame still further, to include all suicide survivors, the relationship showed that the longer the time span after loss, the lower the grief difficulties scores.

Figure 4.1 as follows shows the plots of each of these three associations of years since the death against the different numeric means of grief difficulties.

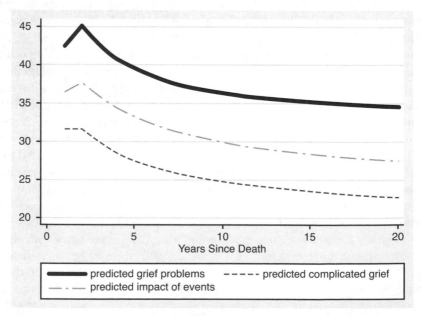

FIGURE 4.1   Predicted Grief Difficulties for Three Measures by Years Since the Death Among Suicide-Bereaved Parents

It should be noted that this figure is based on cross-sectional data. It includes information on different survivors placed along a continuum of different time periods since their loss. It is not based on a single group of survivors who were studied repeatedly over the range of the period depicted. Interestingly, the plot shows a slight upward spike in grief difficulties for survivors on two of the three grief difficulties measures between the first 12 to 24 months after loss. Yet, after the 2-year time point steady declines on all three grief difficulties criteria are shown. Whether we consider the GEQ, the ICG, or the IES, the plots for each measure shows the steepest declines in grief difficulties taking place between the third and fifth years after loss. After 5 years, the declines in grief difficulties scores appear to become more gradual.

INTERPRETING OUR FINDINGS

Although many of the suicide bereaved at support group meetings believe that finding a deceased relative's body at the death scene has greatly increased their posttraumatic stress and grief difficulties, and many clinicians share these beliefs, as well, our data only partially confirmed these perceptions. Our data suggested that these suppositions can apparently only be applied to bereaved mothers but appear to run in the opposite direction for bereaved fathers. Additional future research will be needed before we can place more confidence in these results.

Our data showed the overall importance of time since the loss on the longer term impact of a suicide-bereaved parent's bereavement trajectories. In contrast, seeing the body assumed a comparatively minor role in our regressions analyses. It became a redundant correlate among more newly bereaved survivors, who are less than 3 years past their loss. In addition, it attained only a modest significance in a longer term multivariate analysis along with time since the loss, yielding a correlation coefficient of .10 and a beta weight of .09. The time since loss factor assumed an overshadowing role in explaining differences in grief difficulties in relation to all the other related factors, such as gender differences, a child's prior suicide attempts, and the parent's prior relations with the decedent, outranking all other correlates with a coefficient of $-.32$.

These findings are somewhat at odds with the results obtained by Callahan (2000), who found the exposure-to-the-body variable as a most significant correlate with grief difficulties in his survey. In his study, he found that the exposure variable superseded time since loss as the most significant single correlate in his multivariate multiple regression analyses. Any number of reasons might explain the discrepancies between our results and his. These include the slightly different question wordings between our two studies; the use of the full GEQ scale applied by Callahan and the abbreviated scale employed here; the longer time span covered in this study compared to Callahan's study; and the fact that the Callahan survey studied a mixed group of survivors, whereas ours examined parents exclusively. More research will be needed to better explain these discrepancies. Presently, our research leads us to conclude that as the time interval after the loss widens, the trauma-inducing aspects of close exposure to the death and seeing the body are reduced and therefore their role in contributing to overall reported grief difficulties also recedes.

Although Maple and her associates' (2007) small sample of Australian parent survivors suggested that grief difficulties were more pronounced when parents were greatly surprised at their child's death than when they were less surprised, we found no association between parental surprise and levels of grief difficulties. If anything, on the criteria of the IES differences, we found the associations ran in an opposing direction from Maple's findings. Our results showed grief difficulties higher for less surprised parents. These findings are also consistent with Callahan's (2000) findings on this same subject. When we looked at the number of prior suicide attempts that the deceased made, those parents reporting that their child made three or more suicide attempts showed greater grief difficulties than their counterparts who reported that the suicide represented a first attempt effort. Parents who reported greater surprise at the death tended to report fewer prior suicide attempts. In fact, there was an inverse correlation of $-.40$ between surprise at the death and the number of prior suicide attempts. We also found that reporting that a child had made more prior attempts was associated with encountering greater grief difficulties. Putting these findings together, we speculate that when a child makes more suicide attempts, it may tend to create in their parents greater feelings of guilt and blameworthiness about the death. In fact, our data raise the possibility of a "subtype" of suicide surviving parents who had a negative relationship with their children prior to the deaths, experienced multiple previous attempts by their children, who also may have been less surprised when their children finally completed the acts, but because of all this, are more deeply traumatized by the death.

This study has also identified two important points for clinical practice with the suicide bereaved during their early years of dealing with loss. As Kosminsky's (2006) clinical experiences have demonstrated, prior conflicts with the decedent can impede a survivor's healing. We have obtained empirical confirmation for this from our survey data showing greater grief difficulties for those survivors who had uncertain or negative relationships with their deceased children prior to the death than those parents who reported positive relationships. The data showed a .27 correlation between a negative relationship with the child prior to the death and greater grief difficulties during the first 3 years after the loss. These data point to the importance of assessing for and addressing this point in clinical interventions during the early years of bereavement.

Clinicians working with the bereaved may already be well aware of how a patient's prior relationships with their deceased relatives can become grief "sticking" points. Yet, as these precepts have been verified by this survey research, the knowledge base for clinical applications is thereby extended. The prior suicide attempt history of the decedent appears to be another useful marker for the possible identification of greater grief difficulties, especially as it may occur during the early post-loss years. Multiple prior attempts correlated significantly at .18 ($p = .01$) with higher grief difficulties, among those sustaining child losses 3 or fewer years previously. It seems likely that a troubled relationship with the child and previous suicide attempts are both markers of a child with serious psychiatric illness and may contribute to an increased likelihood of guilt, remorse, and self-blame in the mourning process after the suicide. In a very important sense, survivor parents whose child had a history of prior psychiatric illness and a more problematic relationship with parents may be grieving not only the loss of the child through death but also the many years of a prior lost and troubled relationship with the deceased. It may be that suicide survivors in which the deceased struggled with psychiatric illness for a considerable period before the suicide have an exceedingly complex set of thoughts and emotions about the suicide, ranging from relief that the ordeal is over, to guilt over a feeling of relief, to great sorrow over the troubled life of the deceased and lost dreams of a more "normal" parent–child relationship.

The present investigation has demonstrated the importance of the time span since death as the strongest single predictor of grief difficulties differences among child-death survivors over the course of the life cycle. The method of the suicide, the discovery and viewing of the deceased's body, the prior relationship to the decedent, and the multiple suicide attempts were secondary in importance behind the time span variable when we looked at our entire sample, which ranged from .08 of a year to 27 years in terms of time since the suicide. This conforms with the general findings in thanatology that, for most people, bereavement distress decreases with time (Ott, Lueger, Kelber, & Prigerson, 2007).

Of equal importance, however, are our findings that in the first 4 years of bereavement after suicide, there is either little decrease or even evidence of an increase of grief distress among parent survivors. Time since the death does not appear to matter much in this early phase of bereavement, whereas factors such as the number of previous attempts and the perceived quality of the relationship with the deceased were significantly related to outcome. This fits with an understanding that among the most prominent concerns for suicide survivors is the need to make sense of the death (Jordan & McIntosh, 2011). This need to construct a narrative that helps to explain the reasons for the suicide appears to be one of the most important thematic issues for survivors (Jordan, 2001), and a perceived negative relationship with the deceased may only increase this felt need, particularly for the parents of the deceased.

Lastly, another important corollary of this finding about the impact of time since the death was our results showing—with three different problem indicators—that the steepest declines in grief difficulties occur during the third to fifth years after loss. These results are potentially important to survivors and are convergent with the findings of Murphy, Johnson, Wu, Fan and Lohan, (2003) from their longitudinal study of parent survivors of the traumatic death of a child. This research found years 3 and 4 to be the crucial loss acceptance turning points for the survivor parents. In this first-ever study of survivors who were as far along as 27 years since the death, our results demonstrate continuing declines in grief difficulties taking place over the longer course. These findings deserve further confirmation in future research to see whether the same grief adaptation patterns we found for parent suicide survivors will change in similar ways for survivors of a child's natural death and for other traumatic death survivors. Taken together, these findings can help clinicians to identify parental suicide survivors who are particularly at risk for a complicated mourning trajectory and for whom skillful and compassionate intervention may be needed. Traumatic-loss survivors, too, may be encouraged by the consistency of findings, between the present work and Murphy's, showing a 3- to 5-year time span for the general abatement of acute grief problems. Finally, it is important for clinicians to recognize that the societal and even professional "conventional wisdom" about the normative duration of grief distress may need to be rethought when considering traumatic losses such as the suicide of one's child. For example, although the proposed 6-month duration criterion for the new Prolonged Grief Disorder diagnosis (Prigerson et al., 2009) may work well in terms of achieving an optimal balance between specificity and sensitivity for more normative losses, such as the death of an elderly spouse, our data and the Murphy studies suggest that it is likely to produce far too many "false positives" when dealing with bereavement following the loss of a child to suicide. More research confirming these results should be extremely helpful.

Taken together, the findings from this and the previous chapter, showing important differences between different subgroups of traumatic and nontraumatic-loss survivors can begin to help clinicians differentiate which survivors are at greatest risk for grief difficulties. The supposition that suicide survivors are a homogeneous population is a widely held, untested, and, in our opinion, likely false assumption. Rather, our data suggest that survivor parents who had a difficult relationship with their child prior to the suicide or parents whose child had made more than one attempt prior to the completed suicide are likely to have a more difficult time in their mourning process. It may well be that future research with more nuanced measures of exposure to the body at the time of the death may show that exposure differences—in witnessing the death or in finding the body—could be additional contributors to grief difficulties during the early years after loss.

If we think about what these findings may suggest about the bereavement adaptations of parents losing a child to a drug overdose, the following seems worthwhile to consider. As a group, we often think there is probably a sharp contrast between suicide-bereaved parents and the drug-overdose bereaved. At a workshop devoted to overdose-death bereavement at a recent National Compassionate Friends Conference, a bereaved mother led a session. The audience included some 55 to 60 parents who shared a similar drug overdose loss of a child as the presenter. The facilitator asked attendees to raise their hands showing if they had known about their child's drug problems for 5 or more years before the death. Then, about 20 to 25 hands went up. Next, she asked how many knew about their child's addiction problems for at least

2 years before the death. Then, about 20 more hands were elevated. Last, the question was posed "How many were blind-sided, greatly surprised by the death, and had little to no previous knowledge of their child's drug problems?" To this query, only three or four hands were raised. Thus, most overdose death parents probably share a loss story much like Amy Weiner's story reported in the last chapter, facing what she had termed "a roller-coaster ride to hell." On the basis of the contrasts we are making now, we would imagine that greater numbers of these more highly aware drug-bereaved parents would be more likely to experience relief-related guilt associated with the loss and therefore subjected to more grief difficulties at greater levels during their early loss years compared to other drug-overdose bereaved parents who only learned of their children's addictions by surprise on the child's death. If there are parallels between our findings from these suicide-bereaved parents, it would suggest greater grief difficulties for those parents possessing greater awareness of their children's addiction problems, in contrast to others who may be taken by surprise from them, as they may be initially revealed at the death. It remains for future research to clarify whether the patterns of adaptations noted here for these suicide-bereaved parents may be extended to those bereaved by drug-overdose deaths of a child or to other child-loss survivors.

Finally, the limitations of this study need to be taken into consideration. As we have mentioned elsewhere in this text, our convenience sample may not be representative of all survivors. Although our response rate was a very acceptable one, we simply do not know whether the conclusions apply to all parent suicide survivors or just to those who agree to participate in survivor research, a group that may be different from nonparticipating survivors. Secondly, we have used simple, and in some cases, single-item measures in this chapter. Future research might benefit from the inclusion of more complex measures as well as interview data on some of the key variables under scrutiny here. Lastly, as a cross-sectional and correlational study, we can only demonstrate the associations between different predictor variables and greater bereavement difficulties, not the direction of causality. Longitudinal designs in survivor research would help greatly in furthering our understanding of the likely complex and circular causality between the loss experience itself, the development of psychological difficulties, and diverging bereavement outcomes.

REFERENCES

Asaro, M. R. (2001). Working with adult homicide survivors, part II: Helping family members cope with murder. *Perspectives in Psychiatric Care, 37*(4), 115–124, 136.

Callahan, J. (2000). Predictors and correlates of bereavement in suicide support group participants. *Suicide & Life-Threatening Behavior, 30*(2), 104–124.

Ehntholt, K. A., & Yule, W. (2006). Practitioner review: Assessment and treatment of refugee children and adolescents who have experienced war-related trauma. *Journal of Child Psychology and Psychiatry, 47*(12), 1197–1210.

Horowitz, M. J., Wilner, N., & Alvarez, W. (1979). Impact of Event Scale: A measure of subjective stress. *Psychosomatic Medicine, 41*(3), 209–218.

Jordan, J. R. (2001) Is suicide bereavement different? A reassessment of the literature. *Suicide and Life Threatening Behavior, 31*(1), 91–102.

Jordan, J. R., & McIntosh, J. L. (Eds.). (2011). *Grief after suicide: Understanding the consequences and caring for the survivors.* New York, NY: Routledge.

Kosminsky, P. (2006). *Getting back to life when grief won't heal.* New York, NY: McGraw-Hill.

Maple, M., Plummer, D., Edwards H., & Minichello, V. (2007). The effect of preparedness for suicide following the death of a young adult child. *Suicide & Life-Threatening Behavior, 37*(2), 127–134.

Murphy, S. A., Johnson, L. C., Wu, L., Fan, J. J., & Lohan, J. (2003). Bereaved parents' outcomes 4 to 60 months after their children's deaths by accident, suicide, or homicide: A comparative study demonstrating differences. *Death Studies, 27*(1), 39–61.

Murphy, S. A., Tapper, V. J., Johnson, L. C., & Lohan, J. (2003). Suicide ideation among parents bereaved by the violent deaths of their children. *Issues in Mental Health Nursing, 24*(1), 5–25.

Ott, C. H., Lueger, R. J., Kelber, S. T., & Prigerson, H. G., (2007). Spousal bereavement in older adults: Common, resilient, and chronic grief with defining characteristics. *The Journal of Nervous and Mental Disease, 195*(4), 332–341.

Prigerson, H. G., Horowitz, M. J., Jacobs, S. C., Parkes, C. M., Aslan, M., Goodkin, K., . . . Maciejewski, P. K. (2009). Prolonged grief disorder: Psychometric validation of criteria proposed for DSM-V and ICD-11. *PLoS Medicine, 6*(8), e1000121. doi:10.1371/journal.pmed.1000121

Shulman, L. (2006). *The skills of helping individuals, families, groups, and communities* (5th ed.). Belmont, CA: Thomson Brooks/Cole.

Tang, C. S. (2006). Positive and negative postdisaster psychological adjustment among adult survivors of the Southeast Asian earthquake-tsunami. *Journal of Psychosomatic Research, 61*(5), 699–705.

5

Grief Overload: The Impact of Multiple Losses, Only-Child Loss, and Multiple Stressor Events on Bereaved Parents

In this chapter, we investigate how parents cope with two atypical child-loss situations: multiple losses (including the loss of more than one child or with the loss of a child and a spouse) and the loss of an only child. We also examine how bereaved parents cope with multiple stressor events such as the loss of a job, the termination of a marriage, and other potentially distressing events. The general question we pose is "Do these seemingly additional bereavement challenges impose greater grief difficulties and psychological stresses on these parents compared to other bereaved parents who do not face these challenges?"

In the course of this discussion, we will introduce eight case study vignettes: six from our own interview records and two from published archives, detailing some of the loss and coping challenges parents confront with either the loss of two children or of their only child. These case studies add depth to our understanding, beyond what our survey research results can provide, in a realm that has been generally neglected by bereavement researchers. If there is any single theme that the eight case studies demonstrate, it is a theme of survivor resilience, of parents finding new post-loss roles for themselves, of their attempts to perform good deeds, and of efforts to help others (especially the newly bereaved as they advance with their healing after a loss). We call this particular form of resilience posttraumatic growth (Calhoun & Tedeschi, 2006). Recognizing that some bereaved parents will struggle greatly after their losses and will not be able to follow pathways to posttraumatic growth, we delve more deeply into this subject in Chapter 10, attempting to better understand why some bereaved parents are more likely to experience posttraumatic growth than others.

SUSTAINING MULTIPLE LOSSES

When we began conducting our survey, we were only partially aware of multiple-child losses and did not ask our survey respondents whether they had sustained such losses. Nevertheless, as they completed their surveys, some respondents volunteered that they had experienced multiple-child losses and wanted to acknowledge this. We encouraged them to append any additional comments that explained their unique bereavement experiences and suggested that they use their most recently deceased child as the reference child for the survey. In other cases, some respondents remarked that a spouse had died shortly before or after the death of their child. Here, too, we encouraged these respondents to write in any additional comments that might explain their unique bereavement experiences. Additional parents who had sustained multiple losses, who became known to us in other ways (from telephone contacts, healing conferences, or support group meetings) were also invited to participate and complete surveys. All these respondents were part of the sample that is described in Chapter 1.

Fear of multiple family member losses to suicide often appears in many case studies and memoirs on suicide (see, e.g., Manes, 2003; Rappaport, 2009; Wickersham, 2008; among others). The suicide literature also points to the greater risks of additional suicides within families after an initial suicide occurrence (Jordan & McIntosh, 2011). Previous research suggests there may be as much as a twice greater risk of a future suicide in such a family, compared to other families without histories of suicides (Qin, Agerbo, & Mortensen, 2002; Runeson & Asberg, 2003). The reality of heightened suicides within families encouraged a group of leading suicide-bereavement researchers to highlight this important neglected subject as needing further exploration, at a special conference designed to stimulate more research on suicide survivorship, held at the National Institutes of Health (NIH) in 2003 (NIH, 2003).

Little is known about multiple-loss bereavement. Gauging the magnitude of this potentially problematical behavior is an important question awaiting future research. Our convenience sample of bereaved respondents presented a certain uniqueness in being the largest-ever sample of (nearly 600) parents that reported on the loss of a child. All potential respondents were asked if they had experienced the loss of a child before they were invited to participate in completing the surveys. As respondents filled out their census-like survey form, they realized that, if they had experienced multiple deaths of children in their family, they had to include this information somewhere on their survey forms or had to ask the survey administrator how to handle the recording of this information. From among the total of 575 respondents, 13 reported the loss of two children, indicating a reporting rate of about 2 in 100. Was this 2 in 100 cases rate of occurrence a statistical anomaly? Perhaps, but as future research is conducted among representative samples of bereaved parents, we will be able to learn the true rate of multiple-loss bereavement in the general population, an important question awaiting further research.

The literature on multiple-loss bereavement is at best rather sketchy. [   ] ing on two sources, those surviving the Holocaust (Lifton, 1980) and homosexual men experiencing multiple losses in the AIDS epidemic (Neugebauer et al., 1992), evidence suggests that multiple-loss survivors experience greater grief difficulties than single-loss survivors. Within the frame of discussions of family bereavement, the only study we are familiar with is a memoir written by a mother who lost two sons to suicide 5 years apart (Scovel, 2003). In her book, *Surviving Suicide: My Journey to the Light Within*, Mary Scovel describes her own family as a typical American suburban one. Both parents held advanced educational degrees, with husband Ward, a minister for much of his adult life and Mary, a music educator. They had four children, each born approximately 2 years apart. Two elder daughters were born in the late 1950s followed by two sons, Steve, born in 1961 and Carl in 1963. When the children were young, both boys showed artistic and musical talent. Steve appeared to have a normal childhood and adolescence, completed college, and had hopes of becoming a professional musician. Toward the end of his college studies, he began to show signs of adjustment difficulties, losing some of his zest for academic accomplishment, becoming somewhat reclusive and estranged from his family. Not long after completing college, Steve abruptly left the family home in Ohio, ended up homeless in New York, and was eventually diagnosed with undifferentiated schizophrenia. After a series of abrupt returns and departures from home, punctuated by repeated and desperate efforts by family members to bring him back home, Steve, at age 27, eventually took his life.

Younger brother Carl showed signs of adjustment difficulties in high school and was given a diagnosis of schizophrenia at age 17. He spent the next few years of his life struggling to adapt to society as he was shuttled between his family's home and various treatment facilities, group homes, alternative treatment centers, and hospitals while being managed on psychotropic medications. Sadly, during one of his depressive and anxious cycles, at age 30, he too took his life.

During the early period after the deaths, the Scovels encountered many loss-related problems. The suicides challenged Mary's religious faith. Both spouses experienced frequent bouts of sleeplessness that brought on physical illnesses. Mary assumed a posture of becoming a workaholic to deal with profound anger, guilt, and sadness. Fortunately, the couple used counseling supports and was eventually able to achieve a more harmonious relationship with each other. For a time, the Scovels initiated and co-led a suicide survivors support group, helping newly bereaved families. Later on, they experienced a number of job-related residential moves until they settled into rural South Carolina where they now live, retired, and in proximity to their other family members. Facing many stops and starts along the way, Mary finally completed her book, detailing the family's story of loss and renewal. In a chapter devoted to the mental health system, Mary Scovel details many of the overpowering challenges families with diagnosed schizophrenia face in seeking help for loved ones. Many therapies show inconsistent successes. The psychotropic medications used often present damaging side effects, leading many to put their medications aside, and gaps in insurance coverage are often profound in failing to provide for the costs of good quality care. The stigmatization and discrimination of mental illness often present a barrier for those afflicted and make it difficult for them to gain reentry into society.

Although some of our respondents had experiences much like the Scovels, among our 18 multiple-loss cases there were many different loss scenarios. It should be understood there was no one typical multiple-loss case.

Edwina G. lost her husband of 25 years, Adolfo, who died of lung cancer. (We have changed nonessential details in these case illustrations, such as all names, occupations, places of residence, and so forth, to protect the privacy of our respondents.) Just days before her husband's death, her daughter Carla, age 23, took her life because she too thought she had cancer (although there was never any diagnosis made or evidence collected that suggested she had any malignancies). The prospect of surviving her father's impending death disturbed her so greatly that Carla no longer wanted to live without him. Adolfo was never told of his daughter's suicide before he died. Later, Edwina struggled mightily to cope with her extreme feelings of loneliness and severe economic deprivation. Her husband's death brought down the small surveying business that the family had depended on. As her healing progressed, Edwina found great comfort in writing poetry to ease her profound feelings of loss.

Steven V., a 67-year-old PhD degree holder, recently retired from a civil engineering administrative position in the Boston city government. Father of three children, Steven lost his 29-year-old son to a very aggressive and rare form of skin cancer 10 years ago. Two years ago, after a 3-year-long struggle, his 30-year-old daughter died from breast cancer. He and his wife Maria, married for more than 40 years, became active in cancer fund-raising after their son first became ill. Steven also became a The Compassionate Friends (TCF) chapter facilitator in their suburban Boston community. Steven has been a TCF chapter leader for more than 8 years and occasionally makes presentations at annual conferences. His wife is very active at her local parish church. He remarked,

> Fifteen years ago, I was a 52-year-old happily married man with three children in their mid-to-late twenties. I had a job that I loved, my wife was working, the kids were out on their own and doing well, bills were paid, and we were looking forward to a continued good life. Then illnesses ravaged our family. In addition to taking the lives of two of our children, I lost friends, coworkers, parents, in-laws, and my younger brother. I sometimes have to fight to remember who I was and what life was like before all this happened. I appreciate my family and all the support we've gotten from friends and relatives through these trials. I wonder what the future holds and if I'll be able to handle the coming challenges.

Sarah R. also faced multiple deaths in her family. A retired school social worker 64 years of age who lives in a suburb outside of Baltimore, Maryland, Sarah's first loss happened 12 years ago when her second-born child, Harold, age 16, perished in a commercial plane crash. The family was devastated. Afterward, Sarah and her husband Charles, a surgeon, found that they could no longer communicate readily with each other. After repeated unsuccessful attempts at grief and marital counseling for themselves, the couple decided to part ways. Sarah felt that Charles never tried to get in touch with his feelings about the loss and said it was like living with a zombie. They continued to act cordially to one another and fully cooperated together in supporting their elder daughter, Stephanie, who was 22 at the time of her brother's death. Stephanie appeared to accept the death as well as one might have expected and seemed close to both parents even after their divorce. A decade after her brother's death, after completing medical school, marrying, and living abroad for 2 years, Stephanie set up a medical practice in rural Pennsylvania. Much to her parents' shock and surprise, 2 years later, Stephanie took her life with an overdose of prescription medications. Afterward, Sarah found out that Stephanie had been depressed, and her marriage had soured. She felt overwhelmed by the business aspect of running a medical practice and apparently had never gotten over her brother Harold's death. Now, Sarah lives alone, surprised by the strikingly different reactions she has experienced from other people: how comforting people were after Harold's death and how much less supportive they were after Stephanie died.

Jane D., another respondent, lost her identical twin daughters to suicide. She now lives in a small town outside Albuquerque, New Mexico. A high school graduate, she manages a local restaurant and lives with her mother and a cousin. She is legally separated from her husband although he occasionally seeks temporary refuge in her modest home. Linda, the first child to take her life, experienced a rejection from her fiancée, who terminated their engagement a month before they were to be married. Age 25 years and emotionally immature, she was completely shattered by the rejection and hastily ingested a bottleful of sleeping pills, which brought about her death. Her twin sister, Yvonne, fell apart soon after Linda's death. Both girls had been inseparable and were best friends. Both had been good students at the local college, had graduated with honors, and had distinguished themselves in athletics. Yvonne felt betrayed that her twin sister had opted out of life and left her an "only child." Despite the family's best efforts to get Yvonne into therapy and encourage her to stay the course with it, she eventually withdrew, and her depression and despondency persisted. Two years after her sister died, she was self-treating her depression and took a lethal mix of cocaine along with her psychotropic medications. In the week before she died, Yvonne had told her mother that she had no reason to live any more.

Now, Jane spends a lot of her spare time participating in an Internet support group. She also invests much energy into writing poetry and prose and posting messages at a website she established to memorialize her daughters. She is a suicide prevention advocate in her community and occasionally makes presentations at local high schools and colleges and on talk radio programs. She is very active in fund-raising for suicide prevention causes.

What do these five vignettes tell us about possible bereaved parent attempts to cope with multiple losses? Again, as we stated at the outset, several of these cases show evidence of bereaved parents' resilience. Three of five began writing. Mary Scovel had previously done academic writing in her field of music education. After her boys died, she turned her writing interests in a new direction, doing a memoir of her family's loss story. Edwina and Jane began writing poetry. At least two of the five, Mary Scovel and Steven, assumed positions of leadership as support group facilitators. Two of the five engaged in other acts of helping and advocacy: Steven in giving presentations at the National Compassionate Friends Conferences and Jane in telling her survivor's story at local high schools and on talk radio shows and becoming an active fund-raiser. We imagine that these resilient acts would, in some measure, serve to reduce grief difficulties and psychological problems for these parent survivors. These coping efforts on the part of parent survivors seem to represent adaptive efforts to meet the multiple and complex needs of bereaved parent survivors: to make meaning of what has happened, to move from a passive "victim" status to a position of more active mastery of the traumatic loss, and to find benefit for oneself and others in the midst of the emotional catastrophe (Calhoun & Tedeschi, 2001,2006; Jordan & McIntosh, 2011).

Our multiple-loss respondents showed great diversity in demographic characteristics and in their loss experiences. Most lost two children (13 parents), and a few reported losing a child and spouse (five parents). Some experienced their last loss less than 4 years ago (nine parents), whereas others had their last loss nearly a decade ago or longer; and eight were bereaved for 7 or more years. Death causes of their last lost child varied, as well. Some had experienced a loss of a child to suicide, whereas others had lost children from natural death causes, accidents, or drug-related deaths. Suicide losses predominated: 15 of 18 or 83% reported at least one such loss, which was consistent with the single-child loss reports in the larger sample, where 80% had reported suicide losses of children.

In several informal interviews that we conducted with bereaved parents who had sustained two suicide losses of children, there were reports of extreme avoidance and scorn from some significant others, following their children's deaths. Of the 13 multiple child loss cases in our sample, five were from families who lost two children to suicide. In each of these cases, parents added additional comments on their survey forms reflecting extreme stigmatization.

Jane D. commented,

A "friend" *ran* to keep from having to talk to me. Fingers have been pointed; she's the one. Both of her kids killed themselves. Wonder what she did to them. The whispers, the blame placing, with all this talking behind my back, yet sometimes within earshot, it has often been an incredible ordeal for me.

Sally T., a minister's wife, commented,

People in our church congregation wouldn't talk to me about my boys after they died. My husband sometimes says we have two daughters on this side and our sons are on the other side. Now, I often reply we have two daughters, but our sons died by suicide several years ago. Often, that brings out people's judgments, and although some don't want me to know it, I can see the shock in their faces when I say it. On my vulnerable days, I choose to say we have two daughters and stop there.

Betty M. remarked, "Things were said of us as parents. What did they do to cause this? It must have been the parents' fault."

Ann. C. said, "All my relationships have changed. They are often strained and uncomfortable."

Charlene D. remarked, "In telling a friend about my sons' suicides, she literally backed away and left. I guess she thought it might be catching."

Yet, given the diversity of death cause differences among all 18 multiple-loss respondents in our sample (or among the 13 who lost two children), we found only slight differences in the means on our stigma scale, 4.5 for the self-identified multiple-loss bereaved parents compared with 3.3 for the others. We suspect that had our sample of multiple-loss bereaved been composed entirely of parents losing two children to suicide, there would have been a significantly higher stigmatization exposure experienced by this subgroup (the scale has a top score of 17).

Tests between the multiple-loss subgroup and single-loss survivors, on the measures of years since the death, cause of death, and age of the deceased, showed no significant differences. We also examined whether there were any other demographic differences between multiple-loss respondents and other parent survivors in terms of age, gender, education, family income, and marital status. Comparisons showed no differences in terms of age, gender, and education, although significant differences were noted for marital status and family incomes. When we included all 18 multiple-loss respondents, widows and widowers and lower income respondents were significantly more common among the multiple-loss subgroup than among their single-loss counterparts. Yet, when we omitted the five cases in which a respondent had lost a child and a partner, there were no significant differences. Thus, the multiple-loss respondents were demographically very similar to the larger group of respondents who had lost a single child. None of these tabulations are presented in our tables.

Differences in Grief and Mental Health Problems

We wondered whether multiple-loss survivors encountered more grief and mental health problems compared to their single-child loss counterparts. The previous literature suggests more complicated grief and posttraumatic stress for people experiencing multiple losses compared to those sustaining single losses (Lifton, 1980; Neugebauer et al., 1992). Thus, as we began this comparative analysis of multiple-loss bereavement, we started with one basic hypothesis: We expected that multiple-loss parents would have more grief and mental health problems than those losing a single child.

Table 5.1 suggests negligible and nonsignificant differences in grief difficulties and mental health problems between those losing more than one child or a child and a partner compared to those losing one child, regardless of the cause of death. Responses in both subgroups were very similar to each other on the six criteria selected. Table 5.1 shows nonsignificant differences on (a) grief difficulties, (b) complicated grief, (c) posttraumatic stress disorder (PTSD), (d) mental health difficulties, (measured by our 4-point Index of Personal Psychological Problems; see Chapter 1), (e) overall rates of depression, and (f) frequencies of suicidal thoughts.

Table 5.2 displays several other criteria of potential adjustment difficulties: (a) differences in reports of physical health problems, (b) reports of sleep problems, (c) reports of heavy alcohol use, (d) use of any illegal drugs, (e) life satisfaction reports, and (f) feelings of control over one's life. We added this wider range of comparisons of other lifestyle differences to this particular

Table 5.1
Grief and Mental Health Problems Among Multiple-Loss and Single-Child Loss Bereaved Parents (N = 575)

OUTCOME MEASURE	TYPE OF DEATH	N	M	SD	t	df	SIG.
Grief Experience Questionnaire	1 Multiple	17	38.8	13.5	.12	520	.90
	2 Single	505	39.16	11.4			
	Total	522	39.15	11.5			
Complicated Grief scale	1 Multiple	15	25.7	9.96	.09	539	.34
	2 Single	526	27.9	8.88			
	Total	541	27.9	8.91			
Impact of Event Scale	1 Multiple	15	30.5	9.30	1.24	520	.21
	2 Single	507	33.4	8.88			
	Total	522	33.3	8.89			
Index of Personal Psychological Problems	1 Multiple	18	1.72	1.49	.26	554	.79
	2 Single	538	1.64	1.31			
	Total	556	1.64	1.31			
Eight-item Depression Scale	1 Multiple	16	4.81	2.93	.61	509	.54
	2 Single	495	4.33	3.09			
	Total	511	4.35	3.08			
Suicide thoughts	1 Multiple	18	1.5	.99	.98	565	.33
	2 Single	549	1.76	1.13			
	Total	567	1.76	1.13			

Note. From Survivors Child Loss Survey, 2006–2009.

Table 5.2
**Other Health and Adjustment Problems Among Multiple-Loss and
Single-Child Loss Bereaved Parents (*N* = 575)**

	PERCENTAGE/*n*		Π^2/*df*	*p* VALUE
	MULTIPLE	**SINGLE**		
Perceived physical health				
Poor	0/0	8.3/42		
Fair	44.4/8	25.2/127		
Good	33.3/6	32.1/162		
Very good/excellent	22.2/4	34.3 /173		
Total	100/18	100/504	4.75 (3)	.19
Difficulties falling asleep past year				
Never	5.9/1	8.3/40	.47 (4)	.98
Occasionally	23.5/4	25.9/125		
Sometimes	29.4/5	30.6/148		
Often	29.4/5	22.8/110		
Very often	11.8/2	12.4/60		
Total	100/17	100/483		
Times drunk past year				
Never	72.2/13	73.3/398		
Few times yearly	27.8/5	19.0/103		
Monthly or >	0/0	7.7/42		
Total	100/18	100/543	2.09 (2)	.35
Use of any illegal drug(s)				
One or more	0/0	10.1/56		
None	100.0/17	89.9/498		
Total	100/17	100/554	1.9 (1)	.17
How satisfied are you with your life?				
A great deal	16.7/3	26.2/137		
Somewhat	55.6/10	41.4/216		
A little	16.7/3	22.4/117		
Not at all/none	11.1/2	10.0/52		
Total	100/18	100/522	1.73 (3)	.63
How much control do you feel you have over your life in general?				
A great deal	22.2/4	28.5/151		
Somewhat	44.4/8	41.6/220		
A little	5.6/1	21.2/112		
Not at all/none	27.8/5	8.7/46		
Total	100/18	100/529	9.3 (3)	.03

Note. From Survivors Child Loss Survey, 2006–2009.

analysis so that it may yield a deeper understanding of the multifold adjustments that survivors make following the loss of a child. Although a survivor's grief difficulties and overall mental health is our central focus, if we detect other subtle lifestyle changes following the loss, we penetrate more deeply into how the loss of a child may have upended a parent's overall adjustment.

As Table 5.2 shows, only one statistically significant difference was observed between the multiple-loss respondents and single-child loss respondents, with more multiple-loss respondents feeling they had little to no control over their lives. Nearly 30% of multiple-loss parents felt they had no control over their lives, compared to only 9% among the single-child loss bereaved group. In all other respects about grief, including psychological difficulties and the other adjustment measures, their responses matched those bereaved by the loss of a single child. These results suggest that losses cannot be easily quantified by their sheer number. Each loss seems to stand alone in its own unique way.

LOSING ONE'S ONLY CHILD

Another neglected topic in the bereavement research literature is the subject of losing an only child. Despite exhaustive searching on MEDLINE, PsychLit, and Social Science Abstracts, we were able to find less than a handful of previous research studies on this subject. A Canadian study, based on 20 cases (Barrera et al., 2007), and a Swiss study (d'Epinay, Cavalli, & Guillet, 2009–2010), based on surveying an elderly population, found that depressive symptoms were worse when bereaved respondents who lost their only child were compared with others who had other surviving children. Another investigation, a doctoral dissertation, suggested that bereaved parents reported lower grief scores when they had other surviving children compared to those who did not (Wheeler, 1990). A book length study, *What Forever Means After the Death of a Child* (Talbot, 2002), that is part memoir and part detailed systematic study of 80 mothers sustaining losses of their only child, provides much information on this subject.

It is not known how many bereaved parents of an only child can be found in the U.S. population. Certainly, they must number into the tens of thousands, but it remains a task for future research to delineate the magnitude of the number of these beleaguered survivors. Bereaved parents of an only child often feel like outsiders in the larger society and even from other groups of bereaved parents. Many feel alone and misunderstood. They feel a kindred spirit with one another because of their similarity in experiencing the loss of an only child.

In 1988, two bereaved only-child parents, Kay and Rodney Bevington, created a group expressly aimed at serving the needs of people like themselves after the couple lost their 15-year-old daughter to a malignant tumor. Their group, known as Alive Alone (www.alivealone.org), reaches out to other only-child bereaved parents, forming a national network offering informational resources and support. The Bevingtons' newsletter now reaches a total of some 600–800 parent survivors who live in every U.S. state and seven foreign countries. Presently, Alive Alone holds annual conferences that often coincide with the National Compassionate Friends Conferences.

In the next few pages, we present three vignettes of bereaved parents of a deceased only child that suggest some of the unique concerns and potential problems of these parents. One is from published archives, and two are from our informal interview records. Kay Talbot's (2002) book offers the story of her only child, her 8-year-old daughter, who succumbed to a sudden unexplained brain seizure in 1982. Talbot's story depicts the life of a woman struggling to create a viable family structure for herself. She grew up as an adoptee in her family of origin and eventually became an adoptive parent herself, as she and her husband later confronted the challenge of infertility. Later still, the couple struggled with their daughter's poor health, leading her to be diagnosed as legally blind from diabetic complications and also developmentally disabled because of a variety of other serious ailments. All this frayed the marital bond between husband and wife, leading to divorce. Not many years afterward, as the daughter's health continued to decline, her sudden death occurred before her ninth birthday. Subsequently, Talbot struggled with profound grief and depression, leading her to question her own continuing existence. She eventually found a place for herself in helping others who were bereaved and in completing studies in psychology. Later, she embarked on doctoral studies, eventually leading her to become a psychotherapist and researcher after completing her book on bereaved mothers of only child decedents.

As we collected our survey data from the 575 parents who reported on a child's death, 40 reported that it was their only child who was deceased. These cases were distinct from the multiple-death loss cases because this count was based on parents' reports of those who had a single child during their childbearing years. Again, the two case illustrations we present suggest some of the great diversity in this population. One case, Paul and Cheryl Harvey (pseudonyms) were drawn closer together after their loss, whereas in another case, Silvia Marcus (pseudonym) found that the loss of her only child drove a wedge between her and her husband and fostered Silvia's social isolation.

Survey respondent Paul Harvey, a 68-year-old retired painting contractor, is another example of a parent who lost his only child. His son Jonathan died 12 years ago, after a fall from a high-rise balcony apartment. At the time of his death, Jonathan was traveling in the Far East and was living in Shanghai. Paul said,

> I never found out exactly what caused Jon's death—whether he took his life, whether he was pushed, or if it was an accidental fall associated with drug use. (The last explanation was what the Shanghai Police Department claimed according to their investigations and autopsy.) Jon was 22 when he died, on a year-long trip celebrating his college

graduation. For the longest time, he had a great interest in all things Asian. In Shanghai, he had met a 19-year-old girl with whom he fell head over heels in love. Her family, however, wouldn't hear of the romance and vehemently objected to the idea of their daughter marrying a Westerner, who was also Jewish.

After Jon's unexpected death, the Shanghai Police cooperated with the American consulate and arranged to send Jon's body home to us, sparing us the trip there. I would have gone there but Cheryl (my wife) didn't want to go, and I didn't want to leave her here and alone at that time. After Jon died, we communicated for a time with his girl-friend. She spoke English well and seemed to be almost as upset and distraught about Jon's death as we were.

We knew Jon kept a journal. He fancied himself as a writer, though he never got that far with making a writing career. After he died, his girlfriend promised to send us his journal, and even though we ended up begging her for it, she never complied. We were (and still are) very upset and angry about that. Perhaps it contained some clues about whether he was depressed when he died and what was going on in his mind at the time. We'll never know and that's been a real sticking point to us.

The father continued,

Losing your one and only child is the absolute worst. Cheryl and I keep going over this same conclusion over and over again. Especially at holiday times, it hits us like a ton of bricks; we are the last of our family's line. When we die, that will mark the end of our family's name. Two of the worst holidays for us are Mother's Day and Father's Day. While everybody goes on family picnics and has barbeques on those days, Cheryl and I look at each other, with tears in our eyes, remembering Jon and feeling sad that he's no longer with us.

Cheryl and I are very active in The Compassionate Friends. We're group facilitators, and we've been leading our group for over 10 years. Our group is pretty large; we get anywhere from 30 to 40 people coming to monthly meetings. I took the facilitator training course that Compassionate Friends offered, and we almost always go to their annual national meetings. I put out a newsletter four to six times a year and hold private meetings with new survivors either at my home or at a diner near the church where we hold our meetings. I try my best for the newly bereaved. We know how much they are hurting. I'm also doing occasional grief counseling at a local hospice. I took the training course they offered so that I can do visiting and offer comfort to families losing loved ones to cancer and other terminal illnesses. I guess grief work is the most important thing I do now.

Silvia Marcus, another of our respondents, lost her only son, Randy, to a drug-induced suicide 5 years ago. It took Silvia more than 3 years to put all the pieces together regarding her son's death. As Silvia finally understood it, Randy gave up, hoarded his psychotropic medications until he accumulated enough pills for a sufficiently lethal dose, then methodically killed himself in his college dormitory room, where his body was found after a spring break recess. He left a brief note behind saying he was sorry to take his life, but the pain of living was too great for him. At age 22, Randy had finally surrendered to his near-decade-long struggle with mental and physical illnesses. From his teenage years onward, Randy struggled with anxiety, bouts of depression, and obsessive-compulsive behavior. During these trouble-filled years, Randy visited an almost endless number of psychotherapists and psychiatrists trying to find the right combination of prescription drugs to calm his troubled soul. He was also afflicted with a 3-year bout of chronic fatigue and weakness that suggested the possibility of chronic fatigue syndrome, Lyme disease, or some other rare neurological illness that was never successfully diagnosed or treated. Never at peace with himself, Randy doubted if he was in the right academic program, graphic arts, and wasn't sure he would ever finish it, though his academic advisors repeatedly told him he was a very gifted artist. His horizon was always marked by worry and second-guessing things. Although Silvia was consoled in the belief that Randy finally found relief from his demons, she thought his desperation led him to take the worst possible solution to deal with them.

Unlike many other couples, Silvia and her husband, Mark, did not act kindly to each other after Randy's death. Prior to this immense tragedy, the couple appeared to sail through life effortlessly. Mark, a highly successful patent attorney, and Silvia, an administrator in a city government position, always had ample economic resources. They lived in their large, comfortable home in a prestigious suburb outside Boston, belonged to a local country club, took lavish trips, entertained often, and were able to give their only son unstinting support for his many crises. After Randy died, Mark avoided conversation about him. "Time for us to move on; it's not going to get us any better to dwell on this," he always said. He never accompanied Silvia to the many different support groups she attended. Silvia, by contrast, couldn't stop talking about Randy's death and trying to understand more about this tragedy, including questioning whether they should be suing Randy's psychiatrist. She attended different support groups, often finding fault with them in one way or other. She went to different psychics, hoping to get signs from Randy that he was okay. She saw a number of counselors and psychiatrists, slept fitfully, and couldn't stop searching the Internet for more information about overdose drug death and suicide. After the death, Silvia did not feel ready to go back to her administrative position. She eventually used up all her accumulated leave time and ultimately had to resign. Her relationship with Mark deteriorated to such a point where they seldom spoke. Two years after Randy's death, when Mark indicated he wanted a divorce, Silvia quickly agreed.

As more time passed since the death, Silvia sold the couple's luxurious home to move into smaller quarters. Her generous divorce settlement enabled her to live with economic security and comfort, although she often felt isolated and alone. Her family disappointed her in that they never seemed willing to honor Randy's memory in a way Silvia could appreciate. She made some new friends from her support group contacts, but, unlike the Harveys mentioned earlier, she never advanced far enough to actively help those who were more newly bereaved. Silvia frequently switched doctors, therapists, and treatment programs, always searching for one that would better meet her needs. From time to time, she continued to blame herself for Randy's death, believing that she had completely failed him.

These sharply contrasting vignettes of three different only-child bereaved parents offer insights into some of the adaptations, distinctive concerns, and potential problems of these parents. Again, as we saw earlier, two of the three case studies offer vivid examples of survivor resilience. In the wake of her loss, Kay Talbot assumed a new career as a psychotherapist, researcher, and author, writing a book on only-child bereavement. In the years since she has completed her professional training, Talbot has helped countless numbers of bereaved parents and others struggling with psychological problems. Similarly, the Harveys have helped hundreds of bereaved parents with their leadership in facilitating their The Compassionate Friends group. Paul's additional work as a hospice volunteer extends his helping role even further. We surmise that such acts of posttraumatic growth will be linked to reduced grief and mental health problems for these survivors. In Chapter 10, we will discuss in more detail how our bereaved-parent survey data showed a relationship between posttraumatic growth, diminished grief difficulties, and better mental health.

Paul Harvey's remarks about the special difficulty associated with losing his family's name and inheritance line with his own death was also mentioned by other only-child bereaved parents who were observed at support group meetings. Like Paul, they mentioned the intensified sadness they also felt associated with enduring Mother's Day and Father's Day holidays after losing their only child. They felt their losses more keenly on those days, as they were alone, unlike other families who celebrated those holidays together, with surviving children. Kay Talbot's case studies spotlighted an additional difficulty experienced by only-child bereaved parents: participating in bereavement support groups with other parents. Talbot reported that many only-child bereaved parents feel jealous and envious of other bereaved parents who discuss their surviving children in group sessions, which tends to intensify their feelings of aloneness. Thus, with their children's deaths, the only-child bereaved often shared a common feeling of having been set adrift from the mainstream of American family life.

Our case study material also offered some evidence suggesting that marital strain and possibly breakup may be associated with only-child bereavement. This was noted in Silvia Marcus's experience, where a divorce eventually followed the death of her only son. In Kay Talbot's personal case, also, although her divorce preceded her child's death, there had been a long history of her daughter's serious illnesses that preceded her marriage's eventual termination.

We investigated this possibility with our survey data, contrasting the 40 only-child bereaved parents against the 535 others who reported having had more than a single child. The survey data did not confirm the anecdotal data from the interviews; however, it did show comparability between both groups in rates of post-loss divorces and marital separations. Both groups showed similar rates of divorce and separations since the loss, with divorce rates between 5% and 7% and separation rates between 8% and 12%. Yet, we did discover statistically significant differences between both groups in terms of their marital statuses. Bereaved parents with other children reported a currently married rate at 70%, whereas bereaved parents of only child decedents reported a 48% married rate at the time they completed their surveys. The biggest differences were between those reporting themselves as divorced, with bereaved parents of only child decedents reporting a nearly twice higher divorce rate as parents with other children, 40% as compared to 21%. This difference in divorce experience suggests that marital terminations may have initially led these parents to have smaller families in the first place, rather than the opposite pattern.

That more only-child bereaved parents were not married suggests a potential for problems that currently married bereaved parents might not have. The single parents must shoulder the tragic child-loss experience alone whereas their married counterpart has a sounding board and a potential supporter in carrying the heavy weight of grief and sadness that parents inevitably feel. For the bereaved parent of a deceased only child, there may also be the additional burden of not having other children available to share and support each other with their grief. If we recall our findings from Chapter 2, which showed that grief support from their children superseded all other familial relationships in providing emotional solace to the suicide-bereaved parents, there is evidence to suggest that the absence of other children could make the loss experience more difficult and grief-troubled for the only-child bereaved parents than for their counterparts who have other children.

We also looked to see if there may have been other demographic and loss-related differences between both subgroups that might exacerbate (or lessen) grief problems, such as differences in time since the loss or differences in causes of death between bereaved parents of only child decedents and the other parents with remaining children. Statistical tests showed comparability between both groups in terms of age, gender, education, and socioeconomic status. Both groups were also similar in terms of the age of the child who died, the cause of death, years since the death, and stigma scores.

As we began our comparative analysis of bereaved parents of only child decedents and their counterparts with other surviving children, we expected that bereaved parents of only child decedents would have more grief and psychological problems. This is what the limited past research record had found, and our survey data suggested that the more limited available familial resources might make the grief coping tasks more challenging for those without other children or spouses present at the time of their losses.

Yet, Table 5.3 suggests negligible and nonsignificant differences in grief difficulties and mental health problems between those losing an only child compared to all other survivors. Responses in both subgroups were similar to each other on the six criteria selected, with nonsignificant differences for (a) grief difficulties, (b) complicated grief, (c) PTSD, (d) mental health difficulties, (e) overall rates of depression, and (f) frequencies of suicidal thoughts.

Table 5.4 displays several other criteria of potential adjustment difficulties: (a) differences in reports of physical health problems, (b) frequency of sleep problems, (c) reports of heavy alcohol use, (d) use of any illegal drugs, (e) life satisfaction reports, and (f) feelings of control over one's life. As can be seen among the six criteria examined, two significant differences were observed between the only-child bereaved parents and all other bereaved parents. Those who lost an only child were significantly more likely to report themselves as having poorer physical health. Almost a quarter (24%) reported being in poor health compared with only 7% for those with other children. Physical health reports were matched by life satisfaction reports. A quarter of the only-child

Table 5.3
Grief and Mental Health Problems Among Bereaved Parents Losing Only Children and Those With Other Surviving Children (N = 575)

OUTCOME MEASURE	TYPE OF DEATH	N	M	SD	t	df	SIG.
Grief Experience Questionnaire	1 With onlys	38	40.2	9.0	.57	514	.56
	2 With others	478	39.0	11.7			
	Total	516	39.1	11.5			
Complicated Grief scale	1 With onlys	39	29.3	7.4	1.06	532	.29
	2 With others	495	27.7	9.0			
	Total	534	27.8	8.9			
Impact of Event Scale	1 With onlys	37	34.6	7.6	.96	515	.34
	2 With others	480	33.2	9.0			
	Total	517	33.3	8.9			
Index of Personal Psychological Problems	1 With onlys	40	1.9	1.3	1.31	547	.19
	2 With others	509	1.6	1.31			
	Total	549	1.64	1.31			
Eight-item Depression Scale	1 With onlys	37	4.84	2.96	.99	502	.32
	2 With others	467	4.32	3.09			
	Total	504	4.36	3.08			
Suicide thoughts	1 With onlys	40	1.7	.93	.17	558	.87
	2 With others	520	1.76	1.13			
	Total	560	1.76	1.13			

Note. From Survivors Child Loss Survey, 2006–2009.

Table 5.4
**Other Health and Adjustment Problems Among Only-Child Bereaved Parents and
Those With Other Living Children (*N* = 575)**

| | PERCENTAGE/*n* | | | |
	ONLY-CHILD LOSS	WITH OTHERS	Π^2/*df*	*p* VALUE
Perceived physical health				
Poor	23.5/8	7.0/34		
Fair	14.7/5	26.6/128		
Good	41.0/14	31.5/152		
Very good/excellent	20.6/7	34.9 /168		
Total	100/34	100/482	15.14/(3)	.002
Difficulties falling asleep past year				
Never	6.1/2	8.3/38	6.83/(4)	.14
Occasionally	12.1/4	26.5/122		
Sometimes	42.4/14	30.0/138		
Often	18.2/6	23.5/108		
Very often	21.2/7	11.4/ 54		
Total	100/33	100/460		
Times drunk past year				
Never	65.0/26	73.8/380		
Few times yearly	22.5/9	19.2/99		
Monthly or >	12.5/5	7.0/36		
Total	100/40	100/515	2.12(2)	.34
Use of any illegal drug(s)				
One or more	15.0/6	9.4/49		
None	85.0/34	90.7/475		
Total	100/40	100/524	1.35(1)	.25
How satisfied are you with your life?				
A great deal	17.1/6	26.7/133		
Somewhat	34.3/12	42.5/212		
A little	22.0/8	22.2/111		
Not at all/none	25.7/9	8.6/43		
Total	100/35	100/499	11.48(3)	.009
How much control do you feel you have over your life in general?				
A great deal	25.0/9	28.5/144		
Somewhat	47.2/17	41.4/209		
A little	16.7/6	21.0/106		
Not at all/none	11.1/4	9.1/46		
Total	100/36	100/505	.87(3)	.83

Note. From Child Loss Survey, March 2006–September 2009.

bereaved parents claimed to be not at all satisfied with their lives, compared with only 9% for those parents with surviving children. Interestingly, when we excluded the respondents who reported themselves in poor health ($n = 42$) at the time of the survey, the association between only-child bereaved status and life satisfaction differences no longer was observed. Thus, aside from a 17% differential in the numbers reporting themselves in poor health, there were no other observed differences between the bereaved parents of only child decedents and their counterparts with other children. In terms of their mental health and grief difficulties, both groups reported much the same levels of grief and other mental health problems. These findings were indeed contrary to our expectations.

EXPLORING ASSOCIATIONS BETWEEN OTHER POTENTIAL STRESSFUL EVENTS AND PARENT SURVIVORS' GRIEF

Following her daughter's death, Silvia Marcus's marriage crumbled and she was unable to return to her civil service administrative position. We wondered whether some post-loss experiences—potentially traumatic events such as these—would be associated with more complicated and intense grief difficulties for parent survivors. To investigate this, we asked our respondents whether any one of five different potentially traumatizing events had occurred in their lives since their child had died: the loss of a job; a divorce; a separation from one's spouse or partner; any other deaths in their families; and any other serious life crises, such as the involvement in a law suit, being the victim of a crime, or having a serious health problem in their families. We then explored whether survivors who experienced any one or several of these destabilizing events since the child's death would show more grief difficulties or mental health problems than other survivors who had eluded these experiences.

Table 5.5 shows the frequency of occurrence of these five potentially traumatizing events and how each was associated with grief difficulties and mental health problems. The frequencies data showed other deaths in families

Table 5.5
Correlations Between Types of Experiences of Potentially Traumatizing Events, Grief Difficulties, and Mental Health Problems Among Parent Survivors

POTENTIALLY TRAUMATIC EVENT	N REPORTING THIS EVENT	TOTAL REPORTING N/%	CORREL. W/ GEQ	SIG.	CORREL. W/ MENT. HEALTH PROBLEMS	SIG.
Lost job	67	549/12%	.10	.02	.13	.002
Divorce	31	556/6%	−.01	.75	.03	.50
Separation	44	543/8%	.11	.008	.15	.0003
Other deaths	271	563/48%	−.002	.96	−.01	.73
Crises	250	561/44%	.05	.22	.07	.09

Note. From Survivors Child Loss Survey, 2006–2009.

Table 5.6
Multiple Regression of Grief Difficulties (GEQ Scores) by Various Stressor Events Experienced After the Loss, N = 575

		Number of obs	= 459
		F(5, 453)	= 2.29
		r²	= .02

INDEPENDENT VARIABLES	CORREL. COEFF.	BETA	p
Lost job	.10	.10	.04
Divorced	−.01	−.57	.25
Separated	.11	.12	.02
Other deaths	−.002	−.03	.55
Crises	−.05	.03	.60

Note. p = level of significance. From Survivors Child Loss Survey, 2006–2009.

(with 48%) and assorted crises (with 44%) as the most commonly occurring events that survivors experienced. Family disruptions and job losses were relatively rare, with divorce and separation at fewer than 10% and job loss at 12%.

The associations between each of the five events with grief difficulties and mental health problems were small. Although relatively small, two statistically significant associations stood out as potential correlates of greater grief difficulties and mental health problems: job loss and marital separations.

Table 5.6 presents a regression equation of each of the five potential stressor variables related to grief difficulties. With only two of the five variables showing any bivariate associations with grief difficulties—job loss and marital separations—only 2% of the variance of grief difficulties could be accounted for from these five potential stressor variables.

Table 5.7 presents a similar regression equation but instead uses psychological problems as the dependent (predicted) variable. Again, job losses and marital separations were the only significant correlates related to differences in psychological problems. Here, their contribution to regression variance, while

Table 5.7
Multiple Regression Analysis of Psychological Problems by Various Stressor Events Experienced After the Loss, N = 575

		Number of obs	= 492
		F(5, 486)	= 4.16
		r²	= .04

INDEPENDENT VARIABLES	CORREL. COEFF.	BETA	p
Lost job	.13	.13	.003
Divorced	.03	−.01	.75
Separated	.15	.14	.005
Other deaths	−.01	−.045	.33
Crises	.07	.05	.31

Note. p = level of significance. From Survivors Child Loss Survey, 2006–2009.

somewhat larger at 4%, still represents a small proportion of the variance. It is clear from the foregoing that additional stressors make minor contributions to explaining variance. If they have any significance at all, they are associated with psychological problems more than they are related to differences in grief difficulties.

SUMMARY AND CONCLUSION

Although we began this chapter with expectations that parents sustaining multiple losses of a child or a child and a spouse or of their only child would experience greater grief and mental health problems than their counterparts who sustained a single-child loss but who had other surviving children, the evidence did not confirm either of these speculations. We should also mention that we did explore these same hypotheses with alternative measures of grief difficulties and psychological problems: the Complicated Grief scale, the Impact of Event Scale, and the eight-item Depression Scale. Results were completely consistent with the ones we reported in Tables 5.1 and 5.3, with no significant differences between multiple-loss and only-child bereaved compared to their counterparts with single losses and with other surviving children.

Although we view this exploration as a preliminary and far from conclusive examination of the hypotheses under scrutiny, it is nonetheless important for us to offer some speculation as to why these hypotheses were not supported by the data. Upon reflection, we believe that our findings may suggest some things about the nature of the parental experience of traumatic grief. More specifically, it appears that regardless of whether parents sustained multiple nuclear family losses or whether their loss was of their only child, neither of these distinctive loss features appears to significantly worsen the survivors' grief difficulties when measured by paper-and-pencil outcome measures. All this suggests that the survivor's immediate loss takes center stage, placing them within their present disequilibrated state.

Our findings, showing no grief and mental health differences between multiple-loss and single-loss bereaved parents, calls for more research on the multiple-loss bereaved population. We may wonder whether there are normalizing psychic mechanisms that most bereaved parents rely on to prevent them from experiencing an overload of posttraumatic stress after sustaining multiple traumatic death losses or from multiple deaths within their families. The multiple-loss bereaved represents an important population that can shed new light on the nature of intensified posttraumatic stress.

If a person remains in support groups long enough, he or she will inevitably confront experiences of witnessing competitive discussions between some survivors who debate with one another as to "who has sustained the most tragic loss": Was it the parent who lost their newborn child or another who lost their teenage child? Was it the parent who lost a child who was very accomplished in life or the one losing a child who spent most of his life struggling with different kinds of mental health problems? Was it a parent who lost a child who was married, with a wife and surviving children, or one who lost a child who was unattached? Whether the loss included several nuclear family members or whether it was an only child is another subject in these competitive discussions. As our evidence suggests, whatever the loss, from the survivor's perspective, survivors may still report being utterly depleted and empty afterward. The psychic pain within the survivors rises to a peak, draining their emotional reserves to near zero. Support group facilitators will want to discourage survivors from engaging in rivalrous comparisons not only because it is unhelpful for group dynamics but also because our data do not support such differential comparative ranking of bereavement suffering.

Our comparisons did yield a single significant difference between the investigated subgroups, showing that multiple-loss survivors were more likely to feel that they possessed little to no control over their lives compared to those with single losses. This finding is consistent with "constructivist" approaches to bereavement that suggest significant losses are likely to change the mourner's assumptive world or overall outlook on life (Neimeyer, 2001). It would make sense that losing two children or even one child and a spouse could significantly change the mourner's "locus of control," increasing the individual's sense of helplessness, and reducing his or her perceived ability to regulate the important events in his or her life. The experience of multiple losses itself may engender its own unique sense of having to prevail against what may essentially be perceived as a more uncontrollable world. Although we offer this hypothesis very tentatively, this important question, explaining why and how multiple-loss survivors manage to accept their losses, deserves much greater attention in future bereavement research.

It still remains very puzzling, however, why multiple-loss survivors showed no more elevated levels of grief and psychological distress compared to their counterparts who experienced the loss of a single child. Perhaps the survivors' resilience that so many of the case examples displayed exerted some impact on lessening the cumulative effect of multiple losses. It may be that as bereaved parents engage in acts associated with posttraumatic growth, they counteract the cycle that would otherwise lead them to moods of despondency and hopelessness. To investigate this possibility, we also explored whether multiple-loss bereaved parents showed any differences in posttraumatic growth compared to their counterparts who lost a single child using a scale widely employed in bereavement research called the Hogan Grief Reaction Checklist (Hogan, Greenfield, & Schmidt, 2001). In addition, we investigated whether support group activism—another behavioral manifestation of posttraumatic growth—was any greater among the multiple-loss bereaved compared to its frequency among parents sustaining single-child losses. Here, too, no significant differences were noted between the groups on these two potentially important correlates of survivor resilience.

Another extremely perplexing result was the finding that showed almost no significant differences in grief and mental health problems between only-child bereaved parents and their counterparts with other surviving children. Aside from the single 17 percentage-point difference in poorer physical health reports for the bereaved parents of only child decedents, there were no other differences between these subgroups. We suggest some potential psychological and sociological bases that might help to explain why these groups did not show many grief and mental health differences.

First, there are two sides to the issue of having or not having other children after the loss of a child. The parent with other children may be prone to act with hypervigilance toward their surviving children after a child's death (Dyregrov & Dyregrov, 2008). This is especially true in cases of sudden and traumatic deaths, like drug overdoses and suicides. In our interviews and participant observations, many bereaved parents reported acting with hypervigilance after the death of a child, fearing that other surviving children might succumb to same illnesses or that the death might have a contagion effect on their other children. This is likely to complicate the grief and mental health problems for these parents with other children.

Second, bereaved parents sustaining the loss of an only child may not remain childless indefinitely. Some will add children to their families through procreation or adoption. Younger bereaved parents, especially those sustaining losses of children to sudden infant death syndrome (SIDS), will likely engage in subsequent childbearing. A German study of 141 SIDS-bereaved parents found 71% had conceived additional children 4 to 7 years after the loss of their first child (Vennemann, Rentsch, Bajanowski, & Zimmer, 2006). For parents who feel that biological procreation no longer remains an available option for them, adoption may be seen as a viable possibility for family expansion and a renewal of their parenting roles. Several older intact couples in our sample reported that they had adopted one or more children after the loss of their only child. Married couples will probably be able to add children to their families with greater ease than single bereaved parents, given the general disapproval of and resistance to single-parent adoptions. Yet, if single parents show a willingness to accept children who are older, handicapped, racial minority members, or sibling pairs, they can succeed in the adoptions marketplace, too. Thus, adoption remains a possibility for some only-child bereaved parents.

Another important direction for future research on only-child bereavement will be to investigate the frequencies of post-loss childbearing and child adoptions among these mourners. We will speculate that family augmentations will be greater when parents are younger and when parents come from an intact marriage, thus widening their opportunities to adopt. Older parents and single-parent bereaved will probably remain less inclined to augment their post-loss families, as they take stock of their more limited opportunities to succeed in these endeavors.

In addition to adding children to their families through procreation or adoption, the greatest number of transformations of parental roles of only-child bereaved parents will probably evolve from family change and reorganization processes. It is commonplace in postindustrial American families for marital breakups, remarriages, informal marriages, and modern stepparenthood to be experienced by many people. All of these family changes have the potential to bring more only-child bereaved parents into eventually assuming parental roles, parenting other children during the years after the death of their child. Of the only-child bereaved parents in our sample, 40% reported being divorced at the time they completed their surveys. This presents a large numeric potential for remarriage. A plurality of these respondents will remarry other partners and assume stepparent roles in their new families. This is precisely what happened to Kay Talbot. She remarried and became a stepparent to her second husband's children. We can anticipate some only-child bereaved parents will follow this same pattern.

In other cases, especially when the bereaved parent's deceased child was a parent with young children, the only-child bereaved grandparent may be cast into a new role as caregiver for these grandchildren. This may, to some extent, mitigate some of the feelings of loss created by the death of an adult child, as grandparents "fill the void" through an intensified parenting relationship with their grandchildren. Several of these cases were reported to us by our respondents.

In addition, several of our only-child bereaved parents reported playing active roles as godparents, assuming quasiparental roles with some of their nephews, nieces, and cousins' children. "Godparenting" or enacting a fictive kinship role has had a long-established place in the Afro-American community, as a response to the legacy of slavery (Chatters, Taylor, & Jayakody, 1994; Guttman, 1976), where remote kinship relatives assume roles as quasiparents, occasionally taking over the parental role when the child's parents may be deceased, ill, and/or otherwise unavailable. The practice also has historic and current importance among Latinos, with the *compadrazgo* (coparenthood) system of having close friends and/or other relatives available to help raise children when the original parents become incapacitated or need extra help (Mintz & Wolf, 1950). Although middle-class American culture has not fully embraced the godparenting concept within our mainstream, godparenting still has a certain cultural credibility among many different ethnic Americans. Several of our only-child bereaved parents reported assuming godparenting roles with remote family members' children, reporting that they hosted godchildren as houseguests, took them on special excursions, helped shoulder their higher educational expenses, offered generous gifting, and included some as beneficiaries to their estates. Such behaviors as these bring only-child bereaved parents back into the role of important stakeholders in parenting children.

Although we initially suspected that a spouse or other children would be essential to help shoulder the heavy burdens of grief that only-child bereaved parents experience after the loss, our informal interviews with participants suggests that these parents often find different significant others to help them through this difficult period. We suspect that they rely on other relatives: siblings, cousins, parents, and, of course, close friends, to help them function during the agonizing early months after loss. In all probability, only-child bereaved parents are not usually exclusively dependent on their children or their spouses to do these tasks. Whether the lack of differences we found between these subgroups are statistical anomalies or are part of the suggested patterned differences, such as remarrying and stepparenthood, godparenting, and relying on a wider network of significant others awaits further research. Whether "replacement parenting" is a more common practice among the only-child bereaved than among the bereaved with other children is another worthy question also awaiting future research.

Lastly, the findings that additional stressors and potentially traumatic events experienced after the loss only minimally worsened parents' grief difficulties is somewhat puzzling because it is inconsistent with most bereavement outcome studies that suggest that additional stressors tend to complicate the mourning process (Lobb et al., 2010; Stroebe, Folkman, Hansson, & Schut, 2006). However, this finding is consistent with our multiple-loss findings, suggesting that the loss of a child may be such a "large" and consuming event psychologically that other stressor events in the individual's life have little additional impact. Our data did find statistically significant correlations between the presence of these two stressor events—job loss and marital separations—and heightened grief and mental health difficulties, yet they accounted for only a small amount of the variance of the outcome variables. Based on our findings, clinicians might be well advised to assess for these potentially traumatizing events in the lives of bereaved parents. These changes may have a cumulative effect and be associated with somewhat poorer mental health among survivors. Having said this, in offering grief support, both clinicians and support group facilitators need to focus attention on the more immediate and more all-consuming losses of survivors—their deceased child. Whether these findings can be extended beyond the case of parents losing children to other relationship losses, such as of spouses, parents, siblings, and other family relationships, is another question awaiting future research.

REFERENCES

Barrera, M., D'Agostino, N. M., Schneiderman, G., Tallett, S., Spencer, L., & Jovcevska, V. (2007). Patterns of parental bereavement following the loss of a child and related factors. *Omega(Westport)*, *55*(2), 145–167.

Calhoun, L. G., & Tedeschi, R. G. (2001). Posttraumatic growth: The positive lessons of loss. In R. A. Neimeyer (Ed.), *Meaning reconstruction & the experience of loss* (pp. 157–172). Washington, DC: American Psychological Association.

Calhoun, L. G., & Tedeschi, R. G. (2006). *Handbook of posttraumatic growth: Research and practice*. Mahwah, NJ: Erlbaum.

Chatters, L. M., Taylor, R. J., & Jayakody, R. (1994). Fictive kinship relations in black extended families. *Journal of Comparative Family Studies*, *25*, 297–312.

d'Epinay, C. J., Cavalli, S., & Guillet, L. A. (2009–2010). Bereavement in very old age: Impact on health and relationships of the loss of a spouse, a child, a sibling, or a close friend. *Omega (Westport)*, *60*(4), 301–325.

Dyregrov, K., & Dyregrov, A. (2008). *Effective grief and bereavement support: The role of family, friends, colleagues, schools and support professionals*. London, UK: Jessica Kingsley.

Guttman, H. G. (1976). *Black family in slavery and freedom, 1750–1925*. Toronto, Canada: Random House.

Hogan, N. S., Greenfield, D. B., & Schmidt, L. A. (2001). Development and validation of the Hogan Grief Reaction Checklist. *Death Studies*, *25*(1), 1–32.

Jordan, J. R., & McIntosh, J. M. (2011). *Grief after suicide: Understanding the consequences and caring for the survivors*. New York, NY: Routledge.

Lifton, R. J. (1980). The concept of the survivor. In J. E. Dimsdale (Ed.), *Survivors, victims, and perpetrators: Essays on the Nazi holocaust*. Washington, DC: Hemisphere.

Lobb, E. A., Kristjanson, L. J., Aoun, S. M., Monterosso, L., Halkett, G. K. B., & Davies, A. (2010). Predictors of complicated grief: A systematic review of empirical studies. *Death Studies*, *34*(8), 673–698.

Manes, R. (2003). *The deafening silence: A memoir*. Bloomington, IN: First Books.

Mintz, S. W., & Wolf, E. R. (1950). An analysis of ritual co-parenthood (compadrazgo). *Southwestern Journal of Anthropology*, *6*(4), 341–368.

National Institutes of Mental Health. (2003). *Research on survivors of suicide workshop*. Retrieved from rarediseases.info.nih.gov/asp/html/conferences/conferences/suicide2003

Neugebauer, R., Rabkin, J. G., Williams, J. B., Remien, R. H., Goetz, R., & Gorman, J. M. (1992). Bereavement reactions among homosexual men experiencing multiple losses in the AIDS epidemic. *The American Journal of Psychiatry*, *149*(10), 1374–1379.

Neimeyer, R. A. (Ed.). (2001). *Meaning reconstruction and the experience of loss*. Washington, DC: American Psychological Association.

Qin, P., Agerbo, E., & Mortensen, P. B. (2002). Suicide risk in relation to family history of completed suicide and psychiatric disorders: A nested case-control study based on longitudinal registers. *Lancet*, *360*(9340), 1126–1130.

Rappaport, N. (2009). *In her wake: A child psychiatrist explores the mystery of her mother's suicide*. New York, NY: Basic Books.

Runeson, B., & Asberg, M. (2003). Family history of suicide among suicide victims. *The American Journal of Psychiatry*, *160*(8), 1525–1526.

Scovel, M. (2003). *Surviving suicide: My journey to the light within*. Beaufort, SC: Coastal Villages Press.

Stroebe, M. S., Folkman, S., Hansson, R. O., & Schut, H. (2006). The prediction of bereavement outcome: Development of an integrative risk factor framework. *Social Science & Medicine*, *63*(9), 2440–2451.

Talbot, K. (2002). *What forever means after the death of a child*. New York, NY: Brunner-Routledge.

Vennemann, M. M., Rentsch, C., Bajanowski, T., & Zimmer, G. (2006). Are autopsies of help to the parents of SIDS victims? A follow-up on SIDS families. *International Journal of Legal Medicine*, *120*(6), 352–354.

Wheeler, I. P. (1990). The role of meaning and purpose in life in parental bereavement. *Dissertation Abstracts International: Section B. 52*(04), 2319. (UMI No. 91-17334)

Wickersham, J. (2008). *The suicide index: Putting my father's death in order*. Orlando, FL: Harcourt Books.

Forms of Bereavement Assistance and How They Help Survivors Cope

6

Early Years After Loss: Survivors Get Help and Advance From Their Depths of Despair

In this chapter, we investigate how parent survivors feel in the early years after losing a child and what they do to get bereavement help. In this analysis, we focus on all bereaved parents and we explore how parental grief and help-seeking efforts may differ given the diverging circumstances of a child's death. Based on their in-depth studies of more than 300 Norwegian parents that lost children to suicide, accidents, and SIDS deaths, Kari and Atle Dyregrov (2008) concisely summarize the feelings parents usually experience immediately after the loss.

> Most bereaved people will experience a sense of unreal as the death occurs. . . . The experience can be that of being in a dream . . . as if it were not true. . . . A number of bereaved people will afterwards blame themselves for the way they reacted. Many think that their responses were insufficient. If the death is permeated with drama, as sudden deaths often are, the sense impressions can become "permanently engraved" with an extraordinary intensity. . . . In principle the first shock reaction guarantees quick reaction and a form of mental protection. . . . The shock becomes so intense that the bereaved cannot absorb everything that has happened at once and hours can pass, or days, weeks and even more time, before they realize what has happened. They know it intellectually but not emotionally. . . . Bodily reactions such as shaking, palpitations, nausea, chills or dizziness are not unusual. For some people these symptoms continue beyond the first day and are intensified by a lack of appetite . . . Many bereaved people speak of a "calamity" of different thoughts

racing around in their heads: "What now?" . . . There is so much to be addressed at the same time, and everything appears chaotic and muddled. Others scarcely remember anything from this period of time. Many find that they do not cry until later, at the wake, devotional service, memorial service, or funeral. (pp. 27–28)

In the months that follow, the Dyregovs (2008) suggest, common longer term responses to sudden death include feelings of loss, yearnings and pain, self-reproach and guilt, reliving the events surrounding the death, sleep disturbances, anxiety and vulnerability, concentration and memory problems, irritation and anger, and physical ailments (p. 29). The Dyregovs point out that a feedback loop can be noted between the psychological difficulties newly bereaved persons may feel and physical changes taking place within their bodies. In turn, the physical changes may further compromise a person's psychological adjustment. As the newly bereaved often experience difficulties with getting enough sleep, they are more prone to physical ailments, fatigue, poor concentration, irritation, anger, and feeling dazed. They are also more susceptible to anxiety and worry, especially about surviving children and other family members, worrying whether they too will succumb to the same illnesses or suicidal impulses that already took the lives of loved ones in their families.

The Dyregovs also emphasize the role of socially significant others who will often provide essential help to the newly bereaved during the early grief period when intense shock, bewilderment, and confusion are commonplace. Socially significant others will often be needed to assist the survivor in planning and executing the memorial and funeral services for the deceased. They may also be needed to help survivors navigate through their everyday living tasks when some feel unable to function. Significant others will also be needed to provide emotional support and act as sounding boards for survivors' frequent ruminations about the death and the perceived failure to avert the tragic outcome. As we pointed out in Chapter 2 on stigmatization, when significant others fail to offer survivors the emotional availability and comfort they may be seeking, survivors will be inclined to experience greater grief difficulties and complicated grief. When significant others offer truly supportive responses, they can be important stabilizing forces in survivors' subsequent quests to restart their lives after loss.

Others have noted additional symptoms accompanying the sudden and unexpected death of a child (see, e.g., Finkbeiner, 1996; Rando, 1986; Talbot, 2002, among others). Survivors often feel immobilized, unable to initiate most ordinary daily actions, such as getting out of bed in the morning. Survivors may feel deeply depressed and hopeless, as if the sense of life's purpose and meaning has suddenly been stolen from them. For some, there may also be a reckless disregard for their own safety and a failure to protect themselves from harm or injury. Some child-loss survivors experience thoughts of their own demise or suicide and see little meaning or value to their continued existence.

RESPONSES FROM OUR SURVEY PARTICIPANTS

The self-reports offered by our survey respondents are fully consistent with these claims. Among all parent survivors who lost a child less than 3 years ago ($N = 211$), 65% reported their mental health to be poor or fair; 41% reported fair or poor physical health; 71% reported difficulties falling asleep sometimes or often during the past year; 27% reported missing one or more days from work (during the past month) for mental health reasons; 45% reported little or no satisfaction with their lives; 80% reported themselves depressed in the past year; 40% reported suicide thoughts occasionally or frequently during the past year; 18% reported making a specific plan for suicide; and 3% reported a suicide attempt.

The poor mental and physical health reports offered by the newly bereaved contrast sharply with assessments given by other child-loss survivors who were 3 or more years past their loss. Longer term survivors offered these reports: 34% stated their mental health was poor or fair; 30% reported fair or poor physical health; 63% reported difficulties falling asleep sometimes or more often during the past year; 12% reported missing one or more days from work (during the past month) for mental health reasons; 25% reported little or no satisfaction with their lives; 60% reported themselves depressed in the past year; 16% reported suicide thoughts occasionally or more frequently during the past year; 6% reported making a specific plan for suicide; and 1% reported a suicide attempt. All of these differences, with the exception of the suicide attempts, were statistically significant with the chi-square test. Both of these child-loss survivor groups showed significantly higher incidences of the aforementioned mental and physical health problems than their same age and gender (nonbereaved) counterparts who answered these same questions in the U.S. Midlife adult survey (Wethington, Kessler, & Brim, 1998).

We also investigated the grief difficulties, complicated grief, and posttraumatic stress disorder (PTSD) responses of newly bereaved respondents and contrasted them with the longer term parent survivors in our sample. Newly bereaved respondents who were less than 3 years since their loss scored 7 points higher on the Brief Grief Experience Questionnaire (GEQ) scale, 6 points higher on the Complicated Grief scale and 6 points higher on the Impact of Event Scale, all of which were significantly higher on t test comparison of means. These differences attest to the greater grief problems shared among newly bereaved survivors.

We also examined the substance use among newly bereaved respondents in comparison with those whose losses took place more than 3 years previously. Of newly bereaved respondents, 14% reported using an illegal recreational drug during the past year, as compared to 7% for longer term respondents; 10% of newly bereaved reported getting drunk or very high on alcohol on a monthly or more frequent basis, as compared to 6% for longer term survivors; 16% reported having five or more drinks on drinking occasions (at least monthly or more frequently), as compared to 9% for longer term survivors. Again, all these differences were significant with the chi-square sta-tistic. These data, too, are consistent with the assertion of greater substance use among newly bereaved survivors, compared to longer term parent survivors. All in all, the comparisons show a variety of greater mental health difficulties among the newly bereaved.

HELP-SEEKING ACTIVITIES OF ALL NEWLY BEREAVED PARENTS

The next question we probed were the kinds of help-seeking activities sur-vivors pursued to repair their lives afterward. Some survivors confronted a huge and perhaps bewildering array of choices for getting help after their loss, whereas others probably found fewer helping aids easily accessible. We sought to explore where survivors went to get help and how long after the loss they pursued their different support resources. In this chapter, we pay special attention to the help-seeking activities survivors engaged in during their first 4 to 5 years after the loss, perhaps their most vulnerable time. (Readers are referred back to the graphs at the end of Chapter 4, which display grief problems of bereaved parents after a child's suicide peaking during the second year after the loss and slowly subsiding thereafter until they fall below mean levels for grief problems, 5 or more years after the loss.) In the next chapter, Chapter 7, we focus on parent survivors' longer term help-seeking efforts. In this discussion, we also try to link the differ-ent kinds of resources survivors use with their loss experiences and demo-graphic characteristics.

Betty Lou Williamson (a pseudonym for a parent who lost her 17-year-old son to a suicide) spoke to the first author at a peer support survivor of suicide (SOS) meeting she regularly attended. She said,

> I don't know where I'd be without this group. I come to every meeting. I wouldn't miss a single one for anything. Jimmy, my husband, usu-ally comes with me. We've learned so much from listening to other survivors. But, this group (meeting once a month) is definitely not enough for us. We also go to The Compassionate Friends (also meeting on a monthly basis). And we've had a few visits to psychics, too. I'm also seeing a psychiatrist, now and then, as well. Quite frankly, I need the medications he prescribes. Without the meds, I'd be climbing the walls from not getting enough sleep and from my feelings of depres-sion. But, honestly I feel ambivalent about seeing the shrink. After all the help my Johnny (her deceased son) got for his problems from treatment professionals, what good did it do for him? He hung him-self anyways. They didn't know how to help him. And we faithfully followed all their recommendations. What worries me now is how Ricky, my surviving son, is dealing with all this. He admired Johnny so much. Johnny was his role model. I'm so worried about Ricky—and doing right for him—he's all we have left. Whenever I see him

doing anything that looks like he's following in his big brother's footsteps, I go nuts. Everyday is a struggle, managing without Johnny. His absence has brought us down in so many ways.

Sharon Coleman is another survivor who was interviewed by the first author at a healing conference. She shared her sad story of discovering her teenage son Timothy's body in the garage.

He was slumped over on the floor and had been crouched over when he died. He had attached a heavy clothesline to the overhead steam pipe and managed to strangle himself from some kind of a kneeling position. He must have learned this method on the Internet or something. I keep on having visions of his contorted body on the garage floor. Even though I've already been to two different counselors, my priest and a support group, nothing helped me with the flashbacks. It wasn't until I started getting EMDR treatments with someone recommended by one of the counselors that I was finally able to feel a little better. I can sleep most nights now. I'm not waking up in the middle of the night in agonizing sweats, tormented by all those second-guessing thoughts: "if only I took Timmy to a different treatment place; if only I let him drop out of school," and so on. Slowly, I'm beginning to get to a better place. But, every time I go into that garage, I'm still afraid of seeing his body again; the garage spooks me.

These two cases vividly show how survivors employ a multiplicity of resources to help them with their early grief. We might wonder whether these cases were typical. Do survivors try many different aid resources or do they usually employ one or two different things? We asked our respondents whether they had used any one of the following six different support resources in the past 12 months: general bereavement support groups, SOS support groups, bereavement counselors, all other professional mental health practitioners, clergy, and psychics. Because our sample was disproportionately drawn from the ranks of support group participants, we anticipated that support groups would be the most popular help resource. Table 6.1 shows the

Table 6.1
Frequency of Using Healing Resources During the Past Year ($N = 575$)

RESOURCE	% USING THIS IN PAST 12 MONTHS	N REPORTING
General bereavement support group	51	573
Survivor of suicide support group	42	542
All mental health practitioners	32	571
Bereavement counselors	24	565
Clergy	23	569
Psychics	20	563

Note. From Survivors Child Loss Survey, 2006–2009.

Table 6.2
Parent Survivors' Use of Healing Resources as Time After Loss Changes

YEARS SINCE THE LOSS	MEAN NUMBER OF RESOURCES USED	NO. OF CASES
2 or less	2.6	120
2–4 years	2.2	130
5–10 years	1.5	137
11 or more	1.4	79

Note. From Survivors Child Loss Survey, 2006–2009.

different percentages of all survivors who used each of these six resources at least once during the past year. As expected, support groups were the dominant resource used.

Most survivors reported using more than a single helping agent during the past year. Two was both the mean and the modal number of helping agents used for the past year with the following breakdown: 20% used no outside help at all; 23% used one resource only; 26% used two resources; 14% used three resources; and 17% used four or more resources. Whether one sought help from more than a single resource was negatively associated with time since the loss, with a correlation coefficient of −.26. Those in early stage grief sought more helping agents than those more removed in time from their losses. This is displayed in Table 6.2. Thus, survivors with little time since their loss use significantly more support resources than those whose losses occurred many years earlier, who use significantly fewer support resources.

We also investigated how using different help resources fluctuated over the first 7 years after the loss. The first 7 years covers the deep abyss of grief that survivors fall into after a loss, as well as the beginning of finding a new normal for themselves when acceptance of loss firmly takes hold, usually 5 or more years after the death. Table 6.3 displays the frequency with which survivors of different duration since their loss used various helping resources. Please note that in this table for summary purposes, we have combined all mental health and bereavement counselors into one category. Likewise, we have collapsed general bereavement and suicide-specific bereavement support groups into one category as well. It made sense to do this, given that both types of groups were generally peer led. When we discuss participation in SOS support groups, unless we reviewed other bereaved subgroups' use of these resources, these analyses were confined to the suicide-bereaved parents.

It should also be understood that these comparisons were made between different groups of survivors who were positioned at different periods since their loss. They were not the same group of survivors who were repeatedly studied at different periods. Note also that many survivors were engaged in multiple treatment modalities at the same time. Table 6.3 suggests that seeing counselors on an occasional basis was the most preferred

Table 6.3
Using Different Helping Resources Within the First 7 Years After Loss
%/*n* (*N* = 410)

	2 YEARS OR LESS	2–4 YEARS	4–7 YEARS	TOTALS
Seen a mental health or bereavement counselor past year**				
Never	36.0/50	51.4/72	67.2/88	51.2/210
Less than monthly	48.2/67	31.4/44	27.5/36	35.8/147
More than monthly	15.8/22	17.1/24	5.3/7	12.9/53
Went to a general bereavement or SOS group past year**				
Never	33.1/46	27.9/39	46.6/61	35.6/146
Less than monthly	54.0/75	52.9/74	40.5/53	49.3/202
More than monthly	13.0/18	19.3/27	13.0/17	15.1/62
Seen a clergy person past year*				
Never	65.5/91	79.0/109	80.6/104	74.9/304
Less than monthly	31.6/44	19.6/27	17.0/22	22.9/93
More than monthly	2.9/4	1.4/2	2.3/3	2.2/9
Seen a psychic past year*				
Never	70.0/96	72.5/100	83.0/107	75.0/303
Once or more	29.9/41	27.5/38	17.1/22	25.0/101

Note. From Survivors Child Loss Survey, 2006–2007.
**Chi-square p < .01
*Chi-square p < .05

treatment mode during the earliest loss period—within the first 2 years after loss—when nearly half of all survivors had done so. The table also showed that the small group of survivors who saw counselors very frequently began to cut back on having counseling 4 years after the loss. Occasional users of therapy also reduced their counseling involvements as well. Although most survivors saw therapists (about two-thirds) during the first 2 years after loss, they subsequently reduced therapeutic visits to about one-third by 4 to 7 years after loss. These differences were significant with the chi-square statistic.

Table 6.3 also shows how child-loss survivors used support groups over the first 7 years after loss. Parental use of support groups appeared to follow a somewhat different pattern than use of counseling. About two-thirds used support groups during the earliest grief period, and by years 4 to 7 after loss, close to half still remained affiliated with such groups. (It should be noted that our particular data collection method, relying primarily on support group affiliation, may have inflated the numbers of survivors using support groups during later years after loss.) Support group usage peaked during the 2- to 4-year period after loss, with more than 70% of survivors relying on this particular resource. This contrasts with the peak usage period for counseling, which was during the first 2 years. These findings suggest two different possibilities: There may either be problems in finding support groups or a hesitancy to use them during the earliest loss period for some survivors. Survivors also cut back on their usage of support groups as they moved from the first 4 years after loss to the later 4- to 7-year post-loss period. Again, the differences we observed were significant with the chi-square statistic.

Table 6.3 also displays the pattern of clergy and psychic usage during the first 7 years after loss. These less popular resources were selected by 30% to 35% of all respondents. Use of clergy peaked among those during the earliest grief period, at 35%, then shrank to only about a fifth using this resource at years 4 to 7 after loss. The biggest drop in usage appeared to occur immediately after the early grief period. For psychics usage levels remained at the 30% level during the first 4 years after loss and then diminished to below the 20% usage level at the 4-year loss point. Both these fluctuations were significant with the chi-square statistic.

WHAT HELPS SURVIVORS THE MOST?

We investigated which bereavement resources were thought to be most and least helpful during early bereavement (see Table 6.4). Support groups were reported as the most helpful of all resources, with close to half of all suicide survivors rating these groups as very helpful and little more than a fifth finding them of little help. Psychics were the next most helpful resource, with more than a third finding these services very helpful and about a quarter finding them of little or no help. Yet, fewer than half of all survivors had actually

Table 6.4
Various Help Sources and How They Were Perceived by Survivors as Helpful, Among Child-Loss Survivors With 4 or Fewer Years After Loss, $N = 279$

HELP SOURCE	NUMBER RESPONDING	MEAN HELP RATING	% VIEWING SOURCE AS VERY HELPFUL	% VIEWING SOURCE AS LITTLE OR NO HELP
Survivor of suicide support group[a]	162	3.85	43.8	22.2
General bereavement support group	193	3.64	31.6	25.4
Professional bereavement counselor	141	3.40	27.0	28.4
Psychologist/psychiatrist/ social worker	171	3.32	25.7	33.3
Clergy person	135	3.29	21.5	32.6
Psychic or spiritualist	104	3.63	34.6	24.0

Note. From Survivors Child Loss Survey, 2006–2009.
[a]This was calculated exclusively for suicide survivors.

sought out psychics. General bereavement groups were also seen as more helpful than not helpful.

When we looked at the least effective resources, we found clergy as the least favorably evaluated help resource. Although only about a fifth found them very helpful, a third found them of little help. Similar evaluations to those for clergy were given for all mental health practitioners, although somewhat greater numbers of survivors had used these resources. In each case, the very helpful ratings matched or fell slightly below the percentage viewing them of little help. The mean ratings for each helping resource did not show any considerable differences for any single aid; all were reported in the moderately helpful range. Had we computed statistical significance tests of these means, it is highly doubtful that any would have shown significant differences from the other resources, given the narrow range of mean differences, yet chi-square comparisons of very helpful versus less helpful resources quite possibly might have shown significant differences in percentages regarding resources as very helpful, or less so. Yet, at this early analysis point, we were hesitant to apply one or another of these standards to evaluate the helpfulness of support resources.

TYPE OF LOSS AND DIFFERENCES IN GETTING HELP

We investigated whether the type of loss that parents experienced was related to their pursuit of helping aids. Respondents could list as many as six different helping resources from which they sought help: SOS support groups, general bereavement groups, bereavement counselors, other mental health professionals, clergy, and psychics. We were unable to distinguish whether a given respondent had gone to more than one SOS or general bereavement group. Similarly, we were unable to tell whether respondents had seen a variety of bereavement or mental health counselors and practitioners or just one. We could only determine whether a respondent had seen at least one counseling professional or had attended at least one bereavement support group.

Table 6.5 shows that the use of helping agents during the previous year was associated with the type of loss the parent had experienced. Survivors sustaining suicide losses of children reported using more helping agents in the past year than the other bereaved parent subgroups: parents losing children to drugs, other accidents, and natural deaths. The one-way analysis of variance (ANOVA) test showed these means to be significantly different from one another, $F(3, 518) = 5.88, p < .0001$. Yet, the post hoc Scheffe test showed that the only significant difference was between suicide survivors (with a mean of 2) and the parent survivors of a child's natural death (with a mean of 1).

Table 6.6 displays the use of the six different healing resources by the type of loss. For the most part, a child's death by suicide, drugs, other accidents, or natural causes was not associated with differences in getting help from general bereavement support groups, professional counselors, or from the clergy. No statistically significant differences were noted regarding ever getting help from each of these resources by type of loss. Yet, seeing psychics was significantly

Table 6.5
Numbers of Healing Aids Used During the Past Year
Among Different Groups of Bereaved Parents

TYPE OF DEATH	MEAN NUMBER OF RESOURCES USED	STANDARD DEVIATION	NO. OF CASES
Natural	1.0	.81	19
Suicide	2.03	1.5	432
Drug overdose	1.45	1.2	42
Other accident	1.45	1.2	29

Note. From Survivors Child Loss Survey, 2006–2009.
$F(3, 518) = 5.88$, $p < .0001$

associated with type of loss, with natural death survivors being the least in-clined to ever see psychics and drug-death survivors being the most inclined to use them. We investigated each of these separate associations (not displayed in our tables) and found that each had an independent association with seeing psychics. When we omitted drug-death survivors from the chi-square com-parison, natural death survivors were significantly less likely to use psychics compared to the other loss subgroups. When we omitted natural death survi-vors from the chi-square comparison, drug-death survivors were significantly more likely to use psychics, compared to the other two subgroups. Over half of all drug-death bereaved parents (54%) had used psychics, compared to 31% for all other bereaved parents.

Table 6.6 also shows significant differences between each loss-type sub-group and attendance at SOS support groups. It was obvious that those be-reaved by suicide would attend more SOS groups than other bereaved par-ents. We did not expect parents whose children died from natural causes or from accidents to find much value in these groups, and the data confirmed our expectations, with 74% of suicide-bereaved parents attending SOS groups, 6% for accidental-death bereaved, and no one attending them among natural-death bereaved. We expected that parents whose children died from drug over-doses would find these groups of value, especially given the overlap between many drug deaths and suicides (discussed in Chapter 3), and yet, the survey data showed only 12% of the overdose-death bereaved parents attended an SOS group.

We investigated this further in our interviews and respondents' comments included in their surveys. Several drug-death bereaved parents remarked on their surveys that their affiliations with SOS groups were very valuable to them, including the opportunity for sharing loss stories and finding encour-agement from other grieving parents that things can and will eventually get better. Yet, our field notes, collected over an 8-year period within two different support groups, suggested that few drug-death bereaved parents remained for long in SOS support groups. After coming to a single meeting, they usually never returned.

Table 6.6
Lifetime Use of Different Bereavement Help Resources by
Different Groups of Bereaved Parents

	NATURAL DEATH	SUICIDE	OVER- DOSE	OTHER ACCIDENT DEATH	ALL SURVIVORS	χ^2	*df*	sig
General Bereavement Support Group								
Percent ever used	83	72	83	81	74	5.22	3	0.16
Group size	24	460	48	37	569			
Clergy Help								
Percent ever used	50	48	42	33	47	3.73	3	0.29
Group size	24	456	48	36	564			
Professional Bereavement Counselor								
Percent ever used	25	48	48	49	47	5.06	3	0.17
Group size	24	454	48	35	561			
Any Mental Health Professional								
Percent ever used	48	63	55	47	60	5.62	3	0.13
Group size	23	458	47	36	564			
Spiritualist or Psychic								
Percent ever used	13	30	54	33	31	15.87	3	***
Group size	23	452	48	36	559			
Survivor of Suicide Support Group								
Percent ever used	0	74	12	6	63	148.19	3	***
Group size	20	448	43	31	542			

Note From Survivors Child Loss Survey, 2006–2009.
***$p < .001$.

We interviewed several drug-death bereaved parents who offered comments suggesting why many of these parents did not find SOS groups appealing or useful. Linda Terman (a pseudonym) lost her 22-year-old daughter, Martha, to a heroin overdose. She said,

I went to one SOS group, and I knew right away it wasn't for me. At the meeting, a few shared their stories of finding husbands or children after gun shots and hangings and feeling very horrified by it all. I can understand those feelings. But my own experience was very different. I found Martha's body at home when she died. She succumbed to a heroin overdose. When I found her, she was lying in her child-hood bed and had such a peaceful expression on her face. She looked just like an angel. I knew then when I saw her that she must have gone to heaven. Of course, I was unbelievably sad and have been ever since, but I know she went to heaven. I don't think many suicide sur-vivors have that sensation, so I don't feel being with them is going to be very helpful to me.

Bob Cranshaw (a pseudonym) had a different take on why he never joined an SOS group. He said,

I met several suicide survivors at CF (Compassionate Friends) meet-ings and at healing conferences. I kind of know what some of their issues are, but they are in a very different place than I am. For me, it has been a train wreck waiting to happen ever since Bobby Jr. started junior high school. He went from one drug to another, and we went with him from one treatment program to another, and none of the treatments worked. We played that awful codependency game with him, and then we went on to tough love. We took Bobby to every different type of treatment program they have in this state: residen-tial treatments, day care, drug rehab counselors, psychiatrists, social workers, 12-step programs, NA, AA, spiritualists, and what have you. Bobby tried them all. And then, here we are. I just feel I need to be with other parents that know this situation, and it makes the most sense for us to stay with others like us.

At SOS meetings, a near-constant discussion theme arises around the ques-tion of why the deceased took their lives. Survivors of drug-related deaths sometimes ask this themselves, but usually, the question does not have the same compelling urgency that it may have for a suicide survivor.

We also examined whether survivors with different types of losses judged the six helping aids any differently in terms of their value. The results of these comparisons showed no statistically significant differences between any of the child-loss subgroups in terms of judging one helping aid more helpful than another. However, there was one possible trend in the ratings of general bereavement groups showing parent survivors of a child's drug or suicide death rating this helping aid somewhat less favorably (with a mean of 3.7) than accident and natural-death surviving parents did (with a mean of 4.02), with a p value of .11 on the t test comparison, which was not statistically significant.

Our face-to-face interviews and written-in comments from survey respon-dents yielded remarks that were consistent with this trend, suggesting that many suicide and drug-overdose survivors did not feel greatly supported in the mixed company of general bereavement groups. Some drug-overdose and suicide bereaved even reported hearing negative comments expressed against the mentally ill and the drug-involved at The Compassionate Friends (TCF) meetings. Unfortunately, these reports were not altogether uncommon.

Barbara Ann Montgomery (a pseudonym) said some of the people at her TCF meetings said

> awful things . . . though, I don't think they meant to be malicious or anything like that. They just didn't know any better. But, some [CF members] implied my son's overdose death was something he chose to do. My son was addicted to heroin, and he couldn't regulate his drug taking. So I didn't find those blaming remarks very helpful to me, stated by people who didn't know the first thing about addictions and who didn't seem willing to learn anything more about it beyond what they already knew.

Veronica Walsh (a pseudonym), whose 23-year-old son died from an Oxy-Cotin overdose in his college dorm, said,

> I couldn't believe it. They "kicked" me out of Compassionate Friends! They said I wasn't progressing fast enough. My son died 4 years ago at that time. I don't know what they were expecting. But, I think I must have stuck out there as some kind of an oddity. I got the feeling they thought my son's drug addiction was contagious or something.

Hannah Myers (a pseudonym), whose 17-year-old daughter died after jumping in front of a commuter railroad train, said,

> I could tell that the other CF members didn't know what to say to me. I was the only one there with a suicide loss and a loss that's not so easy to talk about. I couldn't begin to share my loss story comfortably with the others at the CF meetings. I could feel that some were horrified by my daughter's death. I am too for that matter. So I had to join a survivors of suicide group to find some greater comfort, where I knew I would be understood when I needed to talk about my Debbie's death.

These few illustrations suggest some of the difficulties often experienced in mixed bereavement groups, especially for those with stigmatized losses such as drugs and suicide. In addition, other marginalized groups occasionally have also reported difficulties communicating with other bereaved parents in mixed support groups. Kay Talbot (2002), presenting data from her respondents, indicated that bereaved mothers of only child decedents often felt discomfort at TCF meetings in the company of other mothers with surviving children. Some felt jealous of these mothers who could still carry on family life with their remaining children. Although few of the mothers with surviving children seemed disrespectful to the mothers of deceased only child, their presence alone brought greater sadness and feelings of aloneness to these other bereaved parents. Many claimed they needed to be among others like themselves to feel genuine comfort and support.

Talbot's respondents expressed sentiments very similar to Joyce Enright's (a pseudonym), another mother whose 19-year-old son died after a fatal overdose of prescription drugs and cocaine. Joyce said,

> We started our online support group of other drug-death parents so that we could readily talk about our losses together. We all seemed to gravitate to each other (other drug-overdose bereaved) to work toward realizing our common goals. We want to help and support each other. And we also want to work together toward saving the living by disseminating better information about drugs and their lethal consequences. Our Internet group is a combination support group and agent for social change to change public awareness about drugs. We want to make something positive come out of our losses.

Of the 12 drug-overdose bereaved parents who completed surveys, 11 stated that they obtained their most helpful grief assistance in online support groups, composed exclusively of other parents bereaved by a child's overdose death. Other drug-loss bereaved also expressed similar themes about the comfort and support they only obtained in face-to-face GRASP support groups, where they were able to gain validation and support for their long and deeply unsettling losses and ultimate failures to find answers for their children's drug-abuse problems.

Suicide survivors expressed similar sentiments, wishing to be in support groups with one another, feeling that they obtained their best support in groups exclusively populated with others bereaved by suicide. Thus, *being in support groups with others like themselves appears to be of quintessential importance to parent survivors*. In Chapters 7 and 8, we will expand this theme further, exploring the attributes that produce the most positive results for the suicide bereaved in their peer-led support groups.

HOW DID OUR RESPONDENTS USE DIFFERENT HEALING AIDS?

As each of our respondents presented information on their use of the six different healing aids, we were able to assemble a composite picture of the resources used during the previous year by all respondents. Table 6.1 displays the use of each one of the six different types of healing resources we investigated, but it does not show the patterns of how respondents combined their uses of resources. Of our respondents, 29% reported using a general bereavement group and an SOS support group during the previous year. A smaller number, 15%, reported going to both a mental health practitioner and a bereavement counselor during the previous year. Those reporting going to both a support group (of one kind or other) and some kind of a professional counselor represented 29%, whereas 15% had seen a psychic and attended a support group during the past year. In addition, 16% had seen a clergy person and attended a support group, and 11% and 13% respectively combined visits to a psychic and/or a clergy person with seeing any type of a mental health counselor.

Thus, our respondents seemed equally divided between using a combination of multiple support groups and going to support groups and professional counselors in their most recent past. We suspect that the mixing of therapies in this manner offered survivors the best combination of services for addressing their individual and social needs.

THE SOCIAL CHARACTERISTICS OF THOSE AVOIDING ALL PROFESSIONAL MENTAL HEALTH AND PEER HELP ALTOGETHER

Although the vast majority of our respondents used some combination of support groups, professional counseling resources, or both, we did find that a small minority—7% of all our respondents (37 individuals)—reported shunning professional and peer support help altogether.

Perhaps a most puzzling question for readers might be how we may have ever located these respondents, given that most participants were solicited from the ranks of support group members and a smaller number from professional bereavement counselors. These respondents appeared to have been drawn from several sources. As we collected surveys, we acquired the e-mail addresses of many respondents. Toward the end of our data collection period, we sent out solicitation letters to more than 400 members of our sample, asking if they knew of any additional parent survivors (who had not used support groups or therapy) that they could encourage to be respondents to the survey. We also collected additional surveys from spouses who wished to be respondents, some of whom were not engaged in therapeutic activities. One of our most significant respondent sources, Friends For Survival, has a national circulation base of over 3,000 survivors, many of whom became newsletter subscribers after attending healing conferences. A last source, probably some of our therapy-averting survey participants came from associations with other survey participants.

These cases of people who chose not to seek professional and peer group help shared a single common demographic characteristic: They were less well educated than their counterparts A total of 30% of nonparticipants reported having a high school degree or less education, compared to only 16% for those who went to support groups, counselors, or both. In all other demographic characteristics that we examined—age, gender, marital status, family income level, religion, and urbanicity—we found both groups were comparable to one another. We also investigated whether those declining therapies were more likely to see clergy or psychics for help, than therapy seekers. This comparison showed comparability between both subgroups. These data are displayed in Table 6.7.

Table 6.7 also displays some interesting contrasts between the help-seeking participants and those who did not seek help. Although not statistically significant, respondents who did not seek support resources showed a trend to be survivors of a child's natural or accidental death, compared to the therapy seekers who were more likely to include suicide and overdose-drug bereaved (with a p value of .076). Of those parents who never visited a counselor or a

Table 6.7
**Social and Grief Related Differences Between Those Using and Not Using
Support Groups and/or Professional Counselors**

	%/n THOSE NOT PARTICIPATING IN THERAPIES (*N* = 37)	ALL OTHER RESPONDENTS (*N* = 528)	χ² OR *F p* VALUE
Education			
High school or <	29.7/11	15.9/84	.03
Some college or >	70.3/26	84.1/444	
Used clergy help			
Yes	40.5/15	47.5/248	.41
No	59.5/22	52.5/274	
Used help from psychics			
Yes	21.6/8	32.6/169	.16
No	78.4/29	67.4/349	
Death type			
Natural/accidental	18.9/7	9.7/51	.076
Drugs/suicide	81.1/30	90.3/473	
Mean Stigma Scale score	2.29/34	3.49/491	.036
Mean years since the death	4.26/35	5.58/517	.10
Mean GEQ Scale score	35.2/33	39.4/381	.04
Depression status			
Depressed	54.0/20	68.4/360	.071
Not depressed	46.0/17	31.6/166	

Note. From Survivors Child Loss Survey, 2006–2009.

support group, 19% were natural or accidental-death bereaved, compared to only 10% for those that sought help from therapists or support groups, a larger percentage of whom were suicide and drug-death bereaved.

Analyses using *t* tests of means also showed that those not seeking therapy were significantly less likely to experience stigma compared to the therapy seekers, thus suggesting they were more likely to gain grief support from among their social intimates. In contrast, people who sought therapy reported that they felt more blamed by others for their children's deaths, reported being subjected to more avoidance behaviors from others, and experienced greater disenfranchised grief.

Those not seeking support resources tended to have had less time pass since their losses compared to therapy seekers, 4.26 years as compared to 5.6 years. (Ordinarily, we would expect bereaved to be seeking help sooner after a loss, rather than later on.) In addition, they showed significantly less grief difficulties on the abbreviated GEQ scale ($M = 35$) compared to the therapy seekers ($M = 39$) and were less likely to report themselves as depressed, 54%, compared to 68% for the therapy seekers.

Thus, the pattern was a consistent one: Those choosing not to seek out therapy simply appeared to be less troubled. Also, it is possible that some of these bereaved parents who lost children because of natural causes may have received hospice counseling prior to the death. This counseling may have helped prepare them to accept their losses with less difficulty than the parents who had experienced sudden death losses of children. Such scenarios, of course, would not apply to sudden accidental deaths of children where an enormous outpouring of social support from significant others might have offered these bereaved the grief comfort they inevitably might have sought.

SOCIAL AND GRIEF CHARACTERISTICS OF THOSE USING SUPPORT GROUPS AND PROFESSIONAL COUNSELING HELP

Because the contrasts between those choosing or not choosing to use support resources yielded valuable information, we extended this idea further to create a finer subgrouping of all respondents, dividing parents by the kinds of resources they had used. We divided respondents into one of four different groups: (a) those who had used both support groups and professional counseling resources; they were the most common, numbering 63%, $n = 355$; (b) the second largest group, those using support groups exclusively, 21%, $n = 117$; (c) a smaller group, 10% ($n = 56$) using professional counseling resources exclusively; and (d) the group we already reported on, those not participating in any support groups or counseling, 7% ($n = 37$).

Table 6.8 shows several distinctive demographic characteristics for those never participating in any support group or professional counseling resources. For example, they were less well educated. Table 6.8 also shows that more highly educated respondents were overrepresented in using both support groups and professional counseling resources and were more economically advantaged as well. All this corresponded with residence patterns showing higher percentages of big city and suburban residents more inclined to use both support groups and counselors. Only 17% of the group of bereaved parents using both support groups and counselors lived in small towns, which contrasted with the higher percentages for the other subgroups, which ranged from 26% to 36%. This finding suggests a possible problem with finding the full range of bereavement services among those living in small towns.

When we looked for other demographic differences between the help-using subgroups for age, gender, and race, we did not find any significant differences along these dimensions. (None of these contrasts are shown in Table 6.8.)

Striking differences were noted in religious participation, showing that those who used counseling exclusively were less active in conventional religious participation compared to the other subgroups of bereaved respondents.

Table 6.8

Demographic and Grief Related Characteristics Associated With Using Different Combinations of Support Group and Professional Counseling Help

	NO THERAPIES (N = 37)	SUPPORT GROUPS ONLY (N = 117)	PROFESSIONAL HELP ONLY (N = 56) % OR M/n	BOTH PROFESSIONALS & SUPPORT GROUPS (N = 355)	χ^2 OR F p VALUE
Education					
High school or <	29.7/11	20.5/24	21.4/12	13.5/48	.03
Some college or >	70.3/26	79.5/93	78.6/44	86.5/307	
Family income					.001
$40,000 or <	25.0/9	25.7/29	41.8/23	19.4/67	.001
$40,001–$90,000	47.2/17	52.2/59	27.3/15	42.5/147	
$90,001 and >	27.8/10	22.1/25	30.9/17	38.2/132	
Urbanicity					
Large city or suburb	40.5/15	48.3/55	50.0/28	58.7/206	.01
Small city	23.0/10	25.4/29	14.3/8	23.9/84	
Small town/farm	32.4/12	26.3/30	35.7/20	174/61	
Mean of religious participation (1–7)	3.2/37	3.6/117	2.6/56	3.6/350	.006
Mean years since the death (.08–27)	4.3/35	5.6/114	4.0/54	5.8/349	.02
Type of death					
Natural/accidental	18.9/7	14.5/17	3.6/2	9.1/32	.038
Suicide/drug overdose	81.1/30	85.5/100	96.4/53	90.9/320	
Mean stigma responses (0–17)	2.3/34	2.4/110	3.8/52	3.8/329	.0002
Mean grief diffs. (GEQ) scores (16–80)	35.3/33	37.1/106	42.9/52	39.7/323	.003
Mean mental health problems (0–4)	1.3/34	1.3/111	2.1/56	1.7/347	.0002
Mean depression score (0–8)	3.9/29	3.7/102	5.1/52	4.5/321	.03
Mean suicide thoughts (1–5)	1.6/36	1.4/115	2.0/55	1.8/351	.001

Note. From Survivors Child Loss Survey, 2006–2009.

Thus far, we have not mentioned conventional religious participation as a factor in bereaved parents' healing, and yet, we have found correlations in the low .20s, showing conventional religious participation associated with most measures of grief difficulties. The associations show that those who attended churches or synagogues more often were less likely to experience grief difficulties than their inactive counterparts. All this suggests that those attending support groups or not participating in counseling are more likely to gain grief help from their religious activism, but for those who see counselors exclusively, this benefit appears to be experienced less often.

Table 6.8 also shows significant differences with the one-way ANOVA test on years since the loss with the shortest time since the loss associated with those seeing counselors exclusively. Post hoc Scheffe tests yielded mean comparison differences at the .07 probability level, comparing those using counselors exclusively and those going to both counselors and support groups. Thus, this trend could suggest that seeing grief counselors may take place sooner in time after a loss than joining a support group.

As one pores over the data on the various dimensions of grief difficulties, overall mental health assessments, depression, and suicidality, a consistent pattern is demonstrated showing that those with more of these problems more often see counselors exclusively or see them in conjunction with support group attendance. Those reporting fewer grief and mental health problems were linked to either visiting support groups exclusively or to not seeking any type of outside support resource.

We noted previously that natural and accidental death survivors showed a trend to seek neither therapists nor support groups in their bereavement. They were also underrepresented in the category of people who went exclusively to therapists (but not support groups), with only 4% of the natural or accidental death survivors reporting that they had sought only professional counseling. We must acknowledge that some of this underrepresentation may have been a by-product of our sampling method, which relied very heavily on support groups for the recruitment of bereaved parents who lost children to accidents and natural causes. Most of these groups were recruited from TCF groups. Yet, the observation that only 9% had ever seen professional counselors, along with their support groups, suggests that suicides and drug overdoses—as more stigmatized deaths—are associated with more counseling visitations. Differences in experienced stigma appear to be associated with bereaved parents' pursuit of professional counselors exclusively or with going to both support groups and counselors. The post hoc Scheffe test showed that those going to support groups exclusively and those going to them in conjunction with visiting counselors were significantly different from one another in experienced stigma. Thus, a picture has emerged from Table 6.8, showing that more intensely perceived grief and mental health problems are likely to be associated with bereaved parents' seeking out professional counselors and support groups.

SUMMING UP

We began this chapter describing the utterly lost and vanquished feeling bereaved parents may have with the death of a child. For many, the experience brings them down to the lowest point of their lives. Whatever order and meaning they had previously found in their everyday lives, future dreams for fulfillment suddenly vanish, and many are left in a state of chaos, sometimes wondering whether it still makes sense to go on living. Our analysis in Chapter 4, among parent survivors of a child's suicide, suggested that 4 to 5 years might be needed before many bereaved parents will be able to come to a fuller acceptance of their losses and establish "a new normal" for themselves. Some, who had been challenged by psychological adaptation issues prior to their losses, may continue to have persisting psychological and grief difficulties beyond this period or even indefinitely. The substantial majority of bereaved parents will have restarted their lives 5 years after their loss, but even the most resilient among them will occasionally fall into moods of despair triggered by memories of significant events or subtle environmental cues that bring back the vivid image of their lost child. Most accept these reminders as part of the territory of their lifelong grief.

Our survey and interview data suggested that bereaved parents begin their healing in a mood of desperation, reaching out in a number of different directions to grief counselors, support groups, clergy, and psychics, seeking to alleviate their intolerable pain, confusion, and feelings of aloneness. Socially significant others can and usually do play an important part in leading the survivor along on his or her healing journey. Unfortunately, sometimes they may act as impediments to that transition. As our interviews with bereaved parents suggested, the help of a capable therapist or a professionally run support group may sometimes be perceived as a lifeline and turning point for a new beginning after loss.

However, in our interviews with survivors and observations at support groups, there was also much ambivalence expressed toward professionals, especially in cases of children's overdose and suicide deaths, which had been preceded by long histories of failed treatments. In many of these cases, parents were hesitant to rely on professionals for their own self-care, given the past histories of perceived failure of therapists to save their child. Yet, as our Table 6.8 suggested, despite their misgivings, especially stigmatized and intensely grief-troubled parents (those whose children died from drug overdoses and suicide) will rely more heavily on professional supports when compared to other less grief-troubled bereaved parents. Their needs for help and support simply exceed the levels of assistance that may be available from alternative resources.

If there was a single healing resource that captured the most enthusiastic endorsement from bereaved parents, it was the support group. Again and again, many said, in their written-in comments and interviews, that *being among others like themselves* helped them turn a corner from despair to a renewal of hope, enabling them to restart their lives. Although the survey evidence presented here showed that most bereaved parents (about two-thirds) began seeing counselors or going to support groups at similar rates during the first 2 years after a child's death, the evidence from those who used counselors exclusively suggested that these parents had the shortest period since their loss. They averaged 4 years since the loss, whereas those going to support groups averaged 5 and a half years since their loss. This finding could mean that accessibility to counselors may be more easily obtained than opportunities to affiliate with support groups. The evidence also suggested that there may be less access to support groups in America's small towns and rural places. An alternative explanation could also be that in small towns and rural places, some bereaved parents might be reluctant to join support groups because of secrecy and stigma issues, but they would be less hesitant to visit professional counselors.

Our investigation of survivor's healing efforts has shown psychics and spiritual advisers as helpful resources in the arsenal of healing aids for a minority of bereaved parents. Among those parents, 30% reported using psychics in the first 2-year period after their loss, which receded to 10% 5 or more years afterward. Those who are visiting psychics and spiritualists generally reported benefits from their visits, compared to the numbers finding them of little help. For these reasons, the help bereaved experience from psychics is likely to remain an enduring feature in the bereavement resource landscape.

Why natural-death bereaved parents were disinclined to visit psychics while the drug-overdose death bereaved were more inclined to employ them is especially puzzling. One possibility is that in cases of natural-death bereavement, especially where families had used hospice services prior to the death, there was greater reliance on professionally respected and traditional helping resources than on nontraditional ones, like psychics. Hospice professionals can act as gatekeepers, often leading bereaved families to seek help from professional counselors and support groups (especially those that hospice personnel may themselves facilitate) and may lead bereaved families along to pursue conventionally religious auspices to gain help. Some hospice caregiving teams even include religious advisors for families who are receiving their services.

Another possible explanation is the nature of the relational disruption caused by drug usage and mental illness, several examples of which have been offered previously in the chapter. Having a child struggle with an addiction problem and/or a psychiatric disorder often puts great strain on the bond between parent and child, sometimes producing an angry rupturing of the relationship prior to the death. The sudden and self-inflicted nature of both deaths can also sometimes be experienced as a rebuke by the child to the parental connection with the child. In our interviews with drug-overdose and suicide-bereaved parents, psychics often seem to play a special role in helping to heal this psychological rupture of the relationship, allowing for the development of an ongoing "continuing bond" with the deceased child (Klass, Silverman, & Nickman, 1996). Psychics frequently offer comforting reassurance that the child continues on in another plane, that they are well and healed, and that the child wishes the parents to heal and continue on with their lives.

Lastly, findings showing drug-overdose death bereaved parents more inclined to use psychics could be related to the present somewhat limited bereavement resources that these parents now face. We see these parents as having fewer choices available than other bereaved parents. Like suicide survivors, drug-death bereaved parents are likely to occasionally encounter prejudice and discrimination against the mentally ill and the addicted in the mixed groups of bereaved parents in general bereavement support groups. Yet, unlike suicide survivors, who have hundreds of nationwide SOS face-to-face support groups available to choose from, the drug-overdose bereaved find few dedicated groups focused on their unique loss issues. They may find some emerging Internet groups where drug-overdose bereaved may relate and support one another, but these groups presently remain relatively scare. Luckier survivors will find grief comfort in TCF chapters that are facilitated by drug-overdose bereaved parents or others who are empathic to the concerns of these bereaved persons.

Among our findings were results showing support groups as the most favored helping agent compared to all other alternative helping resources. Yet, it would be premature to conclude that support groups are the most helpful of all available resources for bereaved parents suffering the loss of a child. Given our particular sampling methodology, which drew most of our respondents from these groups, we clearly do not have an even-handed method for judging the helping potential from all the various aids available for all bereaved parents. Had we drawn our sample by either equally representing each helping agency or by deriving the sample from an altogether alternative source—such as from death certificate records—we would then be in a better position to make such assessments. This important task, to assess the most and least helpful alternatives and to better understand the different groups of bereaved persons most and least likely to gain from different resources, is a task that awaits future research.

REFERENCES

Dyregrov, K., & Dyregrov, A. (2008). *Effective grief and bereavement support: The role of family, friends, colleagues, schools and support professionals.* London, UK: Jessica Kingsley.

Finkbeiner, A. K. (1996). *After the death of a child: Living with loss through the years.* Baltimore, MD: Johns Hopkins University Press.

Klass, D., Silverman, P. R., & Nickman, S. L. (1996). *Continuing bonds: New understandings of grief.* Philadelphia, PA: Taylor Francis.

Rando, T. A. (Ed.). (1986). *Parental loss of a child.* Champaign, IL: Research Press.

Talbot, K. (2002). *What forever means after the death of a child.* New York, NY: Brunner-Routledge.

Wethington, E., Kessler, R. C., & Brim, O. G. (1998). *Midlife development in the United States (MIDUS): Psychological experiences follow-up study.* Ann Arbor, MI: Inter-university Consortium for Political and Social Research. doi:10.3886/ICPSR02911.v1

7

Later Years After Loss: Identifying the Postvention Needs of Survivors

INTRODUCTION

In this chapter, we focus on another dimly understood bereavement subject: What happens to bereaved parents in later years after loss, especially after a child's suicide or drug-overdose death? Unfortunately, this too, is a question that, for the most part, has eluded researchers' interests. To inform this discussion, we were privileged to have 243 bereaved parents from our sample, who spent an average of 10 years since the death of their child. These parents offered quantitative survey data on their post-loss coping responses.

Among the bereaved themselves, there is a genuine curiosity about longer term bereaved parents. Many newly bereaved parents, especially those caught up in the agonizing pain of early loss, wonder how long they will remain in their depths of despair. Many question whether the pain of loss and the shattering of many of their important life goals will endure for the rest of their lives. As they represent models of perseverance, longer term or "veteran" survivors shed important light on the pathways for the newly bereaved. In the following two chapters, we will discuss what goes on in survivor self-help support groups, important settings where survivors teach each other about the intricacies of their grief. We see many survivors coming together in support groups to learn from one another and offer each other substantive help as they move along with their healing journeys.

The first author attended a suicide survivors' healing event when a number of other newly bereaved fathers met each other for the first time. The fathers had viewed a video at the event, depicting other suicide-bereaved persons, and were asked to discuss the film together and to share their feelings of loss. They sat around in a circle and a 10-year post-loss suicide-loss bereaved father served as the group's facilitator. At the outset, a newly bereaved father, who had lost his son 2 months earlier asked the facilitator, "Can I ever hope to get well again after this? What's the future going to be like for me?" The facilitator responded,

> We are all different, and we each take different amounts of time to put our lives back together again after the tragic suicide death of a child. From my own standpoint, I don't know if I'll ever get "better." To be honest about it, "better" is a word I am not very comfortable with. If getting better means forgetting about my son, obliterating his memory from my thoughts altogether, then I can tell you this: I'll never get better! I'm always going to feel sad when I think about him. I treasure all the memories I have of him, both the good and the bad. If I didn't think about him, perhaps I might be able to escape the blues that I sometimes have when I think of him. There's hardly a day that passes where I don't have some thoughts about him and here I stand, 10 years after his death. Thankfully, my thoughts now do not bring me to the same immobilizing pain they did shortly after his death. Now and then, I occasionally even have private imaginary conversations with my son that give me some comfort. And I accept all this as giving me the best that I can get without him. I'm okay with this, and I think my grief will be a lifelong thing. But that's me, and we're all different. You may come to a different conclusion about your grief than I have.

In this chapter, we address the postvention (or aftercare) needs of bereaved parents who have lost children 5 or more years earlier. There appears to have been only very limited attention focused on this research subject. In a series of articles on a well-designed, longitudinal study of 173 cases of bereaved parents who lost children to suicide, homicide, and accidental deaths, Murphy and her colleagues followed up parents as long as 5 years after their losses (Murphy, 2006; Murphy, Johnson, & Weber, 2002; Murphy, Johnson, Wu, Fan, & Lohan, 2003). This study generally found that traumatically bereaved parents had higher levels of mental distress and posttraumatic stress disorder (PTSD) than population samples up to 5 years after the death and that it required 3 to 4 years' time before the parents were able to report a "new normal" in their functioning after the death of the child. Another study (Bernstein, 1997) based on a very diverse sample of longer term bereaved parents (that averaged 10 years since their losses) was limited to only 50 cases, and the author wisely refrained from generalizing about bereaved parent adaptations given the relatively small number of cases. In still another study (Talbot, 2002), the author studied 80 bereaved mothers who lost children 5 or more years earlier, but this study did not include bereaved fathers; nor did it include parents who sustained suicide and/or drug-related losses of children. Thus, the question of how traumatically bereaved parents adapt 5 or more years after their losses, and their aftercare needs, still remains a mostly unexamined one in the bereavement literature.

Do bereaved parents continue to seek support services in their later years after loss? What kinds of services do they seek? Does their use of services match their need for grief and psychological support? Do bereaved parents still remain an at-risk population many years after their losses? We will try to shed some light on these questions in this chapter.

Another equally important set of questions pertains to the identification of the correlates associated with survivors' longer term post-loss adaptations. What factors are associated with bereaved parents who are experiencing more severe grief and psychological problems, years after the deaths of their children, compared to those who are less troubled by grief and psychological problems?

Let us begin this inquiry by looking at two contrasting cases that help to understand the range of grief and psychological difficulties among longer term bereaved parents. The two examples we present immediately suggest one important point along which longer term bereaved parents may diverge in their bereavement pathways: marital stability. We distinguish between those parents who remain married after their loss (and who in many cases may strengthen their marital bonds) from others whose marriages may have buckled under the strain of the death and who may have experienced marital breakups. These two examples also suggest that differences in posttraumatic growth following the loss may be relevant to explain the differences in bereaved parents' longer term post-loss adaptations. All of the things that we are examining here, differences in grief difficulties, posttraumatic growth, and even marital stabilities can be thought of as being positioned along continuums, with some bereaved parents being situated at higher or lower points along each range than others, rather than as all or none differences.

Evan and Marta Solomon (pseudonyms) lost their 22-year-old son, Michael, 9 years ago. Like many of the suicide-bereaved parents in our sample, Michael died suddenly and unexpectedly, apparently a casualty of undiagnosed depression. Michael was extremely ambitious and perfectionist; he sought a career in medicine to eventually follow in his father's footsteps. When he did not gain acceptances into the top-tier medical schools that he had chosen for himself, he felt extremely ashamed of his failure and could not bring himself to tell his parents about this disappointing outcome. Shortly afterward, he asphyxiated himself by running a family automobile in the enclosed garage at the family home.

After their tragic loss, the parents suffered through years of sadness, regret, and confusion over their son's rashness in taking his life so seemingly impulsively. Immediately after the loss, Evan and Marta found comfort and support from family and closest friends. Some of Evan's professional colleagues, however, treated the death with extreme avoidance and insisted on remaining silent about Michael's life and death. During the early months after the loss, the couple found helpful support from a counselor who offered them a few sessions. Later on, the couple became active in The Compassionate Friends chapter, and their participation offered them much comfort and help with their grief. Eventually, they were asked to cofacilitate this group when the previous facilitator retired and moved to Florida. Beside their TCF group, the Solomons subsequently decided to start their own survivor of suicide (SOS) peer support group after taking a facilitator training course. The couple also became active in SPAN (Suicide Prevention Action Network, USA) and AAS (American Association of Suicidology), attended yearly meetings, spoke out at conference meetings, and were given committee assignments in light of their active participation.

Seven years after the loss, Evan and Marta felt Michael's death had brought them much closer together than ever before. They felt that their activism in suicide bereavement was a good thing and that it helped to positively memorialize Michael. Although they missed Michael greatly at times, they did not have the same depression and feelings of moroseness they experienced during the early years after loss. They felt their loss opened the door for them to help others and change outmoded and stigmatizing views of suicide and mental illness.

Two years later, they reported that their SOS support group eventually disbanded, owing to a declining membership. They also turned the leadership of their TCF group over to another capable and compassionate bereaved parent who was ready to assume the facilitator role. Although they remained committed to advocacy to change conventional views about suicide and mental health, they decided to withdraw from AAS and SPAN, complaining that these organizations were riddled with petty political rivalries. At this same time, the couple found a new interest to pursue: combating illiteracy. Evan said there was a compelling need to help foreign-born families in their community learn English and acquire reading and literacy skills. Now, both he and Marta teach reading skills in their community, 2 days a week. Their new goal coincides better with Evan's recent retirement from his medical practice and with the couple's other goals to travel and make occasional visits to their other children and grandchildren. Although Evan and Marta shifted their allegiances to different projects over time, it appears they are still deeply invested into helping others.

Eight years ago, Jeffrey Sherwood (pseudonym) lost his 22-year-old son, Will, after he took a lethal dose of his psychotropic medications. From Will's teenage years onward, when he was first diagnosed with severe depression and suicide risk, he was in and out of different mental health clinics and treatment facilities. During quiescent periods of his illness, Will, an intellectually gifted student, functioned well in high school. At other times, unfortunately, his illness resulted in excessive absenteeism, school suspensions for drug use, failing grades, and eventual withdrawal from school. He did, however, manage to finish high school with a general educational development (GED) diploma.

Jeffrey had to acknowledge he was totally dumbstruck by his son's drug death. When Will was stable, both father and son had been the closest of friends. They went hunting and fishing together, were avid sports fans, could talk endlessly into the night about politics, technology, movies, and anything else of common interest. Although Will seemed to be somewhat uncertain about his future after getting his GED, his family members were hopeful that with the right psychotropic drugs, he could function acceptably in society and perhaps live a long and productive life. Treatment professionals thought, at that time, it would be best for the family if Will had his own apartment near the clinic and job training center he attended.

There were no immediate warning signs before Will's death of his impending demise. After he died, it was discovered that Will seemed to have wanted to die. He had accumulated and consumed a lethal dose of his medications and was found dead in his apartment, after failing to appear at a job-training workshop.

Afterward, the family, consisting of Jeffrey, his wife Victoria, and their three other teenage children, experienced deeply agonizing grief over Will's death. As he passed the 2-year post-loss mark, Jeffrey still couldn't stop blaming himself for not getting Will into one of the country's better treatment facilities. Of all family members, Jeffrey was the most immobilized by the loss and took a long leave of absence from his job as a traveling salesman.

Several years later, Jeffrey was still deeply mired in the loss experience. He had written poetry and essays, some of which were published in an anthology of bereaved-parent memoirs. Although he had gotten past the deep yearning for his son and the sense of meaninglessness that he initially felt after the death, he still felt depressed most of the time and had an almost insatiable need to talk about Will, probing the question of why he took his life. His wife, Victoria, spurned these discussions. Neither parent had used much grief counseling nor had joined a support group. Jeffrey attended healing conferences with regularity on his own, where he met with a number of other drug-death survivors, received comfort from speaking informally with healing professionals, and found it very helpful to be around other survivors.

Six years after the loss and much to Jeffrey's great surprise, Victoria, his wife of 25 years, suddenly announced that she wanted a divorce. She accused Jeffrey of polluting her memories of their son by the incessant review of his life. He pleaded with her to stay together, but this was unsuccessful; there was no period of separation, and the divorce took place very soon thereafter. When Jeffrey was interviewed 2 years after his wife's departure, he still felt very sad and distraught about the breakup. He felt part of his current malaise was related to this additional loss.

These contrasting case studies strikingly show diverging patterns of how married couples respond to one another after the loss of a child. In Chapter 13, we will investigate this question of couple's post-loss adaptations in greater detail. Now, however, it should be clear that in some cases like the Sherwoods, when a couple does not experience the loss in compatible ways, marital difficulties can add to their burdens of grief and psychological difficulties. In Jeffrey Sherwood's estimation, his grief difficulties were worsened after his marital breakup. For other bereaved parents, the chain of causality may run in an opposite direction, from first experiencing personal bereavement difficulties to eventually having marital conflicts.

INVESTIGATING THE CORRELATES OF GRIEF AND PSYCHOLOGICAL DIFFICULTIES AMONG LONGER TERM BEREAVED PARENTS

In Table 7.1, we show the differences in grief and psychological adjustment difficulties among longer term bereaved parents who reported marital separations in the years that followed their loss and those who did not. Only 10% of longer term bereaved married respondents in our sample reported separating during the years after the deaths of their children. The table shows significantly higher grief and psychological adjustment difficulties for those who reported marital separations since the death, compared to those who did not. Table 7.1 shows a significantly higher mean of 42 for the separated or divorced bereaved parents on their grief difficulties scores, compared to 35 for those who remained married. It also shows a significantly higher mean psychological difficulties score of 2.1 for the separated, compared to those who remained married, with a mean of 1.11. These comparisons were based on the small group of 24 respondents (10% of all longer term bereaved parents) who reported separating or divorcing since their children's deaths, compared to the larger group of parents who reported having intact marriages ($n = 202$).

We also expected that longer term bereaved parents who reported being divorced, separated, or never married at the time of our survey would show higher grief and psychological adjustment difficulties than currently married or widowed. We anticipated that having a marital partner would generally help one endure the agonies and burdens of grief after the loss of a child. When we examined the means on various psychological adjustment criteria for widowed

Table 7.1
Differences in Grief, Psychological Difficulties, and Marital Differences Among Longer Term Bereaved Parents, $N = 242$

	MEAN/N			
	MEAN GEQ SCORE	**SIG.**	**MEAN PSYCH. PROBLEMS SCALE**	**SIG.**
Couple separated since the loss	41.6/22	.001	2.1/24	.001
Did not separate	34.6/192		1.11/202	
Currently married or widowed	34.2/181	.003	1.04/189	.001
Divorced, separated, or never married	39.6/48		1.73/53	

Note. GEQ = Grief Experience Questionnaire. From Survivors Child Loss Survey, 2006–2009.

respondents, we found that the patterns for this subgroup showed more similarity to the patterns of married parents than they did to those for the divorced or separated. When we consider the previous research, demonstrating that widowed women find more readily available social supports than the divorced, this suggests that widowed parents (the mothers at least) may find it easier to gain grief help from their significant others, such as their children, siblings, and other relatives, than the divorced or separated may experience (Kitson, Lopata, Holmes, & Meyering, 1980). Table 7.1 shows significantly higher grief and psychological difficulties for the presently divorced-, separated-, and never married-bereaved parents, ($n = 53$), with a mean of 40 on grief difficulties and 1.73 on psychological problems, compared to means of 34 and 1.04 respectively, for the married- and widowed-bereaved parents ($n = 189$).

As we contrast Jeffrey Sherwood with either of the Solomons, we observe big differences between the cases regarding helping others and assuming roles of support group leadership. Jeffrey Sherwood appeared to be stuck in his quest to gain more information and understanding about his son's death, whereas both Solomons apparently had moved beyond this quest and were trying to "make a difference" and promote various social changes. We call this activism posttraumatic or personal growth (Calhoun & Tedeschi, 2006; Tedeschi & Calhoun, 2008), and we will explore this characteristic in greater detail in Chapter 10. We administered a personal growth scale to our respondents (Hogan, Greenfield, & Schmidt, 2001) and anticipated that those showing evidence of higher personal growth would have fewer grief and other psychological difficulties compared to the respondents that showed less evidence of this. The correlation matrix presented in Table 7.2 shows significant inverse correlations between personal growth and both grief and psychological adjustment difficulties. The table indicates that growth scores correlate $-.27$ with grief difficulties and $-.34$ with psychological difficulties among the longer term bereaved ($p < .001$ for both), confirming our expectation that higher levels of reported personal growth are associated with lower levels of grief difficulties.

In previous chapters, we suggested a number of other correlates associated with differences in grief and psychological difficulties: whether the death was seen as "blameworthy" death (such as a suicide or drug-overdose death might be) compared to one that was not (such as a general accidental death or one from natural causes); the degree of a respondent's religious activism (we asked respondents to describe their frequency of religious participation on a 7-point scale ranging from *never* during the past year to *more than weekly*); gender; the time since the loss; and a respondent's exposure to stigmatization. It seemed plausible to investigate these factors again as potential correlates to grief and psychological problem differences among the longer term bereaved parents.

The matrix in Table 7.2 investigated whether longer term bereaved parents who lost children to drugs and suicide would harbor significantly higher grief and psychological difficulties than parents whose children died from other

Table 7.2
Correlation Matrix of Various Potential Correlates to Grief
and Psychological Adjustment Problems Among Longer Term Bereaved Parents, *N* = 243

| | CORRELATION COEFFICIENT/SIGNIFICANCE LEVEL | | | | | | | |
	GRIEF DIFFS.	PSYCH. DIFFS.	MARITAL DIFFS.	PERSONAL GROWTH	TYPE OF DEATH	RELIG. ACTIV.	TIME FROM LOSS	STIGMA SCORE
Psych. diffs.	0.55***							
Marital diffs.	0.19**	0.24***						
Personal growth	−0.27***	−0.34***	−0.15*					
Type of death	0.30***	0.20**	0.01	0.14*				
Relig. activism	−0.16*	−0.26***	−0.15*	0.31***	−0.01			
Time from loss	−0.24***	−0.29***	−0.05	0.08	−0.28***	0.07		
Stigma score	0.43***	0.39***	0.14*	−0.10	0.15*	−0.10	−0.11	
Gender	0.23***	0.11	0.11	0.01	−0.05	0.03	0.01	0.06

Note. From Survivors Child Loss Survey, 2006–2009.
*$p < .05$. **$p < .01$. ***$p < .001$.

accidents and natural causes. We counted the values for a death as follows: (0) for an accidental and natural death and (1) for drug and suicide death, what we have termed a "blameworthy death." Then we correlated this with grief and psychological problems. The table showed significant associations with .30 for grief difficulties and .20 for psychological problems on this contrast, thus indicating that drug and suicide deaths were associated with more grief and psychological problems. Religious activism showed an inverse association of −.16 with grief and −.26 with psychological difficulties. Gender showed a .23 correlation with grief difficulties and a .11 correlation, with psychological problems with women showing higher scores than men. (A male was defined as a "0" for the correlation, and a female was defined as a "1," thus yielding positive associations with grief and psychological problems.) Time since loss was also significantly correlated inversely with grief at −.24 and −.29 with psychological difficulties. Lastly, fluctuations in stigma scores showed a correlation of .43 with grief difficulties and .39 with psychological difficulties. Thus, all correlates of differences in grief and psychological difficulties identified in previous chapters also held when we looked specifically at the subsample of longer term bereaved parents.

Tables 7.3 and 7.4 present multiple regression equations for each of these two difficulties criteria showing any redundancies of correlated factors that are associated with the dependent variables. Of all the variability in grief

Table 7.3
Multiple Regression of Differences in Grief Difficulties (GEQ Scores) by Various Potential Correlates Among Longer Term Bereaved Parents, *N* = 243

		Number of obs	= 184
		$F(7, 176)$	= 11.15
		R^2	= .31

INDEPENDENT VARIABLES	CORREL. COEFF.	BETA	*P*
Marital diffs.	.19	.05	.41
Growth score	−.27	−.26	.001
Type of death	.30	.19	.005
Relig. activism	−.16	−.01	.84
Time since loss	−.24	−.02	.77
Stigma score	.43	.31	.001
Gender	.23	.21	.001

Note. P = Level of Significance. From Survivors Child Loss Survey, 2006–2009.

difficulties, 31% was explained by this seven-variable model, with only four factors significantly associated. Marital differences, religious activism, and time since the loss did not contribute significantly in this seven-variable model. The four remaining significant predictors were differences in personal growth, gender, the type of death, and differences in stigmatization. Table 7.4 showed that this predictor model did a similar job of explaining the variability in psychological problems, accounting for 33% of all variability in the dimension of psychological difficulty. In this model, personal growth, time since the loss, and differences in exposure to stigma were the most significant predictors. Both models showed persisting stigmatization as the single most significant correlate to both these predictions. This result was fully consistent with the

Table 7.4
Multiple Regression of Differences in Psychological Difficulties by Various Potential Correlates Among Longer Term Bereaved Parents, *N* = 243

		Number of obs	= 192
		$F(7, 176)$	= 13.08
		R^2	= .33

INDEPENDENT VARIABLES	CORREL. COEFF.	BETA	*p*
Marital diffs.	.24	.10	.11
Growth score	−.34	−.27	.001
Type of death	.20	.12	.07
Relig. activism	−.26	−.11	.09
Time since loss	−.29	−.14	.02
Stigma score	.39	.31	.001
Gender	.11	.11	.08

Note. p = Level of Significance. From Survivors Child Loss Survey, 2006–2009.

correlation matrix data. In our data, the regression equations show marital differences and religious activism as redundant to explaining differences in grief and psychological problems among longer term bereaved parents in a multicausal conceptualization. Differences in stigma, personal growth, time since the loss (in the case of psychological difficulties), and gender and the type of death (in the case of grief difficulties) were significant correlates in multicausal schemes.

Some of our interview data and comments offered on survey forms were consistent with these findings on the importance of stigmatization among the longer term bereaved parents. Harriet Rubinsky (a pseudonym) offered these comments, confirming the survey findings. She said,

> My family has been a mixed blessing to me during all the years (presently 8) since Jonathan's death. On the plus side, my younger sister has always been there for me. To give you some idea of the help she has been to me, just last week I got an e-mail from her that was very typical of her helpfulness. She wrote that she experienced feelings of panic as her son was leaving to go back to college after his long winter vacation break. Then she thought of me, and she thought how terrible I must be feeling facing the prospect of never, ever seeing my son again. Tears came to my eyes when I read her note. I know that she never forgets how I occasionally struggle with the loss. Then, there is my older sister, who is another story, a night-and-day contrast. I don't know if she understands anything about grief. We used to be close, but now there seems to be a gulf between us. Whenever I start to say something about remembering Jonathan, she usually changes the subject. My younger sister remembers significant dates, Jonathan's birthday, and the death anniversary. She calls me to see how I'm doing on those dates. But my older sister ignores these painful milestones unless my younger sister "reminds" her. My older sister and I have drifted apart since Jonathan's death. It is almost as if I lost two people with Jonathan, him and my older sister. It's very sad.

Marge Paulson (a pseudonym) said that her mother's persistent attacks about her poor parenting skills and other criticisms have led her to keep her contacts with her mother to an absolute minimum in the 6 years since her son's drug-overdose death. Marge said her mother has been unsparing in her criticism of her for not trying hard enough to keep her marriage together, for having her own drug problem (which Marge claimed she never had), and for not looking around far enough to find a better rehab program for Joey (her deceased son). Marge also remarked that her two brothers always appeared to be the favored offspring, whereas she often was given the "Cinderella" treatment. "Over the years since Joey died, my mother has kept on harping about how, despite her own economic handicaps and being a single divorced mother, she managed to raise three healthy and successful children, while I couldn't even raise one. When I hear things like that, I have to keep my distance."

Bob and Madeline Cranshaw always had a close relationship with long-time friends Jennie and Mike Timlin (pseudonyms), for almost as long as they could remember. The men were former fraternity brothers, and both couples married around the same time and had two children of approximately similar ages. They shared many commonalities around having their children grow up at about the same times. When Jennie and Mike suddenly lost Evan, their 22-year-old son, to a gunshot suicide, their relationship with the Cranshaws suddenly changed and weakened considerably. Although Bob and Madeline attended their friends' son's funeral and expressed appropriate condolences, they felt the need to pull back from their former close friends. They even confided to the Timlins that Jonathan's death made them feel very nervous, and they were afraid their son Jeremy, who had a history of his own depression and teenage drug use and treatment, might be influenced by Evan's suicide. Years passed, and the couples eventually reconnected again, 5 years after the death, at a mutual friend's party. The Cranshaws asked the Timlins how they were doing. The Timlins mentioned they were doing okay at that time, about as well as they might have hoped for. Both were attending a support group; both went to monthly meetings regularly and shared the job of being the newsletter editor for their group. When this information was shared, Bob expressed surprise and said, "Maybe these activities pull you down? Why don't you two do something fun, like go out dancing or something like that, doing something to lift your spirits? And when do you think you will be moving on?" After Mike explained how they expected their grief to be a lifelong experience, it was clear that Jennie and Mike had a different understanding of bereavement after the death of a child. Their reconciliation was not realistic, as their formerly close friendship appeared to have reached its limit, and the couples went their separate ways.

Our qualitative data contain many similar examples of social disconnection following the loss of a child. It is also interesting to note there were no associations between experienced stigma and time since the loss. Experienced stigma was almost as commonly reported among newly bereaved parents as it was among the longer term bereaved.

Although the previous research annals have not investigated whether heightened stigma and grief difficulties are more common among longer term drug-overdose-bereaved and suicide-bereaved parents, past findings are consistent with our data. Kay Talbot's (2002) survey of 80 longer term bereaved mothers showed concurrence. Although her sample embraced a diverging population of natural- and accidental-death surviving parents, she found that mothers who expressed higher levels of grief distress more often reported inadequate support and criticism from family and friends, compared to the less distressed parents, who reported more offers of help from friends and families. Consistent with our findings on the importance of posttraumatic growth, Talbot also found evidence that those displaying more adaptive responses and less grief distress were more likely to report greater participation in support groups, were more likely to be helping other bereaved parents, and feeling better about themselves as a result of the help they offered to others. Many of the growth-inclined bereaved also stated that they found and created new meaning and purpose in life, whereas those that experienced more intense grief distress did not report feeling this way.

Another study from Sweden, following up 449 parents that had lost children to cancer, 4 to 9 years previously, also showed consistency with our findings (Kriecbergs, Lannen, Onelov, & Wolfe, 2007). The authors found that parents reporting that they had shared with others the emotional problems related to their child's illness and death were more likely to report "working through their grief," compared with those who did not report doing this. The study also showed that parents who reported that they talked often to their spouses, families, and friends about their grief difficulties experienced less grief distress and more often reported working through their grief. A Canadian study of 20 bereaved parents who lost children to natural and general accidental death causes also reported concurrence (Barrera et al., 2007). The authors reported that among the parents who reported "integrated grief," a less complicated response than those who experienced being "consumed by grief" or "minimal grief," there were also reports of greater support from friends and family. This study tracked its respondents up to 19 months after their losses. Thus, convergent with our findings, there appears to be evidence from previous research on longer term parental grief for the importance of good social support and connection.

BEREAVED PARENTS' USE OF HEALING AIDS IN LATER YEARS AFTER LOSS, THEIR POSTVENTION NEEDS, AND EXAMINING WHETHER THEY COMPRISE AN AT-RISK POPULATION

Let us now turn our attention to another set of questions that we posed to gauge the longer term grief and mental health aftercare needs of bereaved parents. What are the longer term grief and mental health needs of parents? Just as Chapter 6 outlined the diminishing levels of grief and psychological problems bereaved parents experienced over the first 7 years after their loss, in this chapter we extend this analysis to cover the entire range of the post-loss years experienced by our 575 surveyed bereaved parents, as long as 27 years after the death. Table 7.5 divides the sample into three groups: those sustaining losses of children less than 5 years earlier ($n = 319$ parents); middle term bereaved parents, whose losses occurred between 5 and 9.9 years earlier ($n = 149$ parents); and longer term bereaved parents, whose losses occurred 10 or more years previously ($n = 94$ parents).

The table shows bereaved parents' use of healing aids during the past year. General bereavement and SOS support groups were shown as the most popular healing aids, with over half of all parents using these resources during early bereavement years. As time after a loss passes, the use of general bereavement groups appears to remain stable and declines from close to 60% of

Table 7.5

Frequencies of Using Different Bereavement Treatments During the Past Year Among Shorter and Longer Term Bereaved Parents (*N* = 575)

	<= 4.9 YEARS (*n* = 319) %/*n*	5–9.99 YEARS (*n* = 149) %/*n*	10 OR MORE YEARS (*n* = 94) %/*n*	χ^2 *p* VALUE
Sought help from general bereavement group				
Never	45.3/143	54.4/80	48.9/46	.18
Once or more	54.8/173	45.6/67	51.1/48	
Sought help from suicide survivors support group **(Only among suicide survivors, *n* = 434)**				
Never	42.7/105	59.0/72	54.6/36	.008
Once or more	57.3/141	41.0/50	45.4/30	
Sought help from professional bereavement counselor				
Never	68.5/215	80.6/116	91.1/82	.0001
Once or more	31.5/99	19.4/28	9.9/8	
Sought help from psychiatrist/psychologist/social worker				
Never	56.9/178	76.2/112	85.9/79	.0001
Once or more	43.1/135	23.8/35	14.1/13	
Sought help from a member of the clergy				
Never	73.4/229	79.9/115	82.0/73	.13
Once or more	26.6/83	20.1/29	18.0/16	
Sought help from psychic or spiritualist				
Never	72.5/227	87.6/127	93.0/80	.0001
Once or more	27.5/86	12.4/18	7.0/6	

Note. From Survivors Child Loss Survey, 2006–2009.

all suicide-bereaved parents using SOS groups during their early bereavement period to approximately 40% to 45% thereafter. We cannot be sure whether these trends reflect actual usage patterns in the larger sample of all bereaved parents or whether they are by-products of our particular data collection method: drawing our sample primarily from the ranks of support group members. Our participant observation data, collected from approximately 200 suicide bereaved in survivor support groups, showed declines in participation in parents who were further out in time from their loss. We discuss this pattern at length in Chapter 9, where we discuss some of the numerous reasons why many longer term bereaved parents withdraw from SOS support groups, after feeling they passed their period of acute grief distress.

Use of mental health professionals peaks at between 30% and 40% of bereaved parents visiting them during the first 5 years after a loss, then shrinks to the 20% range among bereaved parents who were 5 to 10 years past their loss, and ultimately shrinks to the 10% to 15% range thereafter. Only about a quarter of all bereaved parents used clergy help during early bereavement years, and this did not change very much with groups that were temporally further from their loss. The interest in psychics and spiritualists peaks at close to 30% using them during early bereavement years, and then drops off to the 10% range thereafter for parents who were in their later years after loss. It is interesting to note that the fee-for-service bereavement resources—mental health and bereavement professionals and psychics—show declining use as time after a loss passes, whereas freely offered services, such as support groups or clergy help, show more consistent use over time.

Table 7.6 shows the grief and mental health problems among different respondents at different time points after a loss. The table shows a consistent trend toward improved mental health taking place over time on all included dimensions of grief and mental health problems. The three criteria of grief difficulties—the Grief Experience Questionnaire, the Complicated Grief scale,

Table 7.6
Differences in Grief Difficulties and Mental Health Problems by Time Since Loss Among All Bereaved Parents (*N* = 575)

	<= 4.9 YEARS (*n* = 319) %/*n*	5–9.99 YEARS (*n* = 149) %/*n*	10 OR MORE YEARS (*n* = 94) %/*n*	χ^2 OR *F* *p* VALUE
GEQ Mean Score	42.2/292	37.2/137	32.8/84	.0001
Complicated Grief mean score	30.1/302	26.6/144	22.5/84	.0001
Impact of Event mean score	35.6/291	32.9/140	26.3/80	.0001
Rating your mental health				
Poor/fair	56.9/173	40.7/55	18.2/16	.0001
Good	30.9/94	26.7/36	39.8/35	
Very good/excellent	12.2/37	32.6/44	42.1/37	
Past year reported depression				
Yes	77.0/245	63.1/94	40.9/38	.0001
No	23.0/73	36.9/55	59.1/55	
Past year suicide thoughts				
Rarely or more frequently	48.9/155	28.6/42	17.8/16	.0001
Never	51.1/162	71.4/105	82.2/74	
Had suicide plan during past year				
Yes	14.2/45	7.6/11	2.2/2	.002
No	85.8/271	92.4/134	97.8/88	
Attempted suicide during past year				
Yes	2.6/8	.7/1	0.0/0	.142
No	97.4/305	99.3/144	100.0/89	
Number of days in past month was unable to work or do household chores because of mental problems				
One or more	27.9/73	14.1/21	5.3/5	.0001
None	77.1/246	85.9/128	94.7/89	

Note. From Survivors Child Loss Survey, 2006–2009.

diminished grief problems for sur-
ath of their child. The mean GEQ
y loss period, to a mean of 37 for the
ean of 33 for those 10 or more years
grief and posttraumatic stress fol-
The mean changes—in GEQ scores,
ct of Event Scale scores—all were
sis of variance (ANOVA) tests. Post
t-, mid-, and long-term range scores
other on these three dimensions.
s in mental health self-reports over
their own mental health at differ-
s of all bereaved parents reported
the early loss years; this percentage
gh 9.9 after their loss, and down to
. Self-reported depression dropped
reporting themselves as depressed
, giving similar reports 10 years or
ts reported having suicide thoughts
s, compared to only about 30% dur-
during the late post-loss interval.
a high of 14% down to 2% for 10 or
oss. The paucity of suicide attempt
when all three time-period groups
reports of days lost from work or
lth problems, over a quarter of all
orts, compared to only 5% among
ir loss.
ereaved parents (of less than 5 years
iddle-term loss year subgroup (of
nificant with the chi-square statistic.
reen the midrange loss group and
statistically significant differences
, suicide thoughts with a difference
where the chi-square *p* value was
equal to .08. These overall trends suggest that the diagram for suicide survivors presented in Chapter 4 depicting the steepest declines in grief and mental
health difficulties taking place during the first 4 to 5 post-loss years and more
gradual declines taking place in the later years may well be the pattern for all
the mental health variables shown in this table. Stated differently, the general
trend is for people's grief distress and mental health to improve after the loss
of a child.

   Another vitally important question needing to be assessed concerns how
bereaved parents compare with other adults in the general population who
have not experienced the loss of a child. Do longer term bereaved parents

show greater mental health difficulties than their same age and gender counterparts who have not had this experience? We found only one previous study
that has examined this question. It compared a sample of 173 bereaved parents
to homicide, suicide, and accidental death losses who were contrasted with
nonbereaved parents. The study measured respondents at a 5-year post-loss
point (Murphy et al., 1999). They concluded, "Although 70% of the respondents indicated that it took 3 or 4 years to put their child's death into perspective and get on with their lives, it is interesting to note that 5 years after the
deaths, parents' reports on objective measures of mental distress and trauma
are two to three times higher than scores obtained from normative samples of
adults in the same age range" (Murphy et al., 2003, p. 55). Presently, as we extend our time line beyond the 5-year mark, we will compare and contrast the
mental health differences of bereaved parents and their nonbereaved counterparts years beyond this somewhat early bereavement measurement point.

As we aimed to contrast our respondents to their comparable peers in the
general population, we selected mental health status and suicidality questions
that appeared in nationally representative surveys. Our questions matched
the suicidality questions that appeared in the National Comorbidity Survey
Replication (NCS-R), 2001–2003, $N = 9,282$ (Kessler, Berglund, Borges, Nock,
& Wang, 2005). The items read as follows: Suicide thoughts: Have you seriously thought of committing suicide at any time in the past 12 months? (1) yes,
(2) no. Suicide plans: Did you make a plan for committing suicide at any time
in the past 12 months? (1) yes, (2) no. Attempted suicide: Have you attempted
suicide in the past 12 months? (1) yes, (2) no (Kessler et al., 2005, p. 253).

The mental health status items we employed were the same questions that
appeared in the National Survey of Midlife Development in the United States
(MIDUS), 1995–1996, $N = 7,108$ (Brim et al., 1998). The measure of depression
was as follows: "During the past year, was there ever a time when you felt
sad, blue, or depressed for two weeks or more in a row? (1) yes, (2) no, (3) not
depressed because of antidepressant medication"(Brim et al., 1998, p. 26). The
question for self-rated mental health was as follows: "How would you rate
your mental health? (1) poor, (2) fair, (3) good, (4) very good, (5) excellent"
(Brim et al., 1998, p. 9). Days lost in the last month to mental health problems
question was as follows: "How many days in the past month were you unable
to work or do household chores because of mental problems?" (Brim et al.,
1998, p.10).

Table 7.7 displays the results of contrasting mental health and suicidality
differences between a combined group of our 5 through 9.9 years-after-loss
suicide survivor respondents and 10-or-more-years-after-loss survivors with
nationally representative samples of their peers who did not sustain losses
of children. We accessed the archival datasets of the MIDUS (ICPSR # 2760)
from the Inter-University Consortium for Social and Political Research (www.
icprsr.umich.edu) and the National Comorbidity Survey Replication (NCS-R),
presently available from a different website, Collaborative Psychiatric

Table 7.7

Comparing Longer Term Bereaved Parents With Their Demographically Matched Peers From Representative Surveys of Nonbereaved U.S. Adults on Mental Health Difficulties

	LONGER-TERM BEREAVED PARENTS, 5 OR MORE YEARS POST-LOSS++		REPRESENTATIVE SAMPLES OF NONBEREAVED ADULTS (AGES 46–99)	
	FATHERS	MOTHERS	MEN	WOMEN
Rating your mental health				
Poor/fair	14.3/5	34.0/67	3.9/14	9.2/45*
Good	31.4/11	32.5/64	34.1/124	29.2/142
Very good/excellent	54.3/19	33.5/66	62.1/226	61.5/299
Past year reported depression				
Yes	43.6/17	56.9/123	18.1/66	25.5/123*
No	56.4/22	43.1/93	81.9/298	74.5/360
Past year suicide thoughts				
Rarely or >	74.4/29	76.3/161	17.8/29	12.1/35+
Never	25.6/10	23.7/50	82.2/134	87.9/255
Had suicide plan during past year				
Yes	0.0/0	6.6/14	9.5/4	6.2/6+
No	100.0/39	93.4/198	90.5/38	93.8/128
Attempted suicide past year				
Yes	0.0/0	.5/1	6.7/2	3.5/3+
No	100.0/39	99.4/207	93.3/28	96.5/82
Number of days past month unable to work or do home chores because of mental problems				
One or more	5.1/2	12.0/26	7.2/2	10.9/5*
None	94.9/37	88.0/191	92.3/26	89.1/41

*Midlife Development in the U.S. Survey, (2005). *Psychological experiences follow-up study, 1998.* Ann Arbor, MI: Inter-University Consortium for Social Political Research.
+National Comorbidity Replication Survey (NCS-R), 2001–2003, R. Kessler, Harvard Med. School, Dept. Health Care Policy, data available from Ann Arbor, MI: Inter-University Consortium for Social Political Research, 2007.
++Survivors Child Loss Survey, 2006–2009.

Epidemiology Surveys (www.icpsr.umich.edu/icpsrweb/CPES), where the very same questions were asked to representative samples of U.S. adults that we presented to our respondents.

Having observed gender differences in the grief and mental health problems among our respondents, we made gender-specific comparisons of our sample's men and women to their same-aged, nonbereaved counterparts in the population at large. In our sample, there were 39 bereaved fathers and 217 bereaved mothers who had sustained losses of children 5 or more years earlier. The MIDUS survey was based on a telephone-based representative sample of 7,108 respondents between 25 and 74 years of age. We confined our comparisons to those aged 46 to 74 years, who represented approximately 90% of the age range of our respondents. We employed the SDA (Survey Documentation and Analysis) online survey analysis tool accessing the data to explore our questions of research interest. We did not apply the survey weights to this analysis; applying the weights would have produced slightly lower estimations of the frequencies for the variables of interest. The National Comorbidity Survey Replication (NCS-R) was based on 9,282 adults, from a nationally representative household survey collected during 2001 and 2003. Again, this data analysis was completed with the SDA online data analysis software, without the survey weights for the 46-year-old and older respondents. As explained, weighting these data would have generated more conservative estimations of the variables of interest.

Table 7.7 shows sharply contrasting mental health status reports for our respondents, compared to their demographic peers in the general population. Comparing our bereaved fathers to their same age counterparts in the population at large showed 3 times more who regarded their mental health as poor or fair (14% as compared to 4%), twice as many reporting themselves as depressed (44% as compared to 18%), and more than 3 times as many reporting suicide thoughts during the previous year (74% as compared to 19%). For the bereaved mothers, it was much the same story, a 3 times greater number reported their mental health as poor (34% as compared to 9%) twice as many reported themselves as depressed (57% as compared to 26%), and 6 times as many reported the presence of suicide thoughts (76% as compared to 18%). All of these six sets of differences were significant with the chi-square test. Chi-square tests did not show significant differences between bereaved fathers and mothers and their same-gender nonbereaved peers in making suicide plans, in suicide attempts, and in missing days from work because of mental health problems.

With only 18 cases of 10-year-or-longer post-loss bereaved fathers, we were especially cautious before making comparisons among these fathers and their nonbereaved peers. The data showed no statistically significant differences comparing these fathers and their same-aged nonbereaved counterparts in the general population in viewing their mental health as poor. None of the 10-year-plus post-loss fathers reported poor mental health compared to 4% for the control population. Yet, significantly, more of the bereaved fathers (39%) reported themselves as depressed, compared to only 18% for the non-bereaved older men ($p < .03$). Then, equivalent numbers of both groups (22%) for the bereaved fathers reported harboring occasional or more frequent suicide thoughts, which compared to 18% for the nonbereaved males.

With the 85 bereaved mothers, we also examined whether their poorer mental health assessments, greater depression, and suicide thoughts would persist when we reexamined these differences between our respondents and their same-aged nonbereaved peers at an interval of 10 years or more since their loss. Here, given the greater number of women in the sample, we can speak more confidently of the contrasting differences. Among 10-years-or-longer bereaved mothers, 21% reported their mental health as poor, compared to 9% for the nonbereaved, a difference that was significant with the chi-square test. Similarly, 44% of 10-years-or-more bereaved mothers reported themselves as depressed, which compared to 26% for the nonbereaved—another difference that was significant with the chi-square statistical test. However, an examination of suicide thoughts for these 10-years-or-more mothers showed no significant differences, 17% as compared to 18%. Thus, 10 years after the loss, some disparity still remains in feelings of greater depression and poorer mental health assessments among bereaved mothers, when compared to their nonbereaved peers. None of these 10-year-or-longer comparisons are presented in our tables. As we take stock of the overall trends, the differences are very striking, showing longer term bereaved parents at a substantially higher risk for mental health problems and suicidality than the nonbereaved.

These differences bring forward an important next question to ask: What were long-term bereaved parents doing about their mental health problems? Were they getting help from mental health professionals? As we saw in Table 7.5, between 32% and 43% of newly bereaved parents reported seeing a professional bereavement or mental health counselor in the past year, and this number decreased to 26% for those seeing one or another type of professional counselor 5 or more years after their loss. This puts bereaved parents on a par with or slightly above the rates shown for those seeking professional mental health care among the population at large. The 2009 National Survey of Drug Use and Health (NSDUH) showed a gender-differentiated rate of use of 10% for men and 18% for women for those who obtained any mental health services during the past year among the aged 35 and older population in the national sample of over 13,000 respondents (United States Department of Health and Human Services, Substance Abuse and Mental Health Services Administration, & Office of Applied Studies, 2009). We computed these rates from the 2009 NSDUH data set, maintained by the ICPSR archival data collection based on a weighted representative sample of 13,399 (ICPSR, Study #29621, accessed with the SDA online data analysis program, 3/27/11). For our 5-year-or-longer post-loss respondents, 23% of bereaved fathers and 27% of mothers reported seeing any mental health or bereavement professional during the previous year, thus displaying parity or slightly elevated levels of seeking professional mental health care among our respondents.

Table 7.8 shows how longer term bereaved parents used therapists and support groups when they reported different levels of mental health problems. The table suggests a possible underuse of professional therapeutic resources, with 40% or fewer of bereaved fathers and mothers reporting they saw a mental health professional when they reported themselves as depressed or as having poor or fair mental health. Only 25% of bereaved fathers and 50% of bereaved mothers who reported they had suicidal thoughts in the past year said they saw any mental health professionals for help. We examined these same questions with the 2009 NSDUH data. The NSDUH data showed somewhat higher professional mental health use rates for 36 years and older men and women in the general population who reported being depressed or having suicidal thoughts during the past year. The survey found

Table 7.8
Identifying the Mental Health Treatment Needs of Longer Term Bereaved Parents, Five or More Years Since Their Loss (N = 243)

	% THAT SAW A MENTAL HEALTH OR BEREAVEMENT COUNSELOR IN PAST YEAR		% THAT ATTENDED A SUPPORT GROUP IN PAST YEAR	
	%/n			
	FATHERS	MOTHERS	FATHERS	MOTHERS
Reported mental health poor or fair (n = 72)	40.0/2	38.8/26	60.0/3	56.7/38
Reported being depressed two or more weeks (n = 139)	23.5/4	35.3/43	58.8/10	59.4/73
Reported past year suicide thoughts occasionally or more frequently (n = 34)	25.0/1	50.1/15	50.0/2	56.7/17
Had suicide plan during past year (n = 14)	0.0/0	57.1/8	0.0/0	50.0/7
Attempted suicide during past year (n = 1)	0.0/0	100.0/1	0.0/0	100.0/1
Reported one or more days in past month that was unable to work or do home chores because of mental problems (n = 28)	0.0/0	53.9/14	100.0/2	61.5/16

Note. From Survivors Child Loss Survey, 2006–2009.

that 58% of both men and women who reported themselves as depressed saw a mental health professional during the past 12 months. For those who seriously thought about killing themselves in the past year, 49% of men and 59% of women had obtained help from some mental health professional for this problem. With chi-square significance tests, we investigated whether our respondents used professional help any less, compared to others in the general population with these problems. The chi-square test showed our depressed respondents significantly less likely to seek professional help (chi-square [1] = 6.3, p = .01 for males; chi-square [1] = 31.44, p = .0001 for females). Although our respondents with suicide thoughts seemed to be less inclined to seek mental health services than those with similar problems in the general population, the chi-square significance tests did not show significant differences in this respect.

Perhaps differences in the wordings for the questions used in the NSUDH national survey to define depression and the definition we employed may explain some of the disparities we have noted between feeling depressed and seeking professional help among our respondents and their depressed counterparts in the population at large. Another possibility may be that our respondents may be less inclined to use professional help, suggesting that important danger signs of potential psychological problems are being ignored. This could lead some bereaved parents to be vulnerable to their own self-harm, failing to consult with mental health professionals when they should be seeking some professional assistance.

It should also be understood that heightened levels of participation of those with psychological problems in support groups, shown at the 60% level, should be considered no substitute for professional care. Most support groups are run by nonprofessionals who do not profess to provide mental health care. These findings suggest that at a minimum, facilitators should maintain lists of local mental health professionals that work well with bereaved populations, and they should be in a position to make appropriate referrals to local professionals for their distressed members. Facilitators should also avail themselves of training offered to help guide them to better identify and make referrals to survivors who appear to be in crisis.

Another matter that should be mentioned is the increased likelihood of suicidality accompanying increased longevity. It must be remembered that as bereaved persons enter into older age groups, their suicide attempts and other manifestations of suicidality may show higher associations to completed suicides. Previous research has shown ratios of approximately 200:1 for suicide attempts to suicide deaths in young people, but it also shows ratios of 4:1 attempts to deaths for those who are much older (Gardner, Bahn, & Mack, 1964). Thus, differences in manifestations of depression and suicidality for the middle-aged and older bereaved must be taken with utmost seriousness.

We began this chapter with the musings of a 10-year post-loss bereaved father, who was like many longer term survivors who feel grateful they have weathered the storms of early loss with various changes taking place in their lives and in their personalities. Although there is no universal adaptation pattern, most probably acknowledge that the coping process has brought bereaved parents a mixture of both positive and negative outcomes. Surely it has brought many to a realization that they have been deeply wounded and diminished by their loss—one of their dearest treasured children has been permanently lost. For some, seeing themselves as perhaps sadder and more contemplative now or perhaps as more compassionate, caring, and empathic may be part of the mixed bag of changes they have experienced. Many longer term bereaved feel they have accomplished a major grief milestone by accepting their losses, something many never imagined possible when they began their healing journeys. Yet, some still struggle with feelings of profound regret and deep yearning to return to their life before the death occurred.

Most survivors have had to rearrange their lives to find more comfortable places for themselves. Being with people who did not understand their grief, who avoided all references to their deceased child, who urged them to "move on," and who cast nets of blame around either the parent or their deceased child, many survivors have learned they may need to avoid people who espouse such views in the interests of preserving their psychological health and well-being. Our quantitative data evidence seems to be consistent with this conclusion. Bereaved parents are probably best advised to maximize contacts with significant others who offer them compassion and support and who thus contribute to their feelings of psychological well-being.

Taking stock of the enduring impact of the loss of a child over many years, we have accumulated evidence showing that this experience has left some bereaved parents vulnerable with elevated levels of depression and suicidality when compared with population norms. Also, it seems that as a group, long-term bereaved parents appear to be somewhat underrepresented in seeking professional care when compared to their counterparts in the general population who are currently troubled by feelings of depression. Chronically depressed bereaved parents should be seeking professional help to find the appropriate psychotherapeutic help and/or psychotropic medications to combat depression and improve overall mental health. Our findings, of course, await further confirmation in representative surveys of bereaved parents in the population at large since our sample has been drawn from volunteers in the support group community, who may or may not be typical of other bereaved parents who do not attend these groups.

REFERENCES

Barrera, M., D'Agostino, N. M., Schneiderman, G., Tallett, S., Spencer, L., & Jovcevska, V. (2007). Patterns of parental bereavement following the loss of a child and related factors. *Omega (Westport)*, 55(2), 145–167.

Bernstein, J. R. (1997). *When the bough breaks: Forever after the death of a son or daughter.* Kansas City, MO: Andrews McMeel.

Brim, O. G., Baltes, P. B., Bumpass, L. L., Cleary, P. D., Featherman, D. L., Hazzard, W. R., . . . Shweder, R. A. (1998). National Survey of Midlife Development in the United States (MIDUS), 1995–1996. Retrieved from http://www.icpsr.umich.edu. Codebook and archival data available from website: http://dx.doi.org/10.3886/ICPSR02760.v7

Calhoun, L. G., & Tedeschi, R. G. (2006). *Handbook of posttraumatic growth: Research & practice.* Mawah, NJ: Erlbaum.

Gardner, E. A., Bahn, A. K., & Mack, M. (1964). Suicide and psychiatric care in the aging. *Archives of General Psychiatry, 10,* 547–553.

Hogan, N. S., Greenfield, D. B., & Schmidt, L. A. (2001). Development and validation of the Hogan Grief Reaction Checklist. *Death Studies, 25*(1), 1–32.

Kessler, R. C., Berglund, P. A., Borges, G., Nock, M., Wang, P. S. (2005). National Comorbidity Survey Replication (NCS-R), 2001–2003. Codebook and archival data available from ICPSR, Collaborative Psychiatric Epidemiology Surveys website: http://www.icpsr.umich.edu/icpsrweb/CPES/files/ncsr

Kitson, G. C., Lopata, H. Z., Holmes, W. M., & Meyering, S. M. (1980). Divorcees and widows: Similarities and differences. *The American Journal of Orthopsychiatry, 50*(2), 291–301.

Kreicbergs, U. C., Lannen, P., Onelov, E., & Wolfe, J. (2007). Parental grief after losing a child to cancer: Impact of professional and social support on long-term outcomes. *Journal of Clinical Oncology, 25*(22), 3307–3312.

Murphy, S. A. (2006). Evidence-based interventions for parents following their children's violent deaths. In E. K. Rynearson (Ed.), *Violent death: Resilience and intervention beyond the crisis* (pp. 175–194). New York, NY: Routledge/Taylor & Francis Group.

Murphy, S. A., Das Gupta, A., Cain, K. C., Johnson, L. C., Lohan, J., Wu, L., & Mekwa, J. (1999). Changes in parents' mental distress after the violent death of an adolescent or young adult child: A longitudinal prospective analysis. *Death Studies, 23*(2), 129–159.

Murphy, S. A., Johnson, L. C., & Weber, N. A. (2002). Coping strategies following a child's violent death: How parents differ in their responses. *Omega: Journal of Death and Dying, 45*(2), 99–118.

Murphy, S. A., Johnson, L. C., Wu, L., Fan, J. J., & Lohan, J. (2003). Bereaved parents' outcomes 4 to 60 months after their children's deaths by accident, suicide, or homicide: A comparative study demonstrating differences. *Death Studies, 27*(1), 39–61.

Talbot, K. (2002). *What forever means after the death of a child: Transcending the trauma, living with the loss.* New York, NY: Brunner-Routledge.

Tedeschi, R. G., & Calhoun, L. G. (2008). Beyond the concept of recovery: Growth and the experience of loss. *Death Studies, 32*(1), 27–39.

United States Department of Health and Human Services, Substance Abuse and Mental Health Services Administration, & Office of Applied Studies. (2009). National Survey on Drug Use and Health, 2009 [Computer file]. Ann Arbor, MI: Interuniversity Consortium for Political and Social Research. doi:10.3886/ICPSR29621

8

The Healing Potential of Suicide
Survivor Support Groups

INTRODUCTION

In this chapter, we examine suicide survivor support groups from the inside looking out. We apply a method frequently used in anthropology of living with or being with the people being studied. In sociology, this method is known as participant-observation. Because the first and fourth authors had experienced the suicide loss of their son, they were welcomed into a suicide survivors' support group that they then regularly attended for more than 5 years, from 2002 to 2007. From their observations during that time span, we now attempt to present a picture of this group's culture, to explain how group members interacted with each other and to identify how they pursued their mutually perceived goals, namely, to offer one another bereavement support in adapting to the suicide death of a loved one.

For this chapter, all names and personally identifying information about support group members have been changed to preserve their anonymity. Both researchers provided a cross-check on one to another, making sure observations were accurately recorded. Yet, throughout this discussion, wherever necessary, nonessential details of observations and persons have been changed to safeguard each participant's privacy and to maintain confidentiality.

Thus far in our analyses, we have seen bereaved parents seeking help with their multifold bereavement needs from a wide array of caregivers: clergy offering pastoral counseling, psychiatrists, psychologists, psychiatric social workers, psychiatric nurses, other bereavement professionals, psychics, and spiritualists. Many also have sought help by joining support groups.

Support groups can vary in terms of their structures and leadership. Some are peer or professionally facilitated, and some are agency affiliated or free-standing community groups. Some groups, known as closed-format types, operate within fixed-length terms (usually 10–12 weeks that may then be renewed), whereas other groups are open-ended (where the group meets for an indefinite period but at a regular time and place). Closed-format groups, typically, are run by bereavement or mental health professionals, whereas open-format groups are most often run by the bereaved themselves as self-help groups. There may even be hybrid groups that attempt to fuse the distinctive features of both these contrasting types (Jordan, 2011).

Survivor groups may also be further differentiated into single-loss types, such as specifically designated "survivor of suicide" (SOS) groups versus general bereavement support groups, which include survivors from a variety of different death causes (people losing loved ones to accidents, natural causes, illnesses, suicides, and/or homicides). One of the best known (peer-based) general bereavement groups, The Compassionate Friends, is an international organization with chapters in most every major U.S. city, available exclusively for parents who sustained the loss of a child. The Compassionate Friends has the longest history of any self-help bereavement group in the United States. Founded in Great Britain in 1969, the earliest U.S. chapters began to appear as early as 1972. Now, chapters have formed in 30 different countries in addition to its many U.S. chapters. Many parents bereaved by suicide find grief support in The Compassionate Friends groups.

Yet, some suicide survivors attending generalized bereavement groups such as The Compassionate Friends report feeling different from other grievers and tend to drop out of these groups (Dunne, McIntosh, & Dunne-Maxim, 1987). Many suicide survivors also shy away from professionally led bereavement groups, preferring to seek help exclusively in survivor-led groups. Criticism against the medical–psychiatric profession is often a dominant theme expressed in peer-led survivor support groups, especially among the newly bereaved. Some frequently expressed criticisms include disappointment with mental health professionals who seemed overly preoccupied with collecting fees, appeared insensitive to the side effects of prescribed medications, and neglected to communicate serious suicide risk concerns with family members. Some survivors even express the belief that had their lost loved one received better care, the person would be alive today. Some participants in peer-led survivor groups also claim that only other suicide survivors can offer meaningful understanding and help to those bereaved by suicide.

Among professionals, criticism and skepticism is often expressed about peer-facilitated support groups. At a recent group work conference, one professional conferee voiced her concerns:

> I'm worried about nonprofessionals running support groups on their own for survivors. I question whether someone without professional training can provide help to such fragile and vulnerable people. I think

there is a real danger that an improperly facilitated group may leave a survivor deeply frightened, exposed, and more at risk. You need professionally trained leadership for these groups.

Obviously, the dialogue between peer- and professional-led bereavement groups eventually leads to a level of complexity beyond the scope of this analysis. For the present, we are simply interested in exploring how peer-led bereavement support groups offer their suicide-bereaved participants meaningful help with their grief and loss experiences. If evidence from generations of Alcoholics Anonymous members offers any guidance, it would seem that self-help bereavement support groups present promising therapeutic possibilities.

As stated earlier, for many survivors today, peer-facilitated groups are the preferred model of help. Garvin (1997) believes that the values of peer-helping are especially important for those who have experienced rejection and/or inadequate services from mental health professionals. He goes on to claim that "there is value in nonprofessionally led groups because of the sense of competence they nurture" (p. 13). Garvin also recommends that professionals include greater cultivation of peer support even in professionally led support groups.

In this chapter, our focus will be primarily on peer-led, specific SOS groups that are open-ended. These groups are probably the largest single locus today where survivors find immediate solace and support following the suicide loss of a loved one (Cerel, Padgett, & Reed, 2009). Yet, little has been written about these groups.

The reliance on peer-led support groups for helping with different personal problems has a long history in the United States, dating back to the mid-1930s, with the creation of the first Alcoholics Anonymous chapters in 1935 in Akron, Ohio, by "Bill W." and "Dr. Bob" (Makela et al., 1996). However, peer self-help groups for suicide survivors appear to have emerged much later in the United States. The earliest mutual aid programs for suicide survivors came into existence in 1979 and 1980, and the current support group movement stands on the shoulders of a few early (survivor) leaders. We will mention four of them, although others could be named as well. For one, there is Adina Wrobleski, who started a group in Minneapolis in 1979 (Wrobleski, 1984–1985). She has written many seminal works on suicide bereavement, guiding survivors to form support groups and to help them advance after a family member's suicide (Appel & Wrobleski, 1987). Another important founder is LaRita Archibald, who started her first "Heartbeat" survivor support group in Colorado in 1980 (http://heartbeatsurvivorsaftersuicide.org/history.shtml). Since that time, many Heartbeat group chapters have been established all over the United States. Iris Bolton is another key figure in the movement, who founded one of the first groups in Atlanta, Georgia, after the loss of her son in 1977 (Bolton, 2006). Bolton is most well known for her widely read memoir, *My Son, My Son*, and for the founding of "The Link Counseling Center" in Atlanta, an important service provider for the bereaved by suicide and for advancing facilitator training. Another important early leader is Karen Dunne-Maxim, who established one of the first support groups in the early 1980s in Piscataway, New Jersey. Dunne-Maxim is one of the cofounders of the American Foundation for Suicide Prevention (AFSP), and was a coauthor of an important early work summarizing the suicide bereavement knowledge, *Suicide and Its Aftermath*. Each of these four early leaders helped to advance suicide survivors' interests and improve their opportunities to find grief support after a loved ones' suicide death. Today, thanks to the efforts of these suicide bereavement pioneers, and to the help of countless others, an examination of the American Association of Suicidology (AAS) or AFSP websites shows more than 300 SOS support groups nationwide, most of which are suicide specific, peer-led open-ended support groups (AAS, 2011; AFSP, 2011).

Among helping professionals, there is much interest in understanding how group participation promotes individual psychic well-being and especially mutual aid. Katz and Bender (1976) state that people helping one another through the exchange of resources and caring are the backbone of our society. Gitterman and Shulman (2005) advance that a powerful healing force is released as people discover they are not alone in their feelings. Groups provide opportunities for multiple interactions and relationships that expand opportunities for problem solving and vicarious learning (Finch & Feigelman, 2002; Reid, 1997).

In groups, there are opportunities to tell one's full story in an accepting atmosphere. Groups also afford their members an ability to help each other and enhance their own self-esteem in the process. Groups also present the availability of successful role models (Garvin, 1997). In this chapter, we apply Shulman's dynamics of mutual aid theory to explain how the healing of survivors is facilitated in support groups (Shulman, 2006). As peer and professional facilitators better understand, appreciate, and foster mutual aid, they can more readily advance goal attainment in survivor support groups.

THE GROUP STUDIED

Members euphemistically referred to their group as "the club none of us ever wanted to join." This group was located in a suburb near one of the country's largest cities. They held monthly 2-hour meetings that began with a brief informal socialization period. Following this, in the formal part of the meeting, the facilitator provided an introduction to the 15–35 people seated in a circle together. Next, the facilitator encouraged group members to participate in an initial "go-around" by briefly introducing themselves, stating their full or first name, their relationship to the decedent (attendees held a variety of relationships to decedents: parents, adult children, partners, spouses, siblings, other relatives, and friends), the self-killing method employed, and the significant survivors of the decedent. New members were offered the option of passing over their turn or editing what they shared if they felt unable to share at that time. After the initial go-around, the facilitator opened the meeting to those wishing to make general remarks and to respond, nonjudgmentally, to each other. Periodically, the facilitator redirected the flow of communication and assured new members opportunities to speak if they wished to do so. At the close of the meetings, the facilitator led the group in a ritualized reading of a serenity prayer, which was then followed by another informal socializing period where members shared coffee and cake together.

Support group members were never explicitly asked for their consent to collect data on their group interactions. That consent appeared implicit in the cooperation offered to the first author, who asked members to participate in the mailed survey that has been discussed throughout this book. With the endorsement and cooperation of the group's facilitator, more than two-thirds of the regularly attending membership completed the survey. Most survey nonparticipants offered apologies to the first author when they found they could not complete the survey. In most of these cases, members expressed appreciation to the first author for doing this survivors' study, but regretted that the painful memories evoked by answering some of the questions prevented them from participating.

It was also known among group members that the fourth author was a clinical social worker with a psychotherapy practice. In view of what has already been said about survivor skepticism toward mental health professionals, it might seem that this author's role would have imposed a barrier to her acceptance within this group, and might have led to her being cast as a potential group enemy. Yet, this never occurred during the course of our data collection. At all times, she was recognized first and foremost as a suicide survivor and often became a valued resource to the group, sometimes supplying insights into mental health problems, professional terms, and technical information about hospitalization and medical insurance questions. Interestingly, her dual status as both a survivor and a professionally trained clinician actually helped some members to feel less guilty about their own losses. As one participant described it at a meeting:

> I have been very hard on myself since Dotty's death, beating myself up for missing important clues that might have prevented her from taking her life, but with you in the same situation as me, and having lost your own child—in spite of all your knowledge and years of professional experience—I've come to realize how mystifying these mental health problems really are. Even mental health experts can be taken by surprise by a suicide in their family. It may not be nice for me to say this, but meeting you and hearing about your experience has made me feel more forgiving of myself.

SURVIVORS PURSUE THEIR COMMON GOALS

In this analysis, we apply Shulman's 10 important dynamic principles of mutual aid to show how healing is advanced in SOS support groups (Shulman, 2006). We present relevant anecdotal observations and excerpts demonstrating how these principles emerge in the course of the suicide survivor support group experience. Shulman offers the following 10 principles to show how people use groups to address their psychosocial needs:

1. The "All-in-the-Same Boat" Phenomenon

   Group members gain support by discovering that other group members have similar problems, concerns, feelings, and experiences. They learn they are not alone (Shulman, 2006). In the initial go-around, as members introduce themselves, they share a very important part about their survivor experience—how their loved one died. This information bonds them together. From the very beginning of the meeting, a clear linkage of common experience is established. Thus, in the suicide survivor support group, people find they are not alone. The shock, isolation, stigma, and confusion impacting on every part of one's life—from the inability to perform simple daily routines to the loss of one's total belief system—all this is shared. Members also begin sharing personal loss stories. Irv, a middle-aged, investment banker recounts his experience of losing his 22-year-old daughter Betsy:

   > When Betsy died, for the first 3 months following her suicide, I didn't want to get up in the morning. I felt my life was over. I would wake up and for a split-second I was okay, everything was normal in my life, but then, I would remember, Betsy was dead. It felt like a knife thrust into my stomach. I've never felt such pain before. I kept hoping I would really wake up and find that this was only a horrible nightmare. I couldn't believe that I would never see her again. During those first months, I felt like I must have been in some kind of trance. I don't know how I got to the office and did my work during that period, I was such a mess.

   Others in the group nodded because they too remembered their early reactions to the suicides of their loved ones. This included the visceral pain, the shifts between denial and reality, and the trancelike functioning in one's daily life.

   After suicide, the original fabric of the family is destroyed and the entire family is forced to reintegrate (Dunne et al., 1987). Frequently, family members react differently to the suicide and are unable to support each other. Some family members come to the group alone, without their partners. For one survivor, Maria, the group is her only place to be heard.

   > I have been coming to the group alone, without my husband Tony, for 3 years now, since right after Pat, our 22-year-old son, took his life. I tried to get Tony to come here with me but he refuses. Tony never was much of a talker about feelings and now, he doesn't want to talk about Pat, period. I think he feels guilty and I know he also blames me—I was the one who insisted that we stop rescuing Pat all the time and hold him accountable for the messes he kept

getting into. I don't feel guilty about Pat's death now and coming to group has been a huge help for me. In the beginning, it was the only safe place to speak about my son. Maybe if Tony came to group, he would feel better too.

2. Discussing a Taboo Area

One member enters a taboo area of discussion, thereby freeing other members to enter as well (Shulman, 2006). The safe culture of the support group allows survivors to challenge the stigma and shame associated with suicide. One openly shares feelings and is not rejected or abandoned; one is allowed to express grief and anger, suicidal thoughts, disappointments with others, and even, for some, the feeling of relief that after years of living with a chronically depressed, suicidal person, the suffering, for everyone, is finally over. The freedom to say these things diminishes the sense of isolation and feelings of guilt.

Sometimes, one member taking the first risk leads the group to a different place. Mary, after several months in group, talking about her son Jeff's impulsivity, depression, and an earlier traumatic experience in college finally takes a risk and shares more of her story.

> The night my son hanged himself, Jeff had been coming down from a cocaine binge. I was ashamed to talk about this here before because I wanted to protect him and me. I was afraid that you would think less of him—his life, his death, and my loss because of his cocaine use. I know how society looks at people who use drugs. Jeff was very talented and loving and he deserves more than that.

After Mary's disclosure, there is silence as she waits to see how others respond. After a brief pause, others in the group begin sharing their own previously withheld stories of loved ones' abuses of alcohol and other substances. Their spirited exchange suggests that members are relieved; their losses are validated and they have one less secret to hide.

3. Mutual Support

Group members provide emotional support to one another (Shulman, 2006). In the survivors' group, members demonstrate acceptance, offer hope that the pain will lessen with time, and suggest concrete ways to cope with problems. Ken and his wife, Robin, acknowledge this mutual support phenomenon:

> When we first started coming here 11 months ago, we felt hopeless and even though we have lots of friends and family, this place felt different—a room full of strangers and yet we felt comfortable. People really understood us. In the beginning, I was amazed to see how some people, here longer than us, were functioning so well, even laughing a little. Now, I meet new people coming here for the first time and I can see that Robin and I are not in the same place.

Our pain feels different. Time does that. Someone once said these meetings work because of talk, tears, and time. I think that's true.

Yalom and Leszcz (2005) talk about the power of expectation, the installation and maintenance of hope, the benefits of the group experience with individuals at different points along a coping–collapse continuum, and the importance of observing the improvement of others. Another aspect of mutual support that is crucial for survivor healing is the ability to forgive others for whatever self-blame and guilt they suffer. A survivor, Betty, describes how by supporting others she was able to eventually let go of her own guilt.

After my son's death, I felt guilty and ashamed. After all, there had been warning signs and I was a trained mental health professional. Years ago, I had even driven one of my patients who had taken an overdose of aspirin to the hospital emergency room and saved her life. How had I failed my own son? In the group, I listened to others tell their stories, many [are] also feeling guilty that they had not prevented the death of a loved one—a husband, a father . . . it went on and on. At first, I distanced myself, believing my guilt was worse. My crime was more severe. Most of these people did not have my skills and expertise. I was more guilty: a horrible mother and an incompetent clinician. Over time, while helping others (including other mental health professionals who were also survivors) feel less responsible for a death they could not have prevented, I began to be less hard on myself. My son had made the decision to end his life in spite of everything I had done or could have done.

4. Individual Problem Solving

The group members help one member to solve a problem, receiving help themselves while offering it to another (Shulman, 2006). In the survivor group, a member has the opportunity to hear from not one but many others, with diverse backgrounds and experiences in dealing with certain similar situations. It is very supportive to have this orchestra of responses available, and in addition, it is also empowering. "It is this very process of picking and choosing which serves to help us feel progressively more in control of our own lives and which makes it possible for us to resume fully our adult lives in the face of this tragedy" (Dunne, 1992, p. 9).

A member, Paula, asks for help with conflict with her in-laws. "I have a problem with my in-laws. My husband, Chris, was cremated 1 year ago and now his family is pressuring me to spread his ashes. I just can't do this." The group is first supportive, "How can they do this to you!"; several members remark at the same time. Next, Paula remarks, "I want to hold onto him, and I can't let go." One member supports Paula's right to determine the time for this ritual to occur, saying "each person grieves differently and you were his wife." Finally, another member, a parent who lost her son, who apparently identifies with Chris' parents, asks Paula: "What about them? Maybe they need some closure as part of their own healing. Didn't they lose their son?" Paula tearfully listens. Finally, another member shares her own solution to this dilemma; she displays a small gold locket containing some ashes of her loved one. She wears this locket close to her heart and says this has allowed her to part with the rest of his remains. Paula listens, appears less disturbed, and nods gently.

5. Sharing Data

Members of the group have had different life experiences, through which they have accumulated knowledge, views, and values that can help others in the group (Shulman, 2006). In the survivors' group, members share specific information about psychiatric disorder, suicide, and the healing process—where they are now, how they were then. Sometimes this information is volunteered and other times it is shared in request to someone asking for help. One member, Lois, almost 2 years since the death of her son John, is feeling pressured to "speed up" the mourning process by seemingly well-meaning friends and family.

> This second year without my son John feels even harder. People expect me to "move on" and to get rid of John's clothing and possessions, but I can't. Is this normal? Will I ever be able to clean out the closet? Do I have to?

Others in the group provide support by saying "take the time you need, only you can make these decisions; it does get easier, with time, to go through possessions." Then another member, Anne, shares how she handled this kind of challenge:

> I couldn't stand to change anything in my son Brian's room for a long time. It was like a "shrine" and I would go in there and cry. But then, my daughter had a baby and I decided to convert the room into a play room for my new grandchild's visits. I changed the wallpaper, the carpeting, and put in some baby things. Now, when I go into the room, of course I still think of Brian and sometimes I still cry a bit, but I also enjoy the new light in my life—my granddaughter. When she visits, we play games, read books, and laugh, and I point to his photos on the wall and tell her stories about her Uncle Brian.

Sometimes, group members talk about how they deal with "toxic" people or give themselves permission to avoid certain painful situations. Other times, they speak about the benefits they derive from supportive therapists or psychotropic medications. For some, visits to psychics or enhanced religious activity or spirituality provide comfort and they talk about this too. Members share traditional as well as more unusual ways they use to cope with their losses. One member, Terry, a survivor who lost her 18-year-old daughter 4 years ago, speaks about her communal visits to gravesites with her "Mothers' Cemetery Club," a small subgroup of women from the survivor group. "We bring flowers but we also bring miniature toys, Halloween candies, holiday decorations, whatever. One New Year's Day, we even brought a bottle of champagne and drank a toast to them and us."

This interchange provides an opportunity for the group to laugh and to experience relief as they talk about this taboo topic so openly.

6. The Dialectical Process

Group members confront each other's ideas. The group is a sounding board and a place for one's views to be challenged and possibly changed (Shulman, 2006). As in other mutual aid groups, the exchange of differing views in the group allows members to examine their personal beliefs and the beliefs of others. This leads to an expansion of thought and facilitates change (Finch & Feigelman, 2002). One member, Fiona, speaking of her brother's suicide, voices her criticism of her brother's fiancée. She says, "I can't help but blame my brother's fiancée for his death. She pressured him and he had no idea where to turn."

The group supports Fiona but then someone adds, "How easy it is for all of us to look for someone to blame: ourselves, the psychiatrist, and others, rather than to accept the fact that someone chose to end their life."

With this last remark, Beth, who lost her fiancé Steven, challenges Fiona.

> I am still blamed for Steven's death by his family and I have to tell you how much it hurts. Steven and I lived together for 3 years, we loved each other, were engaged to be married, and I thought his family accepted me and our relationship. His family knew a little but not the full story of his depression; the different medications he took, the course of his therapy. He wanted to keep it a secret but in the end I lost him. How can they not know that I lost my whole life with his death?

Beth begins to cry. Fiona listens; she too begins to cry.

In another support group session, Joan, a divorced woman who lost her adult daughter, Barbara, 3 months ago, is accompanied to the meeting by her surviving son Matthew, himself a divorced parent with a young son. Matthew is here today, eager to talk about his mother and how her crying and expressions of guilt seem excessive and upsetting to him. "I don't know why she blames herself. I try to bring over my son, he's a great kid, for frequent visits to cheer her up but she is often unable to get up from the sofa." A group member asks him to be more compassionate to his mother, saying: "You lost your brother but your mother lost her child. It's not the same." Matthew responds: "I can't imagine losing

my son. I'd probably flip out." The possibility of such a loss emotionally overwhelms him and he reaches for his mother's hand to comfort her.

7. Mutual Demand

Group members offer each other help by making demands and setting expectations on personal behavior (Shulman, 2006). The survivors group encourages members to move from being victims to becoming survivors by making demands for growth and change. These changes may be small, may be behavioral or attitudinal but, with each change, survivors become more empowered. It is important for survivors to measure their healing progress according to their own yardsticks because there is definitely no "one size or one method fits all." Although the group makes demands for growth, it also acknowledges change in others no matter how small (Dunne, 1992). Sometimes, the discomfort of facing one's peers without having acted on some helpful suggestions motivates members to change and take risks.

Many struggles are universal in the survivor group, such as the conflict between going on with one's life and feeling guilty. One member, Antoinette (a widow), speaks about her difficulty in celebrating the holidays with her children; other members who have already experienced this try to help her.

> I feel guilty because since my husband shot himself on Christmas day 2 years ago, I have been unable to continue with the family tradition of selecting and decorating a large holiday tree. I feel terrible because my kids, ages 10 and 12, are missing out but I don't have the energy.

Members speak of their own experiences and how they push themselves to function, even when it is hard, so that their children don't have to worry about them. "They already lost their father, they don't need to worry that they are going to lose their mother too."

Fred, who lost his son Peter, shares his struggle:

> I was very close to Peter and, for a long time, couldn't think about doing anything fun with my surviving son Rick (or my wife for that matter, either). My wife and I were close to separation over this. Luckily, I realized that this was not fair to my family. Nothing can be done to bring Peter back, and I just had to push myself.

At a subsequent meeting, Antoinette shares her decision to purchase a smaller Christmas tree this year, one with roots that she and the children will decorate and then plant outside after the holiday. Antoinette has responded to the group's mutual demand. She is being a good mother and is also honoring the valued tradition established early on in her marriage.

8. Rehearsal

The group becomes a forum to try out new ideas and skills (Shulman, 2006). In the survivors' group, there is always discussion of how to deal with difficult people and situations, including holidays, birthdays, death anniversaries, and so forth. These are difficult events for families that have lost loved ones and members share their struggles and methods of coping. The rehearsal in group, with the support and feedback from one's peers, greatly reduces anticipatory anxiety and promotes self-esteem. One member, Lisa, speaks of her anxiety about her dead brother's approaching birthday and wonders how she and her family will get through this day. "Next week will be my brother's birthday. He would have been 36 and my family seems to be avoiding the topic. I don't want to upset my mother but I think we should talk and plan something."

Members of the group encourage her to talk about the day, how she would like to spend it and with whom. They also share memorial actions that worked for them: going to a loved one's favorite restaurant, ordering their preferred foods, renting and watching one of their favorite movies, writing birthday messages in a journal, or making memorial donations in their name.

9. Universal Perspective

The group members begin to view their personal situations in terms of universal issues within a social context (Shulman, 2006). In the survivors' group, suicide is viewed not only as something that happened in your life but also as something connected to a larger picture of institutional shortcomings, such as inadequate mental health resources, limited funding for suicide prevention and research, or societal stigma regarding depression, substance abuse, and suicide.

For many survivors, this wider perspective allows them to move away from personal blame and begin to turn their grief into social action. For some survivors, grief becomes a transformative experience (Fielden, 2003) and posttraumatic stress disorder evolves into posttraumatic growth (Tedeschi & Calhoun, 2004). People talk about beginning volunteer work for the first time in their lives, establishing memorial foundations, or writing and publishing memoirs that help others. Although not all survivors move to social action, with time and exposure to the healing support of others in their support group, many achieve greater understanding of suicide as a social problem, its risk factors, preventive interventions, and the need for more research and knowledge. One member, Bud, speaks in group about legislation he is supporting: "I want to tell you about Timothy's Law because it is important for us to get behind this much-needed legislation to get mental health parity. I'd like to pass around a petition for signatures after the group."

Some members, especially those in the early months of bereavement, seem too numb to be interested in doing more than their day-to-day survival routines of getting up and to going to work, but for others, Bud is presenting an opportunity to take action.

10. The "Strength-in-Numbers" Phenomenon

Group members are strengthened to take on difficult tasks through the support of other group members (Shulman, 2006). Members of suicide support groups are strengthened as they unite with other survivors. They become advocates for suicide education, prevention, and legislative social action, and engage in fund raising for improved research. They join other organizations to participate in community events such as the AFSP Annual Out of the Darkness Suicide Walks, or they collaborate with others to lobby in Washington, DC, with Suicide Prevention Action Network USA (SPAN USA; now a part of AFSP). They begin online support groups, create memorial websites, publish support newsletters, and participate in research studies to "tell their stories." They decrease their feelings of shame and isolation and they become empowered. Jerry Reed, executive director of the SPAN USA talks about the power of survivors to make a change: "Survivors are changing the landscape of suicide awareness. By sharing their personal stories, they are able to turn grief into action and communicate the urgent need to take concrete steps to prevent more deaths by suicide" (Myers & Fine, 2006, p. 262).

CONCLUSION

Anchored to Shulman's dynamic principles, we have demonstrated how survivor support groups help survivors advance with their healing after a suicide loss. No longer marginalized, survivors are able to offer each other important mutual aid, helping each other deal with the necessary life adjustments following a suicide loss. As survivors discover their similarities, they are drawn together to form a natural therapeutic environment. Through the successful models of coping behavior survivors offer to each other and their mutually reassuring and supportive responses, survivors are able to move beyond the isolating sadness of loss and once again envision possibilities for hopeful and meaningful future actions.

There is no more convincing proof of the value of support groups than the testimonies survivors themselves offer at group meetings. As Jane stated at a recent meeting:

All my life I have been shy about speaking up about myself. When I first started coming here, I sat like a clam; I was afraid to open my mouth. But now, I'm in a much better place. I'm stronger and I can talk in this group to tell my story and help others. I can even advocate for myself now when I have to. In my early grieving days, I was full of self-doubt and I couldn't think about disagreeing with anyone in my family who said anything about how I was supposed to grieve.

Now, if anyone puts something out there that seems unhelpful to me,
I'll tell them loud and clear.

Mike framed it differently.

You remember how I was a year ago, when I first came to meetings all
I talked about was how I failed Mike Junior. All I thought about was
how my life was over. After work, I just wanted to go home, watch
some dopey TV shows, and call it a day. When my wife suggested we
take the family vacation to Disneyland we had planned before Mike
Junior's death, I snapped at her. I said, "What are you, crazy? How
are we going to enjoy an amusement park? There's no fun in life any
more." But after coming here and talking it out, I've come to understand the selfish stupidity of that idea. I can't bail out on my wife and
surviving son. We all have to make the best of it. Well, you know we
went to Disneyland, and we had a good time down there. We even
talked about Junior there—he loved that place. And we cried and
missed him together. We've got to move on. Junior would not have
wanted us to mope about, and in his loving memory, we won't. I've
come a long way with this group.

Until now, we have focused on the value of support groups for survivors.
However, natural healing is by no means assured within this context. Although
we have not discussed support group deficiencies, we did observe occasional
instances when people expressed dissatisfaction with the support group and
withdrew. Members who withdrew cited a variety of reasons: displeasure
with the facilitator and other group members for monopolizing the group's
meeting time, feeling that the group was overly preoccupied with issues pe-
ripheral to recovery after suicide, and feeling that continued involvement with
the group "brought them down."

No group leadership will successfully address all the many and potentially conflicting interests and needs of members. There are also important
developmental processes going on within survivor support groups. Newly
bereaved survivors enter groups primarily seeking emotional support for
the profound "psychache" they are experiencing. Longer term survivors will
more often approach support group meetings from the vantage point of what
they can give back to the newly bereaved. There are likely to be others who
feel they have moved on with their grief, and no longer benefit from support group participation. These differences in group member motivations may
offer useful leads for future research on how bereavement support groups are
sustained, prosper, and/or break down.

Survivor support group members come from a wide range of social class
memberships. Some bring with them extensive experience from Alcoholics
Anonymous, Weight Watchers and similar groups that follow the self-help
peer support model. Others enter survivor support groups as complete newcomers to self-help. Some enter groups with a vast reservoir of participation

experiences from religious, civic, occupational, and other voluntary associations, whereas others begin support group participation for the very first time.

After sustaining a suicide loss, many survivors initially go on the Internet in their eager and sometimes desperate searches for help. Many survivors presently find considerable help at five important clearinghouses for suicide information: the Suicide Prevention Resource Center (www.sprc.org), the AAS (www.suicidology.org), the SPAN USA (www.spanusa.org; now merged with AFSP), the AFSP (www.afsp.org), and Suicide Awareness Voices of Education (www.save.org). Many find their local support groups through the listings posted at the AAS and AFSP websites.

Yet, at the time of this writing, there is only limited informational assistance available to help survivor-facilitators better manage their support groups. Presently, the only place where group facilitation materials and training are available is through a facilitator training program given by AFSP. Unfortunately, this training is only offered in three or four different cities yearly, and some of the cost of the training must be borne by the participant. AFSP also offers telephone conference call-in opportunities for facilitators on a once a month basis. The manual for the AFSP training, which was also designed to be a "self-study" tool for facilitators who are not able to attend a training event, is available through AFSP (www.afsp.org). Although valuable, this clearly seems insufficient to support the numerous facilitators throughout the country who may need more information and support to better manage their groups and to meet the needs of their members. Such information may include group development, recruitment, publicity, screening, skills for facilitating the work of the group, management of challenging situations, and so forth. We should also not lose sight of the fact that the suicide survivor population is growing at a rate of at least hundreds of thousands yearly, although only a portion of this number will seek help in survivor support groups.

Our recommendation, accordingly, would be to post more support group facilitation training materials on websites that can be easily downloaded by interested parties. We would also suggest the creation of an ongoing information exchange or Internet chat group that would offer professional expertise to survivor group facilitators at least biweekly. In addition, we recommend subsidized mentorships and training workshops for facilitators to acquire and refine their group facilitation skills as other worthy projects for the suicide information clearinghouses to pursue.

This research has demonstrated the value of peer-support groups to suicide survivors. Peer support is an especially low-cost alternative for helping people deal with the crisis of suicide loss. Much more research is needed to better understand how survivor peer support groups work, to better identify which survivors are best helped by them, and to identify those survivor characteristics best matched with alternative treatment approaches. These important questions about these groups remain for future research and exploration.

REFERENCES

American Association of Suicidology. (2007). Retrieved from www.suicidology.org/

American Foundation for Suicide Prevention. (2007). Retrieved from www.afsp.org

Appel, Y. H., & Wrobleski, A. (1987). Self-help and support groups: Mutual aid for survivors. In E. J. Dunne, J. McIntosh, & K. Dunne-Maxim (Eds.), *Suicide and its aftermath: Understanding and counseling the survivors* (pp. 215–233). New York, NY: Norton.

Bolton, I. (2006, October). Personal communication, Suicide Prevention Action Network-USA Annual Conference, Washington DC.

Cerel, J., Padgett, J. H., & Reed, G. A. (2009). Support groups for suicide survivors: Results of a survey of group leaders. *Suicide and Life-Threatening Behavior, 39*(6), 588–598.

Dunne, E. (1992). How to start your own support group. In *Survivors of suicide support group guidelines*. Washington, DC: American Association of Suicidology, Broadway Books.

Dunne, E. J., McIntosh, J. L., & Dunne-Maxim, K. (Eds). (1987). *Suicide and its aftermath: understanding and counseling the survivors.* New York, NY: Norton.

Fielden, J. M. (2003). Grief as a transformative experience: Weaving through different lifeworlds after a loved one has completed suicide. *International Journal of Mental Health Nursing, 12*(1), 74–85.

Finch, J. B., & Feigelman, B. (2002, June). *Training new field instructors: The power of mutual aid in the educational process.* Paper presented at the 24th Annual AASWG International Symposium of Social Work With Groups, New York, NY.

Garvin, C. (1997). *Contemporary group work* (3rd ed.). Needham Heights, MA: Allyn and Bacon.

Gitterman, A., & Schulman, L. (2005). *Mutual Aid Groups, Vulnerable and Resilient Populations, and the Life Cycle.* New York, NY: Columbia University Press.

Heartbeat Survivors After Suicide Organization website. Retrieved from http://heartbeatsurvivorsaftersuicide.org/history.shtml

Jordan, J. R. (2011). Group work with survivors. In J. R. Jordan & J. L. McIntosh (Eds.), *Grief after suicide: Understanding the consequences and caring for the survivors* (pp. 283–300). New York, NY: Routledge Taylor and Francis.

Katz, A. H., & Bender, E. I. (1976). *The strength in us: Self-help groups in the modern world.* New York, NY: Franklin Watts.

Makela, K., Arminen, I., Bloomfield, K., Eisenbach-Stangl, I., Bergmark, K. H., Kurube, N., . . . Zielinksi, A. (1996). *Alcoholics Anonymous as a mutual help movement: A study in eight societies.* Madison: University of Wisconsin Press.

Myers, M., & Fine, C. (2006). *Touched by Suicide: Hope and Healing After Loss.* New York, NY: Gotham Books.

Reid, K. (1997). *Social work practice with groups: A clinical perspective* (2nd ed.). Pacific Grove, CA: Brooks/Cole.

Shulman, L. (2006). *The skills of helping individuals, families groups and communities* (5th ed.). Pacific Grove, CA: Brooks/Cole.

Tedeschi, R. G., & Calhoun, L. (2004, April 1). Posttraumatic growth: A new perspective on psychotraumatology. *Psychiatric Times, 21*(4), 58–60.

Wrobleski, A. (1984–1985). The suicide survivors grief group. *Omega: Journal of Death and Dying, 15*(2), 173–184.

Yalom, I., & Leszcz, M. (2005). *The theory and practice of group psychotherapy* (5th ed.). New York, NY: Basic Books.

9

Suicide Survivor Support Groups: Comings and Goings

INTRODUCTION

In this chapter, we build on the previous discussion, investigating the more dynamic features of support groups for the suicide bereaved, addressing the comings and goings of members. Now, we focus on what attracts survivors to support groups, and why many discontinue their participation as the time after a loss passes.

Because most U.S. survivors of suicide (SOS) support groups are of the open format type (Cerel, Padgett, & Reed, 2009), membership is in a continuous state of flux. As time passes, different newly bereaved members join in and some longer term survivors withdraw. Although this structure may be a challenging one requiring the smooth integration of beginning, middle, and ending transitional phases within each session (Birnbaum & Cicchetti, 2005)—it allows new members to enter the group quickly and to be motivated to share their "stories" sooner as they listen to the level of openness of other more "seasoned" members (Shulman, 2006). On the other hand, the ease by which newly bereaved members are integrated within the group may come at the expense of serving the bereavement needs of longer term group members. These individuals may feel that the focus on early grief issues "brings them down," forcing them to revisit early grief issues and leaving insufficient group time to discuss the longer term adaptation problems of bereaved survivors. Thus, support group leadership remains in the peculiar position of attempting to address the overwhelming grief experienced by the newly bereaved while also serving longer term survivors who have different needs for grief support. Recognizing this dilemma, it is worth investigating why members initially come to a group, how their needs change over time, and why they may eventually decide to leave a group.

Social Factors Associated With Joining a Support Group

The first question we explore is why do people join SOS support groups? We explore several hypotheses that seem plausible to account for the differences in support group participation.

Hypothesis 1: We anticipated that bereaved individuals who were more frequent churchgoers would be more likely to attend support groups than
the less religiously inclined. We see church membership as a manifestation of civic involvement, and numerous sociopolitical studies document
that acts of community participation beget still wider degrees of social
participation (see Skocpol & Fiorina, 1999; Verba, Schlozman, & Brady,
1995, among others).

Hypothesis 2: We anticipated bereaved individuals coming from larger families would be less likely to join support groups than their counterparts
from smaller families. This hypothesis emerges from the classic work
of Emile Durkheim, *Suicide* (1997), in which he claimed that family
attachments—and the larger the number of family obligations that an
individual acknowledges and submits to from them—prevent people
from individuating and thinking about addressing their own personal
needs. Following this line of thought, individuals coming from larger
families would be less likely to acknowledge their personal needs for
grief support and less inclined to join a support group.

Hypothesis 3: We anticipated that those reporting more grief and mental
health distress would be more actively involved in support groups than
those showing fewer grief and psychological problems. This hypothesis
is suggested from the limited literature on bereavement support groups,
including Levy and Derby (1992), who found, in a study of 159 bereaved
widows and widowers, that survivors who reported more stress, depression, anger, and anxiety were more likely to report affiliations with
bereavement support groups than their less distressed counterparts.

Hypothesis 4: Those reporting more unsuccessful and less helpful experiences with bereavement professionals will be more likely to seek out
support groups. This hypothesis assumes that the support group is a
secondary resource used when one perceives one's grief-related needs
unmet by bereavement professionals.

Hypothesis 5: In Chapter 11, we found that suicide-bereaved parents who
felt stigmatized by their families and friends were more likely to belong
to an Internet support group and were more active participants in this
group, as well. Therefore, we anticipated those scoring higher on our
stigmatization scale would be more likely to participate in face-to-face
groups and also to show greater activism in these groups.

To measure the items of interest for this analysis, we included measures for the following:

1. *Frequency of religious participation.* Respondents were asked to report how frequently they attended religious services during the past year on a 7-point scale extending from *never* to *several times a week*.
2. *Number of children.* Respondents reported the number of children they had ever had through biological parenthood, adoption, or step parentage reflecting nuclear family size differences.
3. *Support group affiliations.* Respondents were asked if they ever sought help from any general bereavement groups or SOS support groups. If they answered affirmatively, they were asked two additional questions: if they had been to the group during the past 12 months, and if so, to present their visitation frequency on a 6-point scale ranging from *once to weekly* or *more often*. Respondents were also asked to rate the value of their group (or their professional counselors') helpfulness on a 5-point scale ranging from *not at all helpful* to *very helpful*.

FINDINGS

Frequency of Peer Support Group Participation During the Past Year

Table 9.1 shows how frequently respondents attended an SOS support group or a general bereavement group (like The Compassionate Friends group) within the previous year. Respondents were asked to report on a 6-point scale their frequency of participation in both types of groups, and we combined responses for the past 12 months, creating a composite measure on a 6-point scale ranging from *no participation* to *weekly or greater participation*. Within our sample, drawn primarily from the ranks of those belonging to support groups, it is not surprising that nearly two-thirds (62%) indicated attendance at one or more support group meeting during the past year. The data also showed near-monthly attendance as the modal pattern for those reporting current

Table 9.1
Suicide Bereaved Parents' Participation in SOS or General Bereavement Support Groups During the Previous Year ($N = 462$)

	PERCENTAGE	(*n*)
Reported no participation	38.5	(178)
Once	9.5	(44)
2–5 times	17.8	(82)
6–20 times	19.7	(91)
21–50 times	6.1	(28)
51 or more times	8.4	(39)

Note. From Survivors Child Loss Survey, 2006–2007. SOS = survivors of suicide.

participation, with a figure of 37% reporting near-monthly participation. A small percentage, approximately 14%, reported greater than monthly participation, suggesting that some of these respondents may have belonged to both an SOS group and a general bereavement group.

Throughout this analysis, we separately examined two interrelated dimensions of past year support group participation: (a) contrasting between survivors who did not participate at all in support groups versus those who went to one or more meetings and (b) contrasting survivors whose rates of support group participation differed on a 6-point frequency scale. There is obviously a great deal of overlap between both these aspects of participation, but their correlates may not be entirely synonymous.

Correlates of Current Support Group Participation

Table 9.2 displays the results of the investigation of our five study hypotheses comparing bereaved parents who have participated to any extent in the past year with participants who did not participate at all in a support group. In this table with *t* tests, we compare the means of those attending support groups and those who did not attend them to see whether the differences between each subgroup are consistent with our hypotheses. The *t* test of religious participation shows a significant difference between church going and any amount of participation in a support group. Support group participants reported a significantly higher mean level of religious participation of 3.72 compared to 3.08 for their inactive

Table 9.2
t test Comparisons of Those Attending Peer Support Groups and Those Not Attending These Groups Among Suicide-Bereaved Parents (*N* = 462)

MEAN/(*N*)	NEVER ATTENDED / OR ATTENDED ONE OR MORE GROUP MEETINGS PAST YR.	TOTAL	*t* TEST *p* VALUES
Average number of years since the loss	5.9 yrs .(175)/5.0 yrs. (280)	5.4 (455)	.02
Religious attendance frequency (6-point scale, *never to several times weekly*)	3.08 (176)/3.72 (282)	3.47 (458)	.001
Mean number of children	3.3 (173)/2.9 (283)	3.02 (456)	.0004
Mean GEQ score	40.3 (164)/40.1 (262)	40.2 (426)	.909
Mean number of psychological problems (ranging from 0 to 4)	1.6 (169)/1.70 (281)	1.67 (450)	.47
Perceived helpfulness of professional bereavement counselors (ranging from 0 to 5)	3.04 (73)/3.6 (160)	3.4 (233)	.011
Differences in stigmatization score (ranging from 0 to 17)	3.5 (273) / 3.5 (160)	3.5 (433)	.97

Note. From Survivors Child Loss Survey, 2006–2007.

counterparts. Table 9.2 also shows significant mean differences on the *t* test between support group participants and nonparticipants in terms of family size differences. Participants reported a mean number of children of 2.9 compared to a mean of 3.3 for nonparticipants. This difference was significant at the .0004 level.

Table 9.2 also shows no significant differences in grief problems between support group participants and nonparticipants on the sensitive indicator of grief difficulties in our abbreviated Grief Experience Questionnaire. The same was true in terms of psychological problems. We also examined both of these hypotheses in terms of frequent attendance at support groups and the grief and psychological problems variables. This is also displayed in Table 9.3, where the correlation coefficients show no significant association between differing rates of support group activism and grief and psychological problems. Whether a respondent participated at all in a support group or whether they went to groups with greater frequency than others (during the past 12 months) was simply not associated with any differences in grief or psychological difficulties.

Table 9.2 also failed to show differences consistent with our prediction that support group participants would be more inclined to find mental health professionals less helpful than others less inclined to use these groups. Instead, there was a significant difference contrary to our prediction, which showed support group participants *more* likely to regard professionals as helpful, compared to the mean ratings given by nonparticipants, 3.6 as compared to 3.0, significant at the .01 level. Table 9.2 also shows no significant mean

Table 9.3

Correlation Matrix of Participating in a Support Group During the Past Year and Other Characteristics of Suicide Bereaved Parents ($N = 462$)

	CORRELATION COEFFICIENT / SIGNIFICANCE					
	SUPPORT GROUP ATTEND	YEARS SINCE LOSS	RELIG. PART.	FAMILY SIZE	PSYCH. PROBS.	GRIEF PROBS.
Stigma score	−0.01					
Years since loss	0.09					
Religious participation	0.15***	0.05				
Family size	−0.16***	0.03	0.09*			
Psychological problems	0.03	−0.34***	−0.22***	−0.03		
Grief problems	−0.01	−0.26***	−0.20***	0.04	0.61***	
Frequency of seeing MH professionals	0.12**	−0.26***	−0.01	−0.07	0.32***	0.22***

Note. From Survivors Child Loss Survey, 2006–2007. MH = mental health.
*$p < .05$. **$p < .01$. ***$p < .001$.

differences in stigmatization between those who attended support groups and those who did not during the past year.

The correlation matrix we present in Table 9.3 offers insight into some of these enigmatic results. Note that this table uses data on the 6-point scale of participation from *never* to *several times a week*. It shows that people with higher levels of participation in a support group are more likely to also see mental health professionals. In addition to relying on treatment professionals more often, these respondents who indicated higher levels of help seeking tended to hold more positive views of the professionals (not shown on this table).

Table 9.3 also shows no association between differing degrees of support group participation and differences in stigmatization. This finding contrasts sharply with the results we obtained from the Internet support group affiliates (see Chapter 11), where we found active participation associated with greater stigmatization. There could be an important difference in this respect between Internet and face-to-face group affiliations, an important issue calling for further investigation.

Table 9.3 also shows that time since loss, grief difficulties, psychological problems, and seeing a mental health professional are all moderately intercorrelated with one another. (This is also true of stigmatization, although it is not displayed in this table). Yet attending a support group is only significantly associated with seeing mental health professionals.

Table 9.3 also shows time since the loss as a potential confounder to support group participation; it is significantly related to grief and psychological problems and to seeing professional counselors. Table 9.2 also shows statistically significant mean differences in time since loss between those who belonged to support groups in the past year or who did not, with a *p* value of .02. For these reasons, we thought it could be a potential confounder for the four hypotheses we were investigating. In addition, we also applied a control for gender. Although our own analyses of gender and support group participation did not show any clear association between these two variables, some previous studies (Suitor & Pillemer, 2000) have shown gender and participation associated with one another. Accordingly, we considered gender as another potential confounder to the other variables under consideration.

Table 9.4 presents a logistic regression analysis of the three variables that we found significantly associated with support group participation: church going, family size, and finding professionals helpful. The logistic regression adds time since the loss and gender into the analysis. Results show that even with the consideration of these potentially confounding variables, each of the three variables still maintains a significant association with current support group participation.

CONCLUSIONS: WHO JOINS SUPPORT GROUPS?

There is a widespread supposition among many bereavement professionals that support group affiliates are more distressed and perhaps more stigmatized

Table 9.4
Multivariate Logistic Regression of Current Support Group Participation by Religious Activism, Family Size, Use of Bereavement or Mental Health Professionals, Years Since the Death and Gender (*N* = 444)

MEASURES	OR	(95% CI)	*p* VALUE
Religious participation	1.18	(1.06–1.30)	.001
Family size	.73	(0.62–0.87)	.0001
Use of MH professionals	1.17	(1.02–1.35)	.023
Time since loss	.97	(.93–1.01)	.207
Gender	.89	(0.51–1.57)	.707

Note. From Survivors Child Loss Survey, 2006–2007.

than their bereaved counterparts who do not attend these groups. Yet, our present findings, drawn from the networks of SOS support group affiliates, did not confirm these expectations. We found current support group affiliates no more troubled by grief and psychological problems and no more stigmatized than other bereaved parents who were not presently attending groups. Whether we focused on having a current support group affiliation or on the frequency of support group attendance from never attending to more than monthly attendance, there simply were no differences in grief and psychological difficulties across the range of respondents who did not participate at all in support groups compared to those who were current, highly active members.

We extended these comparisons still further by examining the larger number of suicide-bereaved parents who reported ever having used a support group since the deaths of their children. Of our suicide-bereaved parents, 83% fell into this category. Interestingly, on five *t*-test comparisons of grief and psychological difficulties among the suicide-bereaved parents who had ever used support groups versus those who never used a group, a consistent trend was noted. The data showed prior support group attendees reported less grief and psychological distress than their nonattending counterparts. Two of the five comparisons were statistically significant. This is displayed in Table 9.5.

The differences between our results and those of Levy and Derby (1992) could be explained by any number of divergences between our study and theirs. Differences in sampling procedures alone could account for these differences. Levy and Derby dealt with widows, whereas we focused on parents. Their study embraced a narrow time line from immediately after the loss to less than 2 years afterward. In our study, close to half of the respondents were 5 or more years past their losses. Levy and Derby's work was done nearly 20 years ago, when the availability and social acceptability of support groups may have been far different from its current meaning and standing today. A recent study of suicide survivor support groups showed a nearly 50% expansion in these groups since 1996 (Cerel, Padgett, Conwell, & Reed, 2009). Any or all of these differences could account for the contrasting results. Clearly, more research on this question is called for, especially among representative samples of bereaved populations.

Table 9.5

t test Comparison of Support Group Activism (During One's Lifetime) by Differences in Grief and Psychological Problems Among Suicide Bereaved Parents (*N* = 462)

	MEAN/(*N*)		
	NEVER ATTENDED / OR ATTENDED ONE OR MORE MEETINGS	TOTAL	*t* TEST *p* VALUES
Grief difficulties	41.9 (105)/39.7 (308)	40.3 (413)	.08
Inventory of Complicated Grief	29.4 (112)/27.5 (313)	28.0 (425)	.05
Impact of Events score	35.2 (106)/32.8 (303)	33.4 (409)	.01
Mean number of psychological problems (from 0 to 4)	1.8 (113)/1.6 (324)	1.68 (437)	.09
Mean global depression	4.9 (104)/4.3 (297)	4.4 (401)	.10

Note. From Survivors Child Loss Survey, 2006–2009.

We also see the diversity in grief and psychological problems among SOS support group members as potentially important and a positive issue. Newly bereaved members can readily find other active participants who are at different points in the healing process and at different levels of mental health functioning. This diversity allows newly bereaved members to draw strength from some who are more advanced in their healing. They can also use less troubled individuals as role models as they try to establish new goals for themselves after a loss. These findings seem instructive for understanding how survivors gain help in support groups, showing that active members attending groups include a wide range of survivors, some with serious grief and mental health difficulties and others who are less troubled in these respects. Thus, the diversity in grief and psychological problems among support group memberships becomes a powerful teaching and helping tool.

Our other findings, showing greater support group participation among churchgoers and those from smaller families, are consistent with a large body of sociological studies. We were, however, mistaken in our belief that support groups would comprise a secondary source of bereavement aid when grief counseling failed. For many survivors, it appears that support groups stand on relatively equal footings with gaining help from mental health and/or bereavement professionals. The data did not confirm suppositions that support groups generally function as refuges for the bereaved who are unable to gain grief help from professional caregivers.

The survey data imply that there is an association between seeing bereavement professionals and going to support groups. The correlation between the two suggests a possible synergy, with one or the other awakening greater desire for self-knowledge through interaction with counselors and/or with other survivors. The synergy works both ways, leading some survivors to go from support groups to counseling and others to begin with counseling and eventually participate in groups later. It may also simply be that people who are more "proactive" about getting help for themselves after a traumatic loss are likely to seek many forms of help (counseling and support groups) and that this proactive self-care is associated with a better outcome for people. For now, it should be clear that support groups are an important, first-line healing resource for many suicide survivors.

As we saw in Chapter 7, the use of most healing aids (therapists, bereavement counselors, support groups, clergy help, psychics, and/or spiritualists) declined over the long course after a loss. However, the steepest declines in participation were noted in the use of mental health professionals. Between 30% and 45% of survivors had used counseling during the first 5 years after a loss; a percentage that declined to about 10% to 15% 10 years afterward. For support group participants, starting from a figure of more than half using them during the early years after a loss, declines showed only a 10% drop over this same period. Thus, the survey data clearly reinforce the notion that for many bereaved parents, support groups remain a primary and longer term healing resource.

The limitations of this study need to be taken into consideration when evaluating the implications of our findings. Although this is perhaps the largest sample of parent suicide survivors ever studied, it is nonetheless a convenience sample that may not be representative of all suicide-bereaved parents. Although the response rate was a most acceptable one for this type of study, we simply do not know whether these conclusions apply to all parent survivors or just to those who participate in survivor research, a group that may be different from nonparticipating survivors. It will also be necessary to see whether the conclusions obtained from this support group–based sample can be confirmed with more broad-based samples of survivors.

Finally, as a cross-sectional and correlational study, we can only demonstrate the associations between predictor and outcome variables and not the direction of causality. In the second part of this analysis, based on in-depth interviews with 24 support group members who eventually withdrew from their groups, we are able to assemble a more detailed view of the healing pathways survivors use over time. Of course, given the small number of these case study records, this understanding necessarily will be more tentative and hypothetical.

WHY DO MANY SURVIVORS EVENTUALLY WITHDRAW FROM SUPPORT GROUPS?

Over time, it is widely observable that many support group members will leave their groups. We have observed many support group members who withdrew from their groups, some shortly after joining and others who withdrew after having regularly attended their group for several years or more. For some survivors, it may simply be that they no longer feel the need to receive the support provided by regular participation in the group. We have also heard survivors remark that after a while, continued group attendance "brought them down" and caused them to feel depressed. What then, explains these support group departures? Are these "unplanned endings" (Walsh, 2003) or "early termina- tions" (Northen & Kurland, 2001) a result of dissatisfaction with the group, the facilitator, or environmental constraints, or are these departures actually a reflection of the differing healing pathways that survivors pursue with the passage of time? This is the question we will now explore.

As some survivors depart from support groups, leaders are often inclined to question whether they have failed to serve some of their members' impor- tant needs, although they usually recognize that it may be impossible for them to satisfy all the needs of the membership. Leadership is often mentioned as a critical component affecting whether some survivors decide to stay or leave their groups. Yet, even with the most skillful support group leadership, there are still likely to be many comings and goings of members. Many pursue dif- fering healing pathways with the passage of time. Survivors' healing needs evolve in different ways over their lifelong course of healing. Some leave groups feeling that the group has given them all that it could to help them manage their grief. Others gravitate to different groups with the passage of time because they perceive that their group failed to meet their expectations. In some cases, disappointments arise because their group has undergone some important changes. The group membership may have grown or shrunk, or its composition may have changed. In still other cases, people leave groups be- cause they feel ready to co-lead or start their own peer support groups. We call this last adaptation an example of posttraumatic growth. Still, other reasons explain comings and goings of some members. Clinicians and support group facilitators serving the suicide bereaved, as well as survivors themselves, can benefit from a better understanding of the healing trajectories of survivors and how they use support groups.

For this analysis, we drew our data primarily from our participant obser- vations with people bereaved by suicide at peer support group meetings and healing conferences. With a base of more than 300 survivors who the first and fourth authors have met and became acquainted with over the past 8 years, we were able to quickly identify 26 survivors who had withdrawn from their groups. We selected these 26 with the hope that they would shed light on another poorly understood aspect of survivors' behavior: support group termi- nations. Unlike the survey sample, who were exclusively parents, this follow- up group consisted of a very diverse group of suicide survivors. Some had lost children, others had lost spouses or partners, and still others had lost parents, siblings, other relatives, or friends. Follow-up respondents also ranged greatly in the time since their loss. Some had withdrawn from their groups after a few meetings, whereas others terminated membership after several years of active or semiactive participation. Approximately a third were newly bereaved, who had sustained a loss less than 2 years earlier; whereas the majority were lon- ger term bereaved, who had experienced a loss 5 or more years previously.

One person refused to be interviewed for the follow-up research, and another could not be reached at her last known phone number. Thus, a total of 24 were interviewed. Again, as in every facet of this research, all names and personally identifying information about respondents have been changed to protect respondents' confidentiality. Wherever necessary, nonessential details about observations and persons have also been changed to safeguard each participant's confidentiality.

In our usually hour-long telephone interviews with follow-up respondents, we asked them to reflect back on all the healing aids they had employed—support groups, bereavement counselors, other mental health caregivers, clergy, psychics—and to evaluate the importance of each in advancing their healing efforts. We probed support group use in particular, asked why respondents had affiliated and withdrawn from their groups, and also inquired about their activities and interests directed at promoting various suicide prevention causes. As far as we know, this is one of only a few research efforts asking U.S. suicide bereaved to make assessments of their healing efforts (McMenamy, Jordan, & Mitchell, 2008; Provini, Everett, & Pfeffer, 2000). The only other analogous research—where bereaved were asked to make an overall assessment of their healing—was conducted among Norwegian suicide bereaved by Kari and Atle Dyregrov (Dyregrov, 2004; Dyregrov & Dyregrov, 2008). This discussion also draws on the participant observation data collected by the first and fourth authors, already described elsewhere in this volume.

FINDINGS ON SUPPORT GROUP DEPARTURES

Clarifying the Synergistic Association Between Seeing Bereavement Counselors and Going to Support Groups

Our survey data demonstrated an association between going to mental health professionals and attending support groups. The follow-up interviews, however, enable us to gain a deeper understanding of how the passage of time can impact the synergistic association between seeing counselors and going to support groups. Betty H.'s comments seem to support the notion of this synergistic association.

> When my husband Donny died by shooting himself, I couldn't stop blaming myself for his death. We had been childhood sweethearts and were supposed to always be there for each other, 'til the very end. Then, he went on active duty in Iraq and never was the same afterwards. He came back like a zombie. I guess he was a classic case of posttraumatic stress. After serving 3 months in a combat zone, he came home and shot himself with a handgun.
>
> I was literally shaking with shock, sadness, and self-blame for nearly the whole first year after Donny died. I went to two suport groups,

saw a therapist, and a psychic. I tried everything. But I couldn't take the first therapist seriously. She hadn't lost anyone to suicide; what could she know and tell me that would be of help—she was completely wasted on me. But the support group, that was wonderful! It felt so good to know others in the same boat as me. I was not the only one losing a husband to a suicide. In the group, I learned to stop blaming myself. There was another widow in our group whose husband shot himself right in front of her in their living room. If she could stop blaming herself for her husband's death, then there was every incentive for me to do the same. The support group showed me that I was not the only one with my problems, and I absolutely must stop torturing myself. Later on, I went back to another counselor, and in the second round—after having been in the group—it didn't bother me at all that my counselor wasn't a survivor. If she could help me learn more things about myself and my imperfections, then it was okay. Now, my second counselor is helping me get to a better place. I'm convinced that managing my grief will be a lifelong project, but at least for now, 3 years after Donny's death, I can begin to think about taking on a new job (which was recently offered to me) to serve as a counselor for bereaved military families. I never thought I'd ever come this far, 2 and a half years ago.

Betty's experience clearly shows the interplay between support group participation and being amenable to clinical treatment. Each feeds into the other, helping the survivor use both treatment modalities synergistically. Yet, it should be understood that the interplay between support groups and therapists is far from simplistic.

In another case, Helen J., at a support group meeting, shared her experience of being at a dinner party with a group of strangers and being asked the question many child loss survivors stumble over: "How many children do you have?" Helen had lost her only daughter to suicide about 5 years earlier. At first, she was tempted to pass on the question and simply respond that she had no children. However, before she spoke, she pondered, and as a former teacher, thought this might be a good teachable moment, and she should be honest about her daughter's life, death, and suicide. Helen briefly shared her story and felt relief afterward. At the support group, she received an enthusiastic burst of approval from most members present who praised her courage. Later, she shared this same story with her psychiatrist. By contrast, her psychiatrist questioned Helen's placing any emphasis on this personal revelation and subsequently expressed some puzzlement why her daughter's suicide should have been regarded as different from any other death. Later on, Helen decided there was little value in remaining under the care of this obtuse treatment professional and sought a referral elsewhere.

In some cases, like Helen's, the lack of compassionate caring by a treatment professional—and the contrast of this with the responsiveness of one's surviving peers—makes a clinician's deficiencies seem all the more apparent to the suicide-bereaved individual. Probably, it makes most sense to think of the interplay between peer support group and professional caregivers taking place on a case-by-case basis. Overall, there appears to be a trend toward a pooling together of treatments, of people who seek one modality being encouraged to pursue another. Of course, in many cases, the gravity of an individual's grief problems and other mental health difficulties, especially those prior mental health problems that may have preceded the death, may lead a survivor toward seeking more treatments. In some cases, opening the door to probe one's grief difficulties and personality may encourage one to pursue parallel treatments, fully exploring interpersonal and intrapsychic issues that may have emerged. At the other end of the spectrum, as some bereaved individuals keep the lid on themselves, shying away from joining a support group and denying the idea that counseling help could ever be of any value, they may encounter experiences reinforcing their decisions to avoid treatment and therapeutic opportunities. In Chapter 6, our findings showed that the parents who did not have any support group or counseling experiences tended to be parents who had sustained natural-death losses of children. It is probable that in some of these cases, parents may have received hospice counseling prior to the death and may have felt that this satisfactorily addressed many, if not all, of their bereavement needs. Also, in cases of natural-death losses, socially significant others may more readily offer caring responses to bereaved persons.

In contrast, in the cases of traumatic deaths, parents may be much more likely to be drawn to support groups and to mental health professionals as they try to cope with the sudden and unexpected nature of their losses and with the responses of some of their significant others who may exhibit silence, avoidance, blame, and an absence of compassionate support.

WHY SURVIVORS LEAVE SUPPORT GROUPS DURING EARLY GRIEVING YEARS: FACILITATOR SKILL ISSUES

One reason why people might leave a group, particularly prematurely, is a lack of good facilitation. In the course of this discussion and with illustrative case material, we identify and recommend several facilitator practices to avoid premature attrition in groups.

1. **Good facilitators prevent monopolization.**
   If there is any one important quality associated with good facilitation in peer support groups, it is the facilitator's ability to control the group so that no one member or small group monopolizes the discussion time at meetings. We repeatedly heard this comment made when survivors reported switching from one group to another or leaving groups altogether. Here's an example from our field notes from Mary Ann V.

   > I had to leave Bob and Marta's CF (group name changed) group because it became a colossal waste. It started out okay. My husband and I were in it for over a year, and it was helping us. But then

two mothers who lost young children in swimming pool drowning accidents joined, and after that, that was all we ever talked about. No one else could get a word in edgewise. I was surprised Bob and Marta didn't intervene to give the floor to someone else. But they just let these two mothers go on and on. And they should have known better. Bob is a school social worker and Marta an RN; they must have run groups before. After waiting three or four meetings for them to do something, we finally decided to pick ourselves up and look for a new support group.

2. **Good facilitators gently encourage support group members to participate by regularly scanning the room and responding to the nonverbal cues of attendees.**
   Linda H. went up to her facilitator after one of her first SOS meetings and said,

   > Thanks for calling on me and getting me into the discussion of how to deal with relatives who avoid mentioning our lost loved ones. I'm glad I got into it, even though you said new members didn't have to say anything. I was about to take the easy way out, but I'm glad you called on me to offer something and I put my two cents in. Now I feel more comfortable here. Thanks for helping me to get started.

3. **Good facilitators sometimes keep silent and let other members respond first to help each other.**
   Support group facilitator, Tom, remarked to his wife, Susan, after a support group meeting how glad he was that he had paused before saying anything in response to one member's query about how survivors should talk about the suicide deaths of relatives to young children. He said,

   > I'm so glad I waited because several group members offered helpful advice based on their own experiences, about providing truthful age-appropriate information to kids. It was much better for it to come from them, rather than from us. We can always offer more information if something said is incorrect or incomplete.

As a corollary to this principle, facilitators should try to avoid "doing it all," and should engage other support group members, wherever possible, to share facilitation tasks. Here is a good example: An especially distressed newly bereaved survivor who lost her husband called a group facilitator asking for information about the support group and for grief help. After offering advice on the bereavement issues of concern to this survivor, the facilitator (himself a survivor of child loss) suggested that another member of the group (who had also lost a spouse) could call and support this person until the group's next meeting. The newly bereaved survivor appreciated this demonstration of concern about her welfare and an opportunity was created where a more experienced survivor rendered aid to someone newly bereaved. The more experienced survivor, in turn, felt respected for the acknowledgment of her healing progress. This example follows the model of "sponsorship" applied in Alcoholics Anonymous.

We cannot emphasize enough the facilitator's role in encouraging empowerment among fellow survivors. As we mentioned in Chapter 6, survivors often feel greatly diminished and personally shattered in the aftermath of a suicide. Their self-confidence has often plummeted to an all-time low. Therefore, opportunities to provide caring responses to other survivors often become important stepping-stones along the pathway toward reestablishing a sense of self-worth and self-confidence.

4. **Learning facilitation**
There are few, if any, "natural leaders" of support groups. Most peer survivors need training to develop leadership skills. Annette P. said,

> I had to leave the Terrace Gardens (a pseudonym) support group. After a few months of going to meetings, it was painfully apparent that the group facilitator didn't know what she was doing. She let the same people talk at every meeting, and she rarely paid much attention to helping the new people who came to meetings. Our meetings kept going over the same few issues, from one meeting to the next. She never had an agenda, or never changed the topic from the few subjects her "regulars" were interested in discussing. That's why I had to find a new group.

Peer facilitators interested in improving their leadership skills can find very helpful peer facilitator manuals, including the following sources: Department of Mental Health and Substance Abuse, 2008; Flatt, 2007; and Jordan and Harpel, 2007. In addition, in the United States, the American Foundation for Suicide Prevention (AFSP) periodically offers 2-day facilitator training courses (open to both laypersons and professionals) in different U.S. metropolitan areas. AFSP also runs a monthly toll-free, professionally facilitated helpline where peer facilitators can gain advice and share information with other facilitators. Interested parties can check the www.afsp.org website for details on the call-in and training course schedules.

It should be understood that mutual aid within a support group doesn't just happen spontaneously or naturally. It has to be cultivated, and it requires hard work, but group work techniques can be taught. Good leadership takes compassion and commitment. Leaders should also be mindful to expand their knowledge of the bereavement process, take advantage of learning opportunities, and try to update their listings of available referral resources in their communities.

As facilitators strive to address the compelling needs for grief support among their newly bereaved members, we offer a summary list of best group facilitator practices:

1. Be a good listener.
2. Scan the group regularly to read and respond to nonverbal cues.
3. Rather than present yourself as the only expert, promote sharing and helping among members whenever possible.
4. Be comfortable with group silence, expressions of pain, and verbal expressions of anger.
5. Gently guide others, especially newcomers, to openly express their grief issues as they feel ready to do so.
6. Lead discussions along relevant and meaningful lines to address survivors' grief problems.
7. Swiftly address potential conflict issues before they escalate, resolving issues so that each person's point of view gains respect and legitimacy.
8. Monitor and respond to other potential group problems: monopolizing, proselytizing, or expressions of intense distress.

DEPARTURES AMONG THE NEWLY BEREAVED (NOT ASSOCIATED WITH LEADERSHIP DEFICIENCIES)

Support groups are not for everyone suffering a suicide loss. Although many peer facilitators may perceive the departure of a new member as caused by their own leadership shortcomings, this can often be a mistaken conclusion. The largest number of member withdrawals are usually caused by a wide variety of circumstances. To promote the most realistic assessment of the group, it is good advice to suggest that newer members give the group at least two or three trial visits before deciding whether to remain or to withdraw.

Survivors come to meetings with many diverging needs. What may satisfy one survivor may be perceived as unhelpful to another. Support group meetings necessarily involve all members sharing their discussion time together as equitably as possible. More needy individuals who persistently take over meetings to the exclusion of other members may need to be referred elsewhere for more one-on-one support.

It is sometimes suggested that survivors should not begin attending support groups until a certain amount of time has passed since the loss. Yet, there appears to be no hard–and–fast rule on this. We have seen some survivors benefit from participation as recently as 1 week after the death of a loved one. We have seen others, starting their participation more than a year after a loss, who are still not entirely comfortable and question the value of support group participation. The time interval depends entirely on the individual survivor and his or her capacity to feel sufficiently safe, supported, and in a comfortable place and ready to share loss stories with other survivors.

Some support group features perceived as essential for most survivors may be experienced as shocking or horrific for others. One cornerstone of the success of a support group is the permission it offers survivors to talk about *all* facets of their loss, including some themes viewed as taboo by nonsurvivors. Some survivors will need to share their firsthand traumatic experiences of encountering a suicide, such as finding a loved one's body after a gunshot death. Other survivors, like the couple described hereafter, may be overwhelmed by hearing such graphic death details and feel unable to continue.

Bob and Betty came to their first support group meeting 3 weeks after their daughter's violent death. Their daughter, Carol, died by jumping from their apartment's eighth story balcony. The next day after their first group meeting, Betty called her facilitator to thank her for running a very orderly meeting but said,

> Maybe I made a mistake by starting here too soon after my daughter's death. Maybe we should have waited longer before we started. I just couldn't sit still during the meeting, hearing about others' tragic losses. It was too much for me, and it brought me right back to the scene of my daughter's death. Every time I walk into my apartment building, I see visions of my Carol's body, lying under a blanket, with the police, EMS people, and all those bystanders milling about in front of our building. Then I go upstairs and look at that stupid balcony barrier. I couldn't take it here last night. It was much too distressing. I think my husband and I will try going to a general bereavement support group where it might be easier for us now.

Betty's comments point to a serious problem for a minority of survivors in support groups—the possibility of being retraumatized by hearing other survivors' loss stories. As these stories are shared, some more fragile survivors may become overwhelmed by the similarities to their own death loss circumstances and to the intensity of emotions expressed by others in the room. Occasionally, a new member may quickly exit from the meeting room in an attempt to escape his or her discomfort. Facilitators need to be prepared for such occurrences and if possible, provide extra support before, during, and after the meetings. Participation in a support group requires a certain amount of courage and may not be a useful healing aid for some survivors or at some points during a survivor's healing process. Referring these individuals to professional bereavement counselors who are both compassionate and familiar with trauma and suicide bereavement may be a more appropriate venue for these survivors.

Another somewhat common reason why survivors leave groups relates to the changing composition of the support group.

Marion R. was a member of a support group for over a year. This young woman lost her father to suicide a couple of months before she began attending the group. She was a regular member for over a year and felt the group was very important to her, especially because all her family lived far away. After she abruptly stopped attending meetings, the facilitator called to find out if every-thing was okay. In the conversation, Marion said that the group had changed and was no longer helping her. When she first began, the group had been very helpful for her with about 8 to 10 survivors coming to monthly meetings. How-ever in recent months, with about 15 to 20 people generally attending, the group had lost its feeling of closeness. Also, when she started, the membership was very diverse, with most every relationship loss represented. Now it seemed parents who lost children were the most common group members and took up most of the discussion time, leaving her feeling less supported. Marion said she would probably try to find another smaller group if possible and if not, would probably seek occasional sessions with a bereavement counselor.

Still, another common reason to explain support group shifts pertains to the informal social relations and shared norms that develop between some members. This can cut two ways. On the one hand, it can lead some members to withdraw from a group because it seems too "cliquish." This is precisely what Renata G. reported.

> I was put off by some other members who usually dominated discus-sions. If I could get a comment in between these five big talkers, I was very lucky. After meetings, this same little group and the facilitator usually went out to a diner for coffee.

For Renata, who had little interest (and time available) to join the others at the diner afterward, the strong ties of other members created a barrier for using the group in a personally meaningful way.

On the other hand, we have also seen members leave groups for the con-verse of this reason when the group did not actively encourage much, if any, informal or formal social relations between members.

Alice H. started attending one support group facilitated by a parent who had lost a child and eventually dropped out after discovering that there was little socialization between members after meetings. She was hoping to connect with others and bond together, but in this group after meetings, most everyone shook hands, gave each other hugs, and took off on their separate ways. Several months later, she tried attending a different group, further from where she lived, in the hopes of finding what she was seeking. The new group, run by a single woman, much like herself, who had survived the loss of a partner, included several other single women who had experienced partner losses. The women in Alice's new group befriended her, and as time passed, she became closely attached to some. Alice felt very happy in her new group; it offered her grief assistance, more helpful support for coping with partner loss, and new friend-ships. Her attraction to the second group was an especially powerful one.

Group facilitators remain in an ambiguous situation when encouraging informal social relations among their members. A strictly task-oriented approach discouraging member interaction beyond grief issues can inhibit the development of member rapport essential for facilitating a survivor's healing over the longer course, but a clique-riddled group is likely to discourage many newly bereaved from being attracted to the group. Facilitators tread a fine line in encouraging socializing among their membership. Although the power of within-group friendships helps promote common goals among survivors and helps them work through their grief problems over time, informal social relations can occasionally create conflicted intragroup relations and can impose barriers for the rapid inclusion of the newly bereaved.

In another case, Eileen B. reported having no interest in socializing with the other members of her group after meetings.

> I declined invitations to attend social events that the facilitator or others organized, like summer picnics and occasional dinner parties. However, when I saw the people again at later meetings, I had the feeling that some of them thought I was stuck up and unfriendly. I resented all these additional social obligations beyond the meetings. I preferred spending most of my free time with my family and friends.

Group goals should be clearly identified. Facilitators need to offer group members a comfortable place to express their grief issues—the primary purpose of an SOS group. If a group has an additional social agenda, beyond its grief-related mission, this should also be clearly articulated. With this clarity, stated at the outset, new members will be able to make more informed decisions about participation. Emotional connectedness among support group members is vital to achieve support group goals. Facilitators will need to promote this, without socialization expectations, especially in the groups where grief work is the group's singular focus.

Our follow-up interviews suggested many different reasons that led survivors to depart from support groups, beyond the ones we have already mentioned. In the following paragraphs, we list several additional profiles of departures by newly bereaved survivors.

Gale F. lost her 38-year-old son to suicide 2 months before she started coming to group. She came to three consecutive meetings and felt the meetings to be greatly helpful to her. Much as she wished to continue participating, she said she would have to take a short break until she completed her cataract surgery. As a widow, whose night-driving abilities were limited, she had previously been escorted to meetings by her daughter or son-in-law. She said her son-in-law was very busy, and she couldn't repeatedly impose on him. As for her daughter, she couldn't come again as she became too depressed listening to the loss stories of the survivors. Gale reported being stuck, unable to return to group, until she completed her eye surgery.

Regina G. and her husband Robert started attending group almost immediately after their 17-year-old son killed himself. After being humiliated by some of his school peers in a practical joke, their son drove the family car into a utility pole. Both attended group for four or five meetings, and then Robert stopped coming because his work schedule had changed. Regina continued attending for the next three meetings but then, she too withdrew. In a follow-up interview, Regina voiced her gratitude for the group but said that unless both she and her husband were able to come to the meetings together, the group had little value. She and her husband had always done things jointly and without his involvement, it seemed pointless to continue.

Maureen S. lost her 36-year-old son to a self-inflicted gunshot wound and started attending a support group about 6 weeks after his death. She came regularly to meetings for about 6 months, was a frequent vocal contributor but then abruptly stopped participating. At follow-up, she remarked that she was beginning to get to a better place with her grief, and a lot of good things were now going on in her life. She joined a gym and was getting regular exercise. She was active in her church and had met several new friends there; she participated in an outreach program visiting homebound sick and infirm parishioners. Most important of all, from a bereavement standpoint, through her new church associations, she had connected with four other widows, two of whom had also lost a child. One of these women was even a suicide survivor. The women met monthly, either going to one or another's homes for dinner or out to a restaurant where they spent an entire evening together socializing. She said she now feels very comfortable talking about her grief issues with these other women. In addition, she had reached a new level of rapprochement with her daughter-in-law and with regular communication and access to her young grandson. This latter benefit had previously been denied to her immediately after her son's death.

As we sum up these last three cases, we note that a support group must fit into the framework of a survivor's life. Sometimes, it must mesh also with the needs of other family members. Family members may be needed to facilitate a survivor's access to attend group meetings. In some cases, a survivor may be unwilling to pursue a support group if it places added burdens on their family relations or marital stability. A survivor who already has a core of available social support may feel that continued support group participation to be unnecessary.

DEPARTURES AMONG SURVIVORS WITH LONGER ASSOCIATIONS IN SUPPORT GROUPS

Our follow-up interviews suggested two contrasting departure patterns; among the newly bereaved, grieving needs were often mentioned in the decisions to withdraw from groups. For longer term survivors, by contrast, these concerns were seldom expressed. Many longer term survivors instead expressed the belief that they had come to have only minimal needs for current grief support.

Pam B. shared such a view, as she reflected on her 6-year absence from support groups. She said,

> I was a "regular" in two groups for many years. My older son was
> 14 years old when he died, and it has been 14 years since his death.

This is putting me into a strange new place. Now I've lived more years with the memory of Jackie than I've had of living with him. I still think of him every day, and I'm sure I will for the rest of my life. But I don't need the groups any more. I guess you could say I outgrew them. Mind you, at the beginning, I needed to relive my loss. Hearing other survivors' loss stories helped me to relive mine. I had to come to terms with my loss, and the support group helped me do that. I learned a great deal from it. Part of my problem after my son died was not having much confidence in myself. I was shattered after Jackie died. I kept blaming myself; he was so young. Working through the grief helped me to rebuild my self-confidence. Eventually, I got back enough nerve to return to high school science teaching. It took me about 5 years to do that, and I think I owe it to the groups for helping me. I never relied on therapists. . . . Eventually, I stopped going [to group] I guess because I didn't need to do it for myself any more. The only reason to stay in group after that would have been to make grief work a central thing in my life. And I didn't want to do that, so I ended it. Actually, my husband, younger son, and I are pretty busy nowadays; we lead pretty full lives.

Another survivor expressed her departure from support group in a different way. Lillian G. whose 38-year-old son died by hanging 4 years ago regularly attended a support group until about 7 months ago. She said, "The support group was a godsend; it had made me at home with my grief." At first, she was totally distraught, full of questioning, blaming herself, and not knowing what to do to calm her troubled soul. The support group was "wonderful medicine. I was free to speak my mind, and I knew I would be understood. I felt safe there. There wasn't anything I couldn't talk about in the group. We're all in that same place together." After a while, Lillian felt more at home with her grief and didn't need the group as much as she did immediately after her son's death. She stopped going for another reason—fatigue. She had a physically demanding job cleaning homes and looking after several frail older adults and didn't have much energy left to go out at night to meetings. The glare from night driving was another problem. Lillian said that hearing the loss stories of the newly bereaved survivors didn't bother her much. She said, "If I could say calming things to them, I was glad to do that, but there were other people in the group, who did a better job of it than me. So I was okay with giving it up."

For many longer term survivors, the experience of staying in the group after having worked through their immediate grief problems weighed heavily on them. Loretta M., an 11-year survivor of her 22-year-old son's suicide, remarked,

I was in the group for 7 years; it was enough already. Hearing the new people come in and tell their loss stories—seeing their tears, seeing them all welled up with so much emotion, guilt, and shock—it all brought me down and back to the place I started from. I didn't need this anymore. The support group had been my salvation. I belonged to two of them. I made a half dozen very close friends in the groups over the years. I still see these friends; we all lost children to suicide around the same time, and we comfort each other. This perhaps is the best help for me now—being with my friends. Now, there are a few rare occasions when I do get sad again (such as when we are invited to a wedding and it reminds me of my son not being alive); being with my friends comforts me. My husband and I go out to dinner with some of them, sometimes. We've even taken vacation trips together. We also celebrate difficult days together like Mother's Day. I thank God for their support.

When asked if Loretta was involved in any suicide prevention activities, she said she helped at an annual local community walk fund raiser; she solicited donations and volunteered at the registration desk. She said, "I enjoy doing these things; it helps the cause, and I do it with some of my good friends who I'm always glad to see again. We pitch in and try to do what we can to change things."

Erica K., another long-term survivor, whose 20-year-old daughter took her life 10 years ago, reported making the rounds with her husband in trying almost every conceivable therapeutic resource to deal with their loss.

I think I was lucky to have my husband willing to try all the different therapies together with me. I've seen other families where the wife does all the grief work and the husband stays home watching football games or something. I don't think that's such a good plan. First, my husband and I tried a grief counselor who was a social worker and that was very helpful. After that, we tried Compassionate Friends. The CF people were nice; no one ever said a negative word to us, but we never felt completely comfortable there. I don't think any of those people knew what we were going through with a suicide. You have to be with suicide survivors to get the feeling of true compassion and support. Later on, we went to an SOS group for over 3 years, and that was much better than the general bereavement group, but the best group of all was an 8-week treatment group we completed at a family mental health clinic. They put eight of us, suicide survivors, together into a single group and we bonded. After the 8-week session, we decided to meet at one of our homes and have monthly meetings. We even considered hiring a grief counselor to lead our meetings, but one of us was an experienced social worker, so we didn't need to hire anyone. We did that for about 3 years, and it worked fine. Eventually, we stopped our monthly meetings and just got together with each other informally, which some of us still do now.

My husband took training as a first responder, and every now and then he is called out to counsel a newly bereaved suicide survivor. I can't do that. Once I go back to all those early grief things—blame, shock, confusion, etc.—it pulls me down. I can't go back there. My husband and I do what we can with suicide prevention. We do fund raising, help organize an annual local community walk; we're on a local chapter board for a mental health service organization; I used to go into the high schools with a group of other survivors, giving suicide prevention talks to students, but I don't have the time to do that anymore.

Sally F. lost her son 13 years ago, when he took his life at age 16. She and her husband Hank belonged to an SOS and a general bereavement group and faithfully went to both group's meetings for about 7 or 8 years. They made several close friendships with other survivors in these groups who they still see from time to time. Sally felt that it was the grief support they received from their survivor friends that helped them the most to ultimately accept their loss.

They [her support group friends] have been like a family to me when my own family failed and didn't know what to do or say to us; they still avoid mentioning our deceased son and act as if he had been consumed by the plague or something. Eventually, we didn't need to continue going to the meetings any more, so we stopped. Later on, in my church I was approached to co-lead a bereavement group with another woman who lost her son. We cofacilitated a group for about 3 years. At its peak, we had 14 people in our group. It seemed like a good thing to do, but eventually it petered out, at least for me it did, when I got a new job. At that point, I had to give my part over to my cofacilitator. I still help out at an annual bereavement conference in our community. It's a big conference, and I usually help out with the registration, and I sit at the conference resources table helping newly bereaved attendees make the most of the conference. At the conference, I also give away copies of my book about my son's life and death.

POSTTRAUMATIC GROWTH THROUGH SOCIAL ACTIVISM

Follow-up interviews suggested far more evidence of posttraumatic growth among longer term survivors than among the newly bereaved. As Chapter 10 will examine this subject in greater detail, readers will note that the term refers to a wide variety of different behaviors. In the conceptualization advanced by Tedeschi and Calhoun (1996) the authors emphasize the development of a greater sense of spirituality following a loss. By contrast, Hogan, Greenfield, and Schmidt (2001) in their analogous concept "personal growth," emphasize the development of a greater compassionate and empathic self following a death. Common to both of these conceptualizations is the idea that social activism may accompany bereavement. Posttraumatic growth can be reflected in social change actions when survivors act collectively to alter the fabric of society, to prevent suicide, and to diminish the stigma that now surrounds it and other mental health problems. Survivors support organizations are committed to suicide prevention and take part in many actions at the local and/or national level that address the problems of suicide and mental health treatment availability. Survivors do many of these things: lead or colead survivor support groups, work with others to organize bereavement conferences, engage in fund-raising efforts to provide more support for research on mental health problems, and participate in political action aimed at providing more and better mental health and bereavement services in their communities. A few act as educators, writing books or articles on suicide or mental health issues, giving talks to community groups about suicide, and helping to change the stereotypical thinking about mental health problems and suicide. Many posttraumatic growth efforts are aimed at fund raising for some of the many organizations supporting mental health and suicide research: NARSAD (National Alliance for Research on Schizoprenia and Depressions; The Brain and Behavior Research Fund), NAMI (The National Alliance on Mental Illness), AFSP, SPANUSA (Suicide Prevention Action Network), SPIORG (Suicide Prevention International), and SAVE (Suicide Awareness Voices of Education), among others.

Even newly bereaved survivors may be involved in acts reflecting posttraumatic growth. For example, one newly bereaved survivor successfully advocated in his or her community to establish a first responder's program, to have teams of trained survivors visit the newly bereaved to help them deal with the unbearable shock of suicide loss. Other newly bereaved survivors have initiated memorial walks, golf outings, and similar fund-raising events honoring their lost loved ones and have raised monies for mental health research. For most, these empowering acts have helped channel survivors' grief into socially purposeful enterprises.

Facilitators must be cautious about incorporating fund raising and suicide prevention goals into their discussion time at meetings lest they offend those members who want and need grief work to be their group's exclusive focus. There also may be pot ential conflicts with members advocating for different service organizations. Suggesting that members discuss advocacy matters among themselves after meetings is an effective way to reduce such conflicts. Here again, the facilitator sometimes treads a fine line in possibly offending different factions within their memberships as they allot (or fail to allot) sufficient discussion time to interested advocacy parties. Facilitators need to strike the right balance between emphasizing the personal dimensions of doing grief work and at the same time providing survivors with opportunities to transform their grief into positive activities that are also healing for the survivor. For most of the newly bereaved, there is little energy and interest available to pursue collective goals, but brief discussions of other survivors' activities, after the initial pain of loss, can be important to instilling hope.

SUMMARY AND CONCLUSIONS

We asked the longer term suicide survivors in our follow-up sample, who comprised the majority, to evaluate what had given them their most important help in coping with and transcending the despair of their suicide losses. A few indicated that a very good counselor had been of great help, especially during the months after loss. Yet, as they took stock of their primary help-rendering resources, most said their support group was their mainstay in helping them endure the sometimes treacherous course of life after loss. As Lillian G. said, the support group was her "godsend," "wonderful medicine" for helping her to accept the loss of her son and move forward with her life. Others said they didn't know how they would have made it to the present without the help of their group and the other survivors who they had met since they began their healing journeys.

Generally, survivors felt that in the support group they were "understood" in their new and difficult roles as suicide survivors. Some reported admiration for longer standing survivors who served as role models, demonstrating the possibility of a "new normal" to them. They felt greatly inspired by these other survivors, especially those who appeared to demonstrate profound resilience, (such as the mother who lost two teenage children in a single [nonsuicide] automobile accident, the father who sustained two suicide deaths of children in his family, or another wife whose husband shot himself in her presence). The survivors expressed profound respect for these loss victims and felt that if they could rebound after such extremely tragic loss circumstances, there must be hope for themselves as well, recognizing that there must be something they can learn from participating in their support groups.

In the groups, survivors used one another as reference points for gauging their own healing progress. We repeatedly heard comments suggesting this in our participant observations among those who felt group was an important helping force. As one survivor remarked, "When I heard Ellen talk about her issues—trying to get her other family members to come to meetings, sharing her feelings of immense guilt and anger, etc.—I could see how far I've come since I joined the group."

For some, these actions of sharing loss stories helped them recognize that it may be time for them to move on from group. As Pam B. expressed it, "I don't need to relive others' loss stories any more to help me come to terms with my own loss."

Again and again, we heard that new friendships with other survivors were extremely important to help them to compensate for disappointments from other relationships in their lives. Many survivors found their social networks shrinking after their suicide losses because some close family members and friends said hurtful things about their lost loved one, suggested blame, or neglect for their parts in their loved one's demise. In other cases, significant others failed to acknowledge the loss or avoided contact to minimize their own discomfort. Others bereaved by suicide or other sudden death losses almost always knew what to say to show compassion and to act supportively to a survivor. They remembered each other's important death anniversary dates and for all these and other reasons, provided great comfort.

As survivors meet one another in their support groups at healing conferences or in online chat groups, some now find they have many new friends with whom they can go out dining, spend a social evening together, or even plan vacation trips as a few reported doing. Because many survivors remain active in bereavement or suicide prevention advocacy work, they now have the comfort and pleasure of working together with former support group members reconnecting with one another at these events. Thus, support groups help strengthen the bonds of friendship and community between survivors.

As we assess the support group over time, we recognize that the structure of the open-ended group may become a zone for potential conflicts as the forum offered to the newly bereaved may clash with the expectations and needs of many longer term survivors who feel they have largely accomplished what they set out to do in accepting their losses. Although longer term survivors show support for the newly bereaved and help them openly express their sorrow, anguish, and confusion, some longer term survivors ultimately realize they need to withdraw from the support group to avoid reliving their own painful feelings of suicide grief. Some of these longer term survivors may even be brought to a sad realization that their own healings may not have progressed to the level of their expectations as evidenced by their strong aversions to the deep sorrow and tears of the newly bereaved. For these survivors, images of the newly bereaved offer them painful reminders of their own persisting inabilities to accept loss.

As they understand that grief has many diverging forms and that there is no one single model of "good grief," each survivor seeks to find his or her own personal level of grieving comfort and the things he or she must do to achieve and preserve his or her well-being. Yet, after any overall assessment, most would agree that open-ended support groups are nurturing environments that successfully address the needs of the newly bereaved and serve to generate a cadre of potential peer leaders among longer term survivors.

This analysis suggests numerous other dividing points within an open-ended SOS group. Survivors come to the meetings bearing a diversity of losses of children, partners, parents, siblings, and friends. At meetings, they expect to find sufficient discussion time allotted to their particular bereavement circumstances so that they may feel supported and understood. Yet, in our experience with the comings and goings of members over our 8-year history of participating in and running a support group, the first and fourth author note attachments to support groups of far shorter duration exhibited by those losing siblings and parents, when compared to those losing a child or a partner. Many of the latter two populations remain affiliated in groups for 3 years or more, whereas the former two populations rarely remain affiliated beyond a year. Whether these differences reflect different magnitudes of grieving or whether the partner and child loss groups exert dominating influences, thereby marginalizing sibling and parent loss survivor constituencies, we are unable to say. Future research should investigate whether there is a perceived shortage of available forums for those sustaining losses of parents and siblings in SOS support groups.

Potential division points within support groups also include the delicate balance of encouragement of informal social relations among members and the support of advocacy interests among members. Both of these areas present a challenge for facilitators, to strike the right balance lest they offend significant segments of their membership. Our follow-up interviews gave abundant evidence of the importance of the friendship ties that survivors make with one another along their healing journeys. These ties and the goals that these survivors now share are especially important in connecting survivors in society in new and personally meaningful ways. Many survivors regard these attachments, some made in professionally led therapy groups and others nurtured in open-ended SOS groups, as tremendously important in their post-loss lives. Such ties help to legitimate their new survivor identities and lead them to accept their losses with greater equanimity.

We see clinicians having a key role in helping their survivor patients coordinate their care-seeking efforts in meaningful and constructive ways. This is especially true during the early postlost years when a survivor is likely to rely on clinicians to the greatest degree. This inquiry has shown how focusing on support groups can better illuminate the process by which survivors heal after suicide losses. It is hoped that future research will draw on this readily accessible and especially fertile resource.

REFERENCES

Birnbaum, M. L., & Cicchetti, A. (2005). A model for working with the group life cycle in each group session across the life span of the group. *Groupwork, 15*, 23–43.

Cerel, J., Padgett, J. H., Conwell, Y., & Reed, G. A. (2009). A call for research: The need to better understand the impact of support groups for suicide survivors. *Suicide & Life-Threatening Behavior, 39*(3), 269–281.

Cerel, J., Padgett, J. H., & Reed, G. A. (2009). Support groups for suicide survivors: Results of a survey of group leaders. *Suicide & Life-Threatening Behavior, 39*(6), 588–598.

Department of Mental Health and Substance Abuse, World Health Organization. (2008). *Preventing suicide: How to start a survivor's support group*. Geneva, Switzerland: WHO Press.

Durkheim, E. (1997). *Suicide*. New York, NY: Free Press.

Dyregrov, K. (2004). Bereaved parents' experience of research participation. *Social Science & Medicine, 58*(2), 391–400.

Dyregrov, K., & Dyregrov, A. (2008). *Effective grief and bereavement support*. London, UK: Jessica Kingsley Publishers.

Flatt, L. L. (2007). *The basics: Facilitating a survivors support group*. Washington, DC: SPAN-USA.

Hogan, N. S., Greenfield, D. B., & Schmidt, L. A. (2001). Development and validation of the Hogan Grief Reaction Checklist. *Death Studies, 25*(1), 1–32.

Jordan, J. R., & Harpel, J. L. (2007). *Facilitating suicide bereavement support groups: A self-study manual*. New York, NY: American Foundation of Suicide Prevention.

Levy, L. H., & Derby, J. F. (1992). Bereavement support groups: Who joins; who does not; and why. *American Journal of Community Psychology, 20*(5), 649–662.

McMenamy, J., Jordan, J. R., & Mitchell, A. M. (2008). What do suicide survivors tell us they need? Results of a pilot study. *Suicide & Life-Threatening Behavior, 38*(4), 375–389.

Northen, H., & Kurland, R. (2001). *Social work with groups* (3rd ed.). New York, NY: Columbia University Press.

Provini, C., Everett, J. R., & Pfeffer, C. R. (2000). Adults mourning suicide: Self-reported concerns about bereavement, needs for assistance, and help-seeking behavior. *Death Studies, 24*(1), 1–19.

Shulman, L. (2006). *The skills of helping individuals, families and communities* (5th ed.). Pacific Grove, CA: Thomson, Brooks/Cole.

Skocpol, T., & Fiorina, M. P. (Eds.). (1999). *Civic engagement in American democracy*. Washington, DC: Brookings Institution Press.

Suitor, J. J., & Pillemer, K. (2000). When experience counts most: Differential effects of experiential similarity on men's and women's receipt of support during bereavement. *Social Networks, 22*(4), 299–312.

Tedeschi, R. G., & Calhoun, L. G. (1996). The posttraumatic growth inventory: measuring the positive legacy of trauma. *Journal of Traumatic Stress, 9*(3), 455–471.

Verba, S., Schlozman, K. L., & Brady, H. E. (1995). *Voice and equality: Civic voluntarism in American politics*. Cambridge, MA: Harvard University Press.

Walsh, J. (2003). *Endings in clinical practice: Effective closure in diverse settings*. Chicago, IL: Lyceum Books.

10

Personal Growth After a Suicide Loss: Is It Associated With a Survivor's Mental Health?

INTRODUCTION

In this chapter, we explore the relationships between a survivor's personal growth (PG) or posttraumatic growth after a suicide loss and their mental health. We will begin by defining these two terms, which we will use interchangeably although they emerged from different theoretical traditions and different groups of behavioral scientists. Posttraumatic growth refers to positive changes experienced as a result of a traumatic event. The originators of the term, Tedeschi and Calhoun (1996), refer to its presence in five areas: (a) the perception of new opportunities, (b) a change in relationships with others, (c) an increased sense of one's own strength, (d) a greater appreciation for life in general, and (e) a deepening of one's spiritual life. The PG term emerged later from a different research group—Hogan, Greenfield, and Schmidt (2001). Like the Tedeschi and Calhoun–inspired term, the PG concept and scale to measure it emphasize positive changes arising after a traumatic loss. The person undergoing PG feels he or she has learned better coping skills, is stronger after having endured tragedy, and now has a better outlook on life and has become a more compassionate, caring, and forgiving individual. Both researcher groups maintain that PG or posttraumatic growth is not necessarily a universal experience. Some bereaved persons will experience it, and others will not.

Thus far in our analysis we have noted that many bereaved parents show evidence of resilience after their losses and we have called their resilient acts manifestations of posttraumatic growth or PG. Some of our bereaved-parent

215

respondents help newly bereaved by starting their own support groups and serving as support group facilitators. Others engage in political actions, working to change laws governing mental health and addictions treatment availability. Some engage in fund-raising, helping to amass more resources for research on the problems causing their children's deaths. Still others engage in advocacy work of different sorts, such as teaching, doing research, and writing their own books, to help change societal perceptions and stimulate greater efforts to deal with the problems that contributed to their children's untimely deaths.

Subsequently, we present two examples of suicide-bereaved parents whose tragic losses ultimately led them to reinvent themselves to assume more humanitarian and service-oriented commitments.

With little forewarning, Susan and Michael Wallach (pseudonyms) lost their 18-year-old son Jeremy to suicide about 8 years ago and ever since have been attempting to rebuild their lives. Susan, a high school guidance counselor, found warm and supportive responses from her colleagues at the local school where she works. Her husband, Michael, an ophthalmologist, also gained much solace and support from his colleagues and their many friends in the upscale suburban community where they reside. After seeing several bereavement counselors and attending survivor support group meetings during their first 3 years after the loss, the Wallachs became interested in participating with the American Foundation for Suicide Prevention (AFSP). An idea percolated in their discussions with AFSP personnel to do a fund-raising event in their local community to raise money to make an educational film on depression and suicidality among high school students. With support from friends, family, and their community, the Wallachs staged a fund-raiser at their local temple and succeeded in collecting more than $200,000 to help finance an educational film. Now, 8 years since their son's suicide, the Wallachs still remain active in AFSP fund-raising efforts and serve on the committee to plan their local AFSP chapter's annual fund-raising memorial walk. Presently, neither Michael nor Susan see counselors or attend local support group meetings. They still feel great sadness and pain over the loss of Jeremy, but recognize that they have turned their family's personal tragedy into an opportunity to "make a difference," to join with others and combat the problem of youth suicide.

After a long and torturous course of trying to get help for their young adult son, Vinny Jr., Vinny and Patti Lombardo (pseudonyms) experienced his tragic suicide by hanging 10 years ago at the age of 31. Afterward, the couple never relied much on professional bereavement counseling resources but instead found great comfort and help in support group participation. They became part of a group of cofounding parents of a new support group, with 12 other parents who had lost children to suicide around the same time that Vinny Jr. died. Their support group participation extended beyond attending monthly meetings to include taking occasional vacation trips with some other members, as well as spending dreaded holiday occasions with one another. As time passed, Patti found that continued support group participation brought her down mentally, but Vinny continued to stay active, regularly attending meetings. Recently, he completed training to become a first responder and has already made several visits to comfort newly bereaved families, thanks to a new program funded by local politicians in his community. At support group meetings, Vinny usually makes important contributions to help newly bereaved survivors see that grief becomes more manageable with the passage of time. He feels that "veteran" survivors like him have an obligation to "give back" to the newly bereaved. For him, the support group has been the cornerstone of his recovery and well-being and, for the foreseeable future, intends to remain active to help newly bereaved "get to a better place."

Unlike many of the less well-researched subjects we have been investigating in this book, posttraumatic growth and PG have gained much attention among bereavement researchers. In the professional literature, much has been written about the grief-to-growth theme, and the functional adaptations emerging among the bereaved after a tragedy. A common claim is that grief and trauma present a survivor with a transformative potential, leading some to eventually take their posttraumatic challenges and change them into posttraumatic growth (Tedeschi & Calhoun, 2004). A large number of articles devoted to the grief-to-growth theme are cited in a review chapter by Schaefer and Moos (2001), entitled "Bereavement Experiences and Personal Growth." Some studies have approached this subject in more general and theoretical terms, often drawing upon illustrative case study materials (see, e.g., Nadeau, 1998; Nerken, 1993; Shapiro, 2008, among others), whereas others have approached it from a survey research standpoint, investigating larger numbers of bereaved individuals, usually with established instruments systematically measuring PG. The two most widely employed instruments measuring PG are Tedeschi and Calhoun's Posttraumatic Growth Inventory (PTGI, 1996) and the PG subscale within the Hogan Grief Reaction Checklist (HGRC; Hogan et al., 2001).

As Schaefer and Moos (2001) point out, the grief-to-growth transition is likely to go forward differently, depending on the relationship a bereaved person had with the deceased. The loss of a child will bring a survivor along different recovery pathways when compared to other types of losses, such as the death of a spouse, parent, or sibling. Of course, our intent in this chapter is to focus on how PG emerges among bereaved parents. There is a fast-mounting research literature with the two established scales of PG about the adaptations of parents losing children (see, e.g., Büchi et al., 2007; Engelkemeyer & Marwit, 2008; Polatinsky & Esprey, 2000; Riley, LaMontagne, Hepworth, & Murphy, 2007; Wagner, Knaevelsrud, & Maercker, 2007). The work of the Dyregrovs also bears on this subject (Dyregrov & Dyregrov, 2008; Dryegrov, Nordanger, & Dyregrov, 2000).

Polatinsky and Esprey (2000) focus their work on the gender differences in personal or posttraumatic growth, whereas Büchi et al. (2007) focus their attention on the loss of premature babies. Wagner et al. (2007) examine a mixed group of bereaved individuals with various relationships to the deceased:

parents, partners, siblings, and so forth. Thus, only a smaller number of the studies are of immediate interest to us.

Riley et al. (2007) studied a small sample of 35 bereaved parents, two-thirds of whom had lost children to accidents and neonatal infant deaths. They found PG associated with a positive reframing of the loss and less complicated grief. With a sample of 111 bereaved parents, almost evenly divided between homicide-, accident-, and illness-bereaved, Engelkemeyer and Marwit (2008) found that the intensity of grief was inversely associated with a respondent's growth scores. In a study of 232 Norwegian parents whose children had died by suicide, accidents, and sudden infant death syndrome (SIDS), a percentage of whom were given follow-up interviews, it was found that most of the follow-up respondents experienced positive personal changes or PG in the years after their losses (Dyregrov & Dyregrov, 2008; Dyregrov, Nordanger, & Dyregrov, 2003).

Given the consistency of these results, we speculated that PG would be associated with fewer grief difficulties and better mental health among our respondents. In addition, based on the findings of Dyregrov and Dyregrov (2008), we also speculated that time since the loss would be positively associated with PG.

Given the great similarity between posttraumatic growth and PG conceptualizations and their measurements, we decided to use only one of these scales in our survey work; we chose the Hogan Personal Growth Scale, which was one of several subscales from the HGRC. The authors have asserted that PG is an integral component of bereavement. In their groundbreaking article, they found that longer term survivors scored higher on PG than the newly bereaved (Hogan et al., 2001). They also noted an inverse association between PG scores and measures of grief difficulties, posttraumatic stress, and complicated grief. The HGRC PG subscale consists of 12 questions that probe whether the bereaved respondent feels they have become more tolerant, compassionate, caring, and better persons following their loss.

Although the Hogan PG scale has not been employed in a great many studies, one study (Gamino, Sewell, & Easterling, 2000) employed this scale, with a sample of 85 mourners. They found that higher scorers were more likely to experience "adaptive grieving," suggesting that they were more likely to see some good coming from a death, had a chance to say goodbye to the decedent, experienced intrinsic spirituality, and had spontaneous positive memories of the decedent. Given the built-in redundancies of the scale for our survey, we used an abbreviated version, consisting of its seven highest correlated items, where each showed correlations of .66 or higher with the overall score. These seven items are shown in Chapter 1.

Given the consistency between Hogan's preliminary work with the scale and the other research findings we have already mentioned, we were encouraged to posit several additional hypotheses about PG that we also wanted to explore. With PG presumed to emerge later in the grieving process, we anticipated that among the longer termed bereaved in our sample, people showing higher growth scores would be more active support group participants (and more likely to serve as support group facilitators or to demonstrate higher levels of participation) compared to other longer term bereaved who would have lower PG scores. At the other end of the spectrum, among the newly bereaved, where it is assumed that PG has yet to advance very far, we did not anticipate much, if any, association between the attitudes embracing PG and support group participation. Thus, we were eager to explore whether behavioral manifestations of PG—reflected in support group participation—would be associated with the PG attitudes that bereaved parents affirmed.

Before beginning our analyses, we explored PG among the different death-cause subgroups of our sample and found them to show significant differences from one another. In addition, we found that within each of these same subgroups, there were also significant differences in time since the loss, a key variable to the present analysis. Readers will recall in Chapter 4 that we presented a graphic showing grief problems diminishing for most suicide-bereaved parents as the years after a loss pass. For these reasons, we decided to limit our focus to the 462 parents bereaved by suicide in our sample. This simplified our analyses and limited our generalizations to the PG experiences of suicide-bereaved parents. It will remain a task for future research to investigate whether the findings we obtained for these bereaved parents can be applied more broadly.

In this work, we also sought to better identify the demographic and other social correlates associated with PG. If PG represents an important part of a survivor's mental health and healing, then a better understanding of its dynamics and social bases seems essential in order for clinicians to help bereaved patients move most expeditiously toward healing after loss.

FINDINGS

Table 10.1 presents a correlation matrix for many of the important variables explored in this investigation: PG, brief Grief Experience Questionnaire scores of grief difficulties, time since the loss, the Index of Psychological Problems, and reported suicide thoughts, plans, and attempts. The matrix shows all variables significantly related to each other with one exception: suicide attempts and time since the loss. PG scores are positively associated with time since the loss and inversely associated with suicidality (thoughts and plans), grief difficulties, and mental health difficulties. As expected, our mental health problems indicator was also positively associated with grief difficulties and suicidality (thoughts, plans, and attempts) and inversely associated with time since the loss and PG. Some of the associations were relatively strong, such as the relationship between mental health problems and grief difficulties (.61) and suicide thoughts (.54). Some of the associations with suicide plans and attempts were relatively weak and probably reflect the relative rarity of these experiences among our respondents. (When a sampled variable includes too few cases, it can yield great fluctuations and less reliable estimates.) Only

Table 10.1
Correlation Matrix of Personal Growth, Years Since Loss,
Suicidalities, Grief, and Mental Health Difficulties ($N = 462$)

	PERSONAL GROWTH (PG)	YEARS SINCE LOSS	SUICIDE THOUGHTS	SUICIDE PLANS	SUICIDE ATTEMPTS	GEQ SCORES
	CORRELATION COEFFICIENT/p VALUES					
Years since loss	0.30***					
Suicide thoughts	−0.40***	−0.25***				
Suicide plans	−0.18***	−0.16***	0.62***			
Suicide attempts	−0.12*	−0.09	0.30***	0.36***		
GEQ scores	−0.36***	−0.28***	0.52***	0.31***	0.22***	
Mental health diffs. (IPP)	−0.42***	−0.35***	0.54***	0.32***	0.17***	0.61***

Note. From Survivors Child Loss Survey, 2006–2007.
*$p < .05$. **$p < .01$. ***$p < .001$.

11% of suicide survivors ($n = 51$) reported suicide plans in the past year and 2% reported a suicide attempt ($n = 9$). PG scores showed modest correlations with most of the mental health, suicidality and grief difficulties variables, and time since the loss (ranging at the .30–.40 level).

We also investigated whether PG was simply a reflection of a lack of grief difficulties or mental health problems or whether it stood alone and made independent contributions to explain the variability in suicidality among parent survivors. To probe this, we created a multiple regression equation with the frequency of suicide thoughts as the dependent variable and grief difficulties, mental health problems, and PG as independent variables. We also included in the same equation another important confounder of grief difficulties: time since the loss. Results are displayed in Table 10.2. The model explained 38% of the variance in suicide thinking. All independent variables contributed additional variance to this model except time since the loss. We also reran the same equation omitting PG, which resulted in a statistically significant 4% drop in explained variance. The explained variance dropped to 34% without PG in the equation. This shows its own dynamic importance in this analysis.

The multiple regression findings suggested that PG might offer independent contributions to predict differences in mental health problems over and above other established predictors, such as time since loss. We found this to be the case when we examined the means of mental health problems in our entire

Table 10.2
Multiple Regression Analysis of Suicide Thinking by Grief Difficulties (GEQ Scores), Mental Health Problems, Personal Growth Score, and Time Since the Death

INDEPENDENT VARIABLES	CORREL. COEFF.	BETA	P
GEQ score	.52	.25	.0001
Personal growth (PG)	−.40	−.18	.0001
Years since death	−.25	−.02	.58
Index Psychological Problems (IPP)	.54	.32	.0001

Note. From Survivors Child Loss Survey, 2006–2009.
Number of obs = 391
$F(4,386) = 59.7$
R-squared = .38
p = Level of Significance

sample and its subsamples. We found a mean of 1.67 mental health problems for our entire parent-suicide survivor sample. This mean was reduced to 1.22 for the 195 cases that had lost a child 5 or more years earlier. This mean declined still further to .94 when we counted only those 5-year post-loss survivors who had scored above the mean ($n = 139$) on the PG scale. (This is not displayed in the tables.)

As PG correlated negatively with mental health problems, we plotted both of these variables separately in Figures 10.1 and 10.2 along the continuum of time since loss. The plots suggest that as the time passes after a suicide loss, PG scores rise and mental health problems begin to subside. Figure 10.1

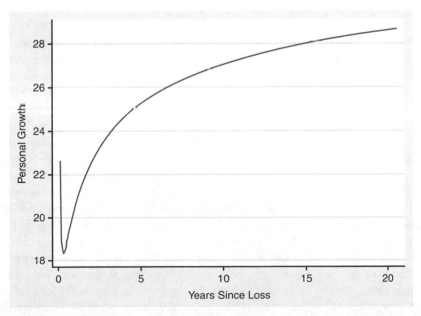

FIGURE 10.1   Lowess-Smooth Functions of Years Since Death by Personal Growth

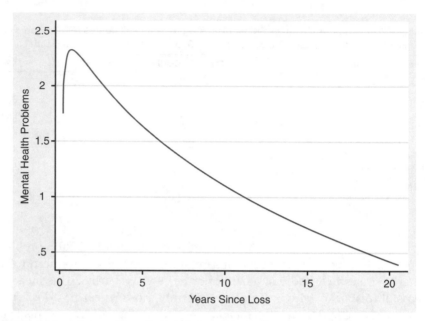

FIGURE 10.2 Lowess-Smooth Functions of Years Since Death by Mental Health Problems

shows, after a slight drop in PG during the first year after a loss, PG scores rise steadily as the years after loss pass. By the fifth year, most survivors exceed the mean PG score. Figure 10.2 shows mental health problems spiking slightly in the first year after loss, and thereafter steadily declining. It should be understood that these figures are based on cross-sectional data from the 462 suicide survivors who offered ratings at different time intervals after their child's death. Only longitudinal research that follows the same sample of survivors over many years would allow us to know for certain that mental health problems decrease while PG increases with time since the death in a given sample of individuals.

We also anticipated that those high in PG would be more active participants in support groups compared to those showing lower PG scores. We expected this hypothesis to be supported only among longer term survivors. This hypothesis was suggested by the data in Figure 10.1 that showed most survivors exceeding the mean scores in PG approximately 5 years (or later) after their losses. The hypothesis also meshed with our field observations collected at support groups, where longer term survivors more often assumed caregiving roles at meetings. Table 10.3 presents the correlation coefficients for support group participation, use of professional help, and PG. Participation was scored on a 3-point scale with the following values: (0) for *no participation*; (1) for *attending 1–5 meetings or sessions during the past year*; and (2) for *going to 6 or more meetings or sessions during the past year*. If we look at support group participation among the newly bereaved survivors who sustained a loss less than 5 years ago, we note no association between support group activism and PG. During this early bereavement period, the only significant association noted is a negative correlation between seeing any mental health professional and experiencing PG. This makes sense if we revisit Figure 10.2, which shows a higher number of survivors above the mean having mental health problems during the period of early bereavement. These survivors are more inclined to seek mental health counselors, to see them more often, and are less likely to experience PG during this period of early survivorship. In Chapter 6, we discussed the findings showing that those seeing professional counselors had poorer mental health and greater grief difficulties during the period of early bereavement. Now, Table 10.3 suggests that PG is another correlate during early bereavement, inversely associated with seeing mental health professionals.

As we shift our attention in Table 10.3 to longer term survivors, we see positive associations between support group participation and PG, perhaps

Table 10.3
Differences In Personal Growth by Participation in Survivor Support Groups and Seeking Counseling Among Shorter and Longer Term Suicide Survivors (*N* = 455)

AMONG SHORTER TERM SURVIVORS, < OR = TO 4.99 YEARS, N = 259	PERSONAL GROWTH SCORE	
	CORRELATION	SIG.
During the past year, how often did you go to a general bereavement support group meeting?	.10	.12
During the past year, how often did you go to a survivor of suicide support group meeting?	.01	.81
During the past year, how often did you go to a professional bereavement counselor?	.001	.99
During the past year, how often did you seek help from a psychiatrist, psychologist, social worker, or psychiatric nurse?	−.21	.001
AMONG LONGER TERM SURVIVORS, > OR = TO 5.0 YEARS, *N* = 196	PERSONAL GROWTH SCORE	
	CORRELATION	SIG.
During the past year, how often did you go to a general bereavement support group meeting?	.16	.02
During the past year, how often did you go to a survivor of suicide support group meeting?	.28	.001
During the past year, how often did you go to a professional bereavement counselor?	−.03	.66
During the past year, how often did you seek help from a psychiatrist, psychologist, social worker, or psychiatric nurse?	−.12	.09

Note. From Survivors Child Loss Survey, 2006–2007.

suggesting that "giving back" becomes a predominant concern among survivors who are further along in the grieving process. Interestingly, we also note no significant association between PG and seeing professional counselors during the later bereavement period. Here again, only longitudinal data can satisfactorily demonstrate what these cross-sectional data seem to suggest— that the passage of time since a loss is associated with fewer mental health problems, greater reports of PG, and a diminished need (or at least going to see someone) for counseling among survivors.

Table 10.4 displays ANOVA test results comparing the means of PG and various demographic differences among our respondents. We collected the following demographic information: gender, age, educational attainments, socioeconomic status, voting participation, political ideologies and preferences, religious affiliation and frequency of participation, and urbanicity, that is, urban versus rural residence. Bivariate comparisons suggested the following significant differences in growth means between respondents: age, voting participation, religious affiliation, and religious participation. Scheffe post hoc comparison tests showed that middle-aged respondents (aged 35 to 45 years) had significantly lower PG scores than both older groups, those 56 to 65 years old and those older than 66 years old. Post hoc tests also showed that Jewish respondents were significantly lower in PG than Protestants and Catholics. Post hoc testing also showed that those attending religious services weekly reported significantly higher PG than those attending services several times yearly or less often.

Some of these factors could potentially be confounded with one another and with the variable of time since loss, another established correlate of PG. We therefore conducted a multiple regression analysis of all significant bivariate correlates of PG. This is displayed in Table 10.5. In this equation, all predictors, except age, explained 18% of the variance in PG scores. We completed an additional regression analysis (not presented in our tables) that omitted all demographic variables and simply gauged the explained variance of time since loss by itself. This equation explained 9% of the variance in PG. Thus, the demographic variables do indeed add predictive power to the model.

SUMMARY AND STUDY LIMITATIONS

Some of our findings may evoke little surprise among suicide survivors and clinicians working closely with this population. It is not uncommon to hear longer term survivors say they are "giving back" and trying to "make a difference" in their support group circles. What is more remarkable is the large number of our longer term respondents who fell into this category. Nearly two-thirds of parents losing children to suicide 5 or more years earlier had PG scores above the mean for this sample. Nearly a third had scores exceeding the mean by one standard deviation unit. The considerable number of survivors who experienced high PG suggest a transformative potential in grief, helping people feel changed by their loss, shaping them into becoming more compassionate, caring, and help-giving

Table 10.4

Differences in Personal Growth by Various Demographic Factors Among Suicide Survivors (N = 462)

	PERSONAL GROWTH					
	MEANS	**SD**	**N**	**DF**	**F**	**SIG.**
Gender						
Male	24.3	6.7	70	1,433	.03	.86
Female	24.4	7.2	365			
Age						
< 45	20.8	5.7	35	3,431	5.2	< .002
46–55	23.7	7.3	165			
56–65	25.4	6.6	166			
66 or older	25.3	7.4	70			
Education						
High school or <	24.1	7.1	72	3,431	1.5	.21
Some college	25.0	6.7	188			
College graduate	23.0	7.6	83			
Postgraduate	24.6	7.2	92			
Family income						
< 20K	21.3	8.6	27	5,423	1.3	.28
20–40K	24.1	6.0	79			
40–60K	24.4	7.4	92			
60–90K	24.9	7.1	100			
90–120K	24.4	7.3	60			
> 120K	24.9	6.9	71			
Voted in last presidential election						
No	21.0	7.1	53	1,419	13.7	< .001
Yes	24.8	6.9	368			
Political affiliation						
Very liberal	24.6	7.6	72	4,422	.16	.96
Slightly liberal	24.6	7.1	91			
Moderate/middle of the road	24.3	7.6	143			
Slightly conservative	23.8	6.1	72			
Very conservative	24.5	6.6	49			
Religion						
Protestant	24.9	6.3	169	4,423	2.8	.03
Catholic	24.7	7.8	112			
Jewish	20.2	7.7	26			
Other	24.5	7.2	81			
None	23.6	6.9	40			

(continued)

Table 10.4
Differences in Personal Growth by Various Demographic Factors
Among Suicide Survivors (*N* = 462) *(continued)*

	PERSONAL GROWTH					
	MEANS	SD	N	DF	F	SIG.
Frequency of religious participation						
Once or twice yearly	21.9	7.3	94	6,425	6.1	< .0001
Several times yearly	23.5	7.1	106			
Monthly	24.1	6.4	53			
2–3 times monthly	25.5	6.4	14			
Every week	27.4	6.2	92			
Several times weekly	26.9	6.5	29			
Residence type						
Urban	25.3	7.4	81	3,429	.73	.53
Suburban	23.9	7.6	143			
Small city	24.2	6.4	112			
Farm or small town	24.6	6.8	97			

Note. From Survivors Child Loss Survey, 2006–2007.

persons. It will remain a task for future research to verify whether these cross-sectional findings can be confirmed in longitudinal research. It will also remain a task for future research to identify whether the high levels of PG shown for these longer term bereaved parents are any higher than the PG attitudes found among the nonbereaved general public.

Perhaps one of our most noteworthy findings is the association between PG and better mental health. This extends the pioneering work of Hogan et al. (2001) who developed the PG subscale, suggesting its value as a clinical assessment tool for gauging survivor's healing after loss. If survivors can be encouraged to participate in more caregiving activities with other survivors in

Table 10.5
Multiple Regression Analysis of Personal Growth by Time Since the Death
and Various Demographic Attributes of Respondents (*N* = 462)

INDEPENDENT VARIABLES	CORRELATION COEFFICIENT	BETA	*p*
Years since death	.30	.25	.0001
Age	.16	.06	.23
Voted	.18	.11	.02
Religion (Jewish vs. All)	.16	.11	.02
Freq. of relig. part.	.26	.22	.0001

Note. From Survivors Child Loss Survey, 2006–2007.
Number of obs = 413
$F(5,407) = 18.42$
R-squared = .18
p = Level of Significance

support groups, they may facilitate their own emotional healing as well as that of others with whom they interact. Likewise, by addressing the wider world of nonsurvivors, suicide survivors who help to change public perceptions of suicide, work toward raising more research funds to study suicide and mental health problems, and widen the availability of mental health services may also feel a sense of personal renewal and significant accomplishment. Working toward these goals may lead survivors along pathways that help to make their lives meaningful again, by making something "good" come from loss.

Also of interest is the relationship between levels of self-reported PG and the frequency of participation in bereavement support groups. Basically, our data suggest that greater utilization of support groups, but not professional mental health services, is associated with greater PG among longer term survivors. This may mean that for many survivors, support groups may be the most helpful form of intervention, even more so than formal intervention by a mental health professional. This accords with the extremely high levels of helpfulness of support groups reported by survivors in the recent pilot study by McMenamy, Jordan, and Mitchell (2008).

Our findings also demonstrate an association between PG and certain demographic factors. Perhaps the most intriguing one is the clear association between participation in religious activities and PG, suggesting the possibility that religious membership may carry salutatory effects for survivors, perhaps in terms of enhancing meaning reconstruction processes in survivors. Likewise, survivors who voted (a marker of civic involvement) also showed greater PG, suggesting that engagement in community activity may be an important part of the healing process for some survivors and may be a valuable activity for clinicians to encourage in their clients. Of course, the correlational and cross-sectional nature of our sample make these conclusions quite tentative because it is equally possible that PG precedes and leads to greater engagement with one's community.

It was puzzling that Jewish survivors reported less PG than other (mostly Christian) religious affiliates. Whether Judaism presents a less receptive climate for promoting PG is a question that needs further investigation in future research among survivors and the general public. It should also be noted that the sample size of self-identified Jewish respondents in our study was much smaller than participants from other religions so that generalizations from this smaller sample must be made more cautiously.

It is very important to note the limitations of our study and therefore the confidence in and generalizability of our findings. This research has examined the relationship between PG, grief difficulties, and mental health problems in a sample of parents who lost a child to suicide. We found an inverse correlation between growth and these other variables. Likewise, frequency of participation in survivor support groups was related to levels of PG in longer term survivors, as was participation in religious activities. However, the correlational and cross-sectional nature of our data limits our ability to know the sequencing and therefore the possible causality of these associations. For example, it is quite plausible that higher PG and lower levels of grief difficulties are the factors that lead to greater support group participation, rather than the opposite. Alternatively, because PG and mental health problems appear to be inversely correlated, it is possible that they are simply reflections of a common underlying dimension of general grief distress (or its absence), rather than orthogonal variables. Only longitudinal studies of survivors, factor analytic work, and some form of structural equation modeling on the data from our study would allow for clearer conclusions about the causal relationship between the development of PG in survivors and the reduction of grief distress, as well as the utility of various coping activities, such as religious or support group participation.

In addition, the Hogan Personal Growth Scale is an attitudinal measurement. It does not include specific behavioral components of compassion, such as the number of support group meetings attended within a specified time frame, positions of leadership taken in suicide prevention advocacy work, hours spent (within a specified time frame) in fund-raising for suicide prevention causes, the number of prevention talks given to youth groups, and other manifestations of compassionate actions. Future research is needed to better understand the relationship between attitudinal dimensions of PG and behavioral manifestations than we have been able to demonstrate here. It is also important to recognize that PG may take many other forms than the kinds of activism that our participant-observations allowed us to observe in group members. For example, survivors may become kinder and more empathic in their associations with partners and children, colleagues at work, and friends, or they might experience a deepening of religious faith. These alternative forms of posttraumatic growth were not available for observation in this study.

Likewise, our sample, although showing an impressive response rate, was drawn disproportionally from the ranks of survivors who were deeply committed to support groups and more actively involved in them. The sample was also limited to parents who had lost a child to suicide. We simply do not know whether the associations that we discovered between PG and reduced mental and grief distress, or between higher participation in community activities and PG, will hold true for survivors who do not participate in support groups (or whose loss was by a death other than suicide). This broader examination of the larger community of survivors who do not become activists but who may still demonstrate considerable PG after a suicide will have to await the type of longitudinal research that attempts to follow all suicide-bereaved parents in the community, rather than just those who may belong to support groups and/ or agree to participate in survivor research (Jordan & McMenamy, 2004).

CONCLUSIONS

These tentative findings offer directions of hope and encouragement for survivors who often feel trapped in a world of enduring sadness, isolation, and meaninglessness following the suicide loss of a loved one. At healing conferences, survivors often swap their stories of healing journeys, sharing accounts of new social service careers they have assumed following loss, of grantseeking efforts (whether successful or attempted) to obtain funding to establish new programs to provide survivors with more postvention services, and of educating the public at large about suicide. Survivors carve out new identities for themselves as they assume these humanitarian enterprises.

Provisional as our present data may be, they suggest that one important way to facilitate survivor healing may be to take the loss out of the private and personal sphere and attempt to weave it into the fabric of society. As survivors do this they may find that their sadness lifts and life assumes new meaning with a sense of purpose. As we have found elsewhere in this volume, following a suicide loss, survivors often encounter rejection (usually in the form of avoidance) and strain in their relations with family and friends. This isolation can magnify and exacerbate survivor grief. Joining with other survivors and working together within and beyond the boundaries of the survivor community may help suicide survivors know they are not alone in their grief. It may also alleviate some of the hurt felt from their loss as they assume these acts of common purpose, make new friendships with other survivors, and broaden their perspectives to find new pathways of growth after a child's suicide. More work is needed to identify whether these findings can be applied across the broader spectrum of child losses, when parents lose children to homicides, natural deaths, accidents, and drug overdoses.

REFERENCES

Büchi, S., Mörgeli, H., Schnyder, U., Jenewein, J., Hepp, U., Jina, E., . . . Sensky, T. (2007). Grief and post-traumatic growth in parents 2–6 years after the death of their extremely premature baby. *Psychotherapy and Psychosomatics*, 76(2), 106–114.

Dyregrov, K., & Dyregrov, A. (2008). *Effective grief and bereavement support*. London, UK: Jessica Kingsley.

Dyregrov, K., Nordanger, D., & Dyregrov, A. (2000). *Support and care for the bereaved by suicide the bereavement study. Report (in Norwegian)*. Bergen, Norway: Center for Crisis Psychology.

Dyregrov, K., Nordanger, D., & Dyregrov, A. (2003). Predictors of psychosocial distress after suicide, SIDS and accidents. *Death Studies*, 27(2), 143–165.

Engelkemeyer, S. M., & Marwit, S. J. (2008). Posttraumatic growth in bereaved parents. *Journal of Traumatic Stress*, 21(3), 344–346.

Gamino, L. A., Sewell, K. W., & Easterling, L. W. (2000). Scott and White Grief Study—phase 2: Toward an adaptive model of grief. *Death Studies*, 24(7), 633–660.

Hogan, N. S., Greenfield, D. B., & Schmidt, L. A. (2001). Development and validation of the Hogan Grief Reaction Checklist. *Death Studies*, 25(1), 1–32.

Jordan, J. R., & McMenamy, J. (2004). Interventions for suicide survivors: A review of the literature. *Suicide and Life-Threatening Behavior*, 34(4), 337–349.

McMenamy, J. M., Jordan, J. R., & Mitchell, A. M. (2008). What do survivors tell us they need? Results of a pilot study. *Suicide and Life-Threatening Behavior*, 38(4), 375–389.

Nadeau, J. W. (1998). *Families making sense of death*. Thousand Oaks, CA: Sage.

Nerken, I. R. (1993). Grief and the reflective self: Toward a clearer model of loss resolution and growth. *Death Studies, 17*(1), 1–26.

Polatinsky, S., & Esprey, Y. (2000). An assessment of gender differences in the perception of benefit resulting from the loss of a child. *Journal of Traumatic Stress, 13*(4), 709–718.

Riley, L. P., LaMontagne, L. L., Hepworth, J. T., & Murphy, B. A. (2007). Parental grief responses and personal growth following the death of a child, *Death Studies, 31*(4), 277–299.

Schaefer, J. A., & Moos, R. H. (2001). Bereavement experiences and personal growth. In M. S. Stroebe, R. O. Hansson, W. Stroebe, & H. Schut (Eds.), *Handbook of bereavement research: Consequences, coping, and care* (pp. 145–167). Washinton, DC: American Psychological Association.

Shapiro, E. R. (2008). Whose recovery, of what? Relationships and environments promoting grief and growth. *Death Studies, 32*(1), 40–58.

Tedeschi, R., & Calhoun, L. (1996). The Posttraumatic Growth Inventory: Measuring the positive legacy of trauma. *Journal of Traumatic Stress, 9*(3), 455–471.

Tedeschi, R., & Calhoun, L. (2004). Posttraumatic growth: A new perspective on psychotraumatology. *Psychiatric Times, 21*(4), 58–60.

Wagner, B., Knaevelsrud, C., & Maercker, A. (2007). Post-traumatic growth and optimism as outcomes of an internet-based intervention for complicated grief. *Cognitive Behaviour Therapy, 36*(3), 156–161.

11

Internet Support Groups for Suicide Survivors: A New Form of Grief Support

INTRODUCTION

In this chapter, we explore a new and rapidly expanding mode for gaining bereavement assistance: Internet support groups. In earlier chapters, we investigated how those bereaved by suicide use various traditional caregivers to help them manage their loss-related grief—mental health professionals, bereavement counselors, psychiatric nurses, psychiatrists, psychologists, clinical social workers, and other helping agents, such as pastoral counselors, general and loss-specific support groups, psychics, and spiritualists. In this study, we have highlighted peer-led support groups, which we see as a mainstay for many survivors of suicide. Yet, our coverage would not be complete if we did not also explore how survivors gain bereavement assistance in the newly emerging online grief support groups.

In recent years, the Internet has become a significant repository of valuable and strategic information guiding the newly bereaved to find bereavement help after a suicide loss (Krysinska & Andriessen, 2010). In 2004, Vanderwerker and Prigerson found that 60% of their sample of 293 bereaved adults from New Haven, Connecticut, reported using the Internet to find grief assistance after a loss, suggesting that this rate might be typical for the national adult bereaved population. However, we suspect that national rates of adult bereaved using the Internet in some fashion might be closer to the 80% level, given the spectacular expansion of computers into Americans' homes in recent years. By 2002, the General Social Survey, a biannual representative sample of U.S. households, reported that 85% of adults had home computers, and 88% reported using the Internet, with the numbers reporting the use of home computers rising from 59% in the 2000 survey to 82% by the 2010 survey (http://sda.berkeley.edu).

Many now find their support groups from the online listings offered by the American Association of Suicidology (www.suicidology.org) and the American Foundation for Suicide Prevention (www.afsp.org). These and many other websites offer the bereaved a huge bounty of helpful information—books, articles, and other informational materials—that many survivors desperately seek when they suddenly find themselves thrust into the state of confusion, sadness, and horror after a loved one's suicide.

Another venue of potential interest to survivors are the online support groups where peer support takes place in cyberspace. *Psychcentral.com,* one of the leading Internet clearinghouses for psychological information and support services, lists some 11 different national or international web-based support groups for suicide survivors: http://psychcentral.com/resources/Suicide _and_Crisis/. (It should be noted that the online listings at Psychcentral are frequently changing. Some are aimed at specific populations, such as for teenagers; some are local in scope [e.g., for San Diegoans]; others are prevention hotlines rather than support groups.)

There are probably additional similar support groups that may not be known to this clearinghouse. Some Internet support groups have been in existence for nearly a decade or more, and others have emerged more recently. Although little is known about these groups, this knowledge gap is beginning to attract a great deal of new scholarly attention.

Behavioral scientists have begun to devote more study of Internet support groups, and a new literature is now emerging on how people use online groups to get help for a range of problems, such as breast cancer (Winzelberg, et al., 2003), diabetes care (Zrebiec & Jacobson, 2001), mental health problems (Gilat & Shahar, 2009; Schneider, Mataix-Cols, Marks, & Bachofen, 2005; Skinner & Latchford, 2006;), occupational stress (Meier, 2000), children's special healthcare needs (Baum, 2004), and traumatic brain injuries (Rotondi, Sinkule, & Spring, 2005). Many recent studies have emphasized the value of sharing medical and technical information among support group members. Others have focused on the emotional support exchanges available in online support groups. Some studies have also been comparative, examining those individuals who rely on Internet groups and comparing them to others involved in traditional face-to-face self-help groups. To date, although one qualitative study has demonstrated how survivors of suicide use Internet and face-to-face groups to come to terms with suicide losses (Hollander, 2001), no studies have investigated suicide survivors quantitatively, surveying how survivors use Internet support groups, what they value in them, whether Internet support groups appeal to distinctive subsets of survivors, and whether they offer meaningful help to suicide survivors. We attempt to address these important informational gaps in the present chapter.

As we began this particular inquiry, we sought to verify a prevailing assumption about online support groups: that they cater to bereaved affiliates living in remote rural locations. The sparse, but rapidly expanding, literature on Internet support groups suggests that Internet affiliates are likely to be concentrated in remote rural areas where residents have less access to face-to-face groups and other professional bereavement services than would be available in the country's metropolitan places (Bacon, Condon, & Fernsler, 2000; Hill & Weinert, 2004; Lieberman et al., 2003). An unstated assumption behind this view suggests that when clients have opportunities to choose between face-to-face bereavement support and support on the Internet, they will generally select the former ahead of the latter. As we began this inquiry, we anticipated and expected to find higher percentages of small city and rural residents using the Internet support groups. We also hypothesized and expected to observe that rural residents would spend more time participating in their Internet support groups because they had fewer available alternatives.

GATHERING THE DATA FOR THIS CHAPTER

This report is based on survey data collected from one of the largest, longest running Internet survivor of suicide support groups called "POS" or Parents of Suicide (www.parentsofsuicide.com/parents.html). POS was started in 1998 by Karyl Chastain-Beal, a survivor of her daughter's suicide. With approximately 750 people presently listed on its membership rolls, at least two-thirds of POS members participate with some regularity, asking questions, making comments, and giving responses to each other in their group. To join POS, one must be a parent who has sustained the loss of a child to suicide. Stepparents, other family members, and friends of the decedent are guided to join an affiliated support group, FFOS, known as the Families and Friends of Suicide. For those wishing to better understand how such a large group can offer meaningful grief support to newly bereaved parents, readers are advised to consult Chastain-Beal (2011). In this chapter, Chastain-Beal explains that an elaborate division of labor has emerged within the POS group with "veteran" survivors and designated mentors reaching out to address the needs of the newly bereaved. This division of labor also brings many members together in acts of common purpose: maintaining a memorial website and periodically publishing memorial books and cookbooks, among other projects. Within the group, members can choose different formats for receiving their e-mails so they are not bombarded by hundreds daily. Many longer term bereaved remain connected to the group for years after their loss, playing caregiving roles and only responding to e-mails of immediate personal interest.

In November 2006, an Internet support group utilization survey was created by the first author at a secured website hosted by Nassau Community College. POS members were invited to participate in a confidential and anonymous survey of their group by visiting a designated website and registering to complete the survey posted there. Respondents could choose to complete the survey anonymously, or they could provide name and address information along with their survey responses. Only six respondents chose to complete the survey anonymously. Support group members were periodically reminded about the deadline to complete this survey by February 2007, at which point 200 members had already participated.

Those furnishing name and address information were invited by mail to complete the longer bereavement survey (see Appendix) discussed throughout this volume, detailing their child-loss experiences. Of 194 potential respondents (who gave name and address information), 163 requested survey forms, and 116 actually completed the longer survey, yielding a 71% response rate to the longer survey. The present analysis is based on both the Internet specific and the longer survey.

Comparisons were made between two groups of participants. The first group consisted of those in the Internet survey who completed the larger bereavement survey and who also reported spending 1 or more hours participating in the Internet support group during the past 12 months ($N = 104$). (Among these 116 respondents completing longer surveys, 12 indicated not participating in POS during the past year.) These Internet participants were contrasted with face-to-face support group affiliates. Face-to-face affiliates were defined as survey respondents who (a) were not already previously identified as Internet support group affiliates, (b) reported themselves as a parent survivor of suicide, and (c) reported prior participation in a peer support group ($N = 297$).

For our purposes, what differentiates the Internet support group from face-to-face affiliates is *current active participation in the Internet group*. In contrast, in the face-to-face group, although 11 out of 297 reported some prior participation in the Internet group, none reported participation in the Internet group during the past 12 months and all reported participation in one or another type of a face-to-face peer-support group.

RESULTS

Use Patterns

A primary concern of our research was to identify how Internet support group members used their group. Table 11.1 subsequently shows the frequency of use patterns for the 200 Internet support group respondents comparing hours of weekly use in the month prior to taking the survey and for the entire previous year. (When respondent numbers fall short of the 200 total, it was because some respondents did not give answers for every question.) If we combine the two higher frequency categories, we observe that approximately half of all respondents spent 6 or more hours weekly participating in the Internet support group. Once an individual joined the group, they usually received about 100 messages daily from other members. Although it could take a considerable amount of time to digest all this information, members received instructional materials from the

Table 11.1
Frequency of Internet Group Participation

During the past *month*, on an average, how many hours weekly did you spend participating?

	FREQUENCY	PERCENTAGE*
None	23	12
Less than 2 hours	42	21
Between 2 and 5 hours	36	18
Between 6 and 10 hours	54	27
More than 10 hours	45	23
Total	200	100

During the past *year*, on an average, how many hours weekly did you spend participating?

	FREQUENCY	PERCENTAGE*
None	20	10
Less than 2 hours	54	27
Between 2 and 5 hours	35	17
Between 6 and 10 hours	28	14
More than 10 hours	63	32
Total	200	100

Note. Online Internet SOS Participation Survey, November 2006–February 2007.
*Totals may exceed 100% because of rounding.

facilitator to help them select items of interest and bypass less relevant items. Members were also given guidance on how to frame their submissions to attract the widest response from other support group participants. In addition, members were also free to carry on separate dialogues between one another, which many do, as well. We did not tabulate these additional off-line interactions.

Table 11.2 subsequently shows that the usage time for Internet support group members still remains high even when survivors participate in face-to-face support groups or see professional counselors. Table 11.2 shows that 47% still spend 6 or more hours weekly in the Internet group even when they report going to face-to-face meetings six or more times yearly, and 45% still spend 6 or more hours weekly on the Internet group even when they see counselors six or more times yearly. When we examined those who attended face-to-face support groups on a more frequent basis—going to 20 or more meetings within the previous year ($N = 24$)—again, 45% still spend 6 hours or more weekly participating in their Internet support group. Among those going to a counselor 20 or more times during the past year ($N = 24$), 57% still spend 6 hours or more participating in the Internet support group. These latter data are not presented in Table 11.2.

Some previous participation in a face-to-face peer-led support group was reported by 56% of Internet support group affiliates. Of that group, 32 (or 29%) reported going to meetings six or more times during the previous year. Private bereavement counselors were reported as the dominant professional group

Table 11.2
Frequency of Internet Group Participation

(Among those attending a support group six or more times yearly, N = 32)

During the past *year*, on an average, how many hours weekly did you spend participating?

	FREQUENCY	PERCENTAGE*
None	2	6
Less than 2 hours	7	22
Between 2 and 5 hours	8	25
Between 6 and 10 hours	6	19
More than 10 hours	9	28
Total	32	100

(Among those seeing a counselor six or more times yearly, N = 65)

During the past *year*, on an average, how many hours weekly did you spend participating?

	FREQUENCY	PERCENTAGE*
None	8	12
Less than 2 hours	18	28
Between 2 and 5 hours	10	15
Between 6 and 10 hours	8	12
More than 10 hours	21	32
Total	65	100

Note. Online Internet SOS Participation Survey, November 2006–February 2007.
*Totals may exceed 100% because of rounding.

(reported as the 3:1 favorite) seen by Internet support group affiliates as they sought additional aid to supplement their online support group. Of those seeking professional assistance (about half of all Internet group respondents), two-thirds saw their bereavement professional six or more times during the previous 12 months. All these data suggest that for a good portion of survivors, no single caregiver source fulfills their needs for bereavement support. Many survivors seek a multiplicity of caregivers—Internet support group, face-to-face group support, and bereavement counselors *at the same time* to help them deal with their loss. It also appears that reliance on alternative help sources does little to diminish these survivors' needs for Internet support group participation. (The data referred to in this paragraph are not shown in our tables.)

What Internet Support Group Members Value About Online Participation

Table 11.3 subsequently presents a ranked display showing what Internet support group participants value in their group. Three items stand out as especially noteworthy, with more than 80% of respondents indicating these as the most important features of their support group: (a) offering help to cope with the pain and sadness of loss (85%), (b) having a safe place to discuss tabooed topics (84%), and (c) sharing information and experiences (84%).

Table 11.3
Importance of Various Support Group Attributes (*N* = 200)

	PERCENT LISTING ITEM AS EXTREMELY IMPORTANT	PERCENT CALLING INTERNET GROUP BEST	PERCENT CALLING F-TO-F BEST
1. Helping me to better cope with the pain and sadness of loss	85	48	8
2. Having a safe place to discuss tabooed topics	84	57	6
3. Sharing information and experiences	84	51	7
4. Having the power and opportunities to discuss grief-related subjects of importance to me	76	58	8
5. Having a help source available whenever survivor problems emerge	74	63	8
6. Memorializing my lost loved one	73	57	9
7. Helping advance goals of suicide prevention and better mental health resources availability	64	46	7
8. Helping to get through the holidays and other difficult times for survivors	64	48	6
9. Being able to help others struggling with suicide loss issues	63	43	11
10. Learning how to talk about suicide openly and publicly when necessary	62	42	10
11. Gaining spiritual comfort and support	51	34	11
12. Helping to fix family difficulties emerging after a suicide loss	48	35	14
13. Gaining aid from effective leadership that leads discussions along helpful directions	48	40	18
14. Getting help to deal with rejection by family members, friends, coworkers, and neighbors	48	42	8
15. Deciding what to tell children about suicide	38	33	7
16. Maintaining my privacy as I reach out for help and support	37	68	5
17. Making new friendships	26	39	14

Note. Online Internet SOS Participation Survey, November 2006–February 2007.
F-to-F = face-to-face.

Several others were ranked at the level of intermediate importance, with a range of between 60% and 70% endorsing these as most important attributes: (d) having the power and opportunities to discuss grief-related subjects of importance to me (76%), (e) having a help source available whenever survivor problems emerge (74%), (f) memorializing one's lost loved one (73%), (g) helping advance goals of suicide prevention and better mental health resources availability (64%), (h) helping to get through the holidays and other difficult times for survivors (64%), (i) being able to help others struggling with suicide loss issues (63%), and (j) learning how to talk about suicide openly and publicly when necessary (62%).

Finally, seven other attributes were regarded as less important, with about half of the sample or less deeming these as most important features of the support group: (k) gaining spiritual comfort and support (51%); (l) helping to fix family difficulties emerging after a suicide loss (48%); (m) gaining aid from effective leadership that leads discussions along helpful directions (48%); (n) getting help to deal with rejection by family members, friends, coworkers, and neighbors (48%); (o) deciding what to tell children about suicide (37%); (p) maintaining my privacy as I reach out for help and support (37%); and (q) making new friendships (26%).

Table 11.3 also displays the responses to rating whether these same attributes were best addressed in an Internet group, in a face-to-face group, in both equally, or in neither. We report in Table 11.3 those who rated the Internet group and the face-to-face group as best, omitting the neither and both equally response categories. Results suggested that respondents were highly satisfied with their Internet support group participation. Between 33% and 68% listed the Internet group as the best place for addressing each specific need, whereas only 5% to 18% rated the face-to-face group as the best place for addressing that need. Even among respondents who were also active participants in face-to-face groups, only about 10% more rated the face-to-face context as the best choice (for each selected criteria). Among affiliates of both group types, no more than 28% deemed any one of the 17 different features as being best served in a face-to-face context. Hardly anyone, fewer than 5% of all respondents, claimed neither group addressed the 17 selected issues. This was true with three exceptions: helping to fix family difficulties, giving spiritual comfort and support, and deciding what to tell children about suicide. In each of these cases, about 25% regarded the support groups as not helpful in addressing these three issues. This finding suggests that neither Internet exclusively respondents nor mixed face-to-face/Internet affiliates thought that support groups could offer them much help in these three respects.

Table 11.3 also shows that about two-thirds of respondents deemed Internet groups as best for maintaining privacy as they reached out for help and having a help source available whenever survivor problems emerged. At least for those who were active participants in them, these data generally suggest that Internet support groups were perceived as the best mechanism for obtaining help even if they were also participating in face-to-face groups.

Reasons for Seeking an Internet Group

We also presented our respondents with a checklist showing six possible reasons for seeking an Internet group. Respondents could endorse as many as they felt appropriate. The results are displayed in Table 11.4. Nearly twice as many endorsed 24/7 availability as the most important reason for their affiliation with an Internet support group when compared to the next most frequently endorsed item, the participatory style of the Internet group (64% as compared to 38%, respectively).

We also included an open-ended section in the Internet survey where respondents could offer additional comments and thoughts about the support group that helped or hindered their healing. We grouped responses into three types: helpful, hindering, and undetermined responses. Tabulations showed that helpful responses outnumbered hindering ones by a margin of at least 2:1. Among the more than 200 responses offered, one in particular appeared to be the most important. Statements offered by 14 survey respondents indicated that were it not for their Internet group, they might have succumbed to the depression, despair, and desire to end their lives following the suicides of their children. The following are several of the comments offered, typifying these responses: (a) "I honestly don't know how I would have made it through the months following my son's departure if this Internet support group hadn't existed"; (b) "The Internet group has been there when no one else was or cared. POS is the main reason I am alive today"; (c) "Without the support that I received, I would be dead from my own suicide. I have suffered from depression"; (d) "The group helped save my life literally as well as figuratively"; and (e) "POS helped me more than mere words can say. I can't even think about how I would be today, if it wasn't for this group."

Hindering responses fell into several different (and sometimes contradictory) types: for some, the group was perceived as having an overly Christian faith bias; for others, it was felt to be insufficiently spiritual; some complained of too much

Table 11.4

Responses to the Question: Why Did You Seek Your Internet Support Group?
(*N* = 200)

	PERCENT ENDORSING THIS
1. The Internet group is consistent with my personality needs, where having 24/7 availability is needed.	64
2. I like the democratic participatory style of the Internet group.	38
3. I like the structured leadership of the Internet group.	34
4. Leadership does a good job harmonizing the diverse elements within our Internet support group.	34
5. I have no other alternative; there are no face-to-face groups within easy traveling distance.	30
6. I am "turned off" by local face-to-face groups.	25

Note. Online Internet SOS Participation Survey, November 2006–February 2007.

repetition to the subjects discussed, whereas others felt they were overwhelmed by the high volume of different items that were never fully processed. Another common complaint was finding it difficult to get responses to one's postings. Others complained that the Internet support group increased their feelings of depression and sadness as the group dealt with the comments of others who appeared to be stuck in their grief or suffering from multiple suicide losses.

Demographic Characteristics of Internet and Face-to-Face Group Affiliates

Table 11.5 subsequently contrasts the demographic characteristics of Internet support group affiliates and those associated with face-to-face self-help groups. This table shows sharp contrasts between the groups. The Internet group included significantly more women: 96% as compared to 80%. Nearly 60% of Internet group members were younger than 55 years of age; this compared to 39% for face-to-face affiliates. Internet affiliates completed less formal schooling compared to face-to-face participants. In the Internet group, 31% had a college degree or more professional training, which compared to 43% for face-to-face affiliates. Consistent with their educational differences, fewer Internet affiliates reported high incomes, with 21% reporting family incomes above $90,000 yearly; this compared to 35% for face-to-face affiliates.

Twice as many Internet affiliates reported having no religious affiliation compared to face-to-face affiliates: 15% as compared to 7%. Internet affiliates were also less likely to participate in any organized religious observances. Twice as many, compared to face-to-face affiliates, reported not attending a religious service during the past 12 months: 32% as compared to 16%.

The comparison between Internet and face-to-face affiliates showed similar patterns of urbanicity for both groups. Also, both groups were evenly matched on the number of children in the household. Yet, two other important demographic differences were noted: the numbers of people living alone and the number having been divorced or separated. More Internet affiliates reported being divorced or separated: 31% as compared to 22%. A remarkably high number, slightly more than half (52%), reported living alone; this contrasted with 19% for face-to-face affiliates. All these contrasting differences were significant at or below the .05 level with the chi-square statistic.

Differences in Grief Difficulties and Mental Health Problems

Table 11.6 displays differences in grief difficulties, rates of depression, and suicidal thinking and shows more elevated levels of these bereavement problems for the Internet support group members. Of all Internet affiliates, 75% reported being depressed when they completed the survey, compared to about 54% of those who belonged to face-to-face groups giving similar reports. In another comparison, 35% of Internet affiliates reported thinking about suicide sometimes or more often during the past year, compared to 23% offering similar reports among face-to-face members. In addition, 10% more Internet affiliates (17% as

Table 11.5
Demographic Characteristics of Internet and Face-to-Face
Support Group Affiliates ($N = 401$)

| | PERCENT/N | | | |
	INTERNET	FACE-TO-FACE	$\chi^2/(df)$	p VALUE
Gender				
Male	4/4	20/58		
Female	96/100	80/239		
Total	100/104	100/297	14.5/(1)	.0001
Age				
35 or <	1/1	0/0		
36–45	9/9	5/16		
46–55	49/51	34/101		
56–65	35/36	42/125		
66 or >	7/7	19/55		
Total	100/104	100/297	16.8/(4)	.002
Education				
High school graduate or <	10/10	13/38		
Some college technology education	44/46	44/132		
College graduate	13/13	20/60		
Postgraduate	18/19	23/67		
Total	100/104	100/297	10.4/(3)	.02
Family income				
20K or less	10/10	5/15		
Over 20K and < 40K	16/16	18/53		
Over 40K and < 60K	21/22	22/64		
Over 60K and < 90K	33/34	20/58		
Over 90K and < 120K	11/11	16/46		
Over 120K	10/10	19/54		
Total	100/103	100/290	13.4/(5)	.02
Religion				
Protestant	31/32	40/118		
Catholic	25/26	27/80		
Jewish	4/4	8/23		
Other	25/25	18/52		
None	15/15	7/20		
Total	100/102	100/293	10.5/(4)	.03
Frequency of religious attendance				
Never	31.7/32	15.5/46		
Yearly	28.7/29	23.0/68		
Several times yearly	7.9/8	14.2/42		
Monthly	5.0/5	3.4/10		
Several times monthly	6.9/7	11.5/34		
Weekly or >	19.8/20	32.4/96		
Total	100/103	100/296	19.5/(5)	.002

(continued)

Table 11.5
Demographic Characteristics of Internet and Face-to-Face
Support Group Affiliates (*N* = 401) *(continued)*

	PERCENT/*N*			
	INTERNET	FACE-TO-FACE	χ^2/(*df*)	*p* VALUE
Residence				
Urban	20/21	19/55		
Suburban	36/37	34/100		
Small city	21/22	28/83		
Small town/farm	22/23	19/57		
Total	100/103	100/294	1.9/(3)	.597
Current marital status				
Married	66/67	69/205		
Divorced	25/26	20/59		
Separated	6/6	2/5		
Never married	0/0	1/3		
Widowed	3/3	8/25		
Total	100/102	100/297	10.4/(4)	.034
Total number of children ever had (adopted, biological, steps)				
One	8/8	7/20		
Two	29/30	36/107		
Three	26/27	30/89		
Four or more	37/38	27/78		
Total	100/103	100/294	4.5/(3)	.212
Present living arrangements				
Lives with others	48/87	81/242		
Lives alone	52/93	19/55		
Total	100/180	100/297	57.5/(1)	.0001

Note. From Survivors Child Loss Survey, 2006–2007.

compared to 7%) reported having a suicide plan during the past year. There were also significant differences reported between both groups in grief difficulties as measured by our abbreviated Grief Experience Questionnaire (GEQ). As a group, Internet support group affiliates displayed a mean of 44 on this scale, significantly higher than the mean of 38 noted for face-to-face affiliates.

Other important grief differences were noted between these groups. Internet group affiliates consisted of more recent survivors than face-to-face group members, averaging 4 years since the loss of their child to suicide, compared to 6 years on average for face-to-face affiliates. Internet affiliates also sustained more stigmatizing responses from family, friends, neighbors, and coworkers. Internet affiliates reported a mean score of 4.9 on our stigma scale, compared to 3.1 for face-to-face affiliates. All these differences were significant as indicated by either the chi-square probability statistic or mean differences using a one-way analysis of variance.

Table 11.6
Time Since Loss, Stigmatization, Adaptations, and Grief Difficulties Among Internet and Face-to-Face Support Group Affiliates ($N = 401$)

	PERCENT OR MEAN/N			
	INTERNET	FACE-TO-FACE	$\chi^2/(df)$	p VALUE
Mean years since loss*	4.1/104	6.1/292		
Depression				
No	17/18	38/114		
Yes	75/78	54/161		
No because of antidepressant medications	8/8	7/22		
Total	100/104	100/297	16.0/(2)	.0001
Frequency thought about taking your life during the past 12 months				
Never	49/50	65/189		
Rarely	17/17	12/36		
Sometimes	19/20	17/49		
Frequently	11/11	4/13		
Very Frequently	5/5	2/5		
Total	100/103	100/292	12.4/(4)	.015
Had plan for suicide in the past 12 months				
No	83/85	93/271		
Yes	17/17	7/21		
Total	100/102	100/292	7.8/(1)	.005
Attempted suicide in the past 12 months				
No	97/100	99/285		
Yes	3/3	1/4		
Total	100/103	100/289	1.0/(1)	.315
Mean Grief Experience Questionnaire score (GEQ)*	43.9/98	38.4/272		
Mean stigmatization score from all personal associates (ranging from 0 to 17)*	4.9/100	3.1/276		

Note. From Survivors Child Loss Survey, 2006–2007.
*One-way mean analysis yielded F probability of $< .001$

As a prelude to a more complex multivariate analysis of the correlates linked to grief difficulties between Internet and face-to-face support group members, we investigated GEQ differences between both groups at varying points since their time of loss. This factor—the length of time passing since a loved one has died—is acknowledged as one of the most important correlates linked to differences in grief difficulties. Table 11.7 subsequently displays these findings. The table shows sharply contrasting patterns of grief difficulties scores for Internet and face-to-face affiliates. For the Internet group over the entire time span range, the numbers show a comparatively flat response with GEQ means peaking between the second and third year after loss at 46, and

Table 11.7
**One-way Analysis of Variance of Grief Difficulties (GEQ Scores) by Time Since Loss
Among Internet, Face-to-Face Support Group Affiliates, and All Others (*N* = 478)**

TIME SINCE LOSS	MEAN	SD	FREQUENCY	F SIGNIFICANCE PROBABILITY
Among Internet Affiliates (*n* = 98)				
Less than 1 year	43.3	12.1	7	.64
1.01–3 years	46.0	9.4	39	
3.01–5 years	42.4	10.5	22	
5.01–9.9 years	42.8	11.6	24	
10 or more years	41.5	11.4	6	
Among Face-to-Face Affiliates (*n* = 269)				
Less than 1 year	43.8	9.5	22	.001
1.01–3 years	43.0	9.4	78	
3.01–5 years	37.2	10.2	46	
5.01–9.9 years	35.7	10.6	72	
10 or more years	34.1	11.0	51	
Among All Other Child-Loss Survivors (*n* = 111)				
Less than 1 year	41.8	12.1	19	.001
1.01–3 years	44.6	12.4	29	
3.01–5 years	33.4	10.9	15	
5.01–9.9 years	37.7	10.7	25	
10 or more years	27.0	9.9	23	

Note. From Survivors Child Loss Survey, 2006–2007. GEQ = Grief Experience Questionaire

thereafter were lower among the longer term bereaved, dropping to a low of 42. This represented a nonsignificant difference with a one-way analysis of variance test. By contrast, for face-to-face affiliates, GEQ scores peaked during the first year after loss at 44 and were steadily lower for those at successively longer time since their loss, eventually showing a low of 34—a significant difference. In the last case, we included all other child-loss survivors: parents losing children to suicide who did not use support groups and those losing children to other-than-suicide death causes. In these 111 cases, GEQ differences peaked during the second and third years and showed a statistically significant low of 27 for those who were at the longest time period after their child-loss. These findings suggest that for Internet support group survivors, grief difficulties did not show the same pattern of abatement over time that they did for the other two survivor subgroups.

Unfortunately, our foregoing analysis does not enable us to confidently conclude whether the greater grief difficulties found among Internet affiliates are associated with any deficiencies from this type of support system or are related to their demographic uniquenesses, such as the relative short-term nature of their loss experiences, the greater stigmatization from their families, and other personal associates, or all/or any of the above. For this, multivariate regression analysis is needed to begin to disentangle the pattern of associations between all potential predictor variables and to discern their associations with differences in grief difficulties.

Table 11.8 begins this task of disentanglement as we examine the interplay between all significant bivariate demographic correlates of grief difficulties and Internet versus face-to-face affiliation in the same model. In this analysis, Internet/face-to-face membership still remains a significant predictor of GEQ differences when demographic variables are included. In this multivariate model, three other demographic factors remained significant: gender, age, and the frequency of religious participation. Religious affiliation, educational differences, marital status differences, income differences, and living alone were found to be nonsignificant to this model and were dropped in the more complete multivariate model that appears next.

In Table 11.9 subsequently, we introduce two new important and potentially confounding variables into the multivariate analysis: the time since loss and the stigmatization scale score. In this new equation, we also include the carryover significant demographic predictors from Table 11.8, as well as the type of support group experience and combine these in a new multiple regression analysis. The new equation has a modest predictive power, accounting for 30% of the fluctuations of grief difficulties. In this equation, five variables were significantly associated with the dependent variable: total stigmatization score, time since loss, gender, age, and religious attendance. In this equation, certain groups showed higher grief difficulties than others: women over men, younger people over older people, the religiously inactive over the religiously active, and shorter term bereaved over longer term bereaved. In this equation, the type of support group experience—whether

Table 11.8

Multiple Regression Analysis of Grief Difficulties (GEQ Scores) by Support Group Type and Various Demographic Attributes

INDEPENDENT VARIABLES	CORRELATION COEFFICIENT	BETA	p
Internet/face-to-face	−.22	−.111	.03
Gender	.19	.146	.004
Age	−.37	−.254	.001
Education	−.19	−.062	.230
Religion	.10	.08	.09
Frequency religious attendance	−.22	−.140	.005
Marital status	.07	.060	.317
Family income	−.16	−.026	.659
Live alone	−.00	−.027	.665

Note. From Survivors Child Loss Survey, 2006–2007.
Number of obs = 358; $F(9,348)$ = 10.40; R^2 = .21; p = level of significance; GEQ = Grief Experience Questionnaire.

Table 11.9
Multiple Regression Analysis of Grief Difficulties (GEQ Scores) by Support Group Type, Various Demographic Attributes, Time Since Loss, and Stigmatization Experiences

INDEPENDENT VARIABLES	CORRELATION COEFFICIENT	BETA	p
Internet/face-to-face	−.22	−.022	.646
Gender	.19	.126	.008
Age	−.37	−.210	.001
Frequency religious attendance	−.22	−.139	.003
Time since loss	−.32	−.116	.018
Total stigmatization score	.43	.339	.001

Note. From Survivors Child Loss Survey, 2006–2007.
Number of obs = 343; $F(6,336)$ = 24.03; R^2 = .30; p = level of significance; GEQ = Grief Experience Questionnaire.

Internet or face-to-face—did not contribute significantly in the presence of these other more powerful predictors. In this equation, the stigmatization score alone accounted for the largest portion of explained variance: 19%. We also tested these five variables' predictive power in accounting for differences in complicated grief. Here, the same model explained 32% of the variance, with two factors proving to be nonsignificant contributors: whether one belonged to an Internet or a face-to-face group and age differences. We did not present these results in our tables.

It should be noted from the correlational data that belonging to an Internet support group is associated with having greater grief difficulties when compared to those who only participated in face-to-face support groups. Yet, when this association is revisited in a multiple regression analysis, it is does not add to the prediction with the presence of the stigmatization score. (If we omit the stigma score from the regression equation, Internet participation still remains a significant correlate with grief difficulties.) Thus, it seems that feeling stigmatized, participating in an Internet support group, and having greater grief difficulties all appear to be inextricably associated with each other.

The last table we present, Table 11.10, addresses the differences in Internet support group participation. We have taken all significant correlates of current Internet support group membership from Tables 11.6 and 11.7 and correlated them with amounts of Internet participation during the past 12 months. Consistent with the hypothesis expressed in the introduction, we expected rural and small city residents to be more actively involved in the Internet support group than big city or suburban residents. However, no significant association was obtained demonstrating such a pattern with the correlation analysis or with a chi-square significance test (that is not displayed here). In fact, there seemed to be a nonsignificant trend with both of these tests in the opposite direction of our hypothesis, showing urban residents more actively involved in the Internet support group as compared to those from all other residence categories.

Table 11.10
Correlations Between Degree of Internet Group Participation and Demographic, Psychological, Stigmatization, and Time Variables

INDEPENDENT VARIABLES	CORRELATION COEFFICIENT	p
Residence: Urban/rural	−.158	.09
Gender	.100	.29
Age	−.01	.91
Education	−.198	.03
Religion	−.02	.83
Frequency religious attendance	.04	.65
Live alone	.04	.54
Marital status	.07	.46
Time since loss	−.149	.13
GEQ score	.07	.46
ICG score	.13	.19
Reported being depressed	.09	.34
Reported poor mental health	−.13	.16
Total stigmatization score	.25	.007

Note. From Survivors Child Loss Survey, 2006–2007. Number of obs = 115; p = level of significance; GEQ = Grief Experience Questionnaire; ICG = Index of Complicated Grief.

Otherwise, Table 11.10 shows the following groups more actively involved in Internet support group participation: people with less formal education and those scoring higher on the stigmatization scale. Thus, one possible interpretation of this relationship is that the Internet support group provides a refuge for these types of people in particular. It is interesting to note that neither the time since loss nor grief nor psychological difficulties per se showed any apparent association with Internet group involvement.

SUMMARY AND IMPLICATIONS

Our analysis of Internet support group affiliates of parents who sustained the loss of a child to suicide has yielded some unexpected findings. Previous discussions of Internet support groups suggest that these groups have particular appeal to clients living in remote rural locations who may be beyond the reach of face-to-face support group alternatives and professional support services. Our research failed to confirm this supposition, and present findings show similar percentages of rural, small city, and larger metropolitan residents affiliated with Internet and face-to-face alternatives. We found as many Internet group members from big city locations such as New York, Baltimore, Philadelphia, or Denver and their surrounding suburbs as we did for face-to-face support group affiliates. It is also interesting to note that many Internet group members participate in face-to-face groups as well. In addition, the data on Internet support group participation did not show any curtailment of Internet participation when members were active in other face-to-face support groups or were seeing counselors. Instead, it appears that participation in on-line support groups was meeting a different need than meeting with other survivors face-to-face or with a counselor.

Instead, our data suggested an entirely diverging set of associations linked with Internet support group participation and with those who were more actively involved in the Internet group. Internet participants and those who were more active in them tended to report more unsupportive and unhelpful responses from families, friends, and coworkers, possibly leading them to have higher scores on our stigmatization scale. Stigmatization scale score was the highest single correlate to being an active participant in the Internet support group. It seems plausible that as survivors encountered more disinterest and/or rejection from their significant others, they felt impelled to seek comfort, validation, and support from their Internet group.

Another noteworthy finding from this inquiry was the revelation of support group member benefits. Although a minority of affiliates, 30% saw their Internet group as the only viable alternative because of lack of access to any support services, and about two-thirds of all respondents perceived the most important benefit of the group to be its 24/7 availability. This factor led all others by a large margin in creating the preference for this type of support system. Another less clearly articulated benefit experienced by Internet support affiliates was the opportunities it presented for more extensive support group involvement. Approximately, half of all Internet respondents spent 6 or more hours *weekly* in support group participation. If survivors had seen a bereavement counselor on a weekly basis and attended two different monthly face-to-face support group meetings, they still would have found it difficult to rival this high level of support group participation. Internet support groups offer members nearly limitless availability for participation. This also appeared to contribute to their distinctive appeal.

Bivariate and multivariate analyses also suggested that survivors with distinctive demographic characteristics were overrepresented in this group. When multivariate controls were applied, more women, younger survivors, and those less connected to conventional religious observances were overrepresented compared to their face-to-face counterparts. Survivors who lived alone, who were divorced or separated, who had lower incomes, and less formal schooling were also more likely to be among the Internet affiliates. We must keep in mind this exploratory research is based on the affiliates of a single Internet survivor support group, the Parents of Suicide. Whether these patterns will hold among samples of nonparent suicide survivors and among parent survivors of different Internet support groups remains a task for future research.

Our data also bear on the question of the helpfulness of Internet support groups in enhancing the adaptations of survivors of child suicide loss.

From several angles, the evidence was unmistakably clear that respondents perceived considerable benefits from their Internet support group experience. Even though more than half of all respondents had exposure to face-to-face support groups also, fewer than 18% of all respondents rated them best on the 17 different criteria of potential support group benefits, whereas anywhere from 33% to 68% rated the Internet group as best on these same criteria. As expressed by respondents in their surveys, two different advantages of online groups stood out: being able to maintain one's privacy while reaching out for help, and having a help resource available whenever survivor problems emerged. Approximately two-thirds appreciated these particular features of their Internet experience.

From the open-ended part of our survey, respondents reported more helping responses from the Internet support group versus hindering ones in a ratio of 2:1. Only six respondents remarked that the Internet support group participation contributed to worsening their feelings of depression, whereas 14 others commented that they perceived this group as their lifesaver, helping them stay alive after having come to their lowest point of depression and despair. With 75% of online support group members describing themselves as presently depressed and 35% harboring suicide thoughts sometimes or more often during the past year, the significance of these lifesaving remarks takes on additional meaning. At least in this sample, the Internet group participants appear to be more depressed, socially isolated, and a group more at risk for being suicidal for whom a traditional "twice a month" support group format is likely to be insufficient. The participants also reported that, contrary to concerns that are sometimes raised about the safety of anonymous social contact through the Internet, they overwhelmingly found the Internet group a great benefit. Again, as additional research is completed among more representative samples of suicide survivors, we will be better able to judge whether the evaluations given by the members of these groups are typical for Internet affiliates generally.

Our cross-sectional survey data do not enable us to identify the chain of causal forces affecting the differences in grief difficulties. This remains a task for future longitudinal study. Yet, for now, we see a possible association between the intensification of grief difficulties survivors encountered as they have difficulty gaining acceptance and bereavement support from families and other personal acquaintances and their affiliation with an Internet support group. The greater failure of their personal communities to provide emotional comfort and support—at their most vulnerable time after loss—may help to create the need for greater support group participation. What distinguished Internet affiliates from their face-to-face counterparts in bivariate analysis—higher grief difficulties—did not yield additional information when stigmatization differences were included in the same multivariate model. Of course, because our data are only correlational in nature, it is also possible that the directionality of the causation may be reversed. That is, rather than being "rejected" by their social networks, people who have more difficulty in relationships in general or in seeking social support from family and friends after the suicide may then seek out a more anonymous arena for social interaction where they are more able to elicit the support that they need in a way that is better suited to their personality and coping style. Again, future studies will need to clarify this issue, one that likely involves a complex and interactive process that leads to a failure of face-to-face bereavement support.

It should also be noted that the unhelpful and unsupportive responses from family and friends following a suicide loss appears to be associated not only with heightened grief difficulties but also with more depression and suicidality among survivors. Thus, stigmatization may put suicide survivors at a higher risk for mental health problems, including their own suicidality. It will be a task for future research to verify whether the patterns demonstrated here from data collected on this single case of parent survivors relying on a particular Internet support group also apply more broadly to different loss relationship situations and to other samples of parents sustaining other traumatic and natural death losses of children.

REFERENCES

Bacon E. S., Condon E. H., & Fernsler, J. I. (2000). Young widows' experience with an Internet self-help group. *Journal of Psychosocial Nursing and Mental Health Services, 38*(7), 24–33.

Baum, L. S. (2004). Internet parent support groups for primary caregivers of a child with special health care needs. *Pediatric Nursing, 30*(5), 381–388, 401.

Chastain-Beal, K. (2011). Parents of suicides–friends and families of suicide internet community. In J. R. Jordan, & J. L. McIntosh (Eds.), *Grief after suicide: Understanding the consequences and caring for the survivors* (pp. 381–388). New York, NY: Routledge.

Gilat, I., & Shahar, G. (2009). Suicide prevention by online support groups: An action theory-based model of emotional first aid. *Archives of Suicide Research, 13*(1), 52–63.

Hill, W. G., & Weinert, C. (2004). An evaluation of an online intervention to provide social support and health education. *Computers, Informatics, Nursing, 22*(5), 282–288.

Hollander, E. M. (2001). Cyber community in the valley of the shadow of death. *Journal of Loss and Trauma, 6*, 135–146.

Krysinska, K. & Andriessen, K. (2010). On-line support and resources for people bereaved through suicide: What is available? *Suicide and Life-Threatening Behavior, 40*(6), 640–650.

Lieberman, M. A., Golant, M., Giese-Davis, J., Winzlenberg, A., Benjamin, H., Humphreys K., . . . Spiegel, D. (2003). Electronic support groups for breast carcinoma: A clinical trial of effectiveness. *Cancer, 97*(4), 920–925.

Meier, A. (2000). Offering social support via the Internet: A case study of an online support group for social workers. *Journal of Technology in Human Services, 17*(2–3), 237–266.

Rotondi, A. J., Sinkule, J., & Spring, M. (2005). An interactive web-based intervention for persons with TBI and their families: Use and evaluation by female significant others. *Journal of Head Trauma Rehabilitation, 20*(2), 173–185.

Schneider, A. J., Mataix-Cols, D., Marks, I. M., & Bachofen, M. (2005). Internet-guided self-help with or without exposure therapy for phobic and panic disorders. *Psychotherapy and Psychosomatics*, 74(3), 154–164.

Skinner, A. E., & Latchford, G. (2006). Attitudes to counseling via the Internet: A comparison between in-person counseling clients and Internet support group users. *Counseling and Psychotherapy Research*, 6(3), 158–163.

Vanderwerker, L. C., & Prigerson, H. G. (2004). Social support and technological connectedness as protective factors in bereavement. *Journal of Loss and Trauma*, 9(1), 45–57.

Winzelberg, A. J., Classen, C., Alpers, G. W., Roberts, H., Koopman, C., Adams, R. E., . . . Taylor, C. B. (2003). Evaluation of an Internet support group for women with primary breast cancer. *Cancer*, 97(5), 1164–1173.

Zrebiec, J. F., & Jacobson, A. M. (2001). What attracts patients with diabetes to an Internet support group? A 21-month longitudinal website study. *Diabetic Medicine*, 18(2), 154–158.

The Impact of a Child's Traumatic Death on Married Couples

12

Gender Differences in Grief After the Death of a Child

In this final section of our book, beginning with this chapter, we address the gender differences between fathers and mothers in adapting to a child's death, especially after a child's suicide or drug overdose. Once men and women better understand the different cultural scripts that prescribe how they are expected to grieve and how they may actually grieve differently, they may reach deeper understandings of each other and minimize conflicts. At first glance, it would seem that when a couple experiences a common tragedy, like losing a child, they would become more closely united. Some married couples actually do find their union strengthened after the tragedy. However, this adaptation does not always happen and some couples sadly find themselves pulled apart, experiencing the upending pressures of the loss in diverging and conflicting ways.

In the next chapter, using our survey data, we directly approach spouse relationships following the death and further investigate several important questions related to the impact of a child's death upon the married lives of parents: Are marriages likely to be strained from this experience? Is the child loss associated with any increases in marital dissolutions? Are some marriages strengthened after the loss, as some analysts such as Reiko Schwab (1998) contend? How does the marital cohesion of our respondents compare to that of their same-aged nonbereaved peers in the population at large? What, if any, are the enduring marital difficulties for these bereaved parents? What may be some of the important correlates associated with differences in the marital cohesion of bereaved parents? Finally, does a child's violent death change these associations in any way? All these questions will be investigated in our next chapter.

For now, we should be aware that differences in grieving patterns between fathers and mothers set the stage for later unity or conflict between them. In the bereavement literature, Therese Rando's (1986) early theorizing on the adverse impact of a child loss on a couple's relationship continues to hold an important place in the discussion of gender differences. She said,

> Difficulties can arise in the best of marriages when normal patterns of relating are disrupted by grief . . . communication dysfunction often develops when one partner asks the other unanswerable questions such as why the death occurred or avoids communicating with the other spouse for fear it may precipitate a mutual downward spiral. . . . Not only are couples always somewhat dissimilar in their grief processes; they also typically lack synchronicity in their grief experiences. It is not unusual for one spouse to be up while the other is down. This asymmetry may occur in four grief work areas: expressing feelings, working and doing daily activities (one may find comfort in work while the other is overwhelmed by it), relating to things that trigger memories of the deceased child (one may desire all photographs to be removed from the house while the other will cling to them), and searching for the meaning of what has happened (one may find solace in religion while the other may relinquish his former faith). . . . Accompanying this is the recognition that the grief experience will change each of them. . . . Another sensitive issue that spouses must confront is that their physical presences and mannerisms can remind one another of the deceased child. . . . A classic and quite frequent problem is the inhibition of sexual response and intimacy in bereaved parents. All these secondary losses place additional burdens of grief, loss, and adaptation on couples already overwrought with responsibilities and demands. These problems contribute to the assertion that there may be higher divorce rates in bereaved couples. (pp. 26–29)

More recently, several analysts (Christ, Bonanno, Malkinson, & Rubin, 2003) have identified five common problems that bereaved couples typically face after a child's death: (a) conflict and anger, at times directly or indirectly blaming the spouse for the death; (b) breakdowns in communication, such as avoiding all discussions of the death or having misunderstandings of it; (c) discordant coping related to differences between men and women, with women using more emotional expression and men engaging in more solution-focused activities; (d) incongruent grieving in which fathers and mothers display different levels of intensity and for different periods of time in relation to the death; and (e) low intimacy in which the combination of incongruent grieving, discordant coping, communication breakdowns, and other misunderstandings as well as different needs for sexual intimacy are thought to contribute to a low sense of intimacy between parents (p. 563).

Evidence supporting these claims of bereaved couples' relationship problems is somewhat limited, coming primarily from studies of bereavement after neonatal death (DeFrain, 1991; Klass, 1986–1987; Lang, Gottlieb, & Amsel, 1996; Murray & Callan, 1988; Parkes & Weiss, 1983; Schwab, 1992).

Few studies have probed the adverse impact of loss on couples whose children died at older ages or who died by violent means. Murphy (2008) examined this question of marital satisfaction longitudinally among her sample of accident-, suicide-, and homicide-bereaved parents over a 5-year period. She found that marital satisfaction and the diminution of grief difficulties were both associated with a parent's ability to make sense of the death. To the extent that a parent was able to do this, grief difficulties diminished and marital satisfaction rose. The study found that although only 12% of respondents had found meaning in the first year after the death, the number rose to 57% 5 years afterward, thereby suggesting that in the long run, marital satisfaction was not adversely affected by the loss.

A debate continues to swirl around the increased likelihood of divorce following a child's death. Rando (1986) concludes that despite the numerous assertions made about the vulnerabilities of bereaved couples, there is still no solid evidence to support the claim of higher divorce rates. In the most exhaustive review of the research literature devoted to this topic, Schwab (1998) concludes that

> the majority of marital relationships survive the strain by a child's death and may even be strengthened in the long run. The time it takes for the bereaved parents to restore their relationship to the level it was before the child's illness and/or death varies depending on the couple and the circumstances involved . . . confusion between marital distress and divorce appears to be partially responsible for perpetuating the myth of a high divorce rate among bereaved parents. It is time for professionals to dispel the myth. (p. 445)

Finally, in another more recent study conducted under the auspices of The Compassionate Friends organization, it was found that only 12% of those who were married at the time of their child's death later divorced (and of these, 75% felt that the death of their child did not contribute to the termination of their marriage; as reviewed in McIntosh, 2006). What does our own survey evidence show about the likelihood of increased marital terminations and conflict among bereaved parents? We will present these findings in the next chapter.

In this chapter, we pay particular attention to the grieving differences between bereaved husbands and wives that might disrupt their relationship. Let us begin by first examining how men and women grieve differently and how this may initiate the need for a better understanding of each other. If there is any subject in this book that has been studied previously, it is gender differences in grief. According to Doka and Martin (2010), in their widely circulated book, *Grieving Beyond Gender*, women are culturally scripted to respond more *emotionally* to loss, to respond more affectively with tears, and to reach out for emotional help, whereas men are expected to respond more *instrumentally*, to express their loss in physical or cognitive ways, to immerse themselves in work, and to accomplish tasks and activities. The authors are careful to point out, however, that these shared stereotypical gender-based tendencies leave bereaved individuals with a great deal of leeway for personal differences and opportunities to blend their grief responses, often times resulting in healthier outcomes. As they say,

> There are many different styles of coping with loss. Each has distinct strengths and limitations. There are advantages in expressing affect and seeking support. But there are also complementary strengths in stoically continuing in the face of loss and in seeking amelioration of pain in cognitive and active approaches. In short, people who draw from a broad range of adaptive strategies are, in fact, likely to do better. People with the widest range of responses, who effectively integrate all aspects of self, seem best able to respond to crisis. One can learn from both types of responses because, after all, different modes of adaptation are just that—differences, not deficiencies. (pp. 11–12)

Following the cultural scripting line of reasoning still further, Worden (2009) asserts that

> gender role expectations are part of the socialization process of our society and its culture. Studies reveal that men are more likely than women to fear the consequences of emotional expression in a social context. Men disclose far less intimate information to others than do women. For men, close friendships are based on shared activities rather than intimacy, and assumed loyalties rather than shared feelings. Bereaved fathers are faced with several double binds as they struggle to cope with their child's death. First, fathers are given little social support, while they are expected to be a major source of support for their wives, children, and other family members. Second, fathers are simultaneously confronted with the culturally idealized notions that grief is best handled through expressiveness and that they need to control such frightening and overwhelming expressions of grief (Cook, 1988). These conflicts between social and personal expectations can lead men to feel frustration, anger, and aloneness in grief. (pp. 226–227)

Worden offers these thoughts more or less speculatively.

In addition, previous research also shows that culturally gendered scripts about grieving and religious participation bring male and female mourners along diverging pathways. Female mourners are much more likely than males to make cemetery visits. Not only do females visit grave sites of deceased family members more than men but also they spend an average of 50% more time on their visits. On visits to children's graves, they are found to spend 91% more time visiting gravesites than men (Bachelor, 2004). It appears that the differences in cemetery visitations between the genders may stem, in part, from differences in religiosity between men and women. According to Francis (1997), females are more likely to believe in God, to attend public worship services, and to engage in personal prayer. These differences are probably at least partly associated with more frequent cemetery visits, as Bachelor (2004) found greater cemetery visiting among active churchgoers than for those who did not profess a faith.

All these differences led us to the expectation that bereaved mothers would be more likely to seek counseling support and join support groups sooner and in greater numbers than fathers. Men also are supposed to solve their own problems and not turn to others for help or let others see them cry or grieve, all of which make it less likely they would seek or attend support groups or therapy. Gender-based expectations again may be important reasons. We believe it was no accident that our bereaved parents sample was so heavily dominated by females, with a ratio of six mothers for every father. Most other studies of the traumatically bereaved have also shown a similar overrepresentation of females over males in the samples. Callahan (2000), for example, whose study parallels ours, having been drawn from support group members, found that 72% and 84% of its Chicago-based subsamples of the suicide bereaved were females. Even Murphy (2008), whose parental bereavement study was drawn from the death certificate records of two states, found that the participation of mothers dominated over fathers by a large margin: 115 to 58. Murphy's data suggest that women may be more inclined than men to participate in bereavement surveys, hence one plausible reason to explain their gender-skewed results, collected from death certificate records, which should have yielded more evenly matched numbers of men and women in the sample. The overrepresentation of mothers in bereavement research is found in other child-loss studies as well (see, e.g., Dyregrov, Nordanger, & Dyregrov, 2003; Séguin, Lesage, & Kiely, 1995, among others).

Based on his many years of experience providing grief therapy to families sustaining the violent death of a child, Rynearson (2011) contends that this form of bereavement usually falls most heavily on mothers who feel an inordinate sense of remorse for having failed to protect their children from such an extremely adverse outcome. This makes these bereaved mothers much more likely to experience greater grief and psychological difficulties, to seek out help from professionals, and probably also to participate to a greater extent in bereavement research.

Women have been noted more than men to seek out mental health professionals. In Chapter 7, readers may recall that we stated that among the middle-aged and older population reporting depressed feelings, women reported a 10% higher rate than men in using mental health counselors in the 2009 National Survey of Drug Use and Health Study.

Table 12.1 subsequently displays the gender differences among all our respondents regarding ever having used various forms of bereavement help. The

Table 12.1
Gender and Use of Bereavement Help Resources

EVER USED	MEN	WOMEN	TOTAL	CHI-SQUARE *p*
		%/N		
General self-help group	74.1/63	74.0/361	74.0/424	.98
Clergy help	40.0/34	48.5/234	47.2/268	.15
Bereavement counselor	45.8/38	47.7/230	47.4/268	.74
All types of professional mental health counselors	51.8/43	62.3/302	60.7/345	.07
Psychics/spiritualists	17.9/15	33.8/162	31.4/177	.004
SOS support groups +	73.9/51	74.1/281	74.1/332	.97
MEAN CURRENT USE				**SIGNIFICANT OF F**
General self-help group	1.84/63	1.76/363	1.77/426	.68
Clergy help	1.05/40	.90/236	.92/276	.52
Bereavement counselor	1.22/40	1.31/242	1.29/282	.76
All types of professional mental health counselors	1.26/47	1.48/307	1.45/354	.37
Psychics/spiritualists	.81/16	.89/163	.89/179	.73
SOS support groups +	1.89/52	1.87/278	1.88/330	.98

Note. From Survivors Child Loss Survey, 2006–2009.
+ Among parents with a child's suicide death.

table shows bereaved mothers almost twice as likely to have used psychics and spiritualists compared to men, 34% as compared to 18%. Like the national data, our survey findings showed a 10% difference between the women and men in ever-using mental health professionals since the loss, 62% as compared to 52%. It should also be remembered that in Chapter 11, we reported that women also used the Internet support group much more so than men. This, too, could represent still another support mode having a greater appeal to women than men. (Future research will be needed to discern whether our findings on this were group-specific or may be generalized to other Internet groups.)

In all other aspects of bereavement help use, our survey data showed no gender differences between bereaved mothers and fathers in terms of joining a general bereavement support group, a survivors of suicide group, or seeking support from clergy or bereavement counselors. Table 12.1 shows the different frequencies by gender in the use of bereavement resources, whether used weekly, monthly, or not at all. Current frequency of use was placed on a 6-point scale ranging from *no attendance during the past year* to *weekly or higher attendance*. The *t* test comparisons by gender did not show any differences in the average level of use between men and women in receiving bereavement services for the past 12-month period.

We might wonder what the impact on marital cohesion might be from diverging rates of participation between men and women in support groups and counseling. Would a couple's differences in using bereavement help be associated with less cohesion between them? Our interview records shed some light on this important issue, although the data did not suggest any firm conclusions.

The case of Joy M. exemplifies the divisive potential when a bereaved father and mother use bereavement help differently. In the months following their son Anthony's death by hanging, Joy M. began attending a peer support group that she felt greatly helped her come to terms with the death. At first, her husband Charles, a mechanical engineer, came with her to the support group meetings, but he stopped attending after a few sessions. He told Joy it didn't make any sense for him to continue with the group. He said, "You have to move on; there's nothing more you can do about losing Anthony; what's the point of hashing it over and over again?"

Joy, however, experienced the group differently. During the early months of attendance, she blamed herself for Anthony's death, believing that since she had a closer relationship with her son, she should have recognized the suicide warning signs. When Anthony stayed in his room for hours on end, isolating himself from friends and family, she felt she should have insisted on getting him into counseling. After many months of support group participation and occasional visits with a grief counselor, Joy eventually stopped blaming herself. She realized that she had been judging herself by hindsight knowledge following Anthony's death. She finally admitted that Anthony's behavior, prior to the suicide, was not all that clear cut; there had been many times when he had seemed happy to be with his family and, probably, there was nothing she could have done to prevent his death.

Joy and Charles drifted further apart in the months that followed Joy's new involvement in the support group. Eventually, Joy was selected as the group's co-facilitator and assigned the task of welcoming newly bereaved survivors into the group. Charles resented Joy's newfound commitment: her many phone calls with new members, inviting some to her home, and her perfect meeting attendance record. When Charles suggested they go on vacation together, Joy refused, reluctant to miss a support group meeting.

For Joy, Charles had become emotionally unavailable. He never asked about her involvement with the group and often made sarcastic comments about it. When Joy eventually suggested that she and Charles begin marital counseling together, Charles initially refused. He was angered at the suggestion, denied he had any problems, and accused her of being overly preoccupied with her group. Eventually, Charles agreed to go for counseling if Joy agreed to reduce her commitments to the group and to the other survivors. Joy rejected this condition. It was her perception that Charles was in denial about their loss because he never talked much about missing Anthony, and if he said anything at all about him, it seemed to include some subtle or not so subtle criticism of her as an inadequate mother. A few months later, with little improvement in their relationship, Joy asked Charles to move out of the house and a separation agreement was subsequently filed.

This case vividly illustrates how one spouse's participation in a support group and the other's resolute disinterest in therapies may have contributed to the destabilization of their relationship. Although the marriage may have been problematic and at risk before the death of their son, the couple's differences in support group participation appeared to be a key factor in bringing about the demise of their union.

In another case, Harold and Hi Lee B. both started attending a suicide survivors support group about a year and a half after their 19-year-old daughter, Jennifer, died from a lethal dose of Benadryl, a medication she found in the family home. Almost immediately after they started participating, Harold reported that it was especially comforting and helpful for him to be there. He appreciated the group's openness and being able to talk honestly and easily about all aspects of their daughter's death, without having to carefully frame his words to avoid offending others. He said the group was very therapeutic for him, where the heavy almost electrical charge of the suicide was greatly lessened by being there. For his wife Hi Lee, however, the group created just the opposite effect: It made her feel tense and retraumatized. It seemed to intensify her feelings of deep sadness over their loss.

Harold added that he had been in and out of therapies all his life: "ESP, Yoga, Primal Scream therapy—I even did Reichian therapy. Both before and since my daughter's death, I have always been in therapies. It has made me a better person. My wife, Hi Lee, has a different take on therapies. She has never had any since we've been married, except just recently after Jenny's death. Hi Lee grew up in Communist China during the Cultural Revolution. She believes that in China, her family life was greatly traumatized by community and group meetings: Family members were occasionally dispossessed or imprisoned, forced out of jobs, or denied social benefits. For her, openness and candor led to shaming, embarrassment, and sanctions."

Harold continued: "We both stopped coming to the group after a few sessions. It was much too upsetting for Hi Lee. We've been to see a few counselors since Jenny's death and that has helped a bit, but we have a long way to go. The death has also led to my wife's sexual unavailability. This is another problem we are struggling with, but it is now just starting to get better. This grief thing is all about making new adjustments, and these adjustments take time. I know things will never be like they were before—when Jennifer was alive. But we have a surviving teenage son that we have to raise and he's been damaged enough by his sister's death. We have to be there for him. It has been nearly 2 years since Jenny's death and although I can't yet see the light at the end of the tunnel, I'm hopeful that things will eventually get better."

These case illustrations show contrasting adaptations following a couple's or partner's withdrawal from support groups or counseling. In the first case, a probably fragile marital relationship succumbed when the couple confronted each other's conflicting views on the value of professional and nonprofessional help following the loss of their son. In the second case, despite the husband's keen interest in support groups, the couple bypassed this option and focused on using professional mental health caregivers in their efforts to adapt after their daughter's death. The couple remained united but sought another, more jointly acceptable treatment option to help them with their bereavement difficulties.

MARITAL COHESION AND HELP SEEKING

We wondered whether the joint participation of husbands and wives in support groups and/or in professional counseling would be associated with greater marital cohesion. It seemed plausible to expect a couple's joint participation to be associated with higher marital cohesion than if only one of the pair had pursued this activity or if neither of them participated. We were able to take a preliminary look into this question with our survey data.

When we first began collecting the surveys, we invited all married respondents to request a second survey for their partner to complete. More than 350 of the respondents indicated they were married at the time they completed their surveys, but only a much smaller number, 45, requested additional surveys for their partners to complete. In all but two of these cases, both partners returned completed surveys. Thus, we were able to investigate the differences between husbands' and wives' use of support groups and mental health professionals and their marital cohesion for only a smaller subsample of our total.

We created a composite scale of marital cohesion from four questions we asked of all respondents. These questions, taken from the National Survey of Family and Households (NSFH, 2001–2003), were somewhat overlapping. They were as follows: (a) Describe your marital relationship (on a 7-point scale) from *very unhappy* to *very happy*; (b) What do you think the chances are that you and your partner will eventually separate or divorce (on a 5-point scale); (c) How often during the past month do you and your partner spend time alone or share any activities (on a 6-point scale); and (d) When you have serious disagreements, how often do you discuss them calmly (on a 5-point scale). Responses to these four questions were highly intercorrelated and generated correlation coefficients of at least .40 within our sample. From these

Table 12.2a
Marital Cohesion and Joint Versus Singular Support Group and/or Counseling
Participation of Husbands and Wives, Husbands Only, (N = 42)

		MEAN MARITAL COHESION SCORE (14–23)				
	N	MEAN	*SD*	*t*	*df*	SIG.
General bereavement support group						
Joint participation	24	20.8	2.2	1.18	39	.25
One or neither participated	17	19.9	2.1			
Total	41	20.4	2.2			
Survivor of suicide support group						
Joint participation	18	20.1	2.7	−.39	33	.70
One or neither participated	17	20.4	1.8			
Total	35	20.3	2.3			
Saw a mental health professional						
Joint participation	15	19.9	2.7	−1.06	36	.30
One or neither participated	23	20.7	1.9			
Total	38	20.3	2.2			

Note. From Survivors Child Loss Survey, 2006–2009.

four questions, we created an additive scale ranging from 14 to 23 for the bereaved fathers and from 11 to 23 for the bereaved mothers. An alpha coefficient of .78 as a scale of marital cohesion was observed.

Tables 12.2a and 12.2b show the results that contrast the differences in marital cohesion for bereaved fathers (Table 12.2a) and mothers (Table 12.2b) who reported jointly going to general bereavement support groups versus where only one or neither of them had ever done so. Respondents were also asked the same set of questions for going to SOS support groups or seeing mental health professionals. Both tables for bereaved husbands and wives show *t* test comparisons between those who jointly used that therapeutic approach compared to those where only one partner reported doing so or where neither of them had done so. The results show no significant differences in cohesion for the husbands or wives who jointly or separately sought bereavement help. Thus, this very preliminary data suggest that there is not likely to be much of a gain in marital cohesion for couples who jointly seek bereavement help, compared to those where only one or neither member of the couple seek help. If we had a larger sample, it would have been possible and worthwhile for us to separately analyze the smaller group of those couples where neither member reported using these forms of support and compared these cases to the other larger subgroups. It should be noted, too, that for only about 12% of the married participants in our survey did their spouse/partner also participate. Therefore, there may be a large selection bias that influenced these findings, complicating our ability to make generalizations from this smaller subsample.

Table 12.2b

Marital Cohesion and Joint Versus Singular Support Group and/or Counseling Participation of Husbands and Wives, Wives Only, (N = 41)

	N	MEAN	SD	t	df	SIG.
		MEAN MARITAL COHESION SCORE (11–23)				
General bereavement support group						
Joint participation	25	19.6	3.4	−.33	38	.74
One or neither participated	15	19.9	2.2			
Total	40	19.7	3.0			
Survivor of suicide support group						
Joint participation	19	20.1	2.9	.53	32	.60
One or neither participated	15	19.5	3.3			
Total	34	19.9	3.1			
Saw a mental health professional						
Joint participation	15	18.6	3.8	−1.58	35	.12
One or neither participated	22	20.2	2.3			
Total	37	19.5	3.1			

Note. From Survivors Child Loss Survey, 2000–2009.

GENDER DIFFERENCES IN GRIEF AND MENTAL HEALTH DIFFICULTIES

Another question we investigated was the gender differences in grief difficulties and mental health problems following the loss of a child. Most comparative studies conclude that females suffer greater grief difficulties and psychological distress than males following the loss of a child, whether the child died in infancy from natural causes or had sustained a violent death in later life (Dyregrov & Matheisen, 1991; Moriarty, Carroll, & Cotroneo, 1996; Murphy, 1997; Parkes, 1996; Raphael, 1984; Sanders, 1989; Schwab, 1996; Sidmore, 2000). Yet, in a few studies, evidence was collected showing that fathers experienced greater mental health difficulties than mothers. Pudrovska (2009), with data from the Wisconsin Longitudinal Study, found that bereaved fathers showed poorer mental health compared to their maternal counterparts. Osterweis, Solomon, and Green (1984) found that fathers experienced higher levels of anger and loss of control following the death of a child. In addition, in a longitudinal study of 171 bereaved parents, who were studied over a 5-year period, Murphy, Johnson, and Lohan (2002) found that mothers experienced the steepest declines in grief difficulties scores between the first 4 and 12 months after the loss. However, for fathers, scores did not decline significantly until 2 to 5 years after the death.

Tables 12.3a and 12.3b review our findings. Table 12.3a offers *t*-test comparisons of all bereaved parents following a child's natural or accidental death on five criteria of grief and psychological problems that we have been examining throughout this book: GEQ scores, the Index of Complicated Grief (ICG), the Impact of Events Scale (IES), the 4-point Psychological Problems Scale, and

Table 12.3a
Grief and Mental Health Problems Among Bereaved Fathers and Mothers:
Among Parents Whose Child Died a Natural or Ordinary Accident Death (N = 61)

OUTCOME MEASURE	GENDER	N	MEAN	SD	t	df	SIG.
Grief Experience Questionnaire	1 Fathers	7	29.3	13.0	−.28	45	.78
	2 Mothers	40	30.6	11.1			
	Total	47	30.4	11.3			
Complicated Grief Scale	1 Fathers	8	20.6	7.3	−1.63	53	.11
	2 Mothers	47	25.7	8.4			
	Total	55	25.0	8.4			
Impact of Event Scale	1 Fathers	8	28.3	9.9	−.70	55	.48
	2 Mothers	49	30.7	9.2			
	Total	57	30.4	9.2			
Index of Psychological Problems	1 Fathers	7	1.14	1.34	.04	55	.96
	2 Mothers	50	1.12	1.26			
	Total	57	1.12	1.25			
Eight-item Depression Scale	1 Fathers	7	2.42	2.7	−.82	50	.41
	2 Mothers	45	3.44	3.11			
	Total	52	3.31	3.05			

Note. From Survivors Child Loss Survey, 2006–2009.

the 8-point general depression scale. The comparisons in Table 12.3a show a consistent pattern of no appreciable or statistically significant differences between fathers and mothers on each of the five criteria. Comparisons shown in this table came from bereaved parents whose children died from natural causes or accidents.

Any number of factors might explain why our results differed from previous research findings. For one, the paucity of males in these comparisons (7 or 8 cases) creates some uncertainty and unreliability that these results may have been attributable to a small number of male respondents. In addition, the greatest number of our cases was based on accidental deaths, with only a few instances of neonatal deaths. Neonatal deaths could be a factor that may have a greater impact on mothers than fathers (Lang et al., 1996). The disparities could also have been caused by changes in response patterns from today's bereaved parents compared to those from earlier periods, some of whom had been studied as long as 25 years ago. Most discussions of grief and grief problems 20 or more years ago would have been "women's only" topics. Today, however, in the current psychological age, discussions of grief and grief difficulties have become fully acceptable parts of the general public discourse. When theatrical plays and books such as *Rabbit Hole* and *The Year of Magical Thinking* have become widely

Table 12.3b
Grief and Mental Health Problems Among Bereaved Fathers and Mothers:
Among Parents Whose Child Was a Suicide or Drug-Overdose Death (*N* = 510)

OUTCOME MEASURE	GENDER	*N*	MEAN	*SD*	*t*	*df*	SIG.
Grief Experience Questionnaire	1 Fathers	73	34.3	9.6	−4.92	469	.001
	2 Mothers	398	41.1	11.1			
	Total	471	40.0	11.1			
Complicated Grief scale	1 Fathers	72	22.8	6.4	−5.66	480	.001
	2 Mothers	410	29.1	8.9			
	Total	482	28.1	8.9			
Impact of Event Scale	1 Fathers	69	28.8	7.9	−5.08	460	.001
	2 Mothers	393	34.5	8.7			
	Total	462	33.6	8.8			
Index of Psychological Problems	1 Fathers	75	1.1	1.12	−4.59	493	.001
	2 Mothers	420	1.8	1.31			
	Total	495	1.7	1.31			
Eight-item Depression Scale	1 Fathers	70	3.0	3.08	−4.32	453	.001
	2 Mothers	385	4.7	3.01			
	Total	455	4.4	3.07			

Note. From Survivors Child Loss Survey, 2006–2009.

shared media events and the public saturates itself by delving into the grief problems of others on the many TV shows like *Dr. Phil, 60 Minutes,* and many others, grief may be said to have taken hold as a fully public matter.

The longer average time span from the time of death to the collection of our bereavement data may have been still another factor that could account for the divergent findings. Any one or a combination of several of these factors might explain differences between the present findings and those from previous research. It remains a task for future research to further investigate this question of gender differences in grief among natural and accidental death-bereaved parents with larger samples.

On the other hand, Table 12.3b shows convergence with the prior research record, with women experiencing greater grief and psychological problems than men among parents who lost a child to suicide or drug overdose. We also separately investigated newly bereaved parents whose children died by suicide or drug overdoses and contrasted these cases against the longer term bereaved with the same cause of death. Mean difference comparisons for the long-term bereaved on each criterion showed great similarity to the differences observed for the newly bereaved. For example, if there had been a mean difference of 5 points between fathers and mothers on the GEQ scale for the newly bereaved, that 5-point differential was still noted among the longer term bereaved parents. These patterns suggest that the declines in the levels of grief and psychological problems may take place more or less evenly for both genders. However, it should be remembered that our data are cross-sectional, that is, they were based on the assessment of different bereaved parents at different points in time after their losses and not on longitudinal remeasurements of the same respondents over time. Longitudinal research has shown gender differences in the abatement of grief difficulties over time (Murphy, 2008).

The greater grief and psychological problems of bereaved mothers, compared to fathers, whose children died from suicides and had drug-related deaths, invites further speculation regarding why there might be contrasts in this respect from the mothers and fathers whose children died from accidents and natural causes. We are especially impressed with the theorizing on this subject offered by Ed Rynearson (2011) mentioned previously. Although Rynearson was primarily referring to bereaved mothers whose children died by homicide, we think there are parallels here to bereaved mothers of suicides and drug deaths of children. We would be inclined to speculate that when the death of the bereaved mother's child was preceded by a long history of failed drug or mental health treatments, such a situation would be especially conducive to creating postdeath guilt and remorse about the failure to find the right treatments to save the child's life. We further surmise that when bereaved mothers share these remorseful sentiments, they would be especially likely to show higher grief difficulties on established quantitative measures. Further investigation of these speculations appears to be a research task of considerable importance for future research.

Given the greater incidence of grief and mental health problems among bereaved mothers compared to fathers of suicide or drug-overdose child deaths, it seemed important to assess the associations between these problems and each partner's view of their marital cohesion. If a wife's greater grief and mental health difficulties are associated with her husband's perception of diminished marital cohesion, then we have a situation that could produce marital difficulties for the couple.

It should be noted that the single strongest correlate to a husband's or wife's cohesiveness score is their partner's cohesiveness score. The two scores had a correlation of .63 within our marital pairs subsample. It is also noted that grief and mental health problems were associated with a husband's or wife's perception of the level of cohesion in their marriage, more modestly, with coefficients ranging between .20 and .40. This was observed both in our larger sample of 387 married respondents and in the marital pairs subsample of 43 cases.

It seemed important for us to gauge the associations between a bereaved husband's or wife's cohesiveness score and their personal grief and mental health difficulties as well as those of their partner. This should enable us to ascertain the answer to the question mentioned earlier: Is there an association between a wife's grief and mental health difficulties and her husband's perceived

Table 12.4

Correlations Between a Bereaved Husband's or Wife's Marital Cohesiveness Score, Their Grief and Mental Health Problems, and Their Partner's Grief and Mental Health Problems (*N* = 43)

	CORRELATION COEFFICIENT/SIGNIFICANCE	
HUSBAND'S SCORES	**HUSBAND'S MARITAL COHESION**	**WIFE'S GRIEF & PSYCH. DIFFS.**
GEQ score	−.18/.25	.08/.62
ICG score	−30/.06	−.17/.31
IES score	−.18/.27	−.04/.81
Index of Psych. Diffs.	−.49/.01	−.04/.79
Depression score	−.42/.01	−.02/.90
WIFE'S SCORES	**WIFE'S MARITAL COHESION**	**HUSBAND'S GRIEF & PSYCH. DIFFS.**
GEQ score	−.17/.31	−.11/.48
ICG score	−.35/.02	−.42/.01
IES score	−.35/.04	−.14/.40
Index of Psych. Diffs.	−.38/.02	−.65/.01
Depression score	−.29/.11	−.50/.01

Note. From Survivors Child Loss Survey, 2006–2009. GEQ = Grief Experience Questionnaire; ICG = Index of Complicated Grief; IES = Impact of Event Scale.

level of marital cohesion? We also explored the obverse to this question: What association may exist between a husband's grief and mental health difficulties and his wife's level of perceived marital cohesion? Table 12.4 subsequently examines these questions.

Table 12.4 shows that a husband's marital cohesion is associated with his own psychological difficulties and depression. There appears to be no significant association with his wife's grief or psychological difficulties. This finding seems important, given the general discrepancy between a wife's usually greater grief and psychological difficulties, compared to her husband's. Apparently, husbands are minimally affected by their wife's grief and psychological problems.

Interestingly, as we examined wives' cohesiveness correlates, we observed a sharply contrasting response from that of their husbands. Women, too, showed their cohesion associated with their own experiences of complex grief, posttraumatic stress disorder (PTSD), and psychological difficulties. They differed greatly from their husbands in their sensitivity to their husband's psychological difficulties. A wife's perceived marital cohesion appears to be negatively associated with her husband's depression or psychological difficulties. Although this finding is correlational in nature, and therefore the direction of causality cannot be determined from our data, the result is, nevertheless, intriguing for what it suggests about the possible interactional nature of complicated grieving responses after child loss. Wives in particular may have their sense of cohesion in the marriage affected not only by their own bereavement struggles but also by the difficulties their husbands are experiencing. This finding deserves further investigation in future bereavement research on the impact of child death on couple relationships.

Overall, based on the Table 12.3b findings, the evidence shows that wives experience greater grief and psychological difficulties than their husbands after the loss of a child to drugs or suicide. Moreover, the Table 12.4 findings suggest that although husbands are little affected by their wives' greater difficulties, a wife's sense of marital cohesion is likely to be diminished when her husband has elevated levels of grief and psychological difficulties. This somewhat rarely occurring circumstance (based on Table 12.3b findings) suggests that when a husband experiences high grief distress, there may be a more serious adverse effect from it on the couple's marital relationship.

Summing up our most significant findings from this chapter, we found that whether both marital partners sought counseling or support group help together (during the previous year), or whether only one of them or neither of them had done so, there were no differences in their levels of marital cohesion. We also found that a wife's experiences of higher levels of grief difficulties were not associated with any diminished perception of marital cohesion by her husband, compared to cases where a wife may have had fewer grief problems. Given the commonality of cases where wives are found to harbor greater grief difficulties than their husbands, this could have presented a serious flash point in couple relations associated with the loss of a child. Of course, given the especially small numbers of our cases where we found these associations, additional confirmation from further research will be needed. Overall, however, in these respects, this chapter's data analysis does not reveal that a husband's or wife's marital relationship is greatly jeopardized after the loss of their child because of their diverging grief patterns.

Further research will also be needed to investigate why bereaved mothers of suicides and drug-overdose deaths experience more grief difficulties than fathers and why these patterns still appear to persist as time after the loss passes.

We end this chapter on a cautionary note. Our marital pairs, with its low response rate, invites speculation about its selectivity biases. We did a preliminary analysis to further investigate this by comparing means on four important dimensions of our research interests: grief difficulties (GEQ scores), complex grief (ICG scores), psychological problems (our index of psychological problems [IPP] scale), and the 8-point depression scale. When we compared the 40–43 bereaved fathers to their 71–74 counterparts in the larger sample, we found virtually no differences between the two subgroups. In the larger sample, the GEQ mean was 33.3; for the marital pairs males, 32.8; and the ICG mean in the larger sample was 22.6 and 23.4 among the marital pairs husbands. On the IPP in the large sample, the mean was 1.05 and within the smaller subgroup, 1.09; depression scale scores hardly differed with a mean of 2.91 in the larger sample and 2.86 within the marital pairs bereaved fathers.

Yet, for the bereaved mothers, an entirely different and contrasting picture was noted. In the larger sample, which ranged between 270 and 297 cases, bereaved mothers had a GEQ mean of 39.0, and within the marital pairs subsample, the mean was 35.1; for the inventory of Complicated Grief, the large sample mean was 27.8 and 25.8 within the smaller subsample; for the psychological problems scale, the large sample mean was 1.53 and 1.3 within the subsample. On the last comparison, scores varied sharply with a mean of 4.16 in the larger sample and 3.11 among the marital pairs bereaved mothers. Clearly, a trend is noted showing bereaved mothers in the subsample to be less grief and psychologically troubled than their counterparts in the larger sample. Given the heavily skewed nature of our sample, with bereaved mothers outnumbering fathers by a 6 to 1 ratio, we suspected that less grief and psychologically troubled mothers were more inclined to urge their husbands to complete surveys than their counterparts who had higher levels of grief and psychological difficulties. Thus, we wonder whether the findings that we have obtained for this subsample of apparently less grief and psychologically troubled bereaved mothers would also be noted where a greater representation of grief and psychologically troubled bereaved mothers were included. Further research will be needed to clarify this additional important question.

REFERENCES

Bachelor, P. (2004). *Sorrow and solace: The social world of the cemetery.* Amityville, NY: Baywood.

Callahan, J. (2000). Predictors and correlates of bereavement in suicide support group participants. *Suicide & Life-Threatening Behavior, 30*(2), 104–124.

Christ, G. H., Bonanno, G., Malkinson, R., & Rubin, R. (2003). Bereavement experiences after the death of a child. Appendix E. In M. J. Field & R. E. Behrman (Eds.), *When children die: Improving palliative and end-of-life care for children and their families* (pp. 553–579). Washington, DC: National Academy Press.

Cook, J. A. (1988). Dad's double binds: Rethinking fathers' bereavement from a men's studies perspective. *Journal of Contemporary Ethnography, 17*(3), 285–308.

DeFrain, J. (1991). Learning about grief from normal families: SIDS, stillbirths, and miscarriages. *Journal of Marital and Family Therapy, 17*(3), 215–223.

Doka, K. J., & Martin, T. L. (2010). *Grieving beyond gender: Understanding the ways men and women mourn.* New York, NY: Routledge.

Dyregrov, A., & Matheisen, S. B. (1991). Parental grief following the death of an infant—A follow-up over one year. *Scandinavian Journal of Psychology, 32*(3), 193–207.

Dyregrov, K., Nordanger, D., & Dyregrov, A. (2003). Predictors of psychosocial distress after suicide, SIDS and accidents. *Death Studies, 27*(2), 143–165.

Francis, L. J. (1997). Psychology of religion. In J. R. Hinnels (Ed.), *The Penguin dictionary of religions* (2nd ed.). London, UK: Penguin.

Klass, D. (1986–1987). Marriage and divorce among bereaved parents in a self-help group. *Omega: Journal of Death and Dying, 17*(3), 237–249.

Lang, A., Gottlieb, L. N., & Amsel, R. (1996). Predictors of husbands' and wives' grief reactions following infant death: The role of marital intimacy. *Death Studies, 20*(1), 33–57.

McIntosh, J. L. (2006). When a child dies: A survey's results dispelling the myth of high divorce rates after the loss of child. *Surviving Suicide, 18*(4), 1, 7–8.

Moriarty, H. J., Carroll, R., & Cotroneo, M. (1996). Differences in bereavement reactions within couples following death of a child. *Research in Nursing and Health, 19*(6), 461–469.

Murphy, S. A. (1997). A bereavement intervention for parents following the sudden, violent deaths of their 12–28-year-old children: Description and applications to clinical practice. *Canadian Journal of Nursing Research, 29*(4), 51–72.

Murphy, S. A. (2008). The loss of a child: Sudden death and extended illness perspectives. In M. S. Stroebe, R. O. Hansson, H. Schut, & W. Stroebe (Eds.), *Handbook of bereavement research and practice: Advances in theory and intervention* (pp. 375–396). Washington, DC: American Psychological Association.

Murphy, S. A., Johnson, L. C., & Lohan, J. (2002). The aftermath of the violent death of a child: An integration of parents' mental distress and PTSD during the first five years of bereavement. *Journal of Loss and Trauma, 7*(3), 203–222.

Murray, J., & Callan, V. J. (1988). Predicting adjustment to perinatal death. *British Journal of Medical Psychology, 61*(Pt 3), 237–244.

National Survey of Families and Households. (2001–2003). *Wave 3 codebook and data files.* Retrieved from www.ssc.wisc.edu/nsfh/codedata3.htm

Osterweis, M., Solomon, F., & Green, M. (Eds.). (1984). *Bereavement: Reactions, consequences and care.* Washington, DC: National Academy Press.

Parkes, C. M. (1996). *Bereavement: Studies of grief in adult life* (3rd ed.). London, UK: Penguin.

Parkes, C. M., & Weiss, R. (1983). *Recovery from bereavement.* New York, NY: Basic Books.

Pudrovska, T. (2009). Parenthood, stress and mental health in late midlife and early old age. *International Journal of Aging and Human Development, 68*(2), 127–147.

Rando, T. A. (Ed.). (1986). *Parental loss of a child* (2nd ed.). Champaign, IL: Research Press.

Raphael, B. (1984). *The anatomy of bereavement: A handbook for the caring professions.* London, UK: Routledge.

Rynearson, E. K. (2011). *Traumatic grief: Understanding the impact of violent death.* Paper presented at the 33rd Annual ADEC Conference, June 23, 2010, Miami, FL.

Sanders, C. M. (1989). *Grief: The mourning after–Dealing with adult bereavement.* New York, NY: John Wiley & Sons.

Schwab, R. (1992). Effects of a child's death on the marital relationship: A preliminary study. *Death Studies, 16*(2), 141–154.

Schwab, R. (1996). Gender differences in parental grief. *Death Studies, 20*(2), 103–113.

Schwab, R. (1998). A child's death and divorce: Dispelling the myth. *Death Studies, 22*(5), 445–468.

Séguin, M., Lesage, A., & Kiely, M. C. (1995). Parental bereavement after suicide and accident: A comparative study. *Suicide & Life-Threatening Behavior, 25*(4), 489–492.

Sidmore, K. V. (2000). Parental bereavement: Levels of grief as affected by gender issues. *Omega: The Journal of Death & Dying, 40*(2), 351–374.

Worden, J. W. (2009). *Grief counseling and grief therapy: A handbook for the mental health practitioner* (4th ed.). New York, NY: Springer Publications.

13

Investigating Whether Child Loss Promotes Harmony or Discord Among Married Couples

In this chapter, we approach the controversial question of whether a child's death diminishes a couple's marital cohesion and even their marital integrity or whether it may, on the other hand, actually bring a couple closer together, strengthening their ties. A debate continues to swirl over whether a child's death creates such upending and unsettling effects on the couple that it may disrupt their marriage. For example, see Christ, Bonanno, Malkinson, and Rubin (2003) for a full exposition of this position and also see the two Compassionate Friends Survey (n.d.) articles (one collected in 1999 and the other in 2006), where the counterclaim is advanced that bereaved parents are no more likely to experience disruptive marriages than the nonbereaved in the general population (www.compassionatefriends.org/media/Surveys.aspx).

In this chapter, we weigh in on this important controversy with our survey data and with data collected from a nationally representative sample of the nonbereaved, the National Survey of Families and Households (NSFH; Bumpass & Sweet, 2008). In addition, in this chapter, we also explore the less often examined question of whether a child's traumatic death and what we referred to in earlier chapters as a "blameworthy" death (such as a drug overdose or a suicide) imposes any different or greater disruptive potential for a couple than a child's nontraumatic or nonblameworthy death.

To begin this inquiry, our participant observation data offer preliminary evidence on both sides of the controversy. We begin with several vignettes. Dr. Larry P. lost his 18-year-old son, Stanley, suddenly, when Stanley slumped over on the living room sofa—as the two were spending an evening together watching *Monday Night Football*. Larry, a cardiologist, examined Stanley carefully and speedily drove him to the nearest hospital. It was too late, however; Stanley died from cardiac arrhythmia, a rare type of heart abnormality that had never been identified previously in yearly medical checkups.

At the funeral service, attended by more than 500 people, the family received an outpouring of support and caring responses from family, friends, and community. In the months that followed, husband and wife began bereavement counseling, but after several sessions, Larry felt it was unnecessary for him to continue. "I verbalize things, have many friends that I can talk to about my grief and you can't buy support." Harriet, his wife, felt differently. Having used counseling and taken prescribed psychotropic medications for several years to combat episodes of depression, she found grief counseling extremely helpful. She also joined a support group, a Compassionate Friends chapter, attended the group regularly, and even had occasional visits with psychics.

As the months passed, Harriet began to blame Larry for Stanley's death. Larry and their older son, Stanley, had often had a stormy relationship together, especially during Stanley's early teenage years. At that time, Stanley was occasionally prone to violent, impulsive outbursts and was diagnosed with attention deficit hyperactivity disorder and Asperger's syndrome. By Harriet's reckoning, Larry never accepted Stanley's mental health problems, was often impatient with him, added to his psychological stress, and perhaps even triggered the sudden fatal heart attack. Larry perceived his relationship with Stanley very differently. He saw the death as a stroke of extremely bad luck. He felt that Stanley had turned a corner with his mental illness, had become a leader among his schoolmates, and that of their two children, Stanley was most like him temperamentally; in fact, he regarded Stanley as his soulmate.

Eight months after Stanley's death, Harriet abruptly told Larry to move out because it seemed that their marriage was over. At first, Larry suggested that they seek counseling, but it was obvious that Harriet was already committed to ending the marriage. Several months later, Larry was presented with a divorce petition naming him as the blameworthy agent in their son's death. Considering the great friction that had emerged between them in the months since Stanley's death, Larry was only too glad to swiftly agree to the terms of the divorce settlement. He acknowledged that he and Harriet had had many differences over their 25-year-long marriage.

Brenda, their younger child, aged 15, had a history of eating disorders, acting out, substance abuse, and self-mutilation. She had numerous psychiatric evaluations with different mental health professionals and had attended different special schools and programs ever since completing primary school.

Harriet and Larry had many disagreements, especially over how to parent their children and whether they should attend special schools or be mainstreamed into the local public schools. They rarely spent quality time together. When Larry thought about it, he had to acknowledge that even if Stanley had not died so suddenly, it was almost a miracle that the marriage had endured this long, considering the length and intensity of their strife. In his opinion, Stanley's death simply accelerated a family breakup that would have been inevitable in any case.

Sally and Bernie M. lost their 21-year-old son, Henry, as a result of a car accident in which Henry was struck as a pedestrian. Henry was killed almost instantly when a drunk driver lost control of his car and swerved into him as he walked along a nearby sidewalk in their neighborhood. For several months after the tragedy, the couple went to a grief counselor, and Sally initially felt the counseling helped both of them to better accept and adjust to their loss. Yet, in the months that followed, Sally began to feel that Bernie was tuning her out and becoming emotionally isolated. He would come home from work as a fire safety inspector, barely speak, and sit endlessly watching TV shows. He often seemed in a daze when he and Sally were together and also became intensely preoccupied with his computer. One time as she passed by, she observed him visiting a porn site. During this time, Bernie's interest in sexual intimacy with Sally seemed to diminish as well. Eventually, Sally confronted Bernie about their marriage and directly asked him if he was committed to the relationship. Bernie's response, while positive, did not show much enthusiasm. Sally suggested they return to counseling, and although Bernie somewhat reluctantly agreed, during the sessions he showed little interest in communicating either with Sally or with the therapist. Several months later, at Sally's initiation, the couple agreed to a divorce.

When interviewed, Sally remarked that she would not have minded if Bernie had had a fling or something, anything, to get himself out of his isolation and into a better frame of mind. She said, "I just couldn't take his passivity and disinterest in things, and his becoming like a zombie to me, especially when I needed his help and support so much now."

Susan and Henry G. lost their teenage son, Ronald, in a tragic bus accident in Europe, 15 years earlier, on a summer travel adventure that was a gift Ronald received from his parents—a reward for his academic accomplishments. At the time of Ronald's death, Susan was a housewife and her husband an electrician. The couple had been childhood sweethearts and had another child, Rhonda, who was 14 when her brother died. The G.'s were always known for their self-sacrificing lifestyle, always available to meet their children's needs no matter how demanding. They were simply devastated at the loss of Ronald, but long-term brooding was never part of their repertoire.

After Ronald died, the couple joined a nearby Compassionate Friends group, which they found helpful. They remained active in this group for the next 5 or 6 years. With the passage of time, the couple attended fewer meetings, sometimes only one or two meetings a year. Six years after Ronald's death, the couple made a bold decision to adopt two homeless brothers (aged 5 and 8) from Guatemala. The boys, Antonio and Miguel, had been living in the streets and in and out of orphanages all their lives. The couple knew that raising two homeless older boys was going to be a major challenge, but they felt ready to take on this new parenting responsibility. Rhonda, their teenage daughter, also offered her approval for the assumption of this daunting task.

As the years passed, the family faced many behavioral and academic challenges, and the boys presented more than their fair share of teenage difficulties. But the couple remained committed to the boys and were motivated to see them both complete high school and paraprofessional programs. By the time the boys entered their early 20s, they had become devoted sons, with regular jobs in the community. Susan eventually took a part-time clerical job in an accountant's office and continued to work until Henry's retirement. When both parents reached their early 70s, they experienced some serious health challenges. Henry had heart valve replacement surgery and Susan had a bout with breast cancer. Through this all, the couple remained deeply committed to their marriage and devoted to each other and their children's welfare. They felt the best way to memorialize their lost son, Ronald, was to remain focused on their child-serving mission and to carry forward their mutually shared goals.

Steve and Louise L. unexpectedly lost their 24-year-old daughter, Linda, while she was away, enrolled in law school at the other end of the state. Linda took her life with a combination of recreational drugs, mixed with antianxiety medications that she took to reduce her tension while studying. The L.'s were a high-achieving family. Steve, a high school guidance counselor, had a master's degree. Louise, with a PhD in psychology, taught at a local community college. Their other daughter, Kendra, 27, was in the last stages of finishing her medical degree, aiming to become an emergency room physician.

When Linda died, the L.'s found great comfort and support from the survivors of suicide support group they joined in their small Northern Michigan town. When the founder of their support group, a 15-year veteran survivor, decided to pass the leadership baton over to the next generation, they were nominated for the job. Having taken a facilitator training course offered by the American Foundation for Suicide Prevention (AFSP), they were eager to run their small support group. The L.'s had also been especially active in fund raising for AFSP. For 4 consecutive years, they had participated in national fund-raising events, walking 20 miles overnight and raising several thousand dollars yearly for this suicide prevention organization. They often did long "power walks" together to help stay fit for their yearly "marathons." They worked together, counseling newly bereaved individuals who contacted their group. They also made joint presentations on suicide prevention at local high schools and colleges within commuting distance from their home. When they reflected on it, they acknowledged that the loss of their daughter Linda had brought them together—working as a team—as never before. Although they experienced periodic bursts of great sadness, profoundly missing their younger daughter, they recognized that they had channeled their own recoveries to help others bereaved by suicide and to fund raise for suicide prevention, subsequently finding a way to make something good come from their loss.

These four vignettes, drawn from our participant observation data, show a wide range of responses following the loss of a child. Although the first case suggests that a marital breakup was in the making prior to the death, the second suggests an emotional numbing brought on by the death, which created an unbridgeable communications barrier between the husband and wife. In contrast, the latter two cases show the unification of the couple's relationship after the death of a child. These anecdotal findings reflect the great diversity in loss responses that we have found to be representative of our sample.

Although these examples alone do not suggest any clear-cut conclusion about the question of whether positive or negative responses will follow after a loss, in general, the evidence from our survey data seemed clear: Positive outcomes were far more common than negative ones. There also was mixed evidence that bears on the question of whether our sampled bereaved parents were any more prone to marital stresses and separations than their non-bereaved counterparts in the general population. In the next section, we will take a closer look at this survey data.

SURVEY DATA

The majority of our 575 respondents reported being married at the time they completed their surveys: 68% married, 23% divorced, 2% separated, 1% never married, and 6% widowed. Most married respondents reported that their child's death brought them into a closer relationship with their partner. As Table 13.1

Table 13.1
Reports of Closer Versus Strained Marital Relations, Harmful or Helpful Spousal Actions, and Marital Separations Following the Death of a Child*

	PERCENTAGE/*N*
Reported closer vs. strained marital relations	
Closer	56.7/239
Weaker/strained	22.8/96
The same	20.6/87
	100.0/423
Partner acted helpfully or harmfully afterward	
Very helpfully	46.9/188
Somewhat helpfully	22.2/89
Neutrally	15.7/63
Somewhat harmfully	8.5/34
Very harmfully	6.7/27
	100.0/401
Reported divorcing after the loss	
Yes	6.0/34
No	94.0/532
Total	100.0/566
Reported separating after the loss	
Yes	8.9/48
No	91.1/494
Total	100.0/542

Note. From Survivors Child Loss Survey, 2006–2009.
*Table values may fall short or exceed 100 percent because of rounding.

shows, nearly three-fifths of the currently married respondents reported their relationship to be closer or stronger afterward, compared to one-fifth who reported weaker, more strained relations. Most married respondents also reported that their partner acted helpfully in the aftermath of the loss, compared to reports of unhelpful and/or harmful actions. This same table shows that more than two-thirds (69.1%) reported that their spouse acted helpfully after the loss, compared to 15% who reported their spouse acting hurtfully or 16% who acted neutrally afterward.

Table 13.1 also displays the percentages of couples who reported becoming divorced or separated since the loss of their child. Among all respondents, 6% reported terminating their marriages and 9% reported separating after their loss. There was some overlap in these reports. Some of the respondents who reported separating from their partners also reported divorcing their partners. When we combined both groups, either separating or divorcing, the combined total was 11.3% of all respondents. We compared this percentage reporting disrupted marriages with the numbers obtained in the NSFH survey (Bumpass & Sweet, 2008), a nationally representative sample. The NSFH, a longitudinal survey whose first wave was conducted in 1987–1988, originally had a total of 4,225 married respondents. That number of still married shrank by 7% when Wave 2 was conducted 6 years later in 1992–1994. The numbers shrank still further to a total of 12% not married, by the time of Wave 3, 7 years afterward in 2001–2003.

It is not easy to compare these differences, because our survey respondents' group rate is based on people who were, *on average*, 6 years since their loss. In contrast, *all* members of the NSFH sample were exactly 6 years after the first data collection period at Wave 1. (In essence, our data were cross-sectional, whereas the NSFH data were longitudinal.) Thus, for our sample, 35% had lost their children more than 6 years previously, whereas 65% had lost their children less than 6 years ago, with an average time since loss of 6 years. However, it does appear that the participants in our sample had about a 4% higher marital termination rate than the representative U.S. sample. Although we were reluctant to compute tests of statistical significance given the fundamental differences in this comparison, if these differences are replicated in other studies and found to be statistically significant, it would suggest that parents who lose a child, particularly in a sudden and traumatic fashion (as most of our sample did), may experience higher rates of marital separation and divorce than the population at large.

We cannot emphasize enough the tentativeness of our findings. It may well be that bereaved parents do indeed have substantially higher marital termination rates than their nonbereaved peers, or perhaps there are no meaningful and statistically significant differences between the bereaved and nonbereaved in this respect. The 4% difference could prove to be within the range of statistical error variability when statistical significance tests are applied. Most importantly, our comparison between the samples did not measure and control for the differences in potential confounders to marital terminations, such as the number of prior marriages, length of marriages, age differences, socioeconomic differences, numbers of cohabitation relationships, numbers of African Americans, and other factors known to be associated with marital terminations. Until such confounders are known and measured for both samples, we cannot ascertain whether the bereavement experience difference remains the important unique one between both groups. It is hoped that future research will address this important issue more satisfactorily.

Marital Solidarity

Table 13.2 shows the responses among our married respondents to four questions reflecting marital solidarity in couples, using the very same questions that had been administered in the second wave of the NSFH. These questions became the basis of our marital cohesion scale, presented in the previous chapter. Here, we mention them again: (a) On a scale of 1–7, with 1 for *very unhappy* and 7 for *very happy*, taking all things together, how would you describe your relationship? (b) Do you think the chances that you and your partner will eventually separate are very low, low, about even, high, or very high? (c) During the past month, how often did you and your partner spend time alone with each other, talking or sharing an activity: never, once a month, two to three times monthly, once a week, two to three times weekly, or daily? and (d) How often do you and your partner discuss your disagreements calmly: never, seldom, sometimes, very often, or always.

Table 13.2

Comparing Bereaved Parents With Nonbereaved Married Persons Older Than 45 Years of Age in NSFH Survey, 1992–1994, on Four Marital Solidarity Questions

	CHILD LOSS Rs			NSFH Rs		
	M	SD	N	M	SD	N
1. On a scale of 1–7, with 1 for *very unhappy* and 7 for *very happy*, taking all things together, how would you describe your relationship?	5.4	1.6	378	6.0	1.4	2,227
2. Do you think the chances that you and your partner will eventually separate are very low, low, about even, high, or very high?	1.4	.8	377	1.3	.7	2,305
3. During the past month, how often did you and your partner spend time alone with each other, talking or sharing an activity: never, once a month, two to three times monthly, once a week, two to three times weekly, or daily?	5.1	1.4	384	5.1	1.4	2,332
4. How often do you and your partner discuss your disagreements calmly: never, seldom, sometimes, very often, or always?	3.6	1.0	379	3.4	1.0	2,300

Note. From Survivors Child Loss Survey, 2006–2009.
National Survey of Families and Households, Wave 2, 1992–1994.

Interestingly, when we place both sets of findings side by side, we see our respondents giving mostly similar responses to the nationally representative sample of married nonbereaved parents, 45 years of age or older. With one important exception, our respondents reported nearly identical means for how often they spent time alone talking or sharing activities together. They reported two-tenths of a rating point higher mean for always discussing their disagreements calmly, 3.6 as compared to 3.4. Also, mean rated likelihood of separating was one-tenth of a rating point higher when compared to the national sample's mean. Where they differed more substantially was in their reports of marital happiness, reporting themselves six-tenths of a rating point below the national sample, with a mean of 5.4 as compared to 6.

We were reluctant to compute tests of statistical significance to compare all these differences given the very large number of NSFH respondents of more than 2,000 cases. With samples that large, nearly any difference, even a small one, would have become statistically significant. In attempting to focus on clinically meaningful and not just statistically significant results, we determined that the marital happiness differences between both groups appeared noteworthy and likely meaningfully significant. Therefore, we compared the means for marital happiness within our bereavement sample to the 95% confidence intervals for marital happiness within the NSFH survey, which ranged from 5.9 to 6.1. This suggested that the marital happiness means for our respondents of 5.4 differed significantly from the nonbereaved NSFH respondents. Close inspection of the frequencies revealed that fewer bereaved parents, 30%, gave themselves the highest rating for marital happiness, compared to 49% of the nonbereaved who reported being at the highest level for marital happiness. Thus, it appears that almost half as many parents who have lost a child indicate lower ratings of their marital happiness than the population at large. Reports of marital happiness among those at the remaining 6 points of the scale did not appear to differ much between the two groups. We further examined the other survey questions in close detail and found several other differences. Among bereaved parents, 8% fewer thought their chances of getting divorced were very low as compared to the nonbereaved (73% as compared to 81% in the NSFH); 13% more of the bereaved respondents reported discussing their disagreements calmly often as compared to the NSFH respondents (43% as compared to 30%). However, in the other respects that were surveyed, the differences between bereaved and nonbereaved were negligible or nonexistent. To summarize, differences in reports of marital happiness appear to be considerable, particularly at the highest end of the scale regarding reports of marital happiness. This finding deserves further empirical exploration.

Interestingly, despite this evidence of lowered levels of marital happiness and possibly higher marital termination rates, our bereaved parents also reported slightly higher rates of calm discussion with their partners and identical rates of shared activity together. These findings are therefore somewhat surprising because one might expect that if there is a general negative effect from losing a child, it would be manifested in greater conflict (i.e., less calm discussion) and less shared activity together. One possible explanation may be that the lowered levels of marital happiness (mostly lower rates of reporting the highest level of marital happiness in the marriage for the bereaved sample) reflect a general anhedonia or loss of ability to feel pleasure in anything. This is a common experience of bereaved parents as well as a common symptom of depression (recall that our sample showed higher levels of depression, even 10 years after the death, than national samples). In some but not all instances, this heightened anhedonia might affect the ability of couples to be emotionally available to one another and might contribute to marital termination or diminished cohesion. These speculations need further research, with more extensive exploration of marital functioning than was possible with our four-item cohesion measure to clarify and replicate these findings.

Demographic Variables

We return now to the last chapter's discussion of previous studies that suggested a close association between the loss of a child and the negative impact on the couple's adjustment and marital satisfaction that could elevate their chances of a marital breakup. At least four studies, undertaken among bereaved parents of a child dying in infancy, found clear evidence of marital difficulties following the loss (Best & VanDevere, 1986; Feeley & Gottlieb, 1988–1989; Lang, Gottlieb, & Amsel, 1996; Vance, Boyle, Najman, & Thearle, 2002).

We should mention that in terms of their demographic characteristics, there are distinctive differences between most parents losing a child to a stillbirth, sudden infant death syndrome (SIDS), or early infant death and the parents of our sample. Parents of early infant deaths are more likely to be younger, with marriages of a shorter duration. By contrast, our sample contained only two cases of parents experiencing early infant deaths, and only two of the accidental death cases were of children who had died before reaching the age of 10. Thus, our sample was, by and large, bereaved parents sustaining losses of teenage or older children. This suggests a very different character of the marriages of the former group as compared to the latter group.

Parents whose children die as infants are more likely to have had marriages of shorter duration, whereas parents of deceased teenagers and older children are more likely to have been married for more than a decade. Andrew Cherlin (1981) notes that most divorces occur within the first 7 years of a marriage and that the divorce likelihood decreases as a marriage endures (Gottman & Levenson, 2004; Heaton, 1991). The early years of a marriage are when the couple is most likely to confront multiple challenges: job failures, career disappointments, unexpected health and economic problems, and in-law interference, among other unexpected relationship difficulties. Once past their first decade of living together, a couple may have learned how to problem solve and cope with many commonplace problems; their marriage bond is likely to have been strengthened, and they may be better able to withstand the shocks and disappointments of everyday life and perhaps even the impact of nonnormative events such as the loss of a child.

The sociological literature suggests that marital partners who are younger, with greater numbers of previously failed marriages, lower incomes (and more unemployment), and greater geographic mobility are more divorce prone than their counterparts without these characteristics (Bahr & Galligan, 1984; Booth & Amato, 1992; Jalovaara, 2003; Monahan, 1959). Table 13.3 explores these associations among the 11% of our respondents (*n* = 65) who either separated or divorced in the years following their child's death and compares them to the larger subgroup of respondents who remained married (*N* = 510).

As expected, the table shows nearly half of those who ended their marriages (48%) reported a weaker relationship with their partner following the death, compared to only 16% among those whose marriages endured. Among those who terminated their marriages, 40% reported that their spouse acted hurtfully after their child died as compared to only 10% of those couples who remained together, and in agreement with the findings of the sociological literature cited earlier, we found more than twice as many who terminated their marriages were 45 years old or younger (16%), compared to 6% in that same age group among married couples who remained together. Almost 4 times more parents who ended their marriages reported family incomes less than $40K as compared to the percentage among parents who stayed together (41% as compared with 11%, respectively). Twice as many reported having three or more previous marriages as compared to the bereaved parents whose marriages remained intact (20% as compared to 10%, respectively). Nearly three-fifths of the bereaved parents who ended their marriages had moved in the past 5 years compared to only about a quarter for those whose marriages had endured (58% in terminated marriages compared to 23% in intact marriages). Significantly, more of those who ended their marriages reported being unemployed at the time of our survey, 8% as compared to 2% among those whose marriages lasted. Thus, all our expectations of anticipated correlates to marital terminations were supported with the bereaved parents' data. Taken together, these findings suggest that what may be termed the *marital resiliency* of the couples who separated was much lower than the couples who stayed together. Further, stressor events such as unemployment, migration from one location to another, and of course, the death of a child, along with youthful lack of marital experience, all likely contributed to this vulnerability of lowered marital resilience.

Psychological Variables

We also investigated numerous other variables that we have been examining throughout this book to see if any were associated with marital terminations. The list included grief and psychological difficulties, stigmatization, type of

Table 13.3
Respondents Separating or Divorcing Following the Death of Their Child Compared With Those Remaining Married on Various Social and Psychological Characteristics, *N* = 430*

	ENDED MARRIAGE	PRESERVED MARRIAGE	χ^2	CORRELATION/ SIGNIFICANCE
		%/N		
Relationship after the loss				
Weaker	48.3/28	15.6/56	85.6 (3) $p = .001$	−.32*/.001
Closer	22.4/13	60.3/216		* defined as:
The same	5.2/3	21.2/76		*closer* = 1
N/A	24.1/14	2.8/10		*same* = 0
Total	100/58	100/358		*weaker* = −1
Spouse's actions after the loss				
Harmful	39.5/15	10.9/37	27.1 (2) $p = .001$	−.27/.001
Neutral	21.0/8	14.7/50		
Helpful	39.5/15	74.4/253		
Total	100/38	100/340		
Age				
Younger than 45	16.9/11	5.7/21	10.1 (1) $p = .001$	−.15/.001
46 or older	83.1/54	94.3/346		
Total	100/65	100/367		
Family income				
Less than $40K	41.3/26	10.7/38	51.4 (3) $p = .001$	−.35/.001
$41−$60K	25.4/16	17.8/63		
$61−$90K	22.2/14	23.7/84		
More than $90K	11.1/7	47.9/170		
Total	100/63	100/355		
Times married				
Once	44.6/29	63.4/232	9.4 (2) $p = .004$	.15/.002
Twice	35.4/23	20.5/97		
Three or more	20.0/13	10.1/37		
Total	100/65	100/366		
Residential changes in the past 5 years				
None	41.5/27	76.6/281	51.7 (3) $p = .001$	.34/.001
One	29.2/19	16.9/62		
Two	15.4/10	5.5/20		
Three or more	13.9/ 9	1.1/ 4		
Total	100/65	100/367		

(continued)

Table 13.3
Respondents Separating or Divorcing Following the Death of Their Child
Compared With Those Remaining Married on Various Social and
Psychological Characteristics, *N* = 430 *(continued)*

	%/N			
	ENDED MARRIAGE	PRESERVED MARRIAGE	χ^2	CORRELATION/ SIGNIFICANCE
Present employment status				
Employed (ft or pt)	64.6/42	56.4/207	10.1 (3) *p* = .02	
Unemployed	7.7/5	1.9/7		
Retired	17.9/11	24.5/90		
Other (school; keeping house)	10.8/7	17.2/63		
Total	100/65	100/367		

Note. ft = full time; pt = part time. From Survivors Child Loss Survey, 2006–2009.
*Table values may fall short or exceed 100 percent because of rounding.

death, number of children in the family, gender differences, and the time since the loss.

This information, presented in Table 13.4, shows the bivariate correlations between each variable and marital terminations following a child's death. The strongest association was the depression score, with a .24 association. Also statistically significant but with slightly lower correlations with marital terminations were grief and psychological difficulties in general and the respondent's score on our stigmatization variable. Some of the other potential correlates

Table 13.4
Correlates of Marital Terminations After the Death of a Child Among All Married
Respondents, Those Whose Marriages Terminated, and Those Whose
Marriages Remained Intact (*N* = 432)

	CORRELATION COEFFICIENT/SIGNIFICANCE
Grief difficulties (GEQ)	.16/.001
Complicated grief (ICG)	.17/.001
PTSD (IES)	.05/.27
Psychological difficulties	.20/.001
Depression Score	.24/.001
Stigma Scale Score	.15/.001
Type of death (nat./acc. vs. drug/suicide)	.09/.06
Type of death (nat. vs. all others)	.06/.25
Number of children	−.02/.64
Time since the loss	.00/.96
Gender	.09/.06

Note. acc. = accidental; GEQ = Grief Experience Questionnaire; ICG = Inventory of Complicated Grief; IES = Impact of Events Scale; nat. = natural; PTSD = posttraumatic stress disorder.

were not significantly related to it (posttraumatic stress disorder [PTSD], whether the death was a traumatic one or a "blameworthy" death, and time since the loss) and appear not to be associated with marital terminations.

With many of these predictor variables only modestly associated with marital terminations, we anticipated considerable overlap and confounding between these variables and their contributions to prediction in a multifactor predictor model. To investigate this possibility, we conducted a logistic regression of all 10 (significant) predictors and their associations with marital terminations (displayed in Table 13.5). As expected, the table shows great overlap between each variable, with seven not contributing significantly to the model and only three uniquely important and necessary to contribute to the explanation of the observed differences in marital terminations: whether the respondent had made frequent residential changes during the past 5 years, whether the household had a low income, and whether the respondents felt their partner was more of a hindrance than a help after the loss. All the other variables failed to add to the prediction, and their import from our results was essentially embodied by these three earlier mentioned factors.

The 10-factor model explained 31% of the variability in marital terminations, demonstrating that the model did indeed have predictive value. The three significant factors alone explained 23% of the marital termination's variability, suggesting that although the seven remaining variables were statistically insignificant in the company of the other three predictors, they nevertheless accounted for an additional 8% of the variance of marital terminations. Perhaps having seen all these numbers and tables, we may wonder, "What can we learn from this?" In other words, do the numbers guide us in any way to a clearer understanding of marital terminations after a child's

Table 13.5

Multivariate Logistic Regression of Various Factors Predicting Marital Terminations Among Bereaved Parents Who Separated or Divorced After Losing a Child Compared to Those Who Remained Married ($N = 276$)

MEASURES	OR	(95% CI)	P
Times moved	2.46	(1.41–4.31)	.002
Family income	0.64	(0.47–0.88)	.006
Spouse seen as helpful vs. hindrance	0.35	(0.35–0.74)	.001
Grief difficulties (GEQ)	0.99	(0.93–1.06)	.91
Complicated grief (ICG)	1.01	(0.94–1.09)	.74
Psychological difficulties	0.67	(0.34–1.33)	.25
Depression Score	1.20	(0.94–1.54)	.16
Stigma Scale Score	1.02	(0.87–1.21)	.76
Age	0.41	(0.11–1.47)	.17
Number of marriages	0.88	(0.45–1.70)	.70

Note. GEQ = Grief Experience Questionnaire; ICG = Inventory of Complicated Grief.
From Survivors Child Loss Survey, 2006–2009.

death and to knowing which couples may be more likely to terminate their marriages afterward?

Our survey data suggest that a small percentage of bereaved parents will likely terminate their marriages following their child's death. Perhaps the most apparent warning sign of a couple's likelihood to later end their marriage is the perception one or both may have that their partner is a hindrance (rather than a help) in dealing with the death (or that a significant strain has emerged in their relationship afterward). This sets the stage for a possible eventual marital termination.

To arrive at an even deeper appreciation as to why some marriages end after a child's death, clarification can be derived from previous sociological studies. Younger couples who are less well established financially, exposed to greater unemployment, have had less success in making their previous marriages last, and who are less well anchored to their communities stand at a higher risk for a marital breakup. In addition, although the "spouse is helpful or a hindrance" variable was the only statistically significant psychological variable in the multivariate model, it remains true when we found that depression, the "grief distress" variables (grief difficulties, complicated grief, psychological difficulties), and stigmatization had statistically significant and modest associations with marital termination in the bivariate analysis. Taken together, the bivariate and multivariate analyses suggest that a combination of grief distress and unhappiness, coupled with stressor events impacting the marriage (lower income, more frequent moves) combine to create the conditions that increase the risk for marital termination after the death of a child. These conclusions stand out from the bivariate correlations and from the logistic regression results.

Of course, the greatest number of our respondents had marriages that had endured for more than a decade. In these cases, partners were not terminating short-duration marriages. For many, a termination may have taken place after the couple had been participants in a long-standing, "conflict-habituated" marriage (Cuber & Harroff, 1965). In these cases, the death of a child brought the schism between the couple into a new and completely untenable place. This is precisely what happened in the first vignette, the case of Dr. Larry and Harriet P.'s breakup, where we noted that the seeds for the breakup were sown over the many years that preceded the child's death and where the couple discovered substantial differences and clashing beliefs emerging between them. The existence of preexisting factors and differences between the couple has also been acknowledged as a precipitant to marital disruptions in previous work (Klass, 1986–1987). We suspect that future research on marital terminations will find much fruitful data by focusing on the marital partners themselves and exploring their perceptions of each other in the years preceding the child's death and their levels of grief distress and depression, and then combining this with the demographic variables of income strains and family mobility that our data have identified. All this together should lead to a deeper understanding of marital breakups following a child's death.

CORRELATES OF INCREASED MARITAL CLOSENESS

Now, let us direct our attention to the larger number of bereaved parents who experienced greater closeness and increased marital cohesion in the years after their child's death. About 60% of our respondents felt that their child's death had brought them closer together. How does one explain why some parents and not others felt closer to their spouse after the loss? A key concept that we feel generally represents marital closeness is the marital cohesion scale, which we introduced in the last chapter. Scale scores on this variable could range anywhere from as low as 4 to as high as 23 on the four-item scale. The mean for the entire sample of 371 currently married respondents was 18.7. We also found that within the smaller marital pairs sample, where we had survey responses from both husbands and wives in the same marriage, many of the grief and psychological difficulties variables being examined throughout this book showed associations with marital cohesion.

As shown in Table 13.6, we present bivariate correlations with our measure of marital cohesion. The variables we examined were as follows: grief difficulties (Grief Experience Questionnaire [GEQ]), complicated grief (Inventory of Complicated Grief [ICG]), the Impact of Events Scale (IES), the index of psychological difficulties, Depression Score, the Personal Growth Score, time since the loss, Stigma Scale Score, whether the child's death was defined as a "blameworthy one" (i.e., contrasting drug and suicide loss cases with natural and accidental deaths) or a natural death versus all other traumatic deaths, and gender. Because we found profoundly sharp contrasts in marital terminations linked to finding the spouse helpful or a hindrance after the death, we also investigated this association and marital cohesion.

Table 13.6
Correlates of Marital Cohesion Among Currently Married Respondents (*N* = 371)

	CORRELATION COEFFICIENT/SIGNIFICANCE
Grief difficulties (GEQ)	$-.38/.001$
Complicated grief (ICG)	$-.35/.001$
PTSD (IES)	$-.23/.001$
Psychological difficulties	$-.40/.001$
Depression Score	$-.26/.001$
Stigma Scale Score	$-.40/.001$
Type of death (nat./acc. vs. drug/suicide)	$-.03/.50$
Type of death (nat. vs. all others)	$-.05/.32$
Personal Growth Score	$.08/.10$
Time since the loss	$.12/.02$
Gender	$-.11/.02$
Spouse's post-loss response (help vs. hindrance)	$.62/.001$

Note. acc. = accidental; GEQ = Grief Experience Questionnaire; ICG = Inventory of Complicated Grief; IES = Impact of Events Scale; nat. = natural; PTSD = posttraumatic stress disorder.

Table 13.6 shows a very strong association between finding one's spouse helpful and a higher marital cohesion score, with a .62 correlation. Many other grief and psychological difficulties measures showed modest to moderate negative associations with cohesion, with correlations ranging from $-.23$ to $-.40$. They were as follows: grief difficulties, $-.38$; complicated grief, $-.35$; IES, $-.23$; psychological difficulties, $-.40$; Depression Score, $-.26$; and Stigma Scale Score, $-.40$. Type of death and the Personal Growth Score were not significantly correlated with cohesion, with .03 and .08 coefficients, respectively. Time after a loss displayed a weak association with cohesion, with a .12 coefficient, suggesting only slight rises in cohesion follow after the passage of time from a child's death. Gender, too, was associated with cohesion, with men reporting somewhat higher cohesion ratings than women, but neither of these latter two relationships suggests that either of these associations could be potentially important in a multipredictor model.

For our multiple regression analysis here, we took all correlation coefficients that exceeded .20 and entered them into a multiple regression equation model (Table 13.7), seeking to establish a more streamlined and efficient predictive model, and hopefully eliminating redundancies of potential predictors. This regression model was a relatively good predictor of differences in marital cohesion, explaining close to half—46%— of the variance. Only three of the original seven predictors were significant in this multifactor model: seeing one's partner as helpful or as a hindrance, psychological difficulties, and depression score. The three grief problem indicators appeared to overlap with other variables already included in this multifactor model.

Perhaps one of the most noteworthy findings was the failure of the Stigma Scale Score to maintain an independent association with cohesion in the presence of these other variables. Throughout this work, we have been

Table 13.7

Multiple Regression Analysis of Marital Cohesion Scores by Grief Difficulties, Complicated Grief, IES Scale, Psychological Difficulties, Depression Scores, Stigma Scale Score, and Spouse's Post-loss Response

MARITAL COHESION SCORES	CORRELATION COEFFICIENT	BETA WEIGHT	SIG. PROB.
Revised stigma	$-.29$	$-.06$	0.32
Grief difficulties	$-.37$	$-.14$	0.08
Complicated grief	$-.35$	$-.04$	0.66
IES Score	$-.23$	.03	0.68
Psychological difficulties	$-.40$	$-.21$	0.02
Depression Score	$-.26$	.19	0.01
Help vs. hindrance	.62	.54	0.001

Note. From Survivors Child Loss Survey, 2006–2009.
Number of obs = 242
$F(7,234) = 28.67$
Prob $> F = 0.0001$
$R^2 = 0.46$

emphasizing the importance of stigma as having a strong association with a variety of other adjustment difficulties. Our initial correlation test showed a moderate association of $-.40$ between the Stigma Scale Score and marital cohesion. Yet, we must acknowledge that in our original formulation of the Stigma Scale Score, we included a spouse's supportive (or harmful) responses and whether they subsequently became a source of comfort or strain to the respondent afterward. This duplicated the very same questions with the spouse's help or hindrance question that we later used separately.

Therefore, we felt that the Stigma Scale Score should be recalculated without these items to obtain a more genuine representation of societal responses to the death beyond the married couple's own responses. We did this, and the revised scale ranged from 1 to 15, whereas the original scale spanned from 1 to 17. The revised scale did not correlate as highly with marital cohesion, dropping from a $-.40$ correlation to $-.30$. As one entered this revised Stigma Scale Score shown in Table 13.7 into the same equation with the other three significant variables, it, too, became nonsignificant in the prediction equation. We also found that the revised Stigma Scale Score held a modest correlation of .25, with reporting a partner's response as helpful. In considering the role of stigmatization in its impact on marital functioning, it is important to remember that our measure of stigma assessed whether people felt more distant (or closer) to their significant others and whether they felt that the significant other had acted in a way that was harmful (or helpful). Broadly speaking, the measure appears to be a measure of perceived social support or abandonment, even overt rejection, by members of the participant's social network. It is possible that stigmatization's impact on marital cohesion is mediated through its impact on general psychological health and self-esteem. From the point of view of a respondent in the face of social criticism, it is perhaps readily understandable how one might become more self-critical, more negative in perceiving their own psychological health, and more generally depressed in the face of such social criticism. This, in turn, may produce more of the general grief distress and anhedonia mentioned previously that may affect marital cohesion and even marital termination rates. Of course, it is also important to bear in mind that our data are cross-sectional, and therefore we cannot make definitive causal statements. Thus, it is possible that psychological difficulties and grief distress may increase perceived social alienation and even rejection by others, including one's spouse. Unfortunately, this exploration awaits future research that can use a longitudinal methodology to establish the direction of causality in this complex set of variables that appears to be associated with marital distress and termination after the death of a child.

SUMMING UP

In this chapter, we approached the controversial question of whether a child's death disrupts the marital bond between husband and wife. Some past studies have found evidence showing greater marital strains and difficulties following a child's death, especially when the couple sustained the loss of a young child or infant. For our sample, by and large, our respondents sustained deaths of teenagers and older children and they showed mixed evidence of marital disruptions, with rates that may be higher than those of non bereaved parents in the general population but based on a comparison that had some serious methodological problems with it. Of our respondents, 11% reported separating or divorcing in an average of 6 years after their loss occurred. Approximately 60% reported that their loss brought them closer together with their spouse. One factor that may have worked to reduce marital disruption in the bereaved sample that we studied was that it was an older population than previous studies of parents who have lost an infant or younger child, and in general, divorce rates are highest in the earliest years of marriage. It is possible that when bereaved parents have been married for more than a decade, and when they are likely to have learned how to approach and solve commonly experienced marital and family problems, they may stand on a more solid position to endure the shock associated with the loss of a child.

If there is anything we might conclude as a potential indicator of whether a married respondent might be destined to a later marital failure, it was the feeling that he or she might have had about the lack of helpfulness of their partner following the loss. Half of those whose marriages dissolved felt their partner had played a hindering role following the death, a three times greater rate than for the couples whose marriages endured. Interestingly, this same factor, the perceived helpfulness (or lack thereof) of the partner, played an important role as an especially powerful correlate to strengthening the cohesive bond between a married respondent and their partner in the larger majority of married respondents who felt the child's death had brought them closer together. Because marital partners serve as attachment figures for one another, providing security and emotional support in the face of life challenges, it seems quite plausible that when one's partner is experienced as a source of increased distress and burden after the devastating loss of a child, rather than a source of support, this would contribute to marital dissolution.

In the minority of bereaved parents in our sample whose marriages subsequently ended, several sociological variables were also associated with the breakups: being younger, of lower income, with higher unemployment, making frequent geographic moves, and having a longer history of failed marriages. For the larger group of our bereaved parents who felt closer to each other following the death, these feelings were likely to be enhanced when the respondents felt better psychologically and nondepressed and had less grief distress. In contrast, for those reporting more depression and greater psychological difficulties, these respondents also felt less closely connected to their partners on our four-item scale of marital cohesiveness.

Other noteworthy results in this investigation were our findings that showed no substantial relationship between marital disruption or cohesion and cause of death. Parents who had sustained the loss of a child by natural causes or by traumatic deaths from accidents, suicide, or drugs were simply not different on either of these two dimensions.

REFERENCES

Bahr, S., & Galligan, R. (1984). Teenage marriage and marital stability. *Youth and Society*, *15*(4), 387–400.

Best, E. K., & VanDevere, C. (1986). The hidden family grief: An overview of grief in the family following perinatal death. *International Journal of Family Psychiatry*, *7*(4), 419–437.

Booth, A., & Amato, P. (1992). Divorce, residential change, and stress. *Journal of Divorce and Remarriage*, *18*(1–2), 205–213.

Bumpass, L. L., & Sweet, J. A. (2008). National Survey of Families and Households, 1987–1988; 1992–1994; 2001–2003 [Computer files]. Madison: University of Wisconsin, Center for Demography and Ecology [producer], 2008. Madison: Center for Demography of Health and Aging, University of Wisconsin-Madison [distributor].

Cherlin, A. J. (1981). *Marriage, divorce, and remarriage*. Cambridge, MA: Harvard University Press.

Christ, G. H., Bonanno, G., Malkinson, R., & Rubin, R. (2003). Bereavement experiences after the death of a child. Appendix E. In M. J. Field & R. E. Behrman (Eds.), *When children die: Improving palliative and end-of-life care for children and their families* (pp. 553–579). Washington, DC: National Academy Press.

The Compassionate Friends. (n.d.). *Surveys*. Retrieved from http://www.compassionate friends.org/media/Surveys

Cuber, J. F., & Harroff, P. G. (1965). *Sex and the significant Americans: A study of sexual behavior among the affluent*. Baltimore, MD: Penguin.

Feeley, N., & Gottlieb, L. N. (1988–1989). Parents' coping and communication following their infant's death. *Omega: Journal of Death and Dying*, *19*(1), 51–67.

Gottman, J. M., & Levenson, R. W. (2000). The timing of divorce: Predicting when a couple will divorce over a 14-year period. *Journal of Marriage and the Family*, *62*(3), 737–745.

Heaton, T. B. (1991). Time-related determinants of marital dissolution. *Journal of Marriage and the Family*, *53*(2), 285–295.

Klass, D. (1986–1987). Marriage and divorce among bereaved parents in a self-help group. *Omega: Journal of Death and Dying*, *17*(3), 237–249.

Jalovaara, M. (2003). The joint effects of marriage partner's socioeconomic position on the risk of divorce. *Demography*, *40*(1), 67–81.

Lang, A., Gottlieb, L. N., & Amsel, R. (1996). Predictors of husbands' and wives' grief reactions following infant death: The role of marital intimacy. *Death Studies*, *20*(1), 33–57.

Monahan, T. P. (1959). The duration of marriage to divorce: second marriages and migratory types. *Marriage and Family Living*, *21*(2), 134–138.

Vance, J. C., Boyle, F. M., Najman, J. M., & Thearle, M. J. (2002). Couple distress after sudden infant or perinatal death: A 30-month follow up. *Journal of Paediatrics and Child Health*, *38*(4), 368–382.

Section IV

Where Do We Go From Here?

14

Suggestions for Future Research

Unlike the earlier chapters where our focus has been on the larger bereavement community of clinicians, caregivers, researchers, and the bereaved, this chapter focuses more narrowly on bereavement researchers. Although a more detailed consideration of research needs regarding suicide bereavement may be found in McIntosh and Jordan (2011), we want to share with researchers what we have learned from this investigation of the traumatic-loss bereaved and to provide helpful guidance for directing future research so that it enhances the bereavement knowledge base in the most meaningful ways possible.

Our experience of conducting this study has been both enlightening and humbling. We have learned a great deal in the course of this investigation and, acting accordingly, have set forth our findings. We hope others who follow after us, in the scientific spirit, will either provide confirmation to our findings or find that our results do not hold up and may not be applied beyond the particular characteristics of our sample and data collection methods. In any case, we are happy to have played a part in the cumulative development of bereavement knowledge.

From our research findings, we have also learned some of the areas where there is a lack of knowledge about bereavement after traumatic loss. Accordingly, new directions for research have been revealed to us. Also, we have a lot more research questions about traumatic-loss bereavement now than we had when we first began this investigation. This is what we mean when we say that our experience has been a humbling one. We now see that much more needs to be known to better understand how those bereaved by traumatic losses repair their lives afterward.

One of the important things we have learned from this study is the keen willingness of the traumatically bereaved to participate in research about their experience. Many know that they have been a much neglected research population and many are eager to change that fact. Based on our own research experience, and of those whose work is cited in Chapter 1, we cannot say that bereaved individuals are any less amenable to being studied and are any more likely to be harmed from research participation than any groups of the non-bereaved would be. We have yet to see any persuasive empirical evidence that supports the exclusion of the bereaved from research participation based on their presumed fragility. As long as bereavement researchers design their studies with the necessary respect, sensitivity, and compassion for the bereaved, they should be able to ask their questions about loss. If bereaved respondents are clearly informed that they can bypass any questions that may bring them painful or disturbing feelings, they should be fully able to participate in the research process.

One of the most striking results of this study has been its ability to measure experienced stigma and to see its associations with grief and psychological difficulties among bereaved parents. As a correlate of grief and psychological stress among longer term bereaved and among those participating in Internet support groups, we noted stigma's far-reaching impact in being associated with diminished healing for many bereaved parents. We would be pleased if future researchers found our stigmatization scale useful in their own research. We would be even more gratified if future research was able to build on our findings showing the different kinds of comments and actions that bereaved parents felt stigmatizing in their associations with significant others. We are convinced that some of these, especially those statements that cast blame on the deceased and/or their loved ones, will be more stress-inducing to the bereaved than others, such as mere avoidance. We demonstrated these associations at the aggregate level, but it remains to be proven at the individual level whether blaming is more stress-inducing than avoidance. Further investigation of how the bereaved evaluate different acts of experienced stigma should help researchers arrive at a deeper understanding of the impact of stigma than we may currently have. Perhaps a more parsimonious measure of stigma exposure will emerge from such investigations as well. In addition, because our measure only asked globally about whether participants felt harmed or helped by the actions of certain significant others, a measure that more precisely assessed different types of harmful actions—perhaps along the lines identified in our classification of the narrative comments of participants (avoidance, implicit criticism, overt blaming, etc.)—or helpful actions (proactive outreach to the mourner, offering nonblaming explanations for the death, encouraging self-forgiveness, etc.) would greatly expand on and potentially refine our findings.

Future research may also find it helpful to further explore numerous other dimensions of stigma that we barely touched in our study. Our field data suggested that secret-keeping of the death, especially of a suicide or an overdose, appeared to be associated with greater grief distress and psychological difficulties. Many questions still abound about how commonplace it may be for the traumatic-loss bereaved to misrepresent these deaths publicly. Among which groups of significant others is secret-keeping most common and among which groups would secret-keeping be likely to generate the greatest amount of grief and psychological difficulties for the bereaved represent additional questions. Openness about traumatic loss would seem to be associated with better mental health. We have evidence from a number of other arenas—from adoptive parents (Kirk, 1964) who openly acknowledge their children's adoption status versus those who do not do so and from homosexuals (Jordan & Deluty, 1998) who openly acknowledge their gay or lesbian identities versus those who remain closeted—which shows that greater openness is associated with higher self-esteem and better mental health. Recent research from suicide bereavement researchers in Norway would seem to confirm this general finding regarding bereavement after suicide as well (Dyregrov, Plyhn, & Dieserud, 2012).

We need more studies on how the bereaved encounter a traumatic death event: whether the bereaved was physically present and a witness to the death or discovered the body in the case of a suicide and if so, the circumstances surrounding that discovery. In our survey, we only had single-question measures of these experiences. We think that future research should study these important factors and their associations with grief and psychological difficulties in far greater detail and should develop and utilize instruments that have demonstrated psychometric reliability and validity.

Another potentially important matter, at least from its discussion at peer support meetings, is the impact that suicide notes may have on the bereaved and their post-loss grief and psychological difficulties. Although suicide notes are not commonly found in most suicide deaths (Holmes & Holmes, 2005), their availability can impact on a bereaved individual; in some cases causing greater grief distress, whereas in other cases relieving distress. It remains to be documented how many suicide-bereaved actually encounter a suicide note and what generally ensues thereafter: greater grief distress, less distress, or no impact at all on grief difficulties. Also, it would be helpful to identify which types of suicide notes generate grief distress and which do not because the content of the note seems likely to account for much of the positive or negative impact on the survivors.

Unfortunately, our investigations of the drug-overdose bereaved failed to probe the extent of the family member's awareness of the deceased's drug use prior to the death. Based on what we have learned from the suicide-bereaved, it seems likely that this is an important matter that may affect differences in grief difficulties and distress, and this subject clearly calls for further investigation.

Many matters that we explored here for the first time will need further investigation to affirm whether the patterns we identified in our data will be observed in different samples, at diverging locales and time periods. Findings about multiple-loss survivors, only-child bereaved, Internet support group affiliates, and the bereaved who do not participate in support groups or counseling should receive further confirmation. Our research also suggested that further study of personal growth following traumatic loss would be of value. It remains to be demonstrated whether the bereaved who exhibit high personal growth after their loss also show matching behaviors of social activism, such as helping other survivors, increased religious involvements, political activism, and so forth. This important aspect of personal growth needs further exploration.

Another potentially important bereavement area that we did not examine in this study was bereavement among families losing loved ones in military suicides. As Harrington-LaMorie and Ruocco point out in their book chapter in Jordan and McIntosh (2011), military suicides have risen sharply in recent years. In the early 1990s, a military widow, Bonnie Carroll, founded a new nationally based network of peer-based support programs called TAPS (Tragedy Assistance Program for Survivors). This new program was designed to increase the level of bereavement services to military families after a loss, whether the loss experienced was in combat, a suicide, an overdose death, or during or shortly after a military tour of duty. Among the questions that might need to be explored for this population are the following: Do military suicides inspire any greater levels of grief difficulties than civilian suicides? Under what conditions would prior military service exacerbate the grief difficulties outcomes for a bereaved military family? How effective and helpful has the TAPS program been for the families that have utilized it, compared to those who have not? So far, we have not seen much, if any, research on bereavement among those dealing with military suicides, another important but neglected area of research.

One of the supreme challenges of traumatic-loss bereavement research is finding sufficient numbers of respondents. Suicide is often said to be a low–base rate behavior problem with about 11 per 100,000 occurrences in the United States annually (Goldsmith, Pellmar, Kleinman, & Bunney, 2002). Even if we assumed that there were six close relatives for every case impacted by each suicide, we would still find it especially difficult to go out into the community at large and find a sample of suicide-bereaved. For the drug-overdose bereaved, the problem would be a comparable one. Although drawing a sample from the network of support groups is one feasible method to find large numbers of the traumatic-loss bereaved, this procedure does not assure representativeness across all survivors. Thus, it can be argued that drawing largely from support group populations, as we have done in our study, is a selective and potentially biased recruitment process with respect to the entire population of traumatic-loss bereaved.

The most appropriate method to obtain representative samples of the traumatic-loss bereaved would be to work from official death records maintained by local medical examiners or coroners and to attempt to contact survivors of every suicide in a given location over a given period. Only two previous researchers have completed their research by this means (Murphy, Johnson, Wu, Fan, & Lohan, 2003; Provini, Everett, & Pfeffer, 2000). This type of "follow-back" research conducted from official death records has the best chance of obtaining a representative cross section of the bereaved population for a given type of death in a particular community. Yet, even with medical examiner support, there is no guarantee of complete representativeness. In the two previously mentioned cases of official death records–based studies, results were less than perfect. In both cases, there were large nonresponse rates of greater than 30%, owing to incomplete or incorrect records and difficulty in reaching next of kin at their last known phone numbers and addresses. Official death records–based studies will certainly be a lengthier and more costly method for conducting bereavement research because there may be some instances where local officials are reluctant to offer help with facilitating the research. However, if researchers cast a sufficiently wide net, they should be able to gain the cooperation of some medical examiners who would be willing to facilitate their research.

Once that is done, it will be possible to verify whether the support group affiliates who were so dominant in the present research are any different from other similarly bereaved individuals who do not rely at all on support groups or who use them only briefly. With a sample drawn from the community at large, it would be possible to place our findings within a more generalized perspective. One of the great shortcomings of past bereavement research, including our own, is the reliance on convenience samples. Only with representative samples will we be able to generalize successfully and confidently to the population at large of the traumatically bereaved.

One of the things we have repeatedly mentioned throughout this book is the need for longitudinal research on bereavement, certainly the most desirable research method to identify causal processes related to changes and transitions over the course of grief and bereavement. Yet, longitudinal research remains the most costly research method to implement because it requires the maintenance of a research staff for the duration of the project to help preserve contacts with the respondent population. Thus far, governmental and private philanthropic funding agencies have not shown much willingness to support longitudinal bereavement research. This could change, especially as survivor advocates begin to organize and attempt to change the status quo on bereavement-related policy issues.

In the meantime, a great deal may still be learned from less costly, cross-sectional studies like the present one. Just as surveys, in-depth interviewing, and field observation have revealed a great deal about bereavement in the present investigation, there is every reason to expect equally rich results in future cross-sectional studies. Readily accessible support groups remain a great resource for generating many new ideas and preliminary findings about bereavement, just as they have in our study. There is much work to be done to fully understand how survivors mend themselves after a loss. The process that has been outlined here for the loss of a child obviously will not be the same for other relationship categories, such as an individual who experienced the suicide or drug-related death of a parent, sibling, or partner. Future research needs to outline how the healing journey proceeds for different types of close relationships.

Another area of research need relates to the postvention resources utilized by survivors after a traumatic loss. One specific example involves the empirical determination of the efficacy of various postvention approaches generally, both in comparison to "no treatment" or "treatment as usual" groups and in comparison to one another. Although clinical opinion and anecdotal evidence abound that the support group and grief counseling approaches to traumatic-loss bereavement are effective, the research evidence on this issue is nearly absent. As with treatment research in other areas of health and mental health, it is important to have well-conducted empirical studies that show the efficacy of the methods employed. In addition to the general studies of efficacy, research that demonstrates which particular aspects of various specific postvention approaches are most effective is also needed. As one example, in the case of support groups for the bereaved, the question whether peer-led groups are as or more effective than professionally led groups would be a valuable area for study. Data-based answers to questions such as these are vital. We need to understand not only the grief journey of the traumatic-loss bereaved but also the approaches that will assist with the healing that takes place over the course of that journey.

Despite evidence that the suicide-bereaved are at an elevated risk for their own subsequent suicides compared to the nonbereaved (Agerbo, 2003; Runeson & Asberg, 2003), and other research findings showing persisting mental health problems among the bereaved many years after their losses, governmental and private philanthropic funding agencies have given bereavement studies minimal support. Instead, within suicidology, most of the available funding resources have been directed into the hands of researchers working directly with suicide prevention, not postvention. As long ago as 1972, Edwin Shneidman argued that suicide survivors represent "the largest mental health casualty area related to suicide" (p. ix). However, it will take concerted action on the part of survivor advocates to gain a more equitable share of the available research support funds. Unfortunately, until things improve, many researchers with limited financial resources will be forced to turn their attention away from bereavement to other more financially supported topics. Our coauthor group wants to change things now to help promote more bereavement research that is directly related to suicide and drug overdose survivors.

We have agreed to forego all future royalty proceeds from this book and instead to have them placed in a special fund, to be created and maintained by the American Association of Suicidology, that will help sponsor research among the traumatic-loss bereaved. A committee will be created among several established researchers in this field and will include several of this coauthor group, who will review applications and make awards for support of worthy projects pertaining to research on traumatic-loss bereavement. If additional benefactors can be found to contribute, the fund will be augmented by their contributions. We want to do whatever we can to promote more of this much-needed research. We strongly believe not only that postvention work with suicide survivors is the compassionate and ethical response of a caring society to the suffering that can follow a suicide but also that, as Shneidman (1972) noted many years ago, postvention with survivors is truly a crucial form of prevention of future suicides.

REFERENCES

Agerbo, E. (2003). Risk of suicide and spouse's psychiatric illness or suicide: Nested case-controlled study. *British Medical Journal, 327*(7422), 1025–1026.

Dyregrov, K., Plyhn, E., & Dieserud, G. (2012). *After the suicide: Helping the bereaved to find a path from grief to recovery.* Philadelphia, PA: Jessica Kingsley.

Goldsmith, S. K., Pellmar, T. C., Kleinman, A. M., & Bunney, W. E. (Eds.). (2002). *Reducing suicide: A national imperative.* Washington, DC: National Academies Press.

Harrington-LaMorie, K., & Ruocco, K. (2011). The Tragedy Assistance Program for Survivors (TAPS). In J. R. Jordan & J. L. McIntosh (Eds.), *Grief after suicide: Understanding the consequences and caring for the survivors* (pp. 403–411). New York, NY: Routledge.

Holmes, R. M., & Holmes, S. T. (2005). *Suicide: Theory, practice, and investigation.* Thousand Oaks, CA: Sage.

Jordan, K. M., & Deluty, R. H. (1998). Coming out for lesbian women: Its relation to anxiety, positive affectivity, self-esteem, and social support. *Journal of Homosexuality, 35*(2), 41–63.

Kirk, H. D. (1964). *Shared fate: A theory and method of adoptive relationships.* New York, NY: Free Press.

McIntosh, J. L., & Jordan, J. R. (2011). Going forward: A research agenda for suicide survivors. In J. R. Jordan & J. L. McIntosh (Eds.), *Grief after suicide: Understanding the consequences and caring for the survivors* (pp. 507–522). New York, NY: Routledge.

Murphy, S. A., Johnson, L. C., Wu, L., Fan, J. J., & Lohan, J. (2003). Bereaved parents' outcomes 4 to 60 months after their children's deaths by accidents, suicide, or homicide: A comparative study demonstrating differences. *Death Studies, 27*(1), 39–61.

Provini, C., Everett, J. R., & Pfeffer, C. R. (2000). Adults mourning suicide: Self-reported concerns about bereavement, needs for assistance, and help-seeking behavior. *Death Studies, 24*(1), 1–19.

Runeson, B., & Asberg, M. (2003). Family history of suicide among suicide victims. *American Journal of Psychiatry, 160*(8), 1525–1526.

Shneidman, E. S. (1972). Foreword. In A. C. Cain (Ed.), *Survivors of suicide* (pp. ix–xi). Springfield, IL: Thomas.

Appendix

Survivors of Child Loss Questionnaire: **Please read this first before answering the survey.**

Dear Respondent,

Many thanks for all your time and trouble to answer this questionnaire. Admittedly, completing this questionnaire is not an easy task. First, the questionnaire itself is rather long, and you will find some places where repetitive questioning appears; unfortunately, all this was unavoidable as we tried to include, within a single survey, some of the most important psychological thinking on grief associated with losing a child. Please also pay close attention to the "skip question" instructions; some questions in the survey may not apply to you and those can be safely passed over.

I realize that completing this questionnaire takes a certain amount of courage and stamina. We have offered you some questions that may lead you to reflect back on your initial saddening experiences and the deeper feelings associated with loss, and I know how hard this may be for some. You may not be able to go through the entire questionnaire in one sitting. Feel free to take a break on it and to return to it at a later time. Much as we would like you to answer each and every question that applies to you, there may be some questions that you may need to leave blank. The most important thing to keep in mind is that it is better to leave a question blank than to give a less than truthful answer to it. Please take your time doing the survey. Please do your best to complete it and return it in the attached self-addressed stamped envelope. Please remember that all responses will be kept strictly confidential. All presentations of the results will always be in a statistical or altered form to protect your privacy.

Hopefully, this study will shed more light on how bereaved parents adapt to loss and how they carry out their lives afterward. Many of us who have experienced child loss still remain a neglected population to social science researchers. Available research heavily relies on clinic patients, on college students, and on people who answered advertisements seeking bereavement study participants. In contrast, this study will rely more on people in the community at large. We deeply appreciate your willingness to share your experiences in this regard as we try to better illuminate how people go on trying to repair their lives, accepting loss, and making the best of it.

If we haven't covered some of the important aspects of your grief issues in our survey questions or if you would like to further explain some of your written responses, I would be glad to talk to you further about these experiences. Please send me your phone number and the times when you can be most easily reached along with your returned survey form and I will be glad to contact you. Please remember I am not a clinician, but I am most eager to learn the specific details about how you have been living with loss and making the best of it. Again, my sincerest thanks for all your valuable cooperation in helping us to better understand how bereaved parents cope with the death of their child.

Sincerely,

William Feigelman, PhD
Director, Child Loss Research Project
Professor of Sociology
Nassau Community College,
Garden City, NY 11530

About You: **ID Number** __ __ __ __

1. Your gender? (Check or circle one)
   a. Male
   b. Female

2. How old are you now? ____ years (write in age) (Check or circle one)
   a. 35 or younger
   b. 36–45 years old
   c. 46–55 years old
   d. 56–65 years old
   e. 66 or older

3. Present employment status (which number mostly applies to you)? (Check or circle one)
   a. Working full time
   b. Working part time
   c. With a job but not at work because of temporary illness, vacation, or strike
   d. Unemployed, laid off, looking for work
   e. Retired
   f. In school
   g. Housekeeping
   h. Other

4. What is (was) your principal occupation?
   Please specify: (e.g., automechanic, physician) _____
   (Write your occupation and check or circle one of the following choices)
   a. Managerial/professional worker
   b. Technical/sales/administrative support
   c. Clerical
   d. Craftsperson
   e. Operative, semiskilled factory worker
   f. Service or laborer

5. Highest level of schooling completed? (Check or circle one)
   a. Less than high school
   b. High school graduate or equivalent
   c. Some college, community college graduate, or finished technical training program
   d. Four-year college degree holder
   e. Masters, doctoral, and/or professional school degree holder

6. Annual household income? (Check or circle one)
   a. Less than $20,000
   b. Between $20,001 and $40,000
   c. Between $40,001 and $60,000
   d. Between $60,001 and $90,000
   e. Between $90,001 and $120,000
   f. More than $120,000

7. What is your religious preference? (Check or circle one)
   a. Protestant: (If Protestant, specify your denomination here) _____
   b. Catholic
   c. Jewish
   d. Other: (If other, please specify your religion here) _____

8. Frequency of your attendance at religious services or events during the last 12 months. (Check or circle one)
   a. Never
   b. About once or twice a year or less
   c. Several times a year
   d. About once a month
   e. Two to three times a month
   f. Every week
   g. Several times a week

9. Number of people in your household and your relationship to them? (List all household members below.) If you live in a single-person household, skip to Question 10.

(Please use these categories: spouse or partner [1], child [2], parent [3], brother [4], sister [5], other relatives [6], boarder [7]). For example, my husband or spouse could be person A; my son or daughter could be person B; and so on, assuming more people were living in the household.

9a. Person A _____ your relationship to this person

9b. Person B _____ your relationship to this person

9c. Person C _____ your relationship to this person

9d. Person D _____ your relationship to this person

9e. Person E _____ your relationship to this person

9f. Person F _____ your relationship to this person

9g. Person G _____ your relationship to this person

9h. Does your household have more than eight persons in it? (Check or circle one)
   a. No
   b. Yes

10. Current marital status? (Check or circle one)
   a. Married
   b. Divorced
   c. Separated
   d. Never married
   e. Widowed (If widowed, how many years since your spouse died? _____ years)

11. Number of times married? (Check or circle one)
   a. Never married
   b. Once
   c. Twice
   d. Three times
   e. Four or more

If you are currently married and now living with your spouse, please answer the next four questions. Otherwise, please skip to Question 12.

11a. Taking all things together, how would you describe your relationship? (Please select the most appropriate number appearing subsequently.)

Very unhappy ——————————————————————— Very happy

   (1)   (2)   (3)   (4)   (5)   (6)   (7)

11b. It is always difficult to predict what will happen in a marriage, but realistically, what do you think the chances are that you and your husband/wife will eventually separate or divorce? (Circle one choice on the following)

a. Very high
b. High
c. About even
d. Low
e. Very low

11c. During the past month, how often did you and your husband/wife spend time alone with each other, talking or sharing an activity? (Circle one choice on the following)

a. Never
b. Once a month
c. Two or three times a month
d. Once a week
e. Two or three times a week
f. Almost every day

11d. When you have a serious disagreement, how often do you discuss your disagreements calmly? (Circle one choice on the following)

a. Never
b. Seldom
c. Sometimes
d. Often
e. Always

12. Number of children ever had? (Please include all births, adoptions, and stepchildren) (Check or circle one)

a. One
b. Two
c. Three
d. Four
e. Five or more

13. Your race or ethnicity? (Check or circle one)

a. Caucasian
b. African American
c. Hispanic
d. Asian/Pacific Islander
e. Native American
f. Mixed race
g. Other

14. How would you describe your political attitudes? (Check or circle one)
    a. Very liberal
    b. Slightly liberal
    c. Moderate, middle of the road
    d. Slightly conservative
    e. Very conservative

15. Which political party do you usually support? (Check or circle one)
    a. Strong Republican
    b. Not very strong Republican
    c. Independent
    d. Not very strong Democratic
    e. Strong Democratic
    f. Other

16. How did you vote in the last U.S. presidential election? (Check or circle one)
    a. Did not vote
    b. Voted for Bush
    c. Voted for Kerry
    d. Voted for Nader or other candidate

17. Type of community you lived in during the past 5 years. (Check or circle one)
    a. Large-sized or medium-sized city
    b. A suburb of large-sized or medium-sized city
    c. Small city (between 10,000 and 50,000 population)
    d. Small town or farm (less than 10,000 population)

18. Number of times you moved in the last 5 years. (Check or circle one)
    a. None
    b. One
    c. Two
    d. Three
    e. Four or more

19. Were you born in United States? (Check or circle one)
    a. Yes
    b. No

    19a. If you were born outside the United States, which is your country of birth? (Please write the name of country in the space provided)
    _____

This is probably the hardest thing to talk about during this interview: the loss of your child.

20. How old was he or she at the time of death? _____ years old

21. His or her gender? (Check or circle one)
    a. Male
    b. Female

22. How long has it been since the death?
    a. Fill the number of **years** in the blank to the right _____
    b. Fill the number of **months** in the blank to the right _____

23. How did he or she die?
    a. Accidental death, specific type here (e.g., boating accident) _____
    b. Natural causes, specify illness (e.g., heart attack, cancer) _____
    c. Homicide
    d. Suicide
    e. Ambiguous circumstances

If your child did not die as a result of a suicide, skip to Question 31. Questions. 24–30 only apply to suicide deaths.

24. If it was a suicide, what method was used? (Check or circle one)
    a. Gun shot
    b. Hanging
    c. Overdose
    d. Asphyxiation
    e. Knife wounding
    f. Jumping
    g. Drowning
    h. Intentional pedestrian or automotive suicide
    i. Other

25. Did you witness the act of suicide itself? (Check or circle one)
    a. Yes
    b. No

26. Did you find the body or were you present when the body was discovered? (Check or circle one)
    a. Yes
    b. No

27. Did you see the deceased's body before it was buried or cremated? (Check or circle one)
    a. Yes
    b. No

28. Initially, how surprised were you at the suicide death? (Check or circle one)
    a. Extremely surprised; it could not have been more unexpected
    b. Very surprised, although not entirely unexpected
    c. Somewhat surprised
    d. Only slightly surprised; I had been worried they might attempt suicide
    e. Not at all surprised

29. To the best of your knowledge, had your child made any prior suicide attempts? (Check or circle one)
    a. No
    b. Yes, one previous attempt
    c. Yes, two previous attempts
    d. More than two previous attempts

30. How would you describe your relationship with your child immediately prior to their death? (Check or circle one)
    a. Extremely positive
    b. Somewhat positive
    c. Unclear or uncertain
    d. Somewhat negative
    e. Extremely negative

Now, please tell us how you felt shortly after your child's death and afterward.

31. People losing loved ones sometimes feel blameworthy that things they may have done (or have not done) could have contributed to the person's death. Does this apply to you and to **how you felt in the first weeks after** your child's death? (Check or circle one)
    a. Almost completely
    b. Mostly
    c. Somewhat
    d. A little bit
    e. Almost not at all

32. **Presently**, do you feel at all blameworthy in the death? (Check or circle one)
    a. Almost completely
    b. Mostly
    c. Somewhat
    d. A little bit
    e. Almost not at all

33. People losing loved ones sometimes feel anger and rage toward the lost loved one, finding it difficult to forgive the person's carelessness and foolhardy actions that placed their family in such a grief-stricken place. Did these feelings apply to you in the **first weeks after** your child's death? (Check or circle one)
    a. Almost completely
    b. Mostly
    c. Somewhat
    d. A little bit
    e. Almost not at all

34. **Presently**, do you feel any anger or hostility toward this child? (Check or circle one)
    a. Almost completely
    b. Mostly
    c. Somewhat
    d. A little bit
    e. Almost not at all

35. People losing loved ones unexpectedly often experience shock and surprise that a person they knew so well could ever do something to contribute to their death. Does this apply to you and to **how you felt when the learned about the death** of your child? (Check or circle one)
    a. Almost completely
    b. Mostly
    c. Somewhat
    d. A little bit
    e. Almost not at all

36. **At present**, do you feel any surprise or bewilderment about the loss of your child? (Check or circle one)
    a. Almost completely
    b. Mostly
    c. Somewhat
    d. A little bit
    e. Almost not at all

Changes in Your Social Relationships

37. People suffering from the tragic loss of a child, and especially when the child dies by violent means, sometimes encounter situations where family members, friends, or coworkers not only fail to offer the support the bereaved parent may be seeking, but these people may also say or do things bereaved parents find especially troublesome or exasperating. Can you enumerate any specific experiences from family, friends, or coworkers that made your adjustments to loss more difficult? First, list the troubling things that people have said to you, then list the troubling things they did or failed to do. Use the last blank pages of this form if the available space is insufficient.

    Things said to me:

    _____
    _____
    _____
    _____
    _____

    Things done to me:

    _____
    _____
    _____
    _____
    _____

38. Sometimes, people experience change in their social relationships after the loss of a child. Sometimes, family members or close associates become uncomfortable after the death and avoid further discussion about the deceased. Or they may say insensitive or hurtful things. In other cases, they may express kind words and offer a compassionate response. The following are mentioned various groups of people in your life. Please indicate whether your relationship to these people has changed since the loss of your child. (On each line on the following table, circle the most appropriate response for each person or group.)

	NOT APPLICABLE	RELATIONSHIP STAYED THE SAME	CLOSER/ STRONGER RELATIONSHIP	WEAKER/ STRAINED RELATIONS
A. Spouse	0	1	2	3
B. Ex-spouse	0	1	2	3
C. Parents	0	1	2	3
D. In-laws	0	1	2	3
E. Children	0	1	2	3
F. Siblings	0	1	2	3
G. Other relatives	0	1	2	3
H. Coworkers	0	1	2	3
I. Closest friends	0	1	2	3
J. Less close friends	0	1	2	3
K. Neighbors	0	1	2	3

39. How helpful have each of the following groups mentioned subsequently been in helping you to deal with your loss during the last 12 months? Please use these numbers: 1 = *very harmful*, 2 = *mildly harmful*, 3 = *neutral*, 4 = *somewhat helpful*, and 5 = *very helpful*. For example, if you felt your relationship with your parents has been *somewhat harmful*, you might circle the number 2 in that row. (On each line on the following table, circle the most appropriate response for each person or group. Circle 0 for not applicable responses.)

	NA	VERY HARMFUL			VERY HELPFUL
A. Spouse	0	1	2	3	4	5
B. Ex-spouse	0	1	2	3	4	5
C. Parents	0	1	2	3	4	5
D. In-laws	0	1	2	3	4	5
E. Children	0	1	2	3	4	5
F. Siblings	0	1	2	3	4	5
G. Other relatives	0	1	2	3	4	5
H. Coworkers	0	1	2	3	4	5
I. Closest friends	0	1	2	3	4	5
J. Casual friends	0	1	2	3	4	5
K. Neighbors	0	1	2	3	4	5

40a. Losing a child is especially distressing. Some people feel afterward the less said about their loss, the better and the easier it is to accept loss and to move on with their life; others feel that being open and talking about loss helps them best to deal with it. On a scale of 1 to 5, how would you describe your willingness to talk to others about your loss? Circle the appropriate number on the following scale.

The less said about it, ⟵————————⟶ I am especially willing
    the better   to talk about it

0	1	2	3	4	5

40b. If your child died from a sudden and violent cause such as a traffic accident, homicide, or a suicide, please describe how willing are you to talk about the specific manner of his or her death. Use 5 for being most willing and 1 for being the least willing. Circle 0 for a not applicable response. Please choose the most appropriate number response.

NA   The less said about it, ⟵————————⟶ I am especially willing
       the better   to talk about it

0	1	2	3	4	5

40c. If someone asks you how many children you have, how do you usually respond? (Circle or check the most appropriate response on the following choices.)
  a. I will only mention my living child(ren) or say I have no children (assuming that my only child had died).
  b. Occasionally, I might mention I had a child that died along with the living child(ren), that is, assuming I had other living children.
  c. Almost invariably, I will mention both the deceased child (or children) and the living children (assuming I had other living children).

Your Health and Feelings

41. How would you rate your physical health presently? (Check or circle one)
  a. Poor
  b. Fair
  c. Good
  d. Very good
  e. Excellent

42. How would you rate your mental or emotional health presently? (Check or circle one)
    a. Poor
    b. Fair
    c. Good
    d. Very good
    e. Excellent

43. Please list the number of days in the past month you were totally unable to go to work or carry out your normal household activities because of your physical or mental health.
    (Fill in the number of days in the past month at the right) _____ days

44. If one or more, how many of those days were due only to physical health, mental health, or a combination?
    a. (Fill in the number of days in the past month at the right) _____ days physical
    b. (Fill in the number of days in the past month at the right) _____ days mental
    c. (Fill in the number of days in the past month at the right) _____ days combination

45. At present, how satisfied are you with your life? (Check or circle one)
    a. A great deal
    b. Somewhat
    c. A little
    d. Not at all/none at all

46. How much control do you feel you have over your life in general? (Check or circle one)
    a. A great deal
    b. Somewhat
    c. A little
    d. Not at all/none at all

47. Do you feel you are able to make and successfully carry out long-range plans for the future? (Check or circle one)
    a. A great deal
    b. Somewhat
    c. A little
    d. Not at all/none at all

48. How would you rate your contribution to the welfare and well-being of other people? (Check or circle one)
    a. A lot
    b. Somewhat
    c. A little
    d. Not at all/none at all

49. How would you rate the following statement, "In many ways I feel disappointed about my achievements in life." (Check or circle one)
    a. Agree strongly
    b. Agree somewhat
    c. Agree only a little
    d. Disagree only a little
    e. Disagree somewhat
    f. Disagree strongly

50a. In the past 5 years, have you lost your job for any reason? (Check or circle one)
    a. No
    b. Yes, once
    c. Yes, twice
    d. Yes, three or more times

50b. (If you answered yes to the previous question) Did it occur before or after the loss of your child?
    a. Before
    b. After
    c. Both before and after

51a. In the past 5 years, have you been promoted at work or taken on a new job? (Check or circle one)
    a. No
    b. Yes, once
    c. Yes, twice
    d. Yes, three or more times

51b. (If you answered yes to the previous question) Did it occur before or after the loss of your child?
    a. Before
    b. After
    c. Both before and after

52a. In the past 5 years, have you married or remarried? (Check or circle one)
    a. No
    b. Yes, once
    c. Yes, twice
    d. Yes, three or more times

52b. (If you answered yes to the previous question) Did it occur before or after the loss of your child?
    a. Before
    b. After
    c. Both before and after

53a. In the past 5 years, have you divorced? (Check or circle one)
   a. No
   b. Yes, once
   c. Yes, twice
   d. Yes, three or more times

53b. (If you answered yes to the previous question) Did it occur before or after the loss of your child?
   a. Before
   b. After
   c. Both before and after

54a. In the past 5 years, have you separated from your spouse or partner for more than 6 months? (Check or circle one)
   a. No
   b. Yes, once
   c. Yes, twice
   d. Yes, three or more times

54b. (If you answered yes to the previous question) Did it occur before or after the loss of your child?
   a. Before
   b. After
   c. Both before and after

55a. In the past 5 years, have you experienced any other deaths in your family? (Check or circle one)
   a. No
   b. Yes, once
   c. Yes, twice
   d. Yes, three or more times

55b. (If you answered yes to the previous question) Did it occur before or after the loss of your child?
   a. Before
   b. After
   c. Both before and after

56a. In the past 5 years, have you experienced any other serious life crisis, something like a law suit, being a victim of a crime, or a serious health problem in your family? (Check or circle one)
   a. No
   b. Yes, once
   c. Yes, twice
   d. Yes, three or more times

56b. (If you answered yes to the previous question) Did it occur before or after the loss of your child?
   a. Before
   b. After
   c. Both before and after

Substance Use

57a. Do you smoke cigarettes now? (Check or circle one)
   a. No
   b. Yes

57b. If yes, how many do you smoke daily? (Check or circle one)
   a. Not applicable
   b. Less than half pack daily
   c. Less than one pack daily
   d. One pack daily
   e. More than one pack daily

57c. At what age did you begin to smoke regularly?

(Only current or former smokers should answer this question): _____ years old

58. On the average, how often in the past 12 months did you have any alcoholic beverages? (Check or circle one)
   a. Never
   b. A few times during the year
   c. About once a month or several times a month
   d. Usually 1 or 2 days a week
   e. Almost daily or 3–6 days a week
   f. Daily

59. During the past year, how many days did you have five or more drinks on drinking occasions? (Check or circle one)
   a. Never
   b. A few times during the year
   c. About once a month or several times a month
   d. Usually 1 or 2 days a week
   e. Almost daily or 3–6 days a week
   f. Daily

60. During the past year, how many times did you get drunk or very high on alcohol? (Check or circle one)
    a. Never
    b. A few times during the year
    c. About once a month or several times a month
    d. Usually 1 or 2 days a week
    e. Almost daily or 3–6 days a week
    f. Daily

61a. During the past year, did you use any illegal drugs or prescription drugs in a way that the doctor did not prescribe (e.g., smoking marijuana, cocaine, or crack or taking methamphetamine)? (Check or circle one)
    a. No
    b. Yes

61b. (If you answered yes to the previous question) How often did you take any of these drugs? (Check or circle one)
    a. A few times during the year
    b. About once a month or several times a month
    c. Usually 1 or 2 days a week
    d. Almost daily or 3–6 days a week
    e. Daily

62. During the past year, was there ever a time when you felt sad, blue, or depressed for 2 weeks or more in a row? (Check or circle one)
    a. Yes
    b. No
    c. Not depressed because of antidepressant medication

63. Thinking of the 2-week period during the past 12 months when these feelings were worst during that time, did the feelings of being sad, blue, or depressed usually last? (Check or circle one)
    a. Not applicable
    b. All day long
    c. Most of the day
    d. Half the day
    e. Less than half the day

64. During this 2-week period, how often did you feel this way? (Check or circle one)
    a. Not applicable
    b. Every day
    c. Almost every day
    d. Less often than that

65. During this 2-week period, did you lose interest in most things? (Check or circle one)
    a. Not applicable
    b. Yes
    c. No

66. During this 2-week period, did you feel more tired out or low on energy than is usual for you? (Check or circle one)
    a. Not applicable
    b. Yes
    c. No

67. During this same 2-week period, did you lose your appetite? (Check or circle one)
    a. Not applicable
    b. Yes
    c. No

68. During the same 2-week period, did you have a lot more trouble concentrating than usual? (Check or circle one)
    a. Not applicable
    b. Yes
    c. No

69. People sometimes feel down on themselves, no good, or worthless. Did you have, in the past year, any 2-week period lasting that long or longer where you felt this way? (Check or circle one)
    a. Not applicable
    b. Yes
    c. No

70. Did you think a lot about death—either your own or someone else's or death in general—during any 2-week period or longer during the last year? (Check or circle one)
    a. Not applicable
    b. Yes
    c. No

71a. During the past year, have you had any sleep disturbances? (Check or circle one)
    a. Never
    b. Sometimes or often

(If you answered sometimes to the previous questions, please answer questions 71b, 71c, and 71d).

71b. During the past year, did you have difficulties falling asleep? (Check or circle one)
  a. Never
  b. Very occasionally, less than once a week
  c. Sometimes, at least once a week
  d. Often, nearly every night
  e. Very often, every night

71c. Did you have difficulties staying asleep? (Check or circle one)
  a. Never
  b. Very occasionally, less than once a week
  c. Sometimes, at least once a week
  d. Often, nearly every night
  e. Very often, every night

71d. Did you have difficulties with early awakening? (Check or circle one)
  a. Never
  b. Very occasionally, less than once a week
  c. Sometimes, at least once a week
  d. Often, nearly every night
  e. Very often, every night

72a. How often during the past 12 months did you think about taking your own life? (Check or circle one)
  a. Almost never or never
  b. Rarely
  c. Occasionally
  d. Frequently
  e. Very frequently

72b. During the past 12 months, did you ever make any specific plan for suicide? (Check or circle one)
  a. No
  b. Yes

73a. During the past 12 months, how many times did you actually attempt suicide? (Check or circle one)
  a. None
  b. One or more times

73b. (If attempted suicide was done in past year)
  Please fill in at the right the number of attempts made: ____

How Your Grief Adjustment Is Progressing

74. In this next section, we are interested in exploring your reactions to the loss of your child. Please use the following set of numbers: 1 = *never*, 2 = *rarely*, 3 = *sometimes*, 4 = *often*, and 5 = *almost always* to refer to how you felt during the past 2 months. Please circle the most appropriate numbers for each statement subsequently, expressing how you felt **during the past 2 months**.

Did you experience this reaction during the past 2 months?

	ALMOST NEVER	RARELY	SOMETIMES	OFTEN	ALWAYS
A. Feel that the person never considered what the death might do to you.	1	2	3	4	5
B. Wonder about the person's motivation for not living longer.	1	2	3	4	5
C. Feel like a social outcast.	1	2	3	4	5
D. Feel like no one cared to listen to you.	1	2	3	4	5
E. Think that the person's time to die had not yet come.	1	2	3	4	5
F. Question why the person had to die	1	2	3	4	5

Did you experience this reaction during the past 2 months?

	ALMOST NEVER	RARELY	SOMETIMES	OFTEN	ALWAYS
G. Think of times before the death when you could have made the person's life more pleasant.	1	2	3	4	5
H. Feel like there is something very important you wanted to make up to the person.	1	2	3	4	5
I. Experienced light-headedness, dizziness, or fainting.	1	2	3	4	5
J. Experienced trembling, shaking, or twitching.	1	2	3	4	5
K. Feel like others may have blamed you for the death.	1	2	3	4	5
L. Feel that, had you been a different person, the person would not have died.	1	2	3	4	5
M. Worry that you might harm yourself.	1	2	3	4	5
N. Intentionally try to hurt yourself.	1	2	3	4	5
O. Avoid talking about the death of the person.	1	2	3	4	5
P. Feel uncomfortable revealing the cause of the death.	1	2	3	4	5

75. Next, we want to ask you a number of questions assessing how troubling your loss has been for you emotionally and the psychic stresses it may have induced.

Please check or circle the number next to the answer best describing **how you have been feeling over the past month**.

75a. How often do you feel yourself longing and yearning for your deceased child? (Check or circle one)
   a. Almost never (less than once a month)
   b. Rarely (once a month or more, less than once a week)
   c. Sometimes (once a week or more, less than once a day)
   d. Often (once a day)
   e. Always (several times every day)

75b. Is the yearning distressing to you or disruptive to your daily routine? (Check or circle one)
   a. No
   b. Yes

75c. To what extent have you had difficulty accepting the death? (Check or circle one)
   a. No difficulty accepting the death
   b. A slight sense of difficulty accepting the death
   c. Some difficulty accepting the death
   d. A marked sense of difficulty accepting the death
   e. Overwhelming difficulty accepting the death

75d. To what extent have you had difficulty trusting people since your child died? (Check or circle one)
   a. No difficulty trusting others
   b. A slight sense of difficulty trusting others
   c. Some sense of difficulty trusting others
   d. A marked sense of difficulty trusting others
   e. An overwhelming sense of difficulty trusting others

75e. To what extent have you felt bitter over your child's death? (Check or circle one)
   a. No sense of bitterness
   b. A slight sense of bitterness
   c. Some sense of bitterness
   d. A marked sense of bitterness
   e. An overwhelming sense of bitterness

75f. Sometimes, people who lose a loved one feel uneasy about moving on with their life. To what extent do you feel that moving on (e.g., making new friends, pursuing new interests) would be difficult for you? (Check or circle one)

a. Moving on would not be difficult
b. Moving on would be a little difficult
c. Moving on would be somewhat difficult
d. Moving on would be very difficult
e. Moving on would be extremely difficult

75g. To what extent have you felt emotionally numb with difficulty connecting with others since your child's death? (Check or circle one)

a. No sense of numbness
b. A slight sense of numbness
c. Some sense of numbness
d. A marked sense of numbness
e. An overwhelming sense of numbness

75h. To what extent do you feel that life is empty or meaningless without your deceased child? (Check or circle one)

a. No sense of emptiness or meaninglessness
b. A slight sense of emptiness or meaninglessness
c. Some sense of emptiness
d. A marked sense of emptiness
e. An overwhelming sense of emptiness

75i. To what extent do you feel that the future holds no meaning or purpose without your child? (Check or circle one)

a. No sense that the future holds no purpose
b. A slight sense that the future holds no purpose
c. Some sense that the future holds no purpose
d. A marked sense that the future holds no purpose
e. An overwhelming sense that the future holds no purpose

75j. To what extent have you felt on edge, jumpy, or easily startled since the death of your child? (Check or circle one)

a. No change in feelings of being on edge
b. A slight sense of feeling on edge
c. Some sense of feeling on edge
d. A marked sense of feeling on edge
e. An overwhelming sense of feeling on edge

75k. Has your edginess caused you any significant impairment either in your social, work, or other important domains of living? (Check or circle one)
  a. No
  b. Yes

75l. (If you answered yes to the previous question) Has this problem lasted for at least 6 months? (Check or circle one)
  a. No
  b. Yes

76. In this next section, we ask you how different things about your loss impacted on you. How do the following statements apply to you **during the past 30 days**? (Check or circle the most appropriate response for each of the 14 statements subsequently.)

	NOT AT ALL	RARELY	SOMETIMES	OFTEN
A. I thought about my child's death when I didn't mean to.	1	2	3	4
B. I avoided letting myself get upset when I thought about it or was reminded of it.	1	2	3	4
C. I tried to remove the death from my memory.	1	2	3	4
D. I had trouble falling asleep or staying asleep because of pictures or thoughts about the death that came into my mind.	1	2	3	4
E. I had waves of strong feelings about it.	1	2	3	4
F. I had dreams about it.	1	2	3	4
G. I stayed away from reminders of it.	1	2	3	4
H. I felt as if it hadn't happened or it wasn't real.	1	2	3	4
I. I tried not to talk about it.	1	2	3	4
J. Pictures about it popped into my mind.	1	2	3	4
K. Other things kept making me think about it.	1	2	3	4
L. I was aware that I still had a lot of feelings about it, but I didn't deal with them.	1	2	3	4
M. I tried not to think about it.	1	2	3	4
N. Any reminder brought back feelings about it.	1	2	3	4

77. In the next section, we would like to know if any of the personality changes mentioned subsequently apply to you. Please use the following set of numbers to describe whether the change applies to you: 1 = *does not describe me at all*, 2 = *does not quite describe me*, 3 = *describes me fairly well*, 4 = *describes me well*, and 5 = *describes me very well*. Considering the thoughts you might have had since your child died, circle the numbers on the following table for each statement that best describes the way you have been feeling **during the past 2 weeks**, including today.

	DOES NOT DESCRIBE ME AT ALL			DESCRIBES ME VERY WELL	
	1	2	3	4	5
A. I have learned to cope better with life.	1	2	3	4	5
B. I feel as though I am a better person.	1	2	3	4	5
C. I have a better outlook on life.	1	2	3	4	5
D. I have more compassion for others.	1	2	3	4	5
E. I care more deeply for others.	1	2	3	4	5
F. I am stronger because of the grief I have experienced.	1	2	3	4	5
G. I am a more forgiving person.	1	2	3	4	5

Getting Help for Your Grief

77H-1. Have you ever been to a general self-help group for people losing children, like Compassionate Friends?
a. No
b. Yes

77H-1a. (If you answered yes to the previous question, answer the next three questions; if no, skip to Question #77H-2.)

Times attended general self-help group since you lost your child:
a. Once
b. 2–5 times
c. 6–20 times
d. 21–50 times
e. 51 or more times

77H-1b. Times attended in past year:
a. Never
b. Once
c. 2–5 times
d. 6–20 times
e. 21–50 times
f. 51 or more times

77H-1c. On a scale of 1 to 5, how would you rate your experience in this or a similar self-help support groups? (Circle or check one choice on the following)
a. Not at all helpful
b. Slightly helpful
c. Modestly helpful
d. Helpful
e. Very helpful

77H-2. Have you ever seen a member of the clergy for help with your loss?
a. No
b. Yes

77H-2a. (If you answered yes to the previous question, answer the next three questions; if no skip to Question #77H-3.)

Times visited members of the clergy since you lost your child:
a. Once
b. 2–5 times
c. 6–20 times
d. 21–50 times
e. 51 or more times

77H-2b. Times seen in past year:
a. Never
b. Once
c. 2–5 times
d. 6–20 times
e. 21–50 times
f. 51 or more times

77H-2c. On a scale of 1 to 5, how would you rate the help you received from members of the clergy? (Circle or check one choice on the following)
a. Not at all helpful
b. Slightly helpful
c. Modestly helpful
d. Helpful
e. Very helpful

77H-3. Have you ever seen a professional bereavement counselor?
a. No
b. Yes

77H-3a. (If you answered yes to the previous question, answer next three questions; if no, skip to Question #77H-4.)

Times visited professional bereavement counselor since you lost your child:
a. Once
b. 2–5 times
c. 6–20 times
d. 21–50 times
e. 51 or more times

77H-3b. Times seen in past year:
a. Never
b. Once
c. 2–5 times
d. 6–20 times
e. 21–50 times
f. 51 or more times

77H-3c. On a scale of 1 to 5, how would you rate the help you received from professional bereavement counselors? (Circle or check one choice on the following.)
a. Not at all helpful
b. Slightly helpful
c. Modestly helpful
d. Helpful
e. Very helpful

77H-4. Have you ever visited a psychiatrist, psychologist, social worker, or psychiatric nurse for help with your loss?
a. No
b. Yes

78H-4a. (If you answered yes to the previous question, answer the next three questions; if no skip to Question #77H-5.)

Times visited any of the previously mentioned caregivers since you lost your child:
a. Once
b. 2–5 times
c. 6–20 times
d. 21–50 times
e. 51 or more times

78H-4b. Times seen in past year:
 a. Never
 b. Once
 c. 2–5 times
 d. 6–20 times
 e. 21–50 times
 f. 51 or more times

78H-4c. On a scale of 1 to 5, how would you rate the help you received from any of the previously mentioned caregivers? (Circle or check one choice on the following)
 a. Not at all helpful
 b. Slightly helpful
 c. Modestly helpful
 d. Helpful
 e. Very helpful

77H-5. Have you ever seen a spiritualist or psychic for help with your loss?
 a. No
 b. Yes

77H-5a. (If you answered yes to previous question, answer the next three questions; if no, skip to Question #77H-6.)

Times visited psychics or spiritualists since you lost your child:
 a. Once
 b. 2–5 times
 c. 6–20 times
 d. 21–50 times
 e. 51 or more times

77H-5b. Times seen in past year:
 a. Never
 b. Once
 c. 2–5 times
 d. 6–20 times
 e. 21–50 times
 f. 51 or more times

77H-5c. On a scale of 1 to 5, how would you rate the help you received from this previously mentioned source? (Circle or check one choice on the following)
a. Not at all helpful
b. Slightly helpful
c. Modestly helpful
d. Helpful
e. Very helpful

77H-6. Ever seen any other professional or nonprofessional caregiver for help? (List here any other groups or people seen that have not been already mentioned. For example, if you attended a hospital-based group for family member survivors of cancer death and you haven't already covered this before, list it here: _____
Type of group or help provider.)
a. No
b. Yes

77H-6a. (If you answered yes to previous question, answer the next three questions; if no skip to Question #77H-7.)

Times visited this caregiving source since you lost your child:
a. Once
b. 2–5 times
c. 6–20 times
d. 21–50 times
e. 51 or more times

77H-6b. Times seen in past year:
a. Never
b. Once
c. 2–5 times
d. 6–20 times
e. 21–50 times
f. 51 or more times

77H-6c. On a scale of 1 to 5, how would you rate the help you received from this previously mentioned source? (Circle or check one choice on the following)
a. Not at all helpful
b. Slightly helpful
c. Modestly helpful
d. Helpful
e. Very helpful

77H-7. Have you ever been to a self-help support group explicitly for survivors of suicide? (Please consider here only those groups that are peer facilitated.)
a. No
b. Yes

77H-7a. (If you answered yes to the previous question, answer next three questions; if no skip to the next section.)

Times visited self-help survivors of suicide support group since you lost your child:
a. Once
b. 2–5 times
c. 6–20 times
d. 21–50 times
e. 51 or more times

77H-7b. Times seen in past year:
a. Never
b. Once
c. 2–5 times
d. 6–20 times
e. 21–50 times
f. 51 or more times

77H-7c. On a scale of 1 to 5, how would you rate the help you received from self-help survivors of suicide support groups? (Circle or check one choice on the following)
a. Not at all helpful
b. Slightly helpful
c. Modestly helpful
d. Helpful
e. Very helpful

78. Answer this part only if you attended one or more peer support group meetings. If you never attended a support group meeting, please skip this section and go on to Question #79. People attending bereavement support groups mention various benefits from participation. Please rate the importance of each of the benefits on the following table in terms of their importance in helping you with your grief.

	NOT IMPORTANT	IMPORTANT	VERY IMPORTANT	MOST IMPORTANT
A. Friendship	1	2	3	4
B. Sharing information and experiences	1	2	3	4
C. Having a sounding board to develop new skills	1	2	3	4
D. A place for discussing tabooed topics	1	2	3	4
E. Being among people like myself	1	2	3	4
F. Helping myself to deal better with my loss	1	2	3	4
G. Helping others to deal better with their losses	1	2	3	4
H. Spiritual benefits	1	2	3	4
I. Banding with others to promote change in mental health care	1	2	3	4
J. Getting help from the group facilitator	1	2	3	4
K. Other, specify:	1	2	3	4

79. (Answer the question that follows only if you are a survivor of suicide loss. Otherwise, skip to the next section.) Survivors of suicide sometimes report difficulties with some of the issues listed subsequently. Please rate each item in terms of whether it posed any difficulty for you. If the matter posed a problem, did your survivors' support group involvement offer any assistance in this respect? An NA (not applicable) response should be used when someone had no difficulty with that issue or did not ever participate in a support group. If your support group(s) did not help with that issue, circle (0); if it helped, circle (7).

	USE 1 FOR NO DIFFICULTY		USE 4 FOR GREAT DIFFICULTY		NA	SUPPORT GROUP	
						DIDN'T HELP	HELPED
A. Difficulty talking about the suicide with some or all family members.	1	2	3	4	9	0	7
B. Family conflict and blame about the suicide	1	2	3	4	9	0	7
C. Deciding what to tell children about the suicide	1	2	3	4	9	0	7
D. Withdrawal of some or all family members from one another	1	2	3	4	9	0	7
E. Difficulty sharing grief with some family members	1	2	3	4	9	0	7
F. Handling other people's questions about suicide	1	2	3	4	9	0	7
G. People avoiding the topic of suicide	1	2	3	4	9	0	7
H. Feeling obligated to keep the suicide a secret	1	2	3	4	9	0	7

	USE 1 FOR NO DIFFICULTY		USE 4 FOR GREAT DIFFICULTY		NA	SUPPORT GROUP	
						DIDN'T HELP	HELPED
I. Difficulty talking about the suicide with friends, relatives, or coworkers.	1	2	3	4	9	0	7
J. Gossip and blame about the suicide from friends, relatives, or coworkers	1	2	3	4	9	0	7
K. Social isolation and withdrawal of friends, relatives, or or coworkers	1	2	3	4	9	0	7
L. Helping to get through the holidays and other events triggering renewed sadness	1	2	3	4	9	0	7

80. (This section should only be answered if you were a participant in a suicide survivors support group; otherwise, skip to the next section.) If you ever participated in a suicide survivors support group, please list to the following blank spaces any particular experiences that helped you to "turn a corner" or move on to a better place psychologically in accepting your loss. Please explain why you felt this event helped you. And if you had an experience in a support group that set you back, please share that as well, explaining why you were hurt or troubled by this event.

Experiences that helped you: _____

_____

_____

_____

Experiences that hindered you: _____

_____

_____

_____

81. Considering everything that has happened to you since your child died, which things would you say assisted you the most in your grief? And, if you can, please explain why these things were helpful. And, again, have there been any important obstacles to your recovery? Please explain how they have interfered with your healing.

Most helpful things: _____

_____

_____

_____

Things that interfered with your healing: _____

_____

_____

_____

Thank you so much for your extremely valuable help with this study!

Index